Transforming 1916

Meaning, Memory and the Fiftieth Anniversary of the Easter Rising

ROISÍN HIGGINS

CORK
cup
UNIVERSITY
PRESS

First published in 2012 by
Cork University Press
Youngline Industrial Estate
Pouladuff Road, Togher
Cork, Ireland

This paperback published 2013

British Library Cataloguing in Publication Data
A CIP catalogue record for this book is available from the British Library.

ISBN-978-185918-486-8 hardback
ISBN-978-178205-057-5 paperback

Typeset by Tower Books, Ballincollig, Co. Cork
Printed in Spain by Grafo

www.corkuniversitypress.com

Contents

Abbreviations

CIÉ	Córas Iompair Éireann
DED	*Dáil Éireann Debates*
GAA	Gaelic Athletic Association
GLA	Gael Linn Archive
GPO	General Post Office
IRA	Irish Republican Army
IWP	Irish Workers' Party
KGA	Kilmainham Gaol Archive
MA DD	Military Archive, Cathal Brugha Barracks, Department of Defence
NAI DEA	National Archives of Ireland, Department of External Affairs
NAI DT	National Archives of Ireland, Department of the Taoiseach
NAI GIS	National Archives of Ireland, Government Information Service
NGA	National Graves Association
NICD	*Northern Ireland Commons Debates*
OPW	Office of Public Works
PRO	Public Record Office (UK)
PRONI	Public Record Office of Northern Ireland

RTÉ   Radio Telefís Éireann

RUC   Royal Ulster Constabulary

UCDA FFA   University College Dublin Archive, Fianna Fáil Archive

UCDC   Ulster Constitution Defence Committee

UVF   Ulster Volunteer Force

Acknowledgements

This book began life as part of a project funded by the Irish Higher Education Authority under the North-South Research Programme. Mary E. Daly at University College Dublin (UCD) and Margaret O'Callaghan at Queen's University, Belfast were the project leaders and I am very grateful to them for the opportunity to work on the subject. Carole Holohan, the other member of the Dublin team, read drafts of many of these chapters, offered advice and has become a very valued friend. Much of the Dublin-based research was done from the Humanities Institute of Ireland at UCD and Marc Caball, Anne Fuchs and Valerie Norton provided support for the project.

The book was completed in Boston College-Ireland and I owe particular thanks to its director, Mike Cronin, who read part of the manuscript and has facilitated a great working environment. I am also grateful to my other colleagues in Stephen's Green: Arlene Crampsie, Regina Fitzpatrick, Thea Gilien, Claire McGowan and Ben Shorten. Part of this book was written during a year spent at the Institute of Irish Studies, Queen's University Belfast and I am very grateful to its director, Dominic Bryan, and the members of the Institute for the research fellowship and for providing me with such a lovely setting in which to work. I was also fortunate to be involved in an Ireland-Australia Bi-lateral Research Group on 'Memory and the uses of the past', funded by the Irish Research Council for the Humanities and Social Sciences and the Australian Academies of the Humanities and Social Sciences. Conferences and workshops were held in Sydney, Canberra, Belfast and Dublin and I am grateful to Mark Finnane, Katie Holmes and Stuart Ward for organising the various programmes.

I very much appreciate the helpful assistance of the staff in libraries and archives consulted during research for this book, including: Bord Fáilte; British Library at Colindale; Dublin Diocesan Archive; Irish Film Institute Archive; Kilmainham Gaol Archive; Labour History Museum, Dublin; Linenhall Library, Belfast; Military Archive, Cathal Brugha Barracks; National Archives of Ireland; National Graves Association; National Library of Ireland; Office of Public Works; Public Record Office of Northern Ireland (PRONI); RTÉ Archives, UCD Archives and UCD Library.

Material from PRONI has been reproduced by permission of the Deputy Keeper of the Records, Public Record Office of Northern Ireland. The Fianna Fáil archives were consulted in UCD with the permission of Fianna Fáil. I am grateful to Maurice McMahon for providing the project with a copy of the script *Seactar Fear Seacht Lá*; Tomás MacAnna very kindly supplied a copy of *Aiséirí* and Hugh Leonard generously gave permission to use the script of *Insurrection*. I am extremely grateful to Garret FitzGerald, Kevin B. Nowlan, Aindreas Ó Gallachóir and Declan White for discussing their memories of the commemoration with me.

I wish to acknowledge the kind permission of the Irish American Cultural Institute to reproduce a version of an article of mine published in its journal *Éire-Ireland*, Vol. 42, nos 3/4, Autumn/Winter 2007, pp. 11–34: 'Projections and Reflections: Irishness and the Fiftieth Anniversary of the Easter Rising'. I also wish to acknowledge the kind permission of the Royal Irish Academy to reproduce versions of chapters published originally in M.E. Daly and M. O'Callaghan (eds.), *1916 in 1966: Commemorating the Easter Rising* (2007): 'I am the Narrator over and above . . . the Caller Up of the Dead: Pageant and Drama in 1966', pp. 148–72 and 'Sites of Memory and Memorial', pp. 272–302.

I am grateful to the staff of Cork University Press for helping to bring this work to completion, especially Maria O'Donovan and Sophie Watson. Tom Dunne's initial encouragement was extremely valuable, and I also benefitted from the helpful comments of the anonymous readers.

In the course of my academic life I have pitched my tent in many places and would like to acknowledge the encouragement and welcome given to me by Alan Sykes at the University of St Andrews; Mike Rose and Andy Marrison at the University of Manchester; Bob Morris at the University of Edinburgh and Ken Brown at Queen's University Belfast. Academic friends and colleagues who have provided support, information and suggestions during the writing of this book include: Kris Brown, Marie Coleman, Catherine Cox, Brian Crowley, Clara Cullen, Mark

Duncan, Lindsey Earner-Byrne, Garrett Finegan, Kelly Fitzgerald, Luke Gibbons, Brian Hanley, Marnie Hay, Éamonn Hughes, Lisa Hyde, Michael Kennedy, Michael Laffan, Gill McIntosh, Ivar McGrath, Maureen Murphy, William Murphy, Úna Newell, Catherine O'Donnell, Aidan O'Malley, Paul Rouse, Ann-Marie Smith, Clodagh Tait and Regina Uí Chollatáin. I would also like to thank my long-serving friends and travelling book club companions Janet Day, Jo Rogers and Louise Day; as well as Barry and Jean Day, Carol de Buitleir, Liz Harris, Suzanne McElligott, Jude McHugh, Ann Milović, Carmel O'Connor and Tom Webster.

Few people can have been so well provided for in terms of their siblings. My brothers and sisters have, at times, read drafts, listened, advised, encouraged and distracted me throughout the writing of this book. Their insights pepper these pages, and it is with profound thanks that I acknowledge the love and support of Geraldine, Vincent, Peter and Claire. I am also grateful to our larger family: Rob, Paula, Maria, Aodan, Liadan and Conor; and to my magnificently large extended family of aunts, uncles and cousins.

My deepest debt is to my parents. This book is dedicated, with love, to the memory of my father Vincey, and to my wonderful mother Mary who taught us all at an early age that the real importance of any event is in its telling.

Introduction

In March 1966 the taoiseach, Seán Lemass, received a letter from an elderly patient in a Dublin nursing home which implored him to withdraw all preparations for the commemoration of the Easter Rising before it was too late:

> I know that you will have serious trouble if this piece of showing the flag goes on . . . It seems to be impossible to rule this very small island and I know your task is difficult but it seems to me . . . that there is going to be very serious trouble if these celebrations go on.[1]

In retrospect many would agree that these concerns were well founded. Although the beginning of the conflict in Northern Ireland is often dated to 5 October 1968 – when police and civil rights marchers clashed in Derry and two days of serious rioting followed – faultlines had been emerging in the years before. The first victim of the Troubles, John Scullion, was shot by loyalists on 11 June 1966.[2] While the commemoration of the Easter Rising did not cause the conflict in Northern Ireland, it has been seen by unionist politicians as central to the build-up of tension and the subsequent breakdown of order.

The fiftieth anniversary of the Easter Rising has been remembered as a moment of unrestrained triumphalism which fuelled divisions between unionists and nationalists. Indeed there exists in Ireland a dual memory through which 1966 has become as mythical and misunderstood as 1916. David Trimble has written that '1916 had a particular legacy for the North, as the 50th anniversary of the rebellion started the destabilisation of Ulster'.[3] For Trimble, the 'orgy of self-congratulation' that accompanied the commemoration had a devastating impact on the position of moderate politics in Northern Ireland.[4] Terence O'Neill, who was prime minister of Northern Ireland in 1966, described it as 'not a very easy year'.[5] In his autobiography O'Neill expressed his frustration at Catholics in Belfast who had 'insist[ed] on celebrating the Dublin rebellion' and recorded, 'It was 1966 which made 1968 inevitable and was bound to put the whole future of Northern Ireland in the melting pot.'[6] The summer of 1966 was also the fiftieth anniversary of the Battle of the Somme. In the months previously, the Ulster Volunteer Force had been resurrected and Conor Cruise O'Brien later argued that the 1966 commemorations favoured a recrudescence of IRA violence and that the nationalist and unionist commemorations in the North, clashing with those of the Rising in the South, also favoured the revival of armed Protestant extremism.[7]

South of the border the view of those who were young in 1966 has helped to sustain the idea that the jubilee was an occasion of unthinking nationalism which had corrosive if less dramatic consequences in the Republic of Ireland. The poet Michael O'Loughlin has argued that 'it is almost possible to speak of a generation of 66' which shared the characteristics of a total alienation from the state, a cynicism with regard to national institutions and an unspoken assumption that everything emanating from official sources was a lie.[8] For this generation the fiftieth anniversary of the Rising is remembered as a moment of betrayal by the Irish state during which the Easter Rising was elevated to the centrepiece of the national story, only to be abandoned in official circles a few years later when it was no longer politically convenient.[9]

Certainly the anniversary in 1966 marked the most elaborate commemoration of Easter Week to date. It was also the first commemoration to be broadcast on the recently established Irish television network Telefís Éireann, and at a point when Ireland was intensely aware of its image in the outside world. The acts of remembrance therefore contained an acute self-awareness which came from the size of the perceived audience. Self-awareness is not the same as self-reflection and there was little or no consideration given to the impact of the commemoration on politics in Northern Ireland, despite efforts at rapprochement between political leaders there and in the Republic in the mid-1960s. Greater thought was given to the way in which the commemoration would be viewed abroad and the possibility that it might be seen as anti-English. Nevertheless, the government in the Republic of Ireland felt entitled to commemorate the Rising and, indeed, believed that it had a responsibility to mark the fiftieth anniversary as a landmark event.

The commemoration was driven by two forces which gained in significance as the commemoration approached: to demonstrate the success of the modern Republic and to sideline the republican movement (as the IRA and its environs were referred to in the 1960s). The fiftieth-anniversary commemoration of the Rising was therefore about the presentation of a new reality as well as a genuflection to an old one. Indeed Seán Lemass was rather uncomfortable with the prospect of the commemoration and it was undertaken at the urging of Fianna Fáil backbenchers. Lemass had become taoiseach in 1959 and the explicit emphasis of his agenda, economically, socially and rhetorically, was one of modernisation. The government was moving the Republic towards membership of the European Economic Community, a Free Trade Agreement with Britain and improved relations with Northern Ireland. The old co-ordinates appeared to be shifting. The jubilee of the Rising operated within this context and was not an inward-looking reference to the past but rather a desire to project outwards a more positive view of Ireland. Internally the Republic of Ireland continued to face serious economic difficulties and an appeal to practical patriotism (which framed official rhetoric rather than zealous nationalism) was a bid to face down current domestic problems and those of longer standing: emigration, the failure to consolidate the position of the Irish language and the 'unresolved' question of partition.

The presidential election in June 1966 would underline for the second time that year the tug between the past and the future in Ireland. Éamon de Valera's candidacy, at the age of eighty-four, represented the lingering life of the revolution. Publicity material for his re-election campaign emphasised his service to Ireland 'from the fire ruins of Boland's Mills' and notes provided for those electioneering on his behalf included the fact that 'He symbolises Ireland and personifies our struggle for freedom'.[10] However, de Valera and the Rising were no longer unproblematic symbols of Ireland, reflecting as they did an ageing past. De Valera's rival for the presidency, Tom O'Higgins (nephew of Kevin O'Higgins), who had been born in 1916, had a family which was likened in the press to the Kennedy clan while de Valera's image, one newspaper noted, was more de Gaulle than Kennedy.[11] The *Northern Standard* described what he represented as 'part of the "ancient heritage" image, traditional, tragic, rooted in the past, a wolfhound and round tower image rather than a greyhound and factory chimney one'.[12] O'Higgins's campaign recognised this weakness and pushed home the idea that the presidency must reflect an image of the real Ireland: 'It must be progressive, and able to personify a nation fit to take its part in the fast-moving world of tomorrow.'[13]

The same was true of the Easter Rising. It had to be reinvented so that it could serve the needs of a changing Ireland. The battle for the presidency was characterised as one between 'the 1916 image versus the 1966 image'.[14] In many ways rather than being seen as an opportunity to replicate the events and values of the Rising, its fiftieth anniversary was a conscious act of reinvention which was, at times, in direct competition with the image of the original. De Valera won the presidential election by less than one per cent of the vote, indicating the growing dislocation between Ireland's past and its present.

This introduction addresses some of the tensions present in the meaning and memory of the Rising and in its commemoration. It considers the complex position of Easter Week in Irish history, noting that its representation was being transformed continually, even before the week was out. Historiographical and commemorative interpretations have had a significant impact on the meaning of the Rising within Irish society. The introduction provides a context for the jubilee in 1966 through a short discussion of the historiographical developments of the 1960s and the problematic nature of commemorations of the Rising in the decades preceding its fiftieth anniversary. Societies remember selectively, and Ireland is not unusual in singling out an event onto which it projects a sense of nationhood. The introduction suggests ways in which commemorations operate in modern societies and the fact that, although appearing to offer a way to stabilise the past in the interests of the state, their popular reception cannot be controlled by governments, and nor does their meaning remain static. Finally, the introduction looks at the meaning of the Rising in 1966 and considers how this impacted not only on subsequent readings of the fiftieth anniversary commemoration but also on the place of the Easter Rising in Irish society.

What does 1916 mean?

For many in Ireland 1916 has become shorthand for the Easter Rising. This underlines the extent to which that event displaced all others of that year, most notably and contentiously the Battle of the Somme. Alvin Jackson has written that 1916 became 'a different sort of "magic number" to different types of Irishman'.[15] Nineteen sixteen did become a signature of Irish nationalism but did not displace 1690 for loyalists: the four digits that could summon the essence of their history and identity. The Easter

Rising is an event as mythical as it was real and has become the touch-stone and lightning rod in the Irish popular imagination.

Even as its shorthand, 1916 means much more than the Easter Rising. It has come to signify not just a battle against the English but a battle among the Irish. Debates around it expose the extremes of both the nation's self-satisfaction and its self-loathing: 1916 signifies everything from a simple respect for the leaders of Easter Week to a complex sense of what it means to be Irish. For many people in Ireland 1916 transcends the state and is the most vivid symbolic representation of the nation. It is this pivotal role in the nationalist story that has made it the subject of such contention. For some it represents a standard against which to judge all subsequent events, while for others it represents a form of sentimental nationalism that helps to obscure the worst excesses of the Irish state and give succour to the violence of the Irish nation. The significance of the Rising far outweighs the events of April 1916 and its meaning alters with each generation.

The event that was to become so central to the Irish historical story was a military campaign that lasted for one week. It involved the actions in Dublin of approximately 1,600 rebels (including the Volunteers, Citizen Army and Cumann na mBan) who seized sites across the city, most notably the General Post Office, in the centre of the capital. The Rising began on Easter Monday, 24 April, and lasted until the insurgents surrendered on 29 April. Supporting actions took place in Wexford, Galway and County Dublin but developments in the days before the planned rising seriously weakened the position of the insurgents. Arms being transported in the German steamer the *Aud* had been captured and scuttled by the ship's captain; and Eoin MacNeill, commander-in-chief of the Volunteers, published an order cancelling all Volunteer movements for Sunday 23 April. These events seriously constrained any prospect of even limited military success. Nevertheless, on the morning of 24 April, a day later than originally planned, the Easter Rising began.

Mobilisation was chaotic. Believing that manoeuvres had been can-celled, some would-be rebels slept-in. Others struggled to make sense of erratic orders and counter-orders.[16] Those who encountered the Volunteers as they assembled did not take them seriously, and one soldier in the Royal Irish Rifles recalled of the rebels who passed near Portobello Barracks, 'as they waved to us we waved to them'.[17] The dis-orderly nature of Volunteer mobilisation was matched by a lack of preparedness on the part of the British administration. At the outbreak of the rebellion there were only 400 troops in 'immediate readiness' out of a total of 120 officers and 2,265 soldiers. Dublin Castle was guarded by only six men. It was the second day of the Rising before the forces of the Crown had taken control of the situation.[18] During Easter Week, 64 insurgents were killed in Dublin along with 132 members of the British forces and approximately 230 civilians. Sixteen of the leaders were executed, including Roger Casement, who was hanged in Pentonville Prison, England.

The speed and perceived brutality of the British response to the Rising, the introduction of martial law and the re-evaulation of the calibre of the executed leaders themselves changed opposition in Ireland into widespread support for the rebels, despite the fact that many had relatives fighting on the British side in the First World War. The rapidity of the adjustment in the attitudes of the general population suggests that there was latent sympathy for the nationalist aims of the rebels and events in the aftermath of the Rising further politicised the general population.[19] The arrest of over 3,500 people, and the internment of over 2,500 of these prisoners in Britain, helped to create a cadre of future soldiers. The conscription crisis of 1918 galvanised nationalist support and provided a critical propaganda tool for Sinn Féin, allowing the party to win a democratic mandate of a republic. In January the following year a revolutionary government was formed and the first actions were taken in the War of Independence. Therefore, it was not just the actions of Easter Week 1916 but the tumultuous events in the years which followed that situated the Rising as pivotal in Irish history. It has been argued that the two most important consequences of Easter Week 1916 were that it brought republicanism from the margins into the mainstream of Irish nationalism and legitimised the physical force tradition.[20] The impact was immediate and dramatic; and its repercussions cast their shadow over the rest of the twentieth century in Ireland.

When asked 'Why a republic?', Tom Clarke is reported to have replied, 'You must have something striking in order to appeal to the imagination of the world.'[21] The Easter Rising operates within Irish history at the levels of both the real and the imaginary. Michael Collins famously described the Rising as having 'the air of a Greek tragedy'. It would subsequently be characterised as 'street theatre' and a 'unique example of insurrectionary abstract art', indicating that interpretation and representation are a crucial part of the Rising's importance.[22] Fearghal McGarry has pointed to the 'remarkable degree of uncertainty about [the Rising's] fundamental aspects', such as whether or not the rebels thought they had any chance of success, whether the blood sacrifice was an aim in itself or if the aim was to seize power and, most crucially, what sort of republic did the rebels want to bring about?[23] These uncertainties have provided the vacuum into which multiple motives and messages have been projected. W.B. Yeats wrote in the aftermath of the Rising, 'As yet one knows nothing of the future except that it must be very unlike the past.'[24] Ninety years after the event, historian of the Rising Charles Townshend, wrote that it 'shifted the horizons of possibility, both at the subliminal and practical level . . . the symbolic effect of the rebellion by the middle of Easter week was to burst the limits of what could be imagined.'[25] It is within this statement that some understanding can be reached of the emotional and political significance of the Rising in the Irish mind. It is a radical moment shot through with possibility; the imaginative leap before reality set in. In 1966, even critics such as Conor Cruise O'Brien, who thought the aims unattainable, nevertheless accepted the integrity of the Easter leaders. For O'Brien, the action of 1916 was to be understood fifty years later not as a programme but as 'a challenge to conscience and courage'.[26]

The Rising's key ideological moment was the reading of the Proclamation, by Patrick Pearse, outside the GPO. As is made clear in this document, this was not the first time the Irish had risen against British rule, nor was it the first insurrection to incorporate a declaration of the Republic. The 1916 Proclamation literally and symbolically recalled previous struggles for independence and somehow enveloped multiple elements of Irish history, drawing its legitimacy from this past. Also, in contemporary Ireland, this meant that whoever had ownership of the Rising had ownership of the entire nationalist tradition. The generic myth of the Rising encapsulates both an idealised Ireland and an idealised heroic model based on David and Goliath: the poet-dreamer-revolutionary who took on the giant foe. The Rising also represented the victory of the tradition of violence over the constitutional politics that had held sway since the 1880s, and this aspect became increasingly difficult in official circles once violence had returned to the streets of Northern Ireland in 1968.

As the organising document of the Rising, the Proclamation ushered in a new state of being and, by virtue of subsequent events, asserted a new constitutional position for the people. It was vital in the after-life of the event as the mass-produced representation of the Rising, and the document's image (as opposed to its detail) became central to Irish nationalist iconography. The Proclamation moved from being a radical manifesto to a commodity for display in the home, saturating everyday life, much like religious imagery. This transition into kitsch provided a stylised articulation of nationalist politics through which the revolution was literally domesticated.[27] The Proclamation encapsulates perfectly the contradictions inherent in the Easter Rising. It is both subversive and conservative; it is a commodity that was once revolutionary.

The Easter Rising – through the reading of the Proclamation – is seen as the formative event in the creation of the Irish Republic mythical and real.[28] Partition, the disputed Treaty with Britain and the civil war that followed meant that independent Ireland sustained a thwarted desire to have a day on which independence could be celebrated as there was little appetite to commemorate the foundation of the state. The Proclamation was ratified at the first Dáil in 1919 and this linked the Rising to subsequent sittings of the Dáil without it being implicated in the Anglo-Irish Treaty and without any association with partition. The Rising had not been in itself an act of completion but instead had required future events to relay its true significance. Therefore it met the needs of an Irish nation which was ambivalent about the actual nature of its freedom after 1921. This network of positions mean that it could be celebrated by nationalists and republicans, north and south of the border: the Rising kept the idea of the Republic alive when the dream of 1916 had failed to come into being.

The Easter Rising was itself a commemorative act in which Pearse, in particular, mimicked the actions of Robert Emmet through the reading of a Proclamation declaring a republic. It was Emmet's speech from the dock that became the signature of his death. For Pearse it was the Proclamation. In reading it he provided the focus of the original event and of subsequent commemorations. The Proclamation provided an organising document for the upheavals of the Rising and its successive reading also provided stability within its commemoration.[29] The meaning of the Rising could change through time but the reading of the Proclamation allowed it to appear unchanging and continuous. Moreover, the original moment – Pearse's declaration of a republic – was mythologised almost immediately. Witnesses to the event later remembered there to be about 200 people gathered in an otherwise quiet Sackville Street (now O'Connell Street). They reported little reaction to what Pearse had said and that 'when he had finished the crowd melted'.[30] However, as early at 1 May 1916 it was reported in the *Chicago Tribune* that huge crowds of civilians thronged the streets while Pearse read the Proclamation, 'attired in some sort of fantastic uniform, with golden tassels and a sword'. When he had finished, the *Tribune* reported, 'thundering shouts rent the air, lasting for many minutes. The cries were taken up all along Sackville Street and the adjoining thoroughfares.'[31] Before the week had ended, this central symbolic moment was recast in dramatic grandeur.

Historiography of the Rising

The 1960s was an important decade for scholarly and critical reassessments of the events of Easter 1916. This process began with the publication by F.X. Martin of two memoranda written by Eoin MacNeill in 1916 and 1917, accompanied by Martin's extensive notes and interpretation.[32] An extraordinary level of attention greeted this work: the *Irish Press* and *Irish Independent* displayed posters announcing the publication of the documents, and it was included in the lunchtime news bulletins. The publication coincided with the forty-fifth anniversary of the Easter Rising, and national newspapers ran a series of articles analysing and commenting on the memoranda.[33] MacNeill's record of events represented a challenge to the accepted historical narrative, which had been shaped by the writings of Patrick Pearse, and Martin's publication was the beginning of his broader project 'to transfer the Rising of 1916 from the realm of mythology to the sphere of history'.[34] His wide-ranging '1916 – myth, fact, and mystery' published in *Studia Hibernia* in 1967, was a lengthy disposition on all that he found objectionable about the conventional historical view. Martin had made extensive use of the papers of Bulmer Hobson in the National Library and his work was instrumental in encouraging Hobson to give media interviews during the fiftieth anniversary of the Rising explaining his position. Hobson has been described by his biographer as 'one of the earliest revisionists of 1916' and it was in the 1960s that interest began to grow in alternative versions of the national story.[35]

The release of official records, begun by the British in 1966, assisted the work of professional historians and helped to challenge further the elevated position given to the Easter Rising (and particularly Patrick Pearse) within the traditional historical narrative.[36] The golden jubilee of April 1916 prompted the publication of significant scholarly work, including Leon Ó Broin's, *Dublin Castle and the 1916 Rising: The Story of Sir Matthew Nathan* and Breandán Mac Giolla Choille's edited *Intelligence Notes, 1913–1916*.[37] F.X. Martin edited *Leaders and Men of the Easter Rising: Dublin 1916*, which was commissioned by Radio Éireann for the Thomas Davis lecture series and included chapters on Edward Carson,

James Craig, John Redmond and Sir John Maxwell as well as the leaders of the Rising. The mixed company within the book's contents indicated immediately that it would not participate in the conventional hagiography of the Easter martyrs.[38] Kevin B. Nowlan was commissioned by the jubilee commemoration committee to edit essays on *The Making of 1916: Studies in the History of the Rising*.[39] This volume contained, in particular, two significant chapters by Maureen Wall which examined the circles of conspiracy within the IRB and drew the focus away from the machinations of Patrick Pearse and instead towards the significance of Tom Clarke and Seán Mac Diarmada.[40, 41] Owen Dudley Edwards and Fergus Pyle produced an edited collection based on the sixteen-page supplement published by *The Irish Times* on the fiftieth anniversary of the Rising.[42] Its most provocative inclusion was the piece 'The Embers of Easter' by Conor Cruise O'Brien, which 'raised eyebrows' in the Department of External Affairs among those who were monitoring coverage of the fiftieth-anniversary commemoration in 1966.[43]

'The Embers of Easter' laid out the compromises that had been made in the creation of a bourgeois republic: a partitioned, English-speaking entity that deluded itself into thinking that it was founded on the ideals of Pearse and Connolly.[44] O'Brien's generation, he said, 'were bred to be patriotic, only to find that there was nothing to be patriotic about; we were republicans of a republic that wasn't there.'[45] O'Brien saw no cause for celebration during the fiftieth anniversary of the Easter Rising, and argued, 'Much of what went wrong was inevitable, like the division of the country. For the rest we are all responsible, in the degree to which we co-operated in nonsense, or failed to expose it, or quietly acquiesced in the injustice being systematically practised against the children of the poor in Ireland.'[46] Criticism was also contained in Fr Francis Shaw's attack on unthinking veneration of the Rising and its leaders and, in 1966, Shaw wrote his famous deconstruction of Pearse and his legacy, 'The Canon of Irish History: A Challenge'.[47] Shaw was vociferous in his criticism of the narrative of Irish history in which 'only the Fenians and the separatists had the good of the country at heart, that all others were deluded or in one degree or another sold to the enemy'. He contended that it was no tribute to the rebels of 1916 'to accept their words and their works in an unthinking and uncritical spirit'.[48] The piece, written for the Jesuit periodical *Studies*, was not considered appropriate for the jubilee edition and, in fact, was not published until 1972, by which time Shaw had died.

These essays by O'Brien and Shaw, and Martin's '1916: Myth, Fact and Mystery', are combative and often brilliant contributions to debates on the significance of the Rising. They participated in a recalibration of the historiography of the period and, significantly, were written before the outbreak of conflict in Northern Ireland influenced all later historical writing on the physical force tradition within Irish history. The underlying fury of these essays is directed not at the Rising itself but at the way in which its myth was propagated and exploited in the years that followed and which was central to the teaching of Irish history in schools. The purpose of this book is not to rehearse again the revisionist debates within Irish history; they have already been sufficiently discussed.[49] Nor does this volume dedicate a chapter to developments in historiography in 1966. Michael Laffan has written three articles on this topic, most recently in 2007, and therefore what historians had to say in 1966 about the Easter Rising has been well documented.[50] Moreover, this book is primarily concerned with the way in which the past was represented in areas beyond the academy: how the Easter Rising continued to live in the public spaces of Irish life.

The meaning and memory of the Rising never escaped the impact of contemporary politics and the conflict in Northern Ireland, from 1968. The Troubles effectively made it impossible for historians to write unencumbered about Irish politics and the acrimony of the revisionist debate echoed through the historiography of the period.[51] When Ruth Dudley Edwards published her biography of Patrick Pearse in 1977, RTÉ dedicated an episode of its *Politics* programme to a discussion of the legacy of Pearse.[52] The irony was not lost on reviewers that members of the Provisional IRA were unable to participate in the programme because Section 31 banned illegal organisations from the airwaves.[53] This underlines well the way in which the history of the Rising could not be regarded as being in the past. In her work on the cultural politics of Pearse's school St Enda's, in 2003, Elaine Sisson wrote that the subject of Pearse remained so contentious that to admit to writing on him 'presupposes that the idea is either to debunk the myths of martyrdom or to reinforce him as an icon of the past'.[54] As a result the topic was seen as off limits and academics generally avoided writing about the Rising and its leaders in the last decades of the twentieth century.

This gap in scholarship has recently begun to be re-addressed. In 2005, Charles Townshend published the first authoritative, and widely praised, account of the Rising and its context, and elements of the events of Easter 1916 have been examined in work by, among others, Foy and Barton, Annie Ryan and James Moran. Fearghal McGarry's recent work is also a significant addition to the scholarship of the period.[55] Edited collections have been produced by Gabriel Doherty and Dermot Keogh, and by Ruán O'Donnell. Joost Augusteijn has produced the first academic biography of Pearse since 1977.[56] Public appetite for the story of the Rising was demonstrated in the fact that when *The Irish Times* produced a commemorative supplement to mark its ninetieth anniversary, it was the fastest-selling issue in the newspaper's long history. The journalists involved, Shane Hegarty and Fintan O'Toole, produced a book which expanded on the supplement.[57]

Despite the recognition in the seminal 1991 publication *Revising the Rising* that Easter 1916 had become a cultural product, and Edna Longley's disquisition in that volume on the vagaries and varieties of historical memory, relatively little has been written on the subject in these terms by historians.[58] Nevertheless Ian McBride's edited *History and Memory in Modern Ireland* provides many important discussions on broader aspects of Irish historical memory, and his work on the Siege of Derry offers an insightful exploration of the myth-making potential of iconic events.[59] Anne Dolan has been the first to address the memory of the Civil War in Ireland in her important monograph *Commemorating the Irish Civil War: History and Memory, 1923–2000*.[60] Guy Beiner's work has also opened up new theoretical possibilities for the field.[61] The bicentenary commemoration of the 1798 rebellion prompted valuable reflection on the relationship between history and official memory (not to mention robust debate) including Tom Dunne's experimental *Rebellion: Memoir, Memory and 1798*.[62] On the Easter Rising specifically, Mary Daly and Margaret O'Callaghan conducted an extensive research project on the fiftieth anniversary in 1966 (out of which this book comes) which dispelled the idea that it was a simplistic glorification of the physical force tradition and, crucially, adopted a North-South framework.[63] More recently, Clair Wills has examined the significance of the GPO in Irish life and, in effect, explored the role of the Easter Rising in Ireland's history and culture.[64]

Commemorating the Rising

The significance of the Easter Rising has not been primarily in its official commemoration. In fact, despite its hold over the Irish population, 1916 has never been altogether successfully translated into a stylised annual ritual. The reading of the Proclamation is the central repeatable annual act but the anniversary itself, with no fixed date, falls somewhere between a partial independence day and a subdued national day. While six counties in the North remain under British rule an independence day is problematic, and the need for it to function as a national day is made redundant by the unparalleled success of St Patrick's Day internationally. Furthermore, the often bitter contest over ownership of the event means that the Rising has had a chequered commemorative history.

The immediate aftermath of Easter week signalled the way in which the event would be most effectively remembered: through songs, pictures, mass cards, flags and calendars. Images of the dead leaders were displayed in almost every shop window on Sackville Street, as Sinn Féin set about mass producing the tools of commemoration.[65] The introduction of martial law, and the fact the only Irish newspapers being produced during the First World War were owned by Redmondites or unionists, meant that propagandists for the Rising used a myriad of unofficial and informal forms to convey their message. Historically the unauthorised commemorations of the Easter Rising have always competed with the official state commemorations for ownership of 1916.

The first anniversary of the Easter Rising, it has been noted, was commemorated in a riot. Twenty thousand people gathered on O'Connell Street to watch the hoisting of a republican flag on the rubble of the GPO. Stone throwing and a police baton charge ensued.[66] The first formal military commemoration of the Rising took place in 1924 under the Cumann na nGaedheal government but, although invitations were issued to all the relatives of the executed leaders, due to the divisive politics of the Civil War, only Michael Mallin's widow attended.[67] On the tenth anniversary of the Easter Rising, Éamon de Valera and Seán Lemass participated in an unofficial commemoration which was organised by republicans in Glasnevin cemetery. In this year too the staging of O'Casey's *The Plough and the Stars* at the Abbey had precipitated a riot in the theatre, organised by female relatives of those who had died in the Rising.[68] The uproar was such that W.B. Yeats was able to take to the stage and mime a speech in defence of the play before heading to a newspaper office to write what he might have said. Townshend has noted that it was almost half a century before *The Plough and the Stars* was endorsed by a significant public figure such was the sacrosanct nature of the Rising in political life.[69] In anticipation of the battles that were certain to surround the twentieth anniversary commemorations, with opposition politicians and militant republicans determined to derail Fianna Fáil's claim to the legacy of 1916, de Valera made 1935 the significant commemorative year by overseeing the unveiling of the statue of Cúchulainn in the GPO. Members of the

Cumann na nGaedheal opposition party were not invited to the event, while, also that year, an estimated 1,000 people marched to Glasnevin cemetery for an alternative commemoration which was addressed by the chief of staff of the IRA, Maurice Twomey.[70]

A three-way division existed in commemorations of the Rising. The Cumann na nGaedheal party preferred to commemorate the founders of the state rather than the leaders of Easter Week and embarked on less than successful attempts to memorialise Michael Collins, Arthur Griffith and Kevin O'Higgins.[71] Fianna Fáil embraced the memory of the Rising and sought to use its commemorations to underline the authority and historical position of the party. For Sinn Féin and the IRA commemorations of the Rising represented opportunities to reiterate the fact that the dream of the Easter leaders had been betrayed and to challenge the legitimacy of the partitioned jurisdictions.

The twenty-fifth anniversary of the Rising in 1941 took place against the background of the Second World War. Pageants and celebratory performances were not deemed appropriate in the circumstances, although the military parade past the GPO was maintained. The presence of 20,000 members of the defence forces and a display that also included aeroplanes, the nursing service and firefighters, represented a significant statement from the Free State government. De Valera's policy of neutrality was part practical and part political. The country had an army of just 7,000 regulars when war broke out; the Marine Service established in November 1939 consisted of two ex-fisheries patrol boats and the Air Corps was equally ill-equipped to fight a war. Nevertheless neutrality was also a clear way to assert Irish independence, and the parade down O'Connell Street demonstrated Ireland's strength in remaining neutral rather than its weakness and was, according to Rosemary Ryan, a direct response to the threats to Ireland's neutrality.[72] When the Irish Free State became a Republic in 1949 it was, of course, at Easter that the transition took place. The failure of Independence Day, Constitution Day or Republic Day to catch the public imagination – although all were initially marked – further consolidated the position of the Rising.

However, through the course of the twentieth century, the Irish state and its citizenry generally have been intermittent in their enthusiasm for commemorations of the Rising. David Fitzpatrick has characterised official commemoration in southern Ireland between 1922 and 1939 as 'often painful and embarrassing'.[73] The failure of the state at any point to claim sole custody of the Rising meant that its anniversary was always a site of contention. In Northern Ireland groups from across the nationalist spectrum such as the Irish National Foresters, the Gaelic Athletic Association (GAA) and trade union groups had traditionally paraded at Easter, but they abandoned this in the late 1960s.[74] Only republicans across the island have commemorated the Rising each year. The outbreak of conflict in Northern Ireland further complicated the political associations of the Rising and meant that its official commemoration at the end of the twentieth century was problematic for all groups within Irish society.[75]

Despite the fact that (and also because) the Rising has been problematic for governments north and south of the Irish border, and has at times been seen as a damaged brand, Easter 1916 remains a resilient commemorative vehicle in Ireland. The politicisation of the Irish population during the centenary of the 1798 rebellion had been a significant part of the broader rejection of British culture and the legitimacy of British rule among nationalists in the years before the Rising.[76] Similarly in 1966 republicans understood that the commemoration of the Easter Rising was an opportunity through which to galvanise nationalist opinion, particularly in Northern Ireland. The performance of Irishness and the rejection of Britishness contained within the narratives of the rebellions of both 1798 and 1916 had a radicalising effect on nationalism in 1898 and 1966 respectively. The Rising of 1916, imbued with all the connotations of Easter resurrection, continued to offer a symbol of reawakening and regeneration.[77] Pearse's sister Margaret proclaimed it the dearest wish of her heart that, during the fiftieth anniversary of the Rising, 'the youth of Ireland will receive a renewal of faith in Ireland's noble destiny'.[78]

Governments have naturally attempted to neutralise the destabilising elements of the message of the Rising and to deploy it on behalf of the needs of the state. This resulted in the events of Easter 1916 being taught in schools as a standardised tale of do-gooders and Catholic martyrs. The leaders of the Rising had not been uncritical Catholics. Pearse had been heavily influenced by his father, a student of English radicalism, and, unusually for a Catholic middle-class school at this time, St Enda's did not produce a single priest.[79] Nevertheless Pearse had carefully constructed an image of himself as a Christ-like figure and the depiction of the other leaders in the immediate aftermath of their deaths helped to transform them into the mould of Catholic martyrs. Forgotten were James Connolly's Marxism (he too received Holy Communion before he died), Tom Clarke's anti-clericalism, Thomas MacDonagh's religious scepticism and Seán Mac Diarmada's hostility towards the political influence of the Catholic church.[80] Anthony Cronin, who was educated in the 1920s and

30s, recalled that within the education system the history of the period leading to the creation of the Free State was so sentimentalised as to make it appear to belong to a different world and that 'Pearse in particular had been turned into an utterly unreal and boring figure, a mother-lover who was without human frailties and, consequently, without human virtues'.[81] Divested of their radicalism, the leaders of the Easter Rising became instead symbols for a conservative Catholic state.

Commemorations of the Rising generally conform to the broader pattern of republican and nationalist remembrance, including parades, speeches and the gathering of people at the graves of the dead. They are not as heavily choreographed as commemorations within the Orange tradition in which participants in parades wear uniforms and where there are clear demarcations between marchers and spectators. Furthermore, the Orange Order has managed to retain a measure of unity for its commemorations while those of republicans have fragmented and are enacted separately by competing groups.[82] Both loyalists and republicans continue a style of parading that can be traced to the late eighteenth and early nineteenth centuries: the former to the paramilitary parading tradition of the Volunteer movement and the latter to the tradition of the funeral procession favoured by Ribbonmen and Freemasons.[83] Pearse, having delivered the oration at the graveside of O'Donovan Rossa in 1915, had already established his place in the canon of republican funerals. The Proclamation had also made it clear that the Easter Rising was being enacted in the 'name of God and of the dead generations from which she receives her old tradition of nationhood'.

Funeral processions were a way of holding political gatherings unofficially. They met the needs of Irish nationalism as a subaltern aspiration in both the nineteenth and twentieth centuries, and graveyards acted as significant spaces of commemoration and contestation. The burial place of Wolfe Tone in Bodenstown became an Easter battleground for ownership of republicanism between Fianna Fáil and republicans. In Northern Ireland graveyards have also retained their significance as alternative political spaces. In 1930 a heavy police presence had ensured that no public gatherings took place at Easter in either Belfast or Derry, but large numbers of people gathered in the Milltown and Brandywell cemeteries in the cities.[84] In 1966 cemeteries continued to be a focus for official and unofficial commemorations and often symbolised defiance. The alternative commemoration organised by the National Graves Association (NGA) in Monaghan attracted 800 people who, it was reported, paraded from the town to the gates of Latlurcan cemetery, which, as every year, were locked.[85] Only one parade was banned in Northern Ireland as part of the commemorations, in The Loup, County Derry, and, in response, hundreds of people went instead to St Patrick's Cathedral cemetery and laid wreaths on the republican plot.[86]

Arbour Hill in Dublin, the detention barracks which contains the bodies of the signatories of the Proclamation, played its part in the commemoration of 1966. The grave site in the prison had been refurbished only a few years earlier. Initial plans for the memorial had raised 'two possible but fundamentally different approaches'. The first would preserve for future generations the original austerity of the prison yard while the second would 'erect an impressive memorial befitting the national and historical importance of the site'. The Commission for Public Works advocated the latter and this view was ratified by the government in 1955.[87] The decision was therefore made to turn what was known as the 'national shrine' into a monument of inspiration. Arbour Hill held the *propria et vera corpora* (proper and true bodies) of the dead. Relics had traditionally been used for the swearing of oaths and were seen as guarantors of compacts and treaties. Therefore it was at Arbour Hill that representatives of the state assembled to renew their rhetorical commitment to the ideals of the dead leaders.

President John F. Kennedy laid a wreath at the graves of the dead in Arbour Hill during his visit to Ireland in 1963, marking a formal acknowledgement that the Easter Rising was a foundational moment. A photograph of the scene was reproduced in 1966 and included in a full page of the commemorative supplement of the *Irish Independent* and in calendars produced for the jubilee. This juxtaposition of Kennedy and Arbour Hill suggests the way in which the Rising operated at levels which were both specific and abstract. No monument directly represented the Easter Rising. Instead it was alluded to and symbolised and suggested across all expressions of Irish heroism, even in the person of the American president. Throughout Ireland commemorations were underscored with references to the full spectrum of Irish republicanism so that the Easter Rising was always located as part of a continuum of the struggle for freedom.

In 1966 the commemoration was broadcast across the country on television, reframing the story of the Easter Rising for a new generation. Television is a medium which has obsolescence at its core and through which images were assigned to oblivion in rapid succession.[88] The *Longford News* pondered the way in which changes to communication and technology had altered Irish life:

> The cars and good roads, radio, telephone and TV, have changed the
> way of life for all in Longford's rural parts, even in the more remote
> and inaccessible districts, and have banished to a great extent the
> element of wonder and surprise and the need for passing on infor-
> mation to groups gathered around farmhouse fires or at pub
> counters. Indeed we are not quite sure if anybody today bothers to
> tell about some adventure or experience or story of the past, even if
> he could get anybody willing to listen.[89]

Television devours and discards vast quantities of information and,
launched on New Year's Eve 1961, Telefís Éireann encapsulated the contradictory nature of modern technology: it both eliminated and created
distance. Television coverage provided a way for the public to share an
experience across the geographical spread of the country and it made a
certain part of the commemorative experience 'virtual'. Mary Maher
reported in *The Irish Times* that, on the opening day of ceremonies, as
events were approaching their climax, 'hundreds, having failed to get into
O'Connell Street, were turning away to return home to watch
television'.[90]

For those who remained on the capital's main street there was a
moment of disorientation. Maher recorded that, as the 'paper words' of
the Proclamation were cracked into reality, doubled and tripled by
amplifiers, the flatness of the reader's accent caused those around to
think at first that it was the voice of an American. 'It's a bloody mid-
Atlantic accent,' someone in the crowd explained. 'But,' Maher wrote, 'it
was still the Proclamation, and [the crowd] didn't speak again.'[91] The
words of that document, familiar and charged with so much significance in Irish history, sounded foreign in the re-enactment. They
occupied a space somewhere, elsewhere, midway between geographical
locations. The Rising had come to float in a virtual time and space. It
has been dramatised, fictionalised and set to music and exists as an
increasing unreality. The step has been preserved on which Edward
Carson stood when he read the Ulster Solemn League and Covenant in
1912 to the Standing Committee of the Ulster Unionist Council.[92] The
steps on which Pearse stood when he read the Proclamation have been
invented.[93] But 1912 has not replaced 1690. Events in many ways have
to be cut loose from time and place in order to function as the central
mythical moment of a nation's identity.

The term '1916' means whatever we want it to. It is an idea, an ideal,
an illusion and a delusion: all bitterly fought over. The Easter Rising has
avoided 'belonging' to a single group in Irish society but has not avoided

excluding groups within that society. Women, for example, were literally removed from the record when Nurse Elizabeth O'Farrell was air-brushed from the photograph of Pearse's surrender to General Lowe on 29 April 1916.[94] The Easter Rising is not remembered primarily through official public commemoration but, in fact, survives best informally in songs, poems and iconic imagery. Primarily the Easter Rising is a dis-cursive space and has been resistant to too much formalised ritual. This created certain challenges for the largest commemoration of the Easter Rising to date in 1966.

Commemorations and Historical Memory

Societies, like individuals, remember in order to forget. Remembering the Easter Rising was a way of forgetting both the First World War and the Irish Civil War. It is now a commonplace to recognise that we cannot possibly remember everything. The conscious narrative of our lives – which we tell to ourselves and others in order to explain who we are – selects details that illustrate the moments in life that have formed us. The same is true of nations.

It has also become something of a cliché to say that Irish people remember too much of their history. In the *New Statesman* in April 1966, the poet W.R. Rogers recalled the story of Cenn Faelad, who received such a severe blow to his head (in the Battle of Moira in AD 646) that, the chronicler noted, 'his brain of forgetting was stricken out of his head' and he remembered everything. Rogers argued that this summed up, in a way, the 'condition of Ireland'.[95] This is to miss the point entirely. Irish histor-ical memory is robust because of the scale of what has been forgotten. It is this selectivity that has allowed unionists and nationalists on the island to construct competing narratives that barely waver in their singular version of events. The 1966 commemoration, in privileging the Easter Rising, excluded or sidelined other narratives, histories and groups.

Commemorations, like human memory, select and narrate the story of the formation of nations, states or communities. However, unlike indi-vidual, private memory, commemoration indicates a coming together, a public recollection of the past. It is their public nature that makes them such a focus for debate and dissent. Commemorations play a significant part in consolidating the narrative of a state's history, isolating events that convey the tale of nation formation or state creation. However, it is when consensus is fragile that commemorations are most intense. This is because the marginalisation of certain versions of the past is more clearly visible. Commemorations are used to confer legitimacy in the present but when that legitimacy is challenged they offer an obvious event around which opposition can cohere.

Post-revolutionary and post-colonial countries inevitably feel the need to reject the old regime and celebrate the events leading to and consolidating the new order. Significance is retrospectively conferred on the single event that encapsulates the narrative that the nation tells of itself. French revolutionaries invented the 'Old Regime' and exaggerated its backwardness and injustices in order to claim that 1789 represented a remarkable leap forward.[96] The Fourth of July was not celebrated nationally in the United States until the 1820s even though the Declaration of Independence was signed in 1776, and in France it was not until 1880 that Bastille Day became a permanent part of the French national calendar.[97] It is only with the passing of time that it is possible to recognise those moments that come to represent victory or clarity. History then becomes constructed in light of subsequent preoccupations and necessities. As E.P. Thompson explained, 'Only the successful (in the sense of those whose aspirations anticipated subsequent evolution) are remembered. The blind alleys, the lost causes, and the losers themselves are forgotten.'[98] Commemorations are a celebration of the dominance of one historical narrative and the defeat of another.[99]

The concept of modernity itself incorporates a need to break with the past. The French Revolution, as the seminal modern moment in the European mind, was marked by the execution of Louis XVI. The regicide was literal and symbolic: the king had been beheaded and the principle of kingship severed. Uniquely the institution of the monarchy was assassinated along with the king, as the throne was not being secured for a successor.[100] More generally, modernity requires a sense of rupture from the traditional; a dramatic departure from all that has gone before.[101] This is why modernity itself is often configured as a state of forgetfulness. The development of an industrial-capitalist economy in the nineteenth century exacerbated this sense of fragmentation and dislocation as mechanical reproduction caused objects to become obsolete at ever increasing speed. In modern societies everything is potentially disposable. Information is produced with increased rapidity and discarded almost immediately. Paul Connerton and other historians argue that a fear of cultural amnesia fed the nineteenth-century cult of commemoration, which was expressed through monuments, anniversaries and jubilees.[102]

Therefore commemorations are generated by a fear of forgetting and, in their selectivity, have forgetfulness at their centre. They represent both a recognition that the past is gone and an attempt to reconstitute that past. By their very nature, commemorations reinvent historical episodes in order to confer respect upon them. They stage the historical moment that represents significant change and turn it into a part of historical tradition. Discontinuity and continuity are somehow entwined; therefore commemorations are always shot through with contradiction. Ultimately they are a negotiation between the old and the new, the past and the future. During the opening ceremony of the fiftieth anniversary of the Easter Rising veterans sat on the viewing platform and watched as 'line after line of striding men' passed by on O'Connell Street.[103] The veterans remained static while their commemorative surrogates strode by in motion.

Accelerated modernisation provided the context for the jubilee of the Rising. Ireland was being asked to embrace change and accept industrial-capitalist ideas of 'progress'. Seán Lemass's project gave international capital effective control over the modernisation of the Irish economy. This necessarily altered political, social and cultural relationships and has been described as 'marking the definitive separation of state nationalism from its traditional ideological underpinnings'.[104] The landscape of economic development – factories and tower blocks – was transmitted across the country on television screens and facilitated a nostalgia, not just for a disappearing Ireland but for a disappearing vision for Ireland. Svetlana Boym has identified a nostalgia (literally a longing for home) across Europe at the end of the twentieth century which was not just a longing for a place but for another time and 'for unrealised dreams of the past and visions of the future which [had become] obsolete'.[105] In this sense the Easter Rising effected a nostalgic agency. It acted as both an assurance during moments of change and a vehicle through which to critique that change.

Given the tensions that operate in the commemorative process, it naturally has the potential to be both stabilising and destabilising. At times of rapid historical change the past is looked to for legitimacy and unity of purpose. In Ireland, north and south of the border, commemorations offer a way of expressing a shared identity in the face of internal opposition and globalised homogeneity. The ritualised form of remembrance suggests cohesion and continuity but, in reality, the ritual provides the form through which the meaning of historical events can shift and adapt. Moreover, official commemorative events may aim to control the historical message encapsulated within the event but this is never entirely possible. In 1966 the Irish government attempted to organise a centrally choreographed spectacle but it could not control all interpretations of the commemoration and the official message was frayed though not unravelled in 1966. Competing narratives such as those of republicans, northern nationalists and unionists meant that the Irish state was never in complete control of the meaning of the jubilee commemoration.

A community can fix the date of a commemoration but it cannot fix its meaning. Even dates mean different things to divergent groups of people: 1916 has alternative resonances within different national stories. Anzac Day (the anniversary of the Allied landing in Gallipoli) was first commemorated in Australia, New Zealand and London on 25 April 1916, the day after the beginning of the Easter Rising. Like the Rising, the Anzac landing was a failed military campaign that has been retold as a heroic-romantic myth. Jenny Macleod has suggested that elevating 'failure in this manner produces an inclusive myth that all can celebrate – from ardent militarists to pacifists'.[106] However, Anzac Day has had a chequered history within the Australian commemorative calendar. In the 1960s, anti-Vietnam protestors challenged its underlying assumptions and in the 1980s feminists attempted to join the parades in order to protest against the 'male glorification of war' inherent in the celebrations.[107] The re-establishment of Anzac Day as a central expression of Australian national identity at the beginning of the twenty-first century has attracted acute criticism both for its militarism and its role as a 'safe place' for white settler commemorations.[108] While the Allied landing in Gallipoli is a historic event, its commemoration is an ongoing process with contemporary meanings and political connotations.

The experience of the 36th (Ulster) Division in the Battle of the Somme in 1916 was relayed as containing the essence of what it was to be an Ulsterman. In reporting the event, the *Belfast Newsletter* offered that 'Ulstermen may be destroyed but they will never yield when they know that their cause is just'.[109] David Officer has written of the Somme, 'The Ulsterman had proved himself on the battlefield – proved to himself that he was as he imagined.'[110] The devastating losses of the Somme could, in many ways, be absorbed only by being incorporated into a familiar history and tradition of Ulster. The Somme was seen to reflect and represent all battles in which Ulstermen had fought. Similar to the Easter Rising for nationalists, it gathered to itself the full lexicon of unionist remembrance. However, the Battle of the Somme is not remembered so vividly in France. It is Verdun which encapsulates the French experience of the First World War despite the fact that 200,000 Frenchmen died at the Somme.[111] Therefore it is not necessarily the scale of sacrifice that determines the events which will come to dominate the public memory.

This is very clearly demonstrated in the Republic of Ireland through the problematic history of the memorial at Islandbridge dedicated to the 49,400 Irish soldiers who died in the First World War. The garden was completed in 1939 and small commemorations under the auspices of the British Legion were held from 1948 until 1969 when they were abandoned because of the outbreak of the Troubles. It was not until the ninetieth anniversary of the Somme in 2006 that the official 'opening and dedication' took place, attended by President Mary McAleese.

These defining moments were all failures in military terms. Over 8,000 Australians were killed as a result of the Gallipoli expedition. Over 2,500 Ulstermen died on the first day of the Somme to secure ground that was later lost due to a lack of military backup[112] and the Easter Rising ended in surrender after six days of fighting. However, the ways in which these events have been narrated and remembered have transformed them into heroic exemplars that encapsulated the essence of the national character. These episodes were ennobled by defeat because they were seen to represent the importance of service over victory. They also take place midway in a longer 'victorious' narrative. What links the commemorations of these signature events is the way in which they are used to confirm a specific national or ethnic identity. The heroism incorporated in the sacrifices is used to underwrite these identities and is reasserted in each act of commemoration.

In Canada, too, a mythical version of the First World War was presented in order to create a 'usable past' from the devastation and loss.[113] In effect the First World War came to be seen as Canada's War of Independence; it gave birth to a Canadian national consciousness (while also consolidating internal divisions between English and French nationalisms). Sixty thousand Canadians died during the First World War and 170,000 were injured. This created a compelling need to make sense of the war by seeing it as directing and driving the history of the Canadian nation. It has been suggested that use of mythological figures to represent the spirit of the Easter Rising helped to transform it into a heroic drama so that public remembrance became a celebration rather than an occasion of mourning.[114] The Rising certainly lacked the devastating numbers of dead that characterised battles of the First World War, but it did carry some of the grief of the Civil War into its commemoration and, while never serving as a vehicle for public mourning, did mix sorrow with celebration.

In the Republic of Ireland it is the Easter Rising and not the First World War around which the narrative of the early twentieth century pivots. The Rising, in some ways, sets the beat to an irregular rhythm in which the Republic opts out of a European periodisation of history in which world wars dominate. For many in Ireland the First World War did not represent a cataclysmic rupture in the historical flow as it did for other European countries. Instead it was subsumed into the longer narrative of the struggle for independence.[115] Rather than seeing the period of 1914–18 as one suffused with loss, death (north and south of the border) was configured as the surety that those enterprises and projects which had begun before the war would be completed.[116] So (unlike Australia and Canada) it is the Easter Rising and not the First World War that was used to make sense of the Irish nation. Therefore, in the Republic of Ireland, the Easter Rising is employed as a similar organising myth as the First World War in other countries. This elevates the significance of the Rising and also puts pressure on it to sustain whatever myth contemporary society requires.

The Meaning of the Easter Rising in 1966

The fiftieth anniversary commemoration of 1916 was used to convey the message of modernisation. In the autumn of 1965, with 'commemoration in the air', *The Irish Times* argued that the most fitting monument to 1916 would be to ask not 'Is this what the men of 1916 wanted?' but instead 'What is *now* best for all the people on the island?' because 'this is a different world we live in – post-Auschwitz, post-Hiroshima, the world of space travel, of television and of the nuclear bomb. The moon in 1916 was still a quarter of a million miles away,' it explained.[117] The moon, in fact, had not moved, but Ireland, historically, had moved quite a bit.

In the 1960s the Republic of Ireland experienced a brief moment of optimism after decades that had required a rather grim determination to survive. The economic upturn was short-lived but its impact was significant. The project of modernisation created a measure of hope in the future but was also destabilising in the present. Across Europe nationalism itself was fragmenting and, in Ireland, the revolutionary generation was getting old and dying. To some extent the commemoration was waged in defiance of this passing of time. However, it was also a celebration of the process of moving on.

Seán Lemass outlined how he saw the commemoration in a piece he wrote for the *Boston Globe*:

> It is inevitable . . . that the occasion [of the commemoration of the Rising] will be used . . . to review the progress of the nation under

freedom, and to measure the achievement of national endeavour against the revolutionary vision of fifty years ago.

The people of Ireland understand very well, in a clear-headed and realistic way, that the past cannot be changed, that it is in the future that our nation must live, and that the nation will continue to need the fullest help of all its citizens and the greatest attainable unity of purpose in striving for our national goals so that its full strength will be available and will be exerted to shape the future rightly.

The greatest change which the intervening years have brought has been in the Irish people themselves. There is now in Ireland a vigorous forward-looking, self-respecting community, with growing experience in the management of its affairs, and confidence born of its achievements.

The slave spirit, born of centuries of foreign rule, which was once the main curse of the Irish, has now virtually disappeared, and the degradation, moral as well as material, which was its fruit has disappeared for ever.[118]

The break with the past was clear. The 'greatest attainable unity' for which Lemass appealed was as much general as it was specific to the commemoration. Economic unrest was a significant problem in Ireland in 1966 and the process of modernisation was not smooth. Modernity itself is fixated with newness and, in Ireland in 1966, there was a great deal of talk about 'new patriotism'. Lemass was attempting to reposition Ireland's image of itself. He told the Annual Congress of Muintir na Tíre in August 1966:

This belief in our capacity to shape the future of our country is the essence of the new patriotism which is now spoken of. The past is history and the record of the past cannot be changed. We must forget the Ireland of the Sean Bhean Bhocht and think of the Ireland of the technological expert.[119]

Lemass was not interested in depictions of Ireland which centred around the 'poor old woman' waiting for freedom and, in 1966, the message of the official commemoration was one of looking to the future. This is not to say that the jubilee created a modernistic landscape. The jubilee was not undertaken in the way of a world fair exhibition or an event such as the 1951 Festival of Britain, at which the architects and planners were attempting to 'build a vision of a brighter future for Britain – a future that was clean, orderly and modern after the dirt and chaos of the war'.[120] The 1951 Festival projected a modern and scientific version of Britain that members of the public could visit and it was both educational and inspirational. The commemoration committee of the Rising did not create an actual and vivid modern model. In fact, the language of modernisation often clashed with the reality of Ireland's lack of technical sophistication. However, the commemoration attempted to embrace modernisation and to make sense of it and befriend it by connecting it to Ireland's past.

Constraining the jubilee celebrations were two concerns: that they would be met with indifference and that they would be met with hostility. Enlisting the Rising on behalf of the authority of the state always ran the risk of killing much of the enthusiasm for its commemoration. It also created a focus for discontent with the government. This was well expressed in a widely quoted address by Rev. Dom Bernard O'Dea, which warned of the dangers of ignoring the poverty of the countryside and the emigration it precipitated:

> To honour these men is a delicate task. It calls for tact, common sense, and above all justice and truth. Should these celebrations be dominated by the 'wagon packed with patriots', should there be a burst of whipped-up enthusiasm, the American 'big hand', should we be deluged by an incessant babble of thinly disguised self-display, should there be any 'cashing in' on the occasion to distract from our economic plight, then our jubilee will end in blight, and a noble cause will have been desecrated . . .
>
> A government says: 'Clap,' and we all clap, and a flood of clap-trap is let loose. Tis leaders we want, not 'cheer-leaders'![121]

There also existed potentially more violent dissent from those who opposed partition. Minister for Justice Brian Lenihan, when appealing to those with extreme outlooks to join in the jubilation, said, 'We should not make a disgrace of ourselves by having incidents that the foreign Press would gloat over and make a laugh of us. It is our duty to honour the patriots of 1916 in a proper and responsible way and see to it that there would be no incident to spoil or besmirch the name of Ireland.'[122]

The question that pressed upon the jubilee, however, was what exactly represented 'proper and responsible' remembrance. When the sculptor Oisín Kelly was designing a sculpture for the Garden of Remembrance, which was to be opened in 1966 as part of the official commemoration, he struggled to find a unifying theme for his statue, 'a gimmick' as he called it. And there is a sense in which all commemorations need a gimmick. As a space the Garden of Remembrance gives an indication of what was taking place. Kelly had been asked to produce a report on his design but responded, 'My only report on my report is that I am reading a lot of mythology and talking to a lot of people and hoping that some phrase of somebody's will click and that is all that is happening.'[123] The phrase that clicked was 'once we were men, now we are epochs'. Kelly incorporated this sense of metamorphosis into his statue of the Children of Lir who are depicted during their transformation into swans and represented, Kelly noted, 'the change of men into history'. The commemoration of 1966 was an act of hesitant transformation.

When the architect of the Garden of Remembrance, Daithí Hanly, was compiling his report for the Office of Public Works, he explained:

> There are many types of memorials and monuments, but mainly they fall into two categories, the monument of victory or glory of the individual, and the mausoleum or tomb. The Garden of Remembrance is neither of these. It is a monument dedicated to all those who gave their lives for Ireland throughout the ages. The freedom that they finally won for most of our land may be the end of the battle of swords, guns, blood and death, but it is the beginning of the challenge of the national future. The garden must therefore contain a challenge or message to this generation and generations to come.[124]

Implicit and explicit was the idea that 1966 was both a continuation of the revolutionary project and a departure from it. Therefore in 1966 the true victory of the Rising was to be evidenced in economic achievement and technological development. Foreign journalists were directed towards images of factories and electricity generators and briefed on declining emigration and unemployment figures. Lemass was much more interested in talking about these things than he was in recounting his experiences of fifty years previously. The commemoration in 1966 was a projection of a 'modern' Ireland. The clear message was that this was all part of the national work which the country had a duty to complete. The idea underlining the official jubilee was that 1916 had made 1966 possible: the Easter Rising legitimised modernisation and modernisation legitimised the Rising.

This message impacted on the meaning of the Rising for those who were young in 1966. Indeed, Dermot Bolger has written, 'For anyone who grew up in the 1960s, the Easter Rising meant 1966 and not 1916.'[125] Fintan O'Toole, born in 1958, remembered that 1966 had its own truth, the images of 1916 were 'renewed and refashioned for a new generation just at the time when they had finally lost all reality'. He continued, 'It was the year when 1916 needed to be divorced from all reality and turned into a movie . . . that would run forever in the minds of a new generation in a new country and keep them loyal to the past.' For

O'Toole the central myth being conveyed through the Rising was that failures would transform themselves into triumphs: '1916 inured us to failure, befuddled us so that we don't know the difference between an inept tragedy of errors and a solid achievement. It has given us a theatrical masochism, content with suffering so long as the gestures and symbols of defiance are right.'[126]

O'Toole's anger is, in fact, directed at 1966 rather than 1916 and it is situated in the 1980s. Those who lived their early adult years in that decade experienced disappointment in the message the commemoration of the Rising was being asked to convey in 1966: that the worst was over and that if everyone pulled together and rededicated themselves to the national project the future would be a secure one.[127] This message clearly could not be sustained twenty years later. It is the myth of Irish modernisation that is being rejected rather than the Easter Rising. Hostility towards 1966 was also generated by the subsequent events in Northern Ireland. In retrospect the fiftieth-anniversary commemoration seemed to glorify armed struggle. The conflict placed huge pressure on the generic myth of the Rising: one of heroic expression of the national identity. Official silence around subsequent commemorations of the Rising also provoked criticism that what Lemass had described as 'a great and decisive event in Irish history'[128] should be forgotten when it was no longer politically expedient, and led to a further alienation from the messages of the state. Michael O'Loughlin wrote that it was almost impossible for anyone of his generation to think about 1916 as an actual event in history, discrete and autonomous.[129] The use of mythology to convey the meaning of the Rising contributed to it being understood as an abstract rather than historical event.[130] Beyond its factual past the Easter Rising has had another life as conveyer of 'truths' or purveyor of fictions. It has operated as a central event upon which the necessary gimmick or myth of the nation could be hung.

This book explores the meaning and memory of the Easter Rising in 1966. It is concerned with the way in which history operated in Ireland at a moment of rapid change. Chapter one provides the context and content of the official commemoration, supplying a narrative introduction to the book. This is counterposed by Chapters two and three, which discuss unofficial commemorations in the Republic and Northern Ireland. Both examine physical commemorative practices such as parades and religious ceremonies, but Chapter two also focuses on discourses of opposition, while Chapter three emphasises material symbolism such as lilies and flags. Chapters four, five and six examine the transmission of history through different forms. Chapter four discusses the way in which the idea of 1916 was refreshed and reinvented through performance in pageant and television drama. Chapter five discusses the reconfiguration of spaces in Dublin as part of the commemorative process and Chapter six considers the ways in which history is interpreted through art. All three chapters demonstrate the fluid nature of historical meaning as it is conveyed through texts, performances, spaces and new technologies. Chapter seven discusses the way in which the commemoration was relayed to and experienced by those abroad and suggests ways in which the message of modernisation was complicated by realities at home and among the diaspora.

Modernisation and modernity are themes that recur in the book. The former refers to the processes of social and economic change that Ireland experienced in the 1960s: increased industrialisation, urbanisation and social mobility. The end of chronic emigration led to population increase and also proportionally a greater number of young people. Census returns showed that the numbers in the age group fourteen to twenty-four years rose by 91,861 or 20.4 per cent in the period 1961–71.[131] Modernity is the product of these changes. It is understood as a condition rather than a process and is generally characterised by a sense of fragmentation, uncertainty and dislocation from established modes of practice and belief. Modernity and tradition might seem to be at odds, however the jubilee of the Easter Rising used the past to help carry the country towards an unknown future. The funeral of Roger Casement was effectively the opening event of the jubilee celebrations of the Easter Rising. Casement's remains had been returned to Ireland by the British government in February 1965 and he was reburied on a grand scale in Glasnevin cemetery on 1 March. However, it has also been noted that 'it was generally recognized that this was a dress rehearsal for de Valera's funeral'.[132] Therefore, the return of what remained of Roger Casement, while setting the stage for the commemoration, was not simply a celebration of the revolutionary generation: it was an anticipation of its ending.

CHAPTER ONE

The Official
Commemoration

The blowing up of Nelson's Pillar in March 1966 happened just in time for the golden jubilee of the Easter Rising. The *Birmingham Post* reported that the shattered stump served as 'a convenient and symbolic vantage point' for Irish television cameras during the opening parade of the commemorative week.[1] Nelson, erected in 1808, had afforded those who climbed to the top a panoramic view of Dublin. By 1966 this old gaze had been replaced by modern technology. The anticipated television audience helped to frame the ceremonies of the commemoration. In drawing up the plans for the opening of the Garden of Remembrance in Dublin, the Department of the Taoiseach noted that because it lent itself to full live television coverage, the ceremony 'can be considered the most important . . . of the celebrations'. It was further explained that 'the primary objective is to mount a dignified spectacle and that the accommodation of guests is only a secondary consideration'. As there were to be television cameras placed strategically around the garden it was anticipated that the 'T.V. viewers, who will far out-number the attendance at the ceremonies, should never lose sight of the President' as he walked through the sunken garden, but 'even if they [do] lose sight of him, the disappearance and appearance of the President [will] add a certain dramatic effect'.[2]

Telefís Éireann, the national television broadcaster, had been launched in Ireland on New Year's Eve 1961. It altered the collective experience of Irish society. In recognising this, those who organised the official commemoration of the Easter Rising understood that, because of their numbers, the vicarious experience of television viewers was more important than the actual experience of those present at the commemoration.

There was no room for intimate remembrance in 1966. A spectacle had to be provided for the unseen audience and, in order to be successful, it had to be relayed with a dramatic effect. It was also important that the spectacle provided by the government would not be upstaged by divisions in Irish society that the commemoration was as likely to exacerbate as resolve.

The government did not embark on the commemoration project without anxiety. There was no certainty that the public would stir in sufficient numbers to support the official commemoration. The decision to include various civic organisations in a public parade on O'Connell Street in Dublin as part of the opening ceremonies had been met initially with a very poor response. Notices in the press had invited organised groups of Irish people to take part in the parade but in the month before the commemoration only fourteen groups had responded, the largest of which was Fianna Fáil (the party in government).[3] Reports from the Department of Defence, which was co-ordinating commemorations in provincial centres, showed that most committees still had no clear programme of events by January 1966. The state had never produced a commemorative event on this scale and for such a sizeable audience and it proceeded tentatively rather than aggressively. The number one song, by Dominic Behan, in the Irish charts during the jubilee proclaimed gratitude that Ireland is surrounded by water: 'The sea, oh the sea is the gradh geal mo croide/Long may it stay between England and me/It's a sure guarantee that some hour we'll be free/Thank God we're surrounded by water.' Therefore the concern that few people would turn out for the commemoration was coupled with the danger that the jubilee would produce nothing more constructive than a spirited burst of anti-Englishness.[4]

The anticipated widespread coverage of the commemoration added to the pressure to present Ireland and its history in the most positive light. The opening ceremony on O'Connell Street was available across Europe through Eurovision.[5] There was also the hope that *The Irish Rising*, a short film by George Morrison which had been commissioned by the Department of External Affairs, would be broadcast by television stations abroad (although in fact the uptake was rather limited).[6] The concern existed that if the Irish government did nothing to provide information and images, other countries would accept the British version of history.[7] In the event few in Britain were whispering against Ireland. The embassy in London reported that BBC news releases on the commemoration would be in the 'hands of an Irishman who is well-disposed',[8] and that

Rediffusion, which made programmes for Independent Television in the United Kingdom, was planning to make a 45-minute film on the Rising with actual film sequences and the singing of rebel songs. The embassy suggested, 'If there is an undue emphasis upon the singing of "rebel" songs, it may be that the programme will not be all we would wish. However, the Producer, Elkan Allan, has told me that the programme is written from the Irish view-point and that "it does not spare the English."'[9]

The concern over how the history of the Rising itself would be conveyed was matched by an anxiety that the commemoration should not contribute to existing fissures within Irish society. The technological means through which the central messages of the commemoration could be disseminated represented a burden as well as an opportunity. It is in the nature of news production that stories of harmony make uninteresting headlines. Even within Irish newspapers, the story of the official commemoration shared front-page headlines with the news of the banning of a parade in The Loup, County Derry. *The Irish Times* reported that armed police moved in groups around the windswept countryside, in constant contact with two helicopters overhead, in what was 'the biggest mobilisation in the north'.[10] The uglier side of Irish life also threatened to be a feature of the commemoration, as there were mutterings about whether or not members of soccer and rugby groups should be included in local parades (the Gaelic Athletic Association's ban on its members playing foreign games was not rescinded until 1971). A ban on the Football Association of Ireland's participation in the commemoration became explicit in Drogheda (although it was eventually withdrawn) and, although deplored by journalists and political leaders across the country, gained a great deal of publicity during the period of the jubilee. A sectarian undercurrent expressed itself in other incidents. A life-size statue of Lord Farnham was daubed in green paint with the words 'Free Ireland, Up the Rebels' in the grounds of a Protestant Hall in Cavan, while a copy of the Proclamation was pasted across a Protestant Hall in County Derry.[11]

As these incidents suggested, the sense of exclusion that accompanied the chauvinism of the commemorative event had potentially more severe consequences because of tensions within Northern Ireland and in the border areas. Yet no real consideration was given to the possible impact of a large commemorative event in the Republic on its relations with Northern Ireland or on the relationship between nationalists and unionists in that jurisdiction. Elaborate public expressions of Irish nationalism were exploited by The Rev. Ian Paisley, whose increasingly extreme unionism and sectarianism posed a threat to unionist unity and to the position of the prime minister, Terence O'Neill.[12] The tension created by the fiftieth anniversary of the Easter Rising hardened lines between and within political constituencies in Northern Ireland. The Stormont government talked up the threat of IRA violence in the months before the commemoration. Police intelligence suggested that the IRA was planning a new campaign in 1966 and these fears were exacerbated during the general election in Northern Ireland in November 1965 which, O'Neill stated, was being moved forward in order to avoid clashing with the commemoration.[13] Tensions were also high during the elections for Westminster in March 1966 which saw Gerry Fitt elected to a seat, giving Republican Labour a voice in London. A special security committee had been set up in Stormont at the beginning of April 1966 which consisted of government ministers and leading members of the Royal Ulster Constabulary (RUC). All police leave was cancelled over the Easter period and the RUC, Special Constabulary and British Army were described as being in a state of 'instant readiness'.[14]

The jubilee of the Rising represented an important anniversary for republicans. They had been organising commemorative events for the Rising for over forty years and did not intend to relinquish this role to the government. Officials in the Republic of Ireland were not excessively exercised by the prospect that the commemoration of the Rising would lead to an increase in support for the IRA but they did have to contend with the amount of space foreign journalists gave to the views of republicans who were heavily critical of the government and the 26-county state. Where the government was most vulnerable to criticism from republicans was in the *de facto* acceptance of the continued existence of the border. The ending of partition was still a key part of the rhetoric of Fianna Fáil. In 1965 Lemass reassured those assembled at the Ard Fheis:

> So long as we keep clearly in mind that the national aim is to secure the permanent reunification of the Irish people based on understanding of our common nationhood, our common problems and common destiny, and never lose faith in its achievement, or weaken our determination to persist on this course, we can face the future in the certainty of this ultimate achievement.[15]

Nevertheless, at the beginning of 1966, he acknowledged that both reunification of the Irish people and the restoration of the Irish language were two fields in which the amount of progress achieved had been less than hoped.[16]

Nationalism and patriotism were embedded in the discourses of the Irish state. This had a practical application in 1966. Lemass was attempting to change Ireland's economic relationship with Britain and Europe. The Free Trade Agreement with Britain (signed in January 1966) and the ongoing policy of seeking membership of the European Economic Community (EEC) had implications for Irish sovereignty and independence. Fianna Fáil addressed those concerns by presenting these economic policies within a clear package of patriotism. The argument for membership of the EEC was couched within its significance for the project of national unity. Lemass argued that economic co-operation would 'help to sweep away some of the arguments which have been used to sustain Partition, and to create a new situation in which the advantages of Unity will become so increasingly apparent that it must help to bring about the political conditions in which it may be realised'.[17] Moreover, to those who pilloried the Free Trade Agreement as a move that would tie the fortunes of Ireland to those of Britain and make a mockery of independence, Lemass argued that independence was 'primarily a matter of being able to stand on our own feet, without artificial props of any kind, and of being able to win trade abroad on the quality of our products in conditions of fair competition'.[18]

The language of progress was tied to an assertion of economic development. Improvements in agriculture, industry, trade and education and higher living standards were referenced by ministers pointing to the advancements made in the previous fifty years. While the commemoration of the Easter Rising offered an opportunity to showcase these successes, it also took place against a background of economic disharmony, with strike action taking place across many sectors of the economy. The end of 1965 and beginning of 1966 saw 'a period of virtual stagnation' as far as the Irish domestic economy was concerned and the peak in personal expenditure, reached at the beginning of 1965, had since declined.[19] Therefore, the initial optimism of the 1960s had tilted into a high degree of labour discontent by the middle of the decade. April 1966 opened with threatened strikes among CIÉ (public transport) workers, which would have disrupted all rail and bus services; by the workers of the sugar, confectionery and food-processing trade; and by the National Farmers' Association. The agricultural sector had been one of those negatively affected by a dock strike in the previous months and, at the beginning of May 1966, all commercial banking north and south of the border was brought to a standstill by a strike by 3,400 junior officials. Workers throughout the Republic were using strike action to regulate their work practices and improve their incomes.

Economic patriotism was a central theme in 1966. Lemass explained that, while sacrifices of the same character may not be required of people in Ireland as those of fifty years previously, there were 'other sacrifices which Irishmen and Irishwomen, desirous of proving themselves worthy of the destiny to which they are called, can make with honour to themselves and with benefit to their country'.[20] It was a subject Lemass continued to promote throughout the year. When addressing Muintir na Tíre in August 1966 he addressed the theme of their conference, 'The New Patriotism', and argued that a new concept of patriotism meant accepting all the obligations of freedom, including the obligation to subordinate individual and sectional interests to the overriding obligation to the country.[21] Government ministers also linked economic and patriotic interests. Erskine Childers, Minister for Transport and Power, told those assembled in Castleblaney, County Monaghan, that the best tribute to the heroes of 1916 'would be a massive drive by management and workers to increase productivity and seek new export markets' and argued for a closer understanding between employers and workers.[22]

Expecting the Irish population to come together to celebrate the Easter Rising was not straightforward. However, Monsignor Hamilton, speaking in Nenagh, County Tipperary, compared the commemoration of the dead of Easter Week to the renewal of baptismal vows.[23] And, in many ways, it was within this spirit that the commemoration unfolded. It requires quite a leap to refuse to reject Satan and all his works if caught within any vestiges of faith. For the Irish population, belief in the virtue of the Easter leaders went very deep. Whatever the criticisms of the government and the economy, few could refuse their support to the men and women of the Rising. Therefore, with varying degrees of enthusiasm, and with gestures extravagant and small, the population of the Irish Republic acted in remembrance.

Commemoration by Committee

In February 1965 Seán Lemass presided over the first meeting of the committee established to co-ordinate the commemoration ceremonies of the fiftieth anniversary of the Easter Rising. The original group included civil servants from six government departments and 'people who were themselves actively associated with the period [1916]'. The taoiseach made clear that there would be no limit to the size of the committee (it expanded to include thirty members) and that it 'need not feel bound . . . by considerations of expenditure' in order that the occasion be 'celebrated on an appropriately grand scale'. [24]

The committee had been constituted on an informal and ad hoc basis. Lemass would explain (in response to concerns from Fine Gael and the Labour Party), 'What happened was that I invited a number of people to come together and asked them to suggest other people, who, in their own knowledge, would be helpful and likely to be interested.'[25] However, the informal appointment of the committee did not mean that it was politically innocent and there was an expressed fear that the commemoration would become unduly associated with Fianna Fáil.[26] The question of the make-up of the committee had been raised by the Labour Party in the Dáil two years prior to the jubilee commemoration. However, Lemass dismissed the possibility of setting up an all-party committee by explaining that the event would be organised, as always, by the army.[27] The reluctance of the Department of Defence to undertake the task on the necessary scale did not make way for all-party inclusion. It was not until July 1965 – when the programme of events had been agreed – that Lemass signalled that he would communicate its 'general character' to Opposition leaders and to the general public.[28]

The original committee was presented with a draft programme (drawn up by the Fianna Fáil National Executive) that did not differ significantly from the one finally undertaken.[29] Certain decisions, however, were revised. Central to the planning of the commemoration was the fixing of a date. The judgement had to be made as to which date constituted the proper anniversary of the Rising: 24 April (the specific date of the event) or Easter Monday, which was 11 April in 1966. The inaugural meeting of the commemoration committee agreed that the celebrations in 1966 should commence on Sunday 24 April rather than on Easter Monday, 11 April. It was noted that the Federation of the Old IRA had been advocating for several years that the annual commemoration of the Rising be held on 24 April, as holding a parade on Easter Sunday 'caused confusion in the minds of the public, who were inclined to associate the parade with Easter rather than with 1916, giving it a religious rather than a historical significance'. It was also argued that Easter was not ideal, as many people went away for the long weekend. There appeared to be little dissent at the first meeting to the general view that 24 April should be declared an annual public holiday with the suggestion 'even, if necessary, the swopping [*sic*] of Easter Monday for it'.[30] Indeed there were good practical reasons for fixing the date of the anniversary. However, in the past, when the Federation of the Old IRA had lobbied that 24 April should be made a national holiday, the Department of Defence had disagreed and advised that the Rising commemoration should be held at Easter, as it was this that determined the timing of the event and not the date.[31] This was also the line of the Department of the Taoiseach in response to the argument that it was offensive to hold military parades at the hour when the Christian churches were celebrating their principal Easter services.[32]

The issue was revisited in April 1965 at the third meeting of the commemoration committee at which Frank Robbins, who had not been present at the previous discussion, expressed a preference for Easter Week for the ceremonies as 'the 1916 leaders had purposely chosen that week as symbolic of a dual resurrection'.[33] It was further suggested by Éamon Martin that efforts to have 24 April declared as Independence Day should not be confused with the committee's task, which was the celebration of the golden jubilee and was a separate issue: 'Independence Day should not be celebrated until independence for thirty-two Counties ha[s] been achieved.'[34]

The official opening ceremony of the commemorative programme took place on Easter Sunday, 10 April 1966. The decision not to fix the date of the anniversary of the Easter Rising allowed it a certain fluidity of function. Its commemoration could remember both the struggle for freedom while incorporating a recognition that part of the Irish nation remained under British jurisdiction. Despite how the commemoration unfolded, the original intention was not that the anniversary of the Rising should become, in effect, Independence Day (which is not to say that it should not celebrate independence). The choice of Easter facilitated a greater sense of re-enactment as well as maintaining the symbolic parallels between the resurrection of the Irish nation and that of Christ.[35] The moveable date also allowed the government to avoid a sense of finality in terms of the work that independence had made necessary. This sense of an incomplete journey was a central part of Irish nationalism and provided political momentum and rhetoric. Emmet's unwritten epitaph had provided a template. In 1966 the initial statements by Lemass and de Valera emphasised continuity, not completion. In his Presidential Address to the People of Ireland at Easter 1966 de Valera directed his listeners towards their responsibilities in continuing the work begun fifty years previously. He began by providing an expansive understanding of freedom:

Political freedom alone was not the ultimate goal [of the leaders of the Rising]. It was, rather, the enabling condition for the gradual building up of a community in which an ever increasing number of its members, relieved from the pressure of exacting economic demands, would be free to devote themselves more and more to the cultivation of the things of the mind and spirit, and so able to have the happiness of a full life . . . We cannot adequately honour the men of 1916 if we do not work and strive to bring about the Ireland of their desire.[36]

Seán Lemass, speaking of the upcoming anniversary at the Fianna Fáil Ard Fheis in November 1965, had a more practical approach to the desired Ireland:

So far as official arrangements for the commemoration ceremonies are concerned, these will be only the formal expression of our people's pride in the devotion and sacrifice of the leaders and men who had the privilege of participating in that heroic enterprise. Their real significance will be in the response they evoke amongst our people of today in relation to the national work which we today have to do and which it is our duty to complete.[37]

The pride Lemass expressed was in the heroic sacrifice – not in an abstract concept of Ireland. The 'real significance' he indicated was in fact the reformulation of the idea of patriotic sacrifice so that it could be applied to the rather tedious process of making the revolution stick.

Concerns over Relevance

The original plan to have a commemoration lasting for two weeks had resulted in a tentative programme the committee judged to be 'a bit thin' in the second week and prompted Lemass to confine the ceremonies to Easter Week. The views of the Federation of the Old IRA and the 1916 Veterans' Association had been sought and they concurred that there would be a danger of public apathy were the ceremonies to be extended over a fortnight.[38] The veterans were not strangers to public indifference and had written in complaint to the Department of the Taoiseach in the past. In 1962 they noted that commemorative parades had become less impressive each year and had ceased to command the respect to which they were entitled from the public. Such was the sense of diminishing returns that the Federation of the IRA informed Lemass:

The citizens of Dublin have become so used to seeing handfuls of old men marching behind the national flag that they no longer turn their heads to look at them, while the drivers of buses and cars hoot them out of the way and break their ranks with indifference, if not contempt.[39]

The Old IRA's depiction of their commemorations vividly expressed the way in which the revolutionary generation was literally being pushed aside by the corollary of modernisation: buses and cars. The task of the golden jubilee committee was to bridge this sense of disconnection between past and present: the Easter Rising and Irish society.

The committee considered combining the commemoration of the past with an explicit celebration of the modern in the form of an industrial parade or exhibition. The possibility was discussed of putting back the St Patrick's Day industrial parade and linking the jubilee of the Rising to the 'Buy Irish' campaign.[40] Despite the fact that the commemoration would become, in effect, an assertion of the success and modernity of independent Ireland, there was no enthusiasm among interested parties for an overt reference in the form of an industrial parade and the idea was dropped.[41] Organisers in provincial centres asked for direction on the matter and received the reply that the central committee had taken the line that an industrial parade would not be appropriate for inclusion on Easter Sunday.[42] The commemoration committee in Cork had decided against a St Patrick's Day type of pageant, having 'firmly ruled out any idea of "Commercializing" any part of the celebrations'.[43] There was not, however, a general prohibition and industrial displays were held in Mayo and Monaghan.[44]

The Official Programme

The final programme issued by the commemoration committee was concentrated in Easter Week 1966 with some events scheduled in the adjoining period. On Good Friday, 8 April, a ceremony was held at Banna Strand where Florence Monteith-Lynch from New York turned the first sod on the site of a memorial to her father Robert Monteith, D.J. Bailey and Roger Casement, who had landed in County Kerry fifty years earlier while attempting to run guns from Germany for the Rising. Members of the crew of the *Aud*, which had been scuttled by the British Navy, were also present.[45]

The central week of ceremonies opened with a military parade down O'Connell Street on Easter Sunday (marshalled by the Organisation of National Ex-Servicemen) and was followed by a people's parade which included political parties, sporting organisations, community and cultural groups and representatives of Irish associations abroad. The parade was watched by 600 veterans in the viewing stand. The Federation of the Old IRA had decided not to march in the parade because of the age of its members.[46] A noticeable number of empty seats in the viewing stand marred the spectacle as approximately thirty people (including ministers of state, leaders of the Opposition parties, the Council of State and former ministers) had not received their invitations. Incompetence rather than conspiracy lay behind the omission and the Department of Defence issued a statement regretting the error.[47]

For the crowd of onlookers numbering around 60,000, and joined by another 140,000 in the areas adjoining O'Connell Street to watch the parade, the atmosphere was expectant rather than celebratory.[48] Radio and Telefís Éireann broadcast the events live and television cameras were placed in O'Connell Street, College Green and on O'Connell Bridge.[49] The audience was national and international. The *Birmingham Post* judged:

> To an outsider's eye, the crowds filling O'Connell Street for the military parade and its symbolic readings of the 1916 Proclamation of Independence might have seemed as indifferent to the event as the Dublin crowds were to the Rising in 1916. But the subdued attitude of the traditionally excitable Irish no doubt reflected their quiet confidence in their national sovereignty after 50 years.[50]

The *Washington Post* reported that the chilly rain of the previous days had lifted for the occasion and a smart spring breeze kept hundreds of green and orange pennants fluttering along the parade route. The bands played 'Kelly of Killane' and 'Step Together' as the honour guard marched into place. 'Jackets Green', 'The Minstrel Boy' and 'A Nation Once Again' were also played.[51] 'The Last Post' sounded and, as The *New York Times* recorded, there was a moment of quiet and only the cries of sea-gulls could be heard above the crowd in O'Connell Street until the words of the Proclamation began to reverberate from loudspeakers. The recording was the only moment of oratory during the event.[52] The *Los Angeles Times* depicted the local response: 'These are to be the days of wine and roses, for the veterans. Who will deny them their sunlit hour denies the honouring of a rich debt. Let it be paid in full.'[53]

Religion and Commemorative Spaces

Commemorative religious services were held across Ireland on Easter Monday in Jewish synagogues, Catholic cathedral churches and diocesan cathedrals of the Church of Ireland.[54] At the outset of the commemorations the leaders of the four main Christian churches issued a joint statement expressing their desire that the events would take place 'in accord with the universal message of the Holy Season of Easter, which is above history and nationality. This is the message of the reconciling of the Risen Christ in men's lives.'[55] However, the positioning of religious groups in the commemoration had required a certain amount of diplomacy and underlined the difficulties inherent in ecumenism in Ireland.[56] In April 1965 the Standing Committee of the Irish Hierarchy of the Catholic Church had agreed to meet the taoiseach's request to participate in the 1916 celebrations. The minutes recorded, 'It was thought advisable, however, to seek out a suitable formula under which the Church's part in the celebrations might be described.'[57] The primacy of the Catholic Church was clearly an issue and, in this regard, the archbishop of Dublin and his representatives provided a masterclass in polite intractability.

For the Protestant churches the establishment of suitable formulas of engagement was no less important. The Church of Ireland did not want to cause internal divisions and it was agreed that in publicity for the commemoration, 'It will be correct to say that "the Church of Ireland will arrange religious services" but not correct to say that "the Bench of Bishops of the Church of Ireland" have decided on these services.'[58] A columnist in the *Church of Ireland Gazette*, which was published in Belfast, described the Easter Rising as representing 'the very vortex of the disagreements of the Irish people' and argued that

> it must be seen as a basic principle that at this juncture – as always – the Church of Ireland must regard and treat her people, whatever their political differences, as an indissoluble whole.
>
> It is clear, therefore, that no action should be contemplated in connection with the forthcoming celebrations which could be interpreted, even by the most tenuous threat of reasoning, as an official alignment of the Church with one side or the other. Any such partisan act could only result in bewilderment and pain for a large section of the Protestant community which is already confused by some aspects of recent swift-moving ecumenism. With the incitement of the over-zealous it could lead to an even deeper division, which would endanger the unity of the Church of Ireland as we know it.[59]

Things were no easier for the Methodist and Presbyterian churches and the opening of the Garden of Remembrance on Easter Monday became a focus for some of these concerns. The garden represented a site in which the spiritual and temporal shared common ground and the question was briefly discussed as to how best it should be blessed. Before other churches had been contacted, representatives of the Taoiseach's Office met with representatives of Archbishop's House to discuss the matter. Fr James MacMahon[60] recorded that the civil servants had explained that the garden was one of remembrance for the dead of Ireland of every religion and that all religious leaders would be invited. He was, however, asked about the archbishop's preference for the blessing:

> I said that the practice hitherto was that the Archbishop alone would bless, the other religious leaders being present. Mr. O'Sullivan [of the Department of the Taoiseach] came back to this point once or twice more, and I told him I was clear that this was the Archbishop's wish . . . Mr. O'Sullivan asked if there would be any objection to giving the other religious leaders some prominence of presence. I said no.[61]

Further exchanges took place as the Department of the Taoiseach attempted to elicit a direct response from the Archbishop. MacMahon telephoned with the information that the Archbishop 'would, in principle, object to: a) a simultaneous blessing or, b) to the circumstances in which he would be present at a successive blessing by non-Catholic and Jewish clergymen'.[62]

In the event, no one else showed any enthusiasm to bless the Garden of Remembrance. The Reverend R.W. McVeigh, chairman of the Dublin District Synod of the Methodist Church, requested a meeting with the taoiseach to discuss the invitation to attend the opening. The Methodist Church had arranged a commemorative service in Dublin at 11 am on Easter Monday, but McVeigh declined the invitation to the garden as his church felt that 'much as they would like to be identified with all the celebrations and however great the sympathy of many of their members with the achievements of the State from the beginning – it might cause embarrassment in other places if they were closely associated with the opening of the Garden'.[63] An unofficial representative was nominated in McVeigh's stead. Samuel Park, moderator of the General Assembly of the Presbyterian Church, also declined the invitation and nominated a representative.[64] Lack of foresight on the part of the commemoration committee prevented Isaac Cohen, the chief rabbi, from attending as the event coincided with Passover.[65] Lack of appetite for militancy prevented attendance from the Society of Friends. Winifred Bewley, clerk of the yearly meeting, replied that, while members 'honour all those who devote their lives to the service of their fellow men', the

Society maintained that war was inconsistent with the teaching of Christ and, therefore, they could not 'in good conscience, take part in the commemoration of any military action'.[66]

At the opening of the Garden of Remembrance on Easter Monday 1966 the representatives of the Church of Ireland and Presbyterian Church General Assembly arrived late and were locked out of the ceremony. In attempting to be discreet in their presence they became conspicuous in their absence. The problem arose because of the rather elaborate entrance gate, which the architect Daithí Hanly was anxious to have incorporated into the opening ceremony. The gate was unique in Ireland: it was 50 feet wide and opened on the pressing of a button, 'sliding into receiving slots on either side in an operation which [took] half a minute to complete'.[67] An ornate key was to be presented to de Valera at the opening ceremony with which the president could press the switch which would open the electrically powered gates. The key was a copy (three times enlarged) of the oldest known key from any Irish archaeological site.[68] The exaggerated replica inadvertently led to adverse headlines, as it was reported that the Church of Ireland Archbishop and representatives of the General Assembly of the Presbyterian Church had been locked out of the Garden of Remembrance while McQuaid conducted his blessing: they had arrived three minutes late and 'the man with the key could not be found'.[69] Dr Simms, who had preached a special sermon at St Patrick's Cathedral earlier in the morning, had been picked up by a state car and was accompanied by the representative of the Presbyterian Church, the Rev. William McDowell, but had arrived to find the gate already locked.[70]

The combination of a replica of the ancient with modern technology symbolised the way in which the commemoration attempted to reproduce the old in such a way that it would facilitate the opening of the new. The bungling, though not malicious, was instructive. Representatives of non-Catholic religions, whom McQuaid had been prepared to tolerate only within a limited capacity, had excluded themselves and been excluded from the Garden of Remembrance. The official commemorative space in the Republic, therefore, continued as almost exclusively Catholic. However, this did elicit small ripples of embarrassment in 1966.

Culture and Education

The first meeting of the commemoration committee recognised that 'the people in the Show business should be asked to play their part in the celebrations by producing suitable programmes'.[71] Certain committee members were also keen to exercise full authority and it was suggested that Radio and Telefís Éireann should submit their proposed programmes for approval, as there was a fear of an unsympathetic approach by the authority to the events being commemorated.[72] Phillis Bean Uí Cheallaigh (wife of the former president Seán T. Ó Cheallaigh and sister of 1916 veteran James Ryan) also favoured a 'veto' of theatre programmes.[73] Although there was no official policy of censorship, there was a clear determination to control output where government funding was involved. It was made clear to Radio and Telefís Éireann and the Abbey Theatre that plays by Seán O'Casey would not be considered 'suitable' for the jubilee.[74]

The controlling eye was also cast over educational output. Kevin B. Nowlan, the University College Dublin academic, had been commissioned (for a fee of 150 guineas) to edit a book providing a general appraisal of Easter Week by historians. Committee minutes recorded that Phillis Bean Uí Cheallaigh, Éamonn de hÓir and others 'had some doubts as to the "sympathies" of some of the contributors' and that Leslie Bean de Barra felt that the committee should 'censor' the book.[75] Fine Gael was also concerned about the content of the book and requested to see a copy before it was sent to the printers in order to avoid controversy in connection with the commemoration.[76] This was not acceded to, officially, on the dual grounds that the publications sub-committee believed the book would not give cause for controversy, as it was in the hands of capable historians, and that, given the strict time schedule, there would not be time for the book to be sent to Fine Gael.[77] Academic timetables, however, can be somewhat fluid and Kevin B. Nowlan's *The Making of 1916* was published in 1969.

Commemorations are important vehicles through which to educate the nation and in 1966 there was a very strong educational element which – given the personal histories of the signatories – was offered *in memoriam*. Investment in education was also seen as a practical, present-centred remembrance. The *Western People* argued, 'Remember the living. And what better way to remember the noble dust of the dead than that we give that which they sought: an opportunity for a living.'[78] The National Executive of Fianna Fáil had recommended to the minister for education that he initiate a scholarship scheme linked to the seven signatories as part of the jubilee commemoration.[79] Launching the Educational Building Society's award of sixteen £50 post-primary school scholarships, the minister for education, George Colley, noted that the Easter Rising 'was an educational thing in the broad sense of the word'. He continued, but did not explain, 'Indeed, I might describe it as a crash course in national education.'[80] The government launched seven new university scholarships – named after the seven signatories – and local authorities throughout the country paid their own tributes. County councils in several parts of the country marked the anniversary in a similar way. Of these, Dublin added four scholarships to its existing scheme; Leitrim provided a 'Seán Mac Diarmada' scholarship worth £300 for a native-born student and Cork provided twelve new scholarships (along with the existing twenty-four).[81] Boland's bakery provided ten £50 scholarships for girls, of four years' duration, to secondary or vocational schools. At the launch of the scheme Colley commended Boland's on its tribute to the women of Easter Week, particularly as there was, he noted, a tendency to forget the contribution of Cumann na mBan. 'Still oftener,' Colley suggested, 'we fail to recall that the sacrifices of the men of those days were silently matched by those of their mothers, sisters, daughters, wives and sweethearts. If we look at these Scholarships in that light, I don't think there is a boy in the entire country who would grudge a single one of them to his sister.'[82]

De Valera, as chancellor of the National University of Ireland, conferred honorary degrees (Doctor of Law) on the nearest surviving relatives of six of the seven signatories of the Proclamation.[83] Margaret McDermott, the older sister of Seán Mac Diarmada, who was eighty-nine, and his younger sister, Rose, aged eighty-two, refused to accept the award. However, Rose did attend the ceremony at which de Valera made special reference to Mac Diarmada in his speech and noted that it was with great regret the Senate of the University had learned that his nearest living relative would not be present, as she was unwilling to accept the degree.[84] The commemoration committee also provided a 'Cultural and Artistic Tribute' to the Rising by organising eighteen competitions in literature, music, sculpture and painting. Categories open to schoolchildren included essays under the headings 'An Easter Week Veteran tells his Story' and '1916–2016'.[85]

Memorials and Mementoes

As part of the official commemorative week in Dublin, the museum exhibition at Kilmainham Gaol was opened by the president on Easter Sunday. The site had been reclaimed by extensive voluntary effort. De Valera told those assembled that he did not know of 'any finer shrine than this old dungeon fortress in which there has been so much suffering and courage so that Ireland should be a nation not only free but worthy of its great past'.[86] A statue was unveiled to Thomas Davis in College Green and de Valera received a statue of Robert Emmet on behalf of the people of Ireland from a group of US congressmen who were representing its owners, Mr and Mrs Francis Kane. Railway stations became retrospective memorials as principal termini across the country were renamed to mark the jubilee. This included the renaming of Kingsbridge station after the executed Seán Heuston, who had been a clerical officer with the railway. It was to be marked by a special plaque, sculpted by Oisín Kelly.[87]

Personal mementoes were also provided, which acted as reminders of the commemoration as much as the original event. Under the headline 'Huge Crowds Queue for 1916 Stamps', the *Irish Independent* reported that there had been

> unprecedented demand for the 1916 commemorative stamps and coins which went on sale yesterday for the first time. There were huge queues at the G.P.O. in Dublin and at 35 Post Office headquarters all over the country, when the first issue of the eight stamps commemorating the Rising was made . . . At the G.P.O. six special counters to cater for the rush were installed, and officials described the crowd as bigger than Christmas.[88]

Eight commemorative stamps had been issued in four denominations. It was also decided that a stamp remembering Roger Casement would be released in August to commemorate his execution and would be available until September.[89] Seven of the eight stamps to be issued in April 1966 bore the images of the seven signatories of the Proclamation and the eighth stamp carried a commemorative image of the Rising designed by Edward Delaney, which was said by the Department of Posts and Telegraphs to join 'symbolically the lives lost in the War of Independence and the theme of Ireland marching into an era of freedom'.[90] Delaney's design and the stamp carrying the image of Pearse, at 5d, were those which would be used for internal letter postage.[91]

A competition was also run for the design of a commemorative badge. This was won by Mrs Una Watters, who depicted 'An Claidheamh Solais', 'The Sword of Light'. Notes in the Department of the Taoiseach recorded that this was a symbol that had been taken up by scholars of the Gaelic revival, and was adopted by the revolutionary thinkers to indicate their dual objective: '(1) an armed rebellion, (2) an Irish cultural renaissance'.[92] This was intended to replace the Easter lily which had become an issue of contention between the government and republican groups. Republicans were less than willing to accept the change and, in Tralee, expressed the fact that they deplored 'the attempt by the "Establishment" to introduce an emblem in opposition to the oft-banned but ever-flourishing Easter Lily. We believe the Irish people will reject this new emblem as decisively as they did a similar Fianna Fail makeshift in the 1930s.'[93]

Young People and the Commemoration

The commemoration committee recognised the importance of making the jubilee relevant to the younger generation. Several members raised the issue at the first meeting and Lemass agreed that 'it was essential that the rising generation should be made fully aware of the significance of the event, so that they should share the pride of the older generation in it'.[94] Therefore it was decided that a Children's Day should form part of the official programme, which would include mass, a youth parade and an open-air concert with bands and choirs. It was also agreed that the Radio Éireann Authority should be approached with a view to having suitable programmes, 'particularly programmes directed at the younger generation, planned in advance'.[95] The Children's Day took place on Sunday 17 April and included a parade past the GPO to Croke Park; community singing led by the Artane Boys' Band and Choir and a special showing of Tomás MacAnna's pageant *Aiséirí – Glóir-Réim na Cása* ('Resurrection – The Easter Pageant').[96]

In designing the pageant, MacAnna expressed his intention to have an event 'which visually, emotionally, and intellectually will be of an impact never before attained in Ireland. We intend it to be an overwhelming experience to both audiences and participants.'[97] *Aiséirí* had as its central theme the concept of republicanism from the 1790s until the Rising. The pageant had been commissioned in March 1965 and a subcommittee had been established to oversee its development.[98] MacAnna, who liaised with the Department of Defence and a commemoration committee sub-committee, had requested that an early meeting 'take place in the room with the very large table as it is my intention to bring along some of my little son's toy soldiers and some pieces to represent the screens etc. to help us in our planning'.[99] If they got the planning right, and if they brought it to effective fruition, MacAnna was convinced that 'this Pageant will prove to be the highlight of the 1916 Celebrations, and certainly will be talked about and well remembered for a long time after the presentation'.[100]

Aiséiri was a lavish production which was performed five times during the commemorative week. MacAnna requested a total of 639
military costumes from P.J. Bourke, the theatrical and historical costu-
mier in Dublin. The list included fifteen American Colonial 1776; fifteen
French 1789; thirty Wexford Pikemen, thirty Antrim Pikemen and fifty
Famine rabble at an estimated cost of £3,830.[101] To keep control of the
budget uniforms were also borrowed from Telefís Éireann and items
including rifles and bayonets were borrowed from the army.[102] During
the week a revolver which had been given to a civilian actor went
missing and, although the case was considered to be serious by the army,
it was believed the gun could not be readily made serviceable.[103] The
matter was passed to the Gardaí, but the revolver remained at large.[104]

Despite MacAnna's high ambitions for the production, bad weather
conspired with Telefís Éireann's airing of their very popular television
drama *Insurrection* (which will be discussed in Chapter Four) to dampen
crowd numbers so that, his son Ferdia MacAnna remembered,
'Insurrectionists sometimes outnumbered the audience by three to one'
on the first two nights. However, Croke Park was full for the final performances.[105] The enthusiastic correspondent of the *Boston Globe*
recorded that it was 'polar cold and windy' but that her cheers and tears
helped to keep her mind off her frozen feet.[106] *Aiséiri* was also televised
(on Telefís Éireann on Sunday 24 April 1966) but did not lend itself well
to black and white transmission. In a slight wrangle between the commemoration committee and Telefís Éireann over the possibility of the
broadcaster giving free the time used to advertise the pageant, the
director general of RTÉ, Gunnar Rugheimer, reminded the committee
that the pageant had cost in excess of £5,000 to televise:

> Our investment of this sum, plus the not inconsiderable effort put
> into the arrangements by Telefís Éireann officials at all levels, repre-
> sents Telefís Éireann's contribution to the Cuimhneachán. We made
> this contribution in the national interest, in spite of our misgivings
> about the suitability of the material for television; misgivings which
> were subsequently borne out by the public reaction.[107]

Beyond the concept of a Children's Day, the commemoration committee had little imagination as to how the youth of Ireland should be
drawn into the story of the Rising. The booklet *Oidhreacht* (published
by the Stationery Office) was commissioned by the commemoration
committee with the intention that it be made available to all schoolchildren. A copy of the Proclamation was sent to all schools with the
recommendation that it be accompanied by a 'simple unveiling

ceremony' performed by the manager, principal teacher 'or possibly, a local I.R.A. veteran or other local dignitary', giving a short address to point to the significance of the occasion. It was also suggested that there would follow a reading of the Proclamation by one of the pupils, and, finally, the playing (or singing) of the national anthem.[108] Religious authorities had been approached to provide services for children on Friday 22 April. School managers had also been asked to organise the attendance of pupils at school for the unveiling of the Proclamation, after which the children were excused from school for the remainder of the day. It was decided that the Proclamation would, in future, be given prominent display in all schools.[109]

Commemorations Nationwide

The commemoration committee, in consultation with the army authorities, designated twelve centres outside Dublin that would host official commemorations.[110] These represented a geographical spread of the country with some link to the Rising. The centres were Cloughjordan (birthplace of Thomas MacDonagh), Cork, Dundalk, Enniscorthy, Galway, Kiltyclogher (birthplace of Seán Mac Diarmada), Limerick, Monaghan (because of its association with James Connolly), Sligo, Tralee, Waterford and Westport (birthplace of John McBride). It was also decided that the army authorities should oversee provincial celebrations and establish, in collaboration with local interested people, sub-committees to arrange the planning and carrying out of commemorative ceremonies.[111] Correspondence from organisations such as the Knights of Hibernia Friendly Society and the Organisation of National Ex-Servicemen, who sought positions on the central commemoration committee, was redirected to the Army and it was suggested they give their support at a local level.[112] Lemass subsequently wrote to Michael Hilliard, minister for defence, in July 1965 noting that it was the intention that the army authorities contact the Old IRA and other relevant groups in local areas and underlining:

> I should like you to take a lively personal interest in seeing that action as proposed is pushed ahead as quickly as possible. I have been somewhat disappointed by the delay in getting arrangements started for these provincial ceremonies, and it is important that no further time should be lost.[113]

Lemass was right to be concerned. Army memoranda from November 1965 and January 1966 show that many regional organisations had formed committees but had formulated no concrete plans.[114]

Care had to be taken when deciding who should take the salute at official events and it was decided that no one still actively involved in politics should fill this role unless this was the wish of the organising committees.[115] Lemass was anxious to prevent allegations that the ceremonies were being exploited by Fianna Fáil for party advantage and had decided to ask a minister to attend only where the desire of the committee was unanimous. Where a committee did request a minister, Lemass nominated someone with no connection to the constituency concerned. He wrote to Frank Aiken explaining this position and to express his concern that Aiken had arranged to take the salute at the parade in Dundalk, which was part of his constituency. Lemass suggested instead that Aiken swap with Jack Lynch, who was coming under pressure to go to his constituency in Cork.[116] Where a minister was requested, he did not always live up to expectations. In Waterford, although the parade was reported to have been the largest and most colourful ever seen in the county, the one big disappointment was 'that the Minister [George Colley] could not see his way to stay for the Jubilee Dinner. It did not go down well and he made a very poor impression of his short stay.'[117]

Local committees were made up generally of men who were in or had a connection to the Old IRA and those who were seen as significant members of the community: farmers, teachers, members of the GAA, a bank manager, an academic, a Knight of Columbanus and those who were described as 'very good organisers' and 'very well liked locally'.[118] Having responded to the government's decision to hold a commemoration in their locality, the committees were faced with the question of how to pay for the celebrations. Cloughjordan explained that, with no urban council or corporation to appeal to for funds, they trusted that the Department of the Taoiseach would provide some assistance.[119] And, as the liaison for the Mayo committee pointed out, since it was the government's request that the Rising be suitably commemorated in these centres, it was a reasonable assumption that the government would take responsibility for reasonable expenditure.[120] While much of the commemorative programmes were put together through voluntary effort, money had to be raised to pay for bands, platforms for the platform parties and refreshments. An allocation of £75 for seven of the official centres of commemoration was finally agreed. However, of the £525 set aside, only £409 13s 6d was claimed by the seven regional committees.[121]

It was made clear to the Department of Defence that, in the government's view, ceremonies 'should not include an oration, or speech-making, although the reading of the 1916 Proclamation or the playing of a recording of the reading of it, would be appropriate'. Moreover, it was decided that if the commemoration ceremony was linked with another function at which speech-making would be appropriate, 'there should be a clear distinction in time and place between both functions'.[122] This marked a perceptible difference between official and unofficial commemorations. Speeches and graveside orations were a central feature of republican events.

Commemorations across the country conformed to very similar patterns: religious service, parade, cultural and sporting events, and lectures deigned 'to stimulate interest in the celebrations' or to provoke discussion, such as the debate in Naas, 'Has Pearse turned in his grave?'[123] Pageants were held in many towns and villages and Bryan MacMahon's *Seachtar Fear, Seacht Lá* formed the basis of several local theatrical productions, including those in Warrenpoint, County Down, and Ballybay, County Monaghan.[124] Mallow staged 'Handing on the Torch', a pageant involving a cast of 2,000, which included workers from the Borden factory, the White Star laundry, the post office, local garages, Clock House Minerals, the farming community and District Dunhallow Hunt.[125] The pageant took place at Mallow racecourse in May 1966 and de Valera was invited by the committee, 'mindful in a special way of his schoolday connections with north Cork'. De Valera, mindful of the upcoming presidential election in June, agreed to attend.[126]

Other cultural tributes were arranged to mark Easter Week. The Ulster Fleadh Cheoil in Clones held a 1916 ballad competition, and similar competitions and commemorative concerts were held in other parts of the country.[127] In Leitrim, the Musical Society, which had planned to stage *Maritza*, decided to postpone the opera 'and concentrate on the production of the commemoration concert'.[128] The *Sligo Champion* responded to 'possibly the most stupid statement to be issued in the Jubilee year' – the decision by the commemoration committee that O'Casey plays would not be suitable – by hailing the Sligo Drama Circle's production of *Juno and the Paycock*.[129] The Little Theatre Company in Carlow staged *The Plough and the Stars*.[130] In Kerry, the Rose of Tralee received a 1916 commemorative medallion along with her other prizes.[131] Birr planted two trees in the grounds of the town hall as a lasting memorial to the Easter Rising[132] and across the country window displays and bunting marked the week of the jubilee. A window display competition in Monaghan was won by two ladies' draperies.[133] An advertisement in the *Northern Standard* urged customers to 'Commemorate Easter and Parade in Fashion: We have a lovely selection of ladies coats, newest styles in all the latest cloths . . . In our readymade department we have a complete new range of Boys, Youths and Men's wear.'[134]

Where possible, localities linked their commemorations to a person or event connected to the Easter Rising. The *Midland Tribune* carried the headline 'Cathal Brugha married Birr girl' followed by a profile of Brugha.[135] Fermoy in Cork framed itself as the only place outside Dublin to commemorate events that had actually taken place in the locality: the fight by the Kents of Bawnard.[136] Major General Joseph Sweeney, as the only Donegal man to take part in the Rising, attended events in Ballybofey and Letterkenny.[137] Con Colbert was honoured in his home town of Monalena, Castlemahon, and in Athea in Limerick the main street was renamed in his honour.[138] The North Kerry Memorial Committee unveiled plaques to three local men who died in Dublin in 1916: The O'Rahilly in Ballylongford, Paddy Shortin in Ballybunion and Michael Mulvihill in Ballyduff.[139] De Valera travelled to Limerick to unveil a plaque to the Fenian John Daly and his nephew Ned, who had been a commandant in Dublin in 1916.[140]

The commemorative year was also used as a way to mark events connected to the War of Independence. Eyre Square in Clones was renamed Matt Fitzpatrick Square in honour of the famous local patriot who was shot in 1922.[141] Five thousand people turned up in Crossbarry for the unveiling of a monument to the Kilmichael and Crossbarry engagements in 1920.[142] Members of the Old IRA joined a commemorative parade to the grave of Bernard Marron, who had also been killed in the War of Independence, in Ardragh, Monaghan.[143] In Sligo, the Old IRA gathered to lay wreaths at the graves or memorials of those who had died in the War of Independence and the Civil War. A spokesman for the brigade said, 'It is intended that the brief informal ceremonies should be a public gesture of reunion, a burial of past dissension in the true spirit of the martyrs of Easter Week and, as such, an acceptable tribute to their ideals and an example to those who follow them.'[144]

Sport and the Commemoration

The GAA provided a national structure that could be utilised during the commemoration and was keen to use the anniversary to promote the idea of its special place in Irish society.[145] The organisation commissioned a pageant in Croke Park, *Seachtar Fear, Seacht Lá* and published a book of essays, *Bearna Baol*, edited by T.P. O'Neill. It also sponsored a series of ballad competitions with prizes totalling £200 and urged all county boards and clubs to participate in the commemoration.[146] At the convention of the Connacht Council, it was noted that it was 'only fitting that the G.A.A. should play a leading role in honouring all those who died in the cause of freedom. We must all be conscious of the part we have played, and must continue to play, as a National Organisation.'[147] In Cavan it was noted, 'It is a soberly thought but a true one and let us not forget that were it not for the sacrifices made by these gallant men who gave their lives for Ireland that our national game might today be the "banned" ones [*sic*] in this, our native country.'[148] The West Mayo convention also noted that the importance of the GAA was not simply in the organisation of games but that its all-important purpose was 'the organisation of native pastimes and the promotion of athletic fitness as necessary factors in the preservation of our historic Gaelic State'.[149] The president of the GAA, Alf Murray, speaking at the annual congress in Dublin, stated that the importance of the organisation in the years surrounding the Rising was its spiritual contribution, which made 'the fight for freedom something more than a mere attempt at changing the form of government and turned it into a people's struggle for national identity'. He appealed to members of the organisation to use the jubilee year to develop a new approach to their roles within the organisation and to speaking their own language and expressions of 'love of country in everyday lives'.[150]

Given its reach, it was inevitable that the GAA would be caught in some of the tensions that emerged around the country during the course of the jubilee year. Attending the Ulster Convention in March, Murray appealed to members in the North to use their influence with the local 1916 commemoration committees to see that nothing bearing the slightest semblance of provocation should be associated with the forthcoming celebrations and that parades should be held in nationalist areas to avoid causing strife and disunity.[151] Fears of disunity were not confined to Northern Ireland and the Kerry Board of the GAA issued a statement declaring the right of every GAA member to determine his own way of commemorating the jubilee, in order that the association would not be seen to be endorsing either the official or unofficial celebrations.[152]

Controversy surrounded the Drogheda celebrations due to the decision of the committee to ban members of rugby and soccer clubs from joining their parade.[153] Cumann na mBan withdrew its two delegates from the committee in protest at what fast became known in the press as 'the Drogheda affair'.[154] John Healy in the *Western People* believed the majority of the people in the country were 'on the side of the brave old

Cumann na mBan woman [Kathleen Dempsey] who stood out in Drogheda and said all the sporting clubs should march together. God Bless her.'[155] This kind of incident was very much a local rather than a national response to the commemoration and was criticised across the political spectrum. Michael O'Riordan characterised 'the wheel of silly suggestions' in Drogheda as 'a godsend to those who wish to obscure the anti-imperialist character of the 1916 Rising'.[156] The Drogheda ban was lifted shortly afterwards but replaced by another which stipulated that uniformed members of the armed forces could not take part in the commemoration parade.[157]

During the FAI Cup Final in Dalymount Park in Dublin de Valera attended as over two hundred veterans paraded in the middle of the field and were met by the minister for health, Donagh O'Malley, and the president of the Football Association of Ireland. The commemorative ceremony included the sounding of 'The Last Post' and Reveille by the St James Brass and Reed Band and the drummers of the Fintan Lalor Pipe Band.[158] Sporting events were held across the country, including a relay race which was run from Pearse's house in Rosmuc, County Galway, to Kilmainham Gaol in Dublin. Seventy athletes comprising seven teams took part. Each team carried a banner of one of the signatories of the Proclamation and the batons used were also inscribed with the name of a signatory. On completion, runners laid a wreath at the GPO. The event was sponsored by 'a prominent participant of the Rising' who wished to remain anonymous.[159]

The State Reception

The week ended with a state reception hosted by the taoiseach and Mrs Lemass in St Patrick's Hall, Dublin Castle. It was attended by the president, religious leaders, members of the diplomatic corps, representatives of civic bodies and voluntary bodies, and veterans of the Rising and their relatives.[160] An internal report from the civil service on the reception recorded a mildly chaotic scene as the invitees arriving at the door 'were pushed from behind and were "catapulted" past the stewards. Invitation cards were brandished at us rather than submitted for examination . . . There was very little way of knowing whether the card bearers were bona fides.'[161]

The attendance, including stewards and the band, was estimated to be 1,703 people. Their liquid consumption was recorded as including 835 bottles of minerals (soft drinks); 80 bottles of squash; 414 bottles of ales and stouts; 7 gallons of wine; 346.25 bottles of spirits and 2,709 tonics and sodas.[162] The stewards and the band can, it would seem, be included in this consumption count. The civil service report on the reception noted that the author had 'searched the State Apartments for two stewards who were supposed to be on duty at the Main door. One was "entertaining" some people in the Throne room and the other was wandering absently around the Apartments,' and, the report concluded, 'I think it would not be out of place if those in charge of the cloakroom arrangements were to instruct their subordinates that sobriety is an essential requirement for the smooth despatch of their business.'[163]

Closing Ceremony

The ceremonies ended at the GPO on Saturday 16 April. The tricolour was lowered as army trumpeters played 'Sundown' and lights in the vicinity were extinguished as 'The Last Post' was sounded; then the president was introduced with a fanfare.[164] When de Valera had concluded, the band sounded a fanfare and a firing party of 120 men fired a *feu de joie* from the roof of the GPO. A 21-gun salute was also fired from guns in the grounds of Trinity College. The ceremony concluded with the national anthem.[165]

A speech had been drafted for de Valera but he abandoned the script and spoke extempore.[166] He addressed the two tasks he believed still had to be accomplished: reunification of the island and the restoration of the Irish language. Regarding Northern Ireland, de Valera said the method of reuniting the Irish nation must be that of forgetting past differences and dissension: 'Thanks be to God the dissensions [*sic*] and differences we have had down here are now past. We are all on the straight road marching again side by side and we can look forward to the people of the North wishing to be with us.' He remarked that he could not believe that the land of the O'Neills, the Ó Catháin, the McDonnells, the Maguires and the McGuinnesses would permanently be severed from the rest of Ireland and that 'All that is necessary is that the power which is at present retained in the British Parliament should be transferred to a representative all-Ireland Parliament'.[167] Terence O'Neill issued a statement in response. Ironically, he perceived the speech as 'evidently a prepared statement of policy by the Head of State of the Irish Republic', and therefore felt compelled to make his position, and that of the government of Northern Ireland, 'unmistakably clear'. O'Neill totally rejected the idea of an all-Ireland Parliament and asserted that politically, socially and economically Northern Ireland and the Republic were 'poles apart'. In conclusion, O'Neill clarified, 'Let no one suppose that, in our readiness to promote more friendly relations with the South, we are one whit less determined than our forefathers to retain our loyalties to the British Commonwealth and to prosper as an integral part of the United Kingdom.'[168]

Conclusion

The officially endorsed programme of the commemoration engaged all aspects of Irish society – sporting, cultural, educational and religious – and attempted to create a coherent narrative of Irish history and society. The staples of Irish commemoration – parades, masses and congregation around the graves of the dead – and the existing social structures within Irish society – the Catholic Church, the GAA and other civic groups – were all mobilised in the organisation of events. The position of the Rising in the historical narrative was such that it could find representation in many disparate forms. However, there was always the risk that the existing tensions within Irish society would be made more visible by the commemoration of the Rising. The government had to attempt to project a unifying rhetorical echo for the Irish population (and, like the event it commemorated, this did not take any account of the unionist position) and to provide a unifying image of Ireland that looked to the future. The question was whether or not the Easter Rising would successfully provide a bridge to modernity and whether its jubilee would be the occasion of celebration or of a damning critique of independent Ireland.

CHAPTER TWO

Alternatives to the
Official Commemoration

Writing in the *Irish Socialist* in June 1966, Michael O'Riordan applauded those who had offered critical readings of Irish society during the jubilee of the Easter Rising. He welcomed them as an important antidote to the 'adman's clichés of Lemass and Co., who sound more and more as if their true vocation lay in writing cigarette commercials'.[1] The message of the government's commemoration was that independent Ireland was modern and successful. The message of those who rejected the official celebrations was that the 26-county government was selling something that was doing Ireland harm.

Beyond the columns of student newspapers, few were arguing that the Easter Rising had been a mistake.[2] Dissent, where it existed, lay over the legacy not the event and was situated in the gap between official rhetoric and reality. Those who were disaffected included Irish-language groups, educationalists and artists, all of whom could make valid cases against government policy. However, only the republican movement had the capacity to organise significant alternatives to the official celebration. Its position was further strengthened by the fact that it had been holding commemorations of the Rising for over forty years. The move to the left by the IRA meant that anti-partitionism was accompanied by detailed critiques of the government's economic policy – particularly the Free Trade Agreement with Britain that had been signed in January 1966 – and republicans were often joined by socialists and communists in their old traditions of parading and pamphleteering.

The Easter Rising had developed what might be described as a strong brand. In other words, it had come to signify something much greater than the sum of its parts. Association with the brand could confer credibility and legitimacy. The republican movement had reasonable claim on the Rising; but they had an even better claim of ownership over its commemoration. Successive governments in the independent state had struggled to find consistency and unity in remembering Easter Week. Official commemorations invariably had been accompanied by separate republican events that rejected the government's right of custody over Easter 1916. While governments vacillated over how best to remember the Rising, the republican movement took responsibility for ensuring that it was commemorated annually across the country, and by 1966 an organisational structure was in existence, primarily through the National Graves Association. The NGA was founded in 1926 with the aim of recording, renovating and preserving patriot graves. It provided an umbrella structure for republicans, many of whom were former and current members of the IRA. Therefore the government's decision to set up commemoration committees to organise the jubilee met with opposition from republicans who already had an established network of committees. There was also a certain amount of local sympathy for those who had been consistent in their commemorative observations.

Commemoration is itself a form of revivalism and the republican movement attempted to use the jubilee as an opportunity to return to the original texts and recommit to the ideals of the leaders of 1916. Central to their commemoration was a discussion on the true meaning of independence. As with all revivals, however, a return to origins alters the meaning and, for some leading republicans, the rereading of the works of Connolly and Pearse provided the authority for a shift in the ideological direction of the movement.

A 'New Departure'

The republican movement entered the 1960s in need of some repair. The border campaign of 1956–62 had come to an end amid the unbridled apathy of the broader nationalist population. The IRA was short of funds, guns and volunteers.[3] Liam McMillen, OC of the IRA in Belfast, described the defeat of the campaign as having had a traumatic effect on the IRA which caused a full-scale re-evaluation of strategy and tactics; with the clear recognition that physical force alone had failed.[4] Cathal Goulding replaced Ruairí Ó Brádaigh as chief of staff in 1962 and took charge of an estimated 657 members in the Republic.[5] Goulding was a charismatic, attractive figure of republican pedigree who attempted to broaden the radical agenda of the IRA to include a comprehensive economic and social programme. He was influenced by left-wing thinkers such as Roy Johnston and Anthony Coughlan, who in their turn had been influenced by Desmond Greaves, a leading member of the Connolly Association in Britain.[6] Goulding spent the commemoration in prison, on remand for the possession of a Luger pistol and 3,000 rounds of ammunition. During his detention he was replaced by Seamus Costello who, it is argued, used the opportunity to push through changes even more radical than those envisioned by Goulding.[7]

In 1963 republicans commemorated the 200th anniversary of the birth of Wolfe Tone and the organisational structure gave birth to Wolfe Tone clubs the following year. These were radical discussion groups which sought, in Roy Johnston's words, 'new approaches to the question of national unity and independence' and which helped in 'the learning process' the republican movement was undergoing. They were seen to represent a return to classical republicanism and a departure from the more recent tradition of 'shoot first and explain afterwards'.[8] The Wolfe Tone Society became an arena in which republicans, socialists and communists could meet and debate contemporary politics.[9] Johnston and Coughlan, through the Wolfe Tone Society, would also be pivotal figures in the establishment of the Northern Ireland Civil Rights Association in 1967.[10] Left-wing veterans such as Peadar O'Donnell and George Gilmore re-entered a debate which was part of their legacy to the republican movement and younger radicals emerged who embraced the mix of republicanism and socialism.[11]

The IRA had not abandoned the principle of armed struggle and in 1966 it was reported that the Army Council had set up a special military council to plan a new northern onslaught.[12] However, there were clear divisions as to how the movement should proceed. Gerry Adams has written that there are traditionally three tendencies within the republican movement: the militaristic and fairly apolitical tendency, the revolutionary tendency and the constitutional tendency. By the mid-1960s, the republican movement was moving towards politicisation rather than militarism.[13] This decade saw evidence of a 'new departure', which placed emphasis on economic and social agitation. The IRA and Sinn Féin became involved in rural co-operatives, set up a housing action committee in Dublin that staged sit-ins to highlight poor living conditions, and organised illegal 'fish-ins' on exclusive salmon runs in the west of Ireland.[14] At the beginning of 1966 Sinn Féin announced a reorganisation strategy which had at its centre the large-scale education of republicans in order to impart to them 'an understanding of the social questions of the day together with an appreciation of the part the movement will play in securing for the people the guarantees enshrined in the 1916 Proclamation'.[15] Much more contentious was the decision to contest elections in the twenty-six counties. Traditionalists and progressives clashed over the direction of the movement while dissident groups condemned both sides for their lack of radicalism. The recently established *An Phoblacht* (published by Jim Lane in Cork[16]) pilloried both the IRA and Sinn Féin, arguing, 'you know, we know, and everybody with a grain of commonsense knows that: 1) Ireland is not going to be freed by talking; 2) THAT THE BOURGEOISIE, who presently monopolize Irish affairs, are not going to relinquish their position of privilege on request.'[17]

The arrest in May 1966 of Seán Garland, a leading IRA figure, while he was in possession of a document drawn up after the 1965 IRA army convention, confirmed the political direction of the republican movement. The government took the unprecedented step of laying the document on the Table of the Dáil and released aspects of the non-military campaign into the public domain. The Irish press covered the story extensively and, despite the fear that might have been engendered by the unseen military plan, the public reaction was not altogether negative.[18] An indication of how things stood in 1966 can be seen in the fact that *The Times* of London carried the story on page ten, and described the IRA policy as 'a terrorist plan to infiltrate the Irish labour movement and develop a social policy under their Chief of Staff'.[19] However, it has been pointed out that the government was clearly in possession of this information prior to the capture of Garland and it was this intelligence that fed much of the hype and tension surrounding IRA activity in the months before the jubilee.[20]

In the mid-1960s there was a certain fluidity of ideas passing among republicans, socialists and communists who shared an unhappiness with the status quo. However, there was no sense that the republican movement was in the ascendant within Irish politics. The Westminster elections in March 1966 saw Sinn Féin's vote drop by more than 20,000 compared to 1964.[21] Moreover, there was optimism rather than foreboding among those attempting to bring about change in Northern Ireland: the descent into thirty years of conflict was unimaginable.

Partition

For the government in Dublin a rhetorical commitment to the reunification of the island sat uneasily with the determination to celebrate the successes of the Republic despite partition. The concern over how the commemoration would be viewed abroad was not just a question of how the memory of the Rising would be received but how the failures of the completion of its agenda would be relayed. Dissent and disagreement inevitably steal headlines. The *New York Times* reported that Sinn Féin and the IRA regarded the state's commemoration as a funeral ceremony for the Republic that had been proclaimed fifty years previously. Their bitterness was located in the continued British control of the six counties and the failure of the Republic to revive the Irish language.[22] An interview with three veterans (McSweeney, Burke and Reidy) living in San Francisco illustrated well the double-think that existed in the majority of the population regarding the North:

> 'We accomplished what we set out to do,' McSweeney [said]. 'We united the 26 counties of Ireland. And the British, don't you know, they're stuck with the other six in the north.' He chuckled. 'They've got to subsidize them just to keep them going!' 'We'll be getting them back someday,' Burke put in. 'And just who says we won't?' Reidy shot back, looking for all the world as though he'd re-enlist if anyone else said different.[23]

Enlistment was linked to any attempts to disrupt theoretical belief in unification of the island. No action, however, was proposed against the reality of continued partition, which accommodated a clear antipathy by southerners towards the six counties. The circumscribed geography of the Republic also provided an explanation for the circumscribed nature of its successes: paradise was postponed because of partition. *Look* magazine reported that emigration was still a scourge in Ireland and the remedy, many were reported to believe, 'When we get back the six counties . . .'[24]

The politics of Northern Ireland stretched into the Republic. Seán McEntee told the *Washington Post* that the greatest disappointment in his career was the continuation of the border, which cut like a scar through the island. He conceded that concern over IRA violence during the jubilee had been unsettling but argued that the surprising aspect of Ireland after fifty years was not the sporadic violence but the impressive stability of its republican government.[25] Increased security measures were judged to be necessary in the North because of anticipated violence and gave momentum to the story that the jubilee would be marred by IRA activity. This added an extra frisson to stories, which journalists found difficult to ignore. Embassies in Washington and Canberra complained of undue emphasis on 'sporadic acts of violence' and that 'various disturbances and distractions served mainly to allow the press to belittle the occasion'.[26] The blowing up of Nelson's Pillar was the only event of spectacle provided by disaffected republicans, yet the threat of upheaval clung to the commemoration.

Dana Adam Schmidt in the *New York Times* reported that religious and patriotic feelings, political tensions and the fear of violence intermingled in Dublin on the eve of the jubilee celebrations.[27] He noted that tension had risen following four petrol-bomb attacks in the previous two months. In the last of these a bomb was thrown at a wooden hut in the grounds of the Holy Cross Roman Catholic girls' school in the centre of Belfast. Schmidt quoted Terence O'Neill saying that the 'creation of communal disorder would . . . not only besmirch the good name of Ulster but also play into the hands of the IRA, who would clearly welcome an opportunity to exploit such a situation'.[28] The *Washington Post* described how Ireland nervously celebrated its history 'with a perfusion of enthusiasm and just a slight trace of goose flesh' due to persistent rumours that the IRA may contribute 'an unwelcome noisy stunt to the commemorations'.[29] Two bomb blasts in Belfast were also reported and an angry mob attacked three girls wearing Irish republican tricolour rosettes.[30] The embassy in Berne reported that the commemoration in Dublin received little coverage in Switzerland, with more interest being taken in measures to prevent fresh outbursts of violence than in the actual celebrations themselves.[31] On 1 March, an attempt was made to set fire to the residence of Brigadier R.N. Thickness, British military attaché, who lived in Donnybrook, Dublin. A police report recorded that a tin of petrol was thrown into the kitchen of the house and ignited. An accompanying note requested that the attaché leave the country by Easter Sunday, as he was 'a symbol of Partition and a representative of British Occupied Forces'.[32]

A disproportionate number of the minor incidents that took place in the period surrounding the jubilee occurred in Kilkenny. These were largely the work of Richard Behal, who aimed to draw attention to the brutality meted out to republican prisoners. Most incidents involved the blocking of roads and damage to telephone exchanges. The most significant was the blowing up of a telephone exchange in Kilmacow.[33] This caused enough of a sensation to be reported in the international press; the *New York Herald Tribune* noted that the area had been cut off from Dublin and the village then raked with machine-gun rifle fire.[34]

Behal was something of a celebrity during the jubilee, as he had escaped from prison in Limerick with the use of bed sheets in February 1966. He had a history of activism and had been imprisoned in 1964 for non-payment of fines connected to the sale of Easter lilies. He had gone on hunger strike in protest as he had not been accorded the status of a political prisoner.[35] In 1966 Behal was serving a nine-month sentence for assaulting a garda following the firing of shots at a British torpedo boat off the coast of Waterford in September 1965. Sightings of him in various locations were reported throughout the commemorative period, leading *The Irish Times* to comment on one such report that it added the 'dramatic touch of the Scarlet Pimpernel to the whole affair'.[36] The IRA ensured he remained elusive; Behal was abducted and sentenced to death for unofficial action, seizure and unofficial use of IRA weapons. The sentence was transmuted on condition that Behal leave the country. The Gardaí received information that he left for England on 27–8 May 1966.[37] He was later heard from in New York.[38]

The tone in the foreign press was set by United Press International reports, which were filed from Dublin. Donal O'Higgins reported in early March of a national recruiting drive by the IRA and the belief that the organisation would use the occasion of the jubilee to stage a demonstration in Northern Ireland. Shipments of arms and ammunition were also believed to have reached the organisation via Cobh from sympathisers in the United States.[39] The consulate in San Francisco reported that coverage in its area had been due mainly to the wire services operating out of Dublin, and to a lesser extent Belfast. The *Los Angeles Times* was the only newspaper in the region to send its own staff reporter. The consulate noted that 'Inevitably much space was devoted – either in isolation or as part of general reports – to acts of violence, protest, security measures etc.' The wire services had reported 'Tight Security Measures Against IRA Attacks' followed by reports from Belfast, 'Ireland's Violence Cools Off'. The consulate also recorded that the Irish-language hunger strike received considerable coverage and other items included the crossing of the border by British forces, the sealing of the border, and the efforts of the Gardaí to seize an illegal banner.[40] Others reported that the trade agreement with Britain, which was to come into effect on 1 July, would be the target for militant fringe groups. Levi Sedin in the *New Times*, Moscow, argued that resentment against the agreement had produced subterranean political tremors from time to time, including the attack on the stone Nelson, which had 'fallen victim to human passions'.[41]

It was the focus on the revived fortunes of the IRA that made the government sensitive to an article by Tim Pat Coogan in the *Sunday Telegraph*. Illustrated with photographs of republicans training and arms piles, the article 'The I.R.A. Fights On' reported that fears had risen steadily that the commemoration would be 'the signal for the kick-off to yet another bloody replay of the Patriot Game'. Membership of the IRA, which was estimated to number up to 2,000, was said to consist of 45 per cent farm workers, 45 per cent tradesmen with the remaining 10 per cent professional men ranging from auctioneers to doctors. Coogan asserted that training sessions were undertaken once a week, with considerable organisation required to transport the guns and uniforms. As many of these sessions took place at night – to avoid detection – members often went to work without any sleep, having spent the night carrying guns across mountainous terrain. 'Unemployment is another hazard facing the potential IRA man,' he wrote. 'Very few firms will give jobs to someone who spends his spare time training to overthrow the State.' This group of men, he told his readers, was armed with the latest type of sub-machine guns and small arms, which they obtained from an international network of 'unscrupulous arms dealers'.[42]

Despite his rather grand claims for the IRA, Coogan inclined towards the view that it would have ceased to exist in ten years' time but cautioned against being dogmatic.[43] The article had caused discussion of its author between Paul Keating at the embassy in London and Frank Coffey at the Department of External Affairs. Keating admitted to not knowing Coogan personally, but gathered that 'his judgement is somewhat faulty and I hope he will be discreet in what he says about modern Ireland'. He did not advocate trying 'to nobble' the journalist but suggested that if Coffey could employ means of 'persuading him that statements one can make easily at home are liable to be greatly distorted abroad, it might do no harm'.[44] In an *aide memoire* Coffey recorded that in a telephone conversation Coogan said

> he had sent in the article some time ago . . . (it would appear that it was in train well before the recent bombings and was not therefore inspired by them as suggested by Mr. Keating) . . . Mr. Coogan said that he had the reputation of the country very much in mind, particularly as he was writing for an influential British publication.[45]

Nevertheless the *New York Times* reported that the president of Sinn Féin, Tomás Mac Giolla, had confirmed as 'probably about right' recent reports that the IRA had about 2,000 men in secret training armed with weapons, including the latest United States Army machine guns.[46]

There was a growing concern among official circles that the IRA was regrouping for a renewed campaign. British records reveal that Lemass viewed reports of the IRA as tending towards exaggeration, 'but this did not mean that he was taking them lightly'.[47] The Department of

External Affairs, in looking for clarification from Lemass in May 1966 on the position of the IRA, noted that it generally tended 'to play down their [the IRA's] importance completely and to suggest that they constitute no significant element of public opinion in Ireland and very little danger to the maintenance of good relations between Britain and Ireland'.[48] The administration in Northern Ireland, however, tended to play up rather than down suggestions of IRA activity. O'Neill was certainly less sanguine than Lemass and reported that IRA members who had been trained were 'impatient for action' and that in 'many aspects the present situation is on a par with that which prevailed immediately before the last IRA campaign was mounted in 1956'.[49] Roy Jenkins, as home secretary in Britain, submitted a lengthy report to Harold Wilson in May 1966 which suggested that the IRA threat was a real one and that its membership had been building steadily in the year prior to the jubilee and had reached a point of having 'some 3,000 trained members or supporters who could be called out in an emergency. Military training has been carried out at camps held secretly in various parts of Ireland, and an adequate supply of arms and ammunition is held.'[50]

The most comprehensive assessment of republican activity south of the border was contained in a Garda report to the Department of Justice, which estimated the total active strength of the IRA in October 1966 to be 1,039 members, with 312 people regarded as likely to take part in armed activities if ordered to do so (the figures are broken down by county and do not include Northern Ireland).[51] It noted that the organisation had 'a fairly considerable amount of arms, ammunition and explosives at its disposal' but was not making many strides in obtaining a substantial arsenal.[52] An *aide-mémoire* in the Department of Justice in December 1966 recorded that, although drilling with firearms continued to take place, there was no particular reason to conclude that a campaign of violence would take place. Indeed the *aide-mémoire* noted 'fairly strong signs' that the policy of force might be left in abeyance while public support was sought in municipal and Dáil elections. However, it made clear that a strong recrudescence of feeling running through the country may be reflected in violence if nationalists in the North were denied their fair share of public appointments and participation in public affairs.[53]

Throughout the jubilee period, members of the republican movement accused governments in the North and South of whipping up tension. The *United Irishman* noted that the reaction of republicans 'was one of surprise' to Stormont home affairs minister Brian McConnell's claim, in January 1966, that the IRA was about to renew its campaign.[54] In March, a statement from the Irish Republican Publicity Bureau criticised the regimes in Stormont and Leinster House and stated, 'The drums of sectarian strife have boomed before to the advantage of the Stormont regime. Now they are made to sound again.'[55] In his interview with the *New York Times* Tomás Mac Giolla accused British security forces of 'deliberately fostering tension in Ulster . . . to divide the Catholics and Protestants and to provoke the I.R.A. into premature actions'.[56] Nationalist politicians in Northern Ireland echoed these complaints and Harry Diamond, the Republican Labour Stormont MP for the Falls, charged the government with deliberately creating tensions in the community.[57]

In the mid-1960s the fault lines along which the republican movement would split by the end of the decade were already present: physical force versus political force and the role of republicans north and south of the border. The Garda Report of 1966 noted that the appointment of Roy Johnston as director of political education was a 'complete departure from former IRA policy' in associating with communist or left-wing groups.[58] This did not mean that the republican movement had abandoned the principle of physical force but the emphasis had shifted. The commemoration of the Easter Rising provided an event around which ideas could be discussed and formulated. The IRA and Sinn Féin did not attempt to use the jubilee to start a war. Neither, however, did they intend to pass up the opportunity to stir the political pot.

Republicans and the Commemoration

Republicans opposed to the official government programme of events in April 1966 established the 1916 Golden Jubilee Committee, Coiste Cuimhneacháin Seachtain na Cásca. The committee president was the veteran republican Joseph Clarke, who had fought during the Rising at Mount Street Bridge and was one of the founding members of the National Graves Association.[59] At a press conference to launch the programme (the day before the launch of the official programme of events) the committee chairman, Éamonn Mac Thomáis, said that it had no connection with 'any commemoration organised by those who stand for a connection with England'. The committee claimed that it was not a Sinn Féin organisation but was simply renting Sinn Féin offices in Gardiner Place.[60] The Department of Justice, however, reported that the ten-person committee consisted of the IRA, Sinn Féin and Cumann na mBan.[61] This alternative commemoration programme also began on

Easter Sunday, 10 April, and included 10 o'clock mass in St John the Baptist Church, Blackrock, followed by a parade to the republican plot at Dean's Grange cemetery. A second parade at 3 pm took place from the Custom House to the republican plot at Glasnevin cemetery. Mac Thomáis explained at the launch that it would be the same as in any other year, 'with the exception that there would be more commemorative lectures'.[62] A concert was also planned for the Gaiety Theatre on Easter Sunday evening. The notice for the event (and others) in the *United Irishman* included the note, 'Wear an Easter Lily.'[63] It was announced that 'full-scale preparations' were also under way in 'British occupied Ireland'. This would include parades and rallies in Belfast and various towns across Northern Ireland. It was intended that film shows, lectures, céilithe and concerts would take place in each county during the commemorative period.[64]

Joseph Clarke, who was on crutches in Glasnevin cemetery on Easter Sunday, turned down invitations to the official ceremony at the GPO and to the state reception in Dublin Castle. He was certain that 'If the men they killed in '16 were alive today they'd be up here with us. Our parade is much closer to what they fought for than the one in O'Connell Street.'[65] He also stated his intention to go to the Belfast parade the following week. Clarke's letter to the taoiseach turning down an invitation to the state reception concluded, 'do not forget there are young men in BELFAST JAIL, LIMERICK JAIL, MOUNTJOY JAIL – their only crime being they are following the teachings of all true Republican Leaders from Tone to Plunkett – BREAK THE CONNECTION WITH ENGLAND'.[66] It was retained 'on file'.[67]

The parade in Dublin was joined by nationalist groups, unwelcome at the official commemoration, from Wales, Scotland, Brittany, the Isle of Man, Cornwall and Belgium. A spokesperson for Pleidiol Wyf I'm Gwlad, the Welsh Home Rule body, said, 'We came here to join this parade to show our hatred of England.'[68] After a wreath-laying ceremony at the grave of the republican Patrick McGrath, a public meeting was held outside the cemetery. Speakers, addressing the crowd from the back of a lorry, included Paul Donohoe from Dublin, who joined greetings from the Army Council with praise for the co-operative movement in the west of Ireland which would 'eventually spell the end of the Irish neo-colonialist economy'. It was within this context that he issued the appeal to Irish youth 'to join us in the ranks of the IRA and help to hasten the day when foreign domination of our country will be ended'. *The Irish Times* reported that at the end of the meeting 'some young people approached the platform party to inquire about joining the republican movement'.[69]

A month before Easter representatives of the 1916 Golden Jubilee Committee – also known as the National Committee – Mac Thomáis and Jack Butler – met with Piaras Mac Lochlainn, the secretary of the official commemoration committee, to discuss the co-ordination of parades. Mac Thomáis and Butler had asked for assurances that the official (closing) ceremony on Saturday 16 April would conclude by 8.15 pm so as to avoid a clash with their planned event. Mac Lochlainn reported that after 'a long and very amicable discussion' it was agreed that the official ceremony would be over and the platform party gone by 8.45 pm and the unofficial parade would not reach the GPO until 9 pm. Mac Lochlainn also recorded:

> They asked that I advise the Gárda Superintendent at Store Street that we are satisfied with that arrangement and I have done that. (It seems the Superintendent had told Mr. Mac Thomais that they would have to cancel their parade. The Superintendent is satisfied that such will not now be necessary).[70]

The parade began in Parnell Square and stopped in Moore Street, where Mac Thomáis delivered a short speech on its importance in Irish history. The parade then passed into Parnell Street where the marchers were similarly educated before going to the GPO where an open-sided lorry provided the platform for five prominent republicans. The meeting was chaired by Joseph Clarke, as the original chair, Cathal Goulding, was on remand. It was estimated that a revolving crowd of approximately four hundred people looked on.[71]

The final event of the National Committee programme was the unveiling of the National Graves Association plot in Glasnevin cemetery on 24 April 1966. The work on the memorial had been overseen by Lorcan Leonard, who was also the driving force behind the Kilmainham Gaol restoration.[72] Glasnevin had long operated as a commemorative site of opposition to state nationalism.[73] Lemass had corresponded with Jim Gibbons regarding what was perceived to be the 'unsuitable and unworthy' scheme for the NGA plot but felt limited in how the government could respond. Lemass wrote to Gibbons, 'I agree that we should not be associated with the design which is likely to evoke adverse public comment, and particularly one which cannot be completed by next Easter.' However, he did believe it to be 'important that as much as possible should be done to improve the appearance of the Plot by Easter next, and I think it would be advisable to urge the Cemeteries

Committee to do everything in their power to this end, offering them financial help if this is required'.[74] This illustrated well the official position in the run-up to the commemoration. There was distaste rather than outright hostility towards republican groups. A letter to the *United Irishman* from Seán Fitzpatrick, secretary of the NGA, noted that despite a widely publicised campaign for funds in the media, 'the response in Ireland had been virtually nil'.[75] However, the National Graves Association maintained its independence and the chairman, Seosamh Mac Gráinne, issued an appeal, particularly to industrial concerns, for subscriptions to the fund necessary to restore the graves of the rank-and-file Easter Week men. Financial help for the headstone, which was estimated at £5,000, was deemed by Mac Gráinne as 'one of the most urgent gestures in this jubilee year'.[76]

Much of the funds obtained by the NGA were raised in the United States, including the receipt of $500 from the Transport Workers' Union of America.[77] The treasurer of NGA branches in the United States, Joseph O'Connor (originally from Roscommon) attended the ceremonies in Dublin and presented the association with a further cheque from Irish exiles.[78] The New York branch of the NGA organised a chartered flight, headed by O'Connor, from which 137 passengers were due to stay for almost the whole of April.[79] The American connections of the association were indicated in the presentation of souvenir copies of the Proclamation with an attached gift plaque to J. O'Connor, New York; T. Finn, Philadelphia; Mrs McGuinness, Chicago, and L. Leonard, Dublin.[80] Mrs O'Connor and Mrs McGuinness were also present, in their personal capacity, at the handing over of the Robert Emmet statue in Iveagh House.[81]

The plot in Glasnevin held the bodies of the 'unknown soldiers' of the Rising, who had been buried before their relatives could be found to claim them.[82] It contained sixteen of the sixty-four rebels killed in action during Easter Week. Tomás Mac Giolla gave the oration on 24 April and Rev. Fr Livincus blessed the plot.[83] Minutes of the National Graves Association record that all organisations had been requested to have as many flags as possible to provide colour.[84] The parade, which started at 3 pm from St Stephen's Green, was scheduled to reach Glasnevin by 4.30 pm.

Marchers clashed with police along the route as the gardaí had drawn their batons when they saw a colour party carrying a flag that they described as 'an emblem'. The blue flag was that of the Dublin Battalion of the IRA. The result was a number of running scuffles during the afternoon parade and at a rally later in the evening, during which a number of marchers were badly beaten by the gardaí.[85] Nine people were admitted to hospital; none had suffered serious injury.[86] Seven people were arrested and appeared in Dublin District Court on 27 April. Six were charged with obstructing gardaí and were remanded in custody; the seventh was charged with assaulting a garda and was sentenced to six months' imprisonment.[87] Seán Ó Brádaigh issued a statement on behalf of Sinn Féin, accusing the police of brutality and comparing them with the Royal Ulster Constabulary (RUC) in Belfast.[88] Members of the Irish Workers' Party (IWP) and of labour and trade union groups had participated in the event and the IWP also issued a statement saying that the actions of the gardaí were not only directed at the flag, which had been carried on public parades in the past, but that:

> These actions would appear to be a deliberate attempt at intimidation against all those who rightly consider that the ideals of Easter Week were betrayed by the recent signing of the Anglo-Irish Free Trade Agreement, which will bind the country closer than ever to Britain economically and can lead to a form of political reunion.[89]

The unveiling ceremony in Glasnevin was attended by 2,500 people (the Gardaí estimated that 5,000 had taken part in the initial parade).[90] The memorial contained the dates 1798, 1803, 1848, 1867, 1882 and 1916 and the inscription 'We know their dreams. They dreamed and are dead.' At the ceremony, Joseph O'Connor said that it was unfortunate that some followers of the men who died in 1916 had gained the power 'to rule and to ruin this designedly divided Ireland'. In his oration, Tomás Mac Giolla said that the commemoration had taught young people the true meaning of republicanism: 'For a brief moment the fog of lies and deceit has been swept aside and they have seen a gleam of truth . . . They shall never be the same again.'[91]

A rally held later in the evening called for the release of republican prisoners. Approximately 200 supporters marched from Parnell Square to the GPO, where there were again scuffles with gardaí as the Dublin IRA flag was once more carried publicly. Some marchers chanted, 'We want Behal, we want Behal.' Éamonn Mac Thomáis said, 'The streets of Dublin today were reminiscent of the Larkin days. If the Free State wants to put the gun back into politics let them be prepared to take responsibility for it. We have only one enemy. That enemy is the British military.' He added, 'We are not here to create trouble, but if they want it we will give it to them.' The blue flag had been carried in Belfast in a parade to Casement Park on Easter weekend. The RUC had made no attempt to seize it.[92]

Unofficial Commemorations outside Dublin

In the twelve officially designated sites of commemoration outside Dublin, the government established its own committees which did not take account of existing networks of commemoration and this caused friction which, in some cases, resulted in the holding of two parades. The most high profile was in Kiltyclogher, chosen as one of the official sites of commemoration because it was the birthplace of Seán Mac Diarmada. In December 1965 a letter was sent by Patrick O'Rourke (one of those who had organised the erection of the Seán McDermott Memorial) to Lemass stating that an event had already been planned in Kiltyclogher and seeking information on the government's intentions, as 'Should the Government Commemoration be arranged for Easter Sunday a very awkward situation could arise.'[93] The official event was being co-ordinated by the Department of Defence and a report in January 1966 on the progress being made in all designated centres of commemoration included the following information on Kiltyclogher: 'Arrangements to establish an active and firmly controlling official committee are now progressing.'[94]

Despite this, an awkward situation did indeed arise, as the sisters and a niece of Seán Mac Diarmada publicised their objection to the 'Free State Army' coming to Kiltyclogher on Easter Sunday morning. They endorsed the commemoration being organised by the National Graves Association and asserted, 'We are true to the 32-county Republic for which all these Leitrim men, including Sean, died and we object to Commemoration ceremonies organised by those who have accepted less.'[95] The result was two ceremonies in Kiltyclogher on Easter Sunday. The *Sligo Champion* reported that the official military parade was held 'in the presence of only a couple of hundred onlookers, while the afternoon ceremony, organised by the National Graves Association, was attended by a huge crowd'.[96]

In Monaghan, the annual commemoration for Ferghal O'Hanlon, who was killed in an IRA attack on Brookeborough army barracks in County Fermanagh in January 1957, offered an alternative for those who did not subscribe to the official programme. It was reported to Fianna Fáil that a prominent member of the North Monaghan Comhairle Ceantair had advocated that those attending the official parade should also participate in the second parade. The party's response made it clear that it would be 'incompatible with the membership of Fianna Fáil' to take part in the O'Hanlon parade.[97] The Monaghan Commemoration Committee had initially raised concern that the two parades would clash and appeared at a loss to find a suitable schedule. However, a private memorandum in the Department of Defence recommended that these references be disregarded as 'these conclusions have been arrived at mainly in the hope that the parade might yet go to another town in the County'.[98]

Approximately 800 people gathered on Easter Sunday to join the republican parade from the town to the gates of Latlurcan cemetery, which, as every year, were locked.[99] The *Northern Standard* reported that the parade was 'one of the biggest in recent years and included a contingent from Monaghan Co. Board G.A.A.' The oration was given by Jerry McCarthy from Cork, who criticised the collaboration of the state forces on both sides of the border, which were attempting to destroy the efforts of true republicans. McCarthy referred to the 'hot line' between Dublin and Belfast as a 'spying, renegade and cut-throat line'. Despite such things, however, he said the struggle for freedom would continue and each new generation would prove themselves as great as those who came before them.[100]

In Tralee conflict arose between the Easter Week Commemoration Committee, which had been organising events annually for over forty years, and a separate group, which had emerged in the months before the jubilee. The second group was chaired by Thomas Ellistrim, who was a member of the Old IRA and also a TD for Fianna Fáil. It was the latter association that caused tension. Members of the Labour Party and Sinn Féin were heavily critical of the membership of the new commemoration committee because of its decided Fianna Fáil bearing. At a heated meeting of the county council in February, J. Godlay said he did not see 'why people should butt in now on the fiftieth anniversary of 1916 and try to organise ceremonies when only one section of the people had been organising ceremonies for the past fifty years and at times, despite intimidation'.[101] Killarney Urban District Council decided not to participate in the Tralee commemorations because its members did not want to 'ally themselves' with either of the two bodies organising the celebrations.[102]

Therefore there were two parades in Tralee on Easter Sunday. The official parade culminated in high mass celebrated on the steps of Thomas Ashe Memorial Hall. The annual republican parade moved from Denny Street to Rath cemetery at 3 pm where a decade of the rosary was recited and 'The Last Post and Reveille' sounded. The parade then returned to Denny Street where, the *Kerryman* reported, orations were delivered from a platform erected near the '98 monument, which had recently been renovated by the republican movement. Sinn Féin's Kevin Barry of the urban district council presided over events and attacked the Free Trade Agreement with Britain, saying that co-operative movements in the west of Ireland indicated the way in which neo-colonial economics could be defeated. He called on the trade unions to develop a policy of active resistance to 'this treacherous economic policy of England and her Irish allies'.[103] The attendance at the parade was the largest for many years. These events were followed in the evening by the annual Easter Week concert in Thomas Ashe Memorial Hall, which included a programme of song, comedy and dancing.[104]

Two parades were also organised in Limerick when the existing commemoration committee refused to take part in the official parade, which was being organised by the city council. Members of the committee which had, again, been organising the commemoration for years refused to participate in a parade which included the army and the Gardaí.[105] The committee described itself as being made up of the Republican Trades Council.[106] In March the mayor of Limerick, Councillor Frank Leddin, announced that it had been impossible to reach agreement on a single parade but that were he invited to participate in the republican parade he would do so.[107] After some rather public wrangling an accommodation was reached in the city among all those commemorating the Rising and it was reported that over 3,000 people took part in the two parades: the first, official parade to Sarsfield Bridge and the second, at which 'thousands' took part, to the republican plot at Mount St Lawrence cemetery. The parade was headed by a colour party of young men and followed by republicans, the Old IRA, the mayor and members of the corporation in their robes. Mass had been celebrated at 9 am at St Michael's church on behalf of the republican movement, for all those who died for Ireland.[108]

Donegal had not made it to the final list of official designated sites, so the Republican National Commemoration Committee organised events in that county. The celebrations centred on Stranorlar from where a parade made its way to Drumboe Castle (close to where four republicans had been shot by the Free State Army in March 1923). The oration was given by Seán Gorman from Tuam, who wondered how the 26-county politicians could 'say they were free and independent when a few miles from where they stood there was a British army of occupation . . . What freedom had they when they were tied hand and foot to the British treasury and the Bank of England?'[109]

The lexicon of republican commemoration was exhausted without being reinvented during the jubilee of the Easter Rising. Parades,

prayers and concerts formed the basis of events locally and internationally. In the aftermath of the jubilee Roy Johnston wrote to the *United
Irishman* criticising the tradition of holding commemorations in
Catholic cemeteries or, if on unconsecrated ground, reciting the rosary
which, he argued, made the events sectarian.[110] Seán Mac Stíofáin, who
was then commander in Cork and South Kerry, ordered that distribution of this edition of the *United Irishman* be stopped in as wide an area
as possible. He received a six-month suspension from the IRA which
was reduced to two months on appeal.[111] Virtually the entire membership of Kerry Sinn Féin resigned in protest over the controversy.[112] Mac
Stíofáin would write later that the 'real target of this Marxist criticism
[by Johnston] was not sectarianism, but religion as such'.[113] He had
objected to Johnston becoming a member of the IRA Army Council as
the regulations forbade membership to communists.[114] Mac Stíofáin's
actions had as much to do with his opposition to the new departure
which would 'divert the IRA into the never-never land of theoretical
Marxism and parliamentary politics'[115] as it did religion or practices of
remembrance. However, the incident underlined the residual conser-
vatism of many members of the IRA and the limits of their
commemorative imaginations.

The Blowing up of Nelson's Pillar

The most dramatic and widely discussed of the unofficial commemorative gestures was the blowing up of Nelson's Pillar on O'Connell Street
in Dublin on 8 March 1966. In what was described by specialists as 'a
really expert job' a necklace of explosives blew off the top of the pillar at
1.30 am. Despite the fact that there were people on O'Connell Street at
the time, no one was injured. The explosion was heard over a wide area
and people within half a mile felt a tremor and saw a flash of light. The
explosion left Nelson's head lying at the foot of the pillar, his eye looking
down North Earl Street.[116] 'They'll go wild about this in America,' said
one onlooker.[117]

   As a result, on the eve of the jubilee, police kept a more watchful eye
over other British monuments and residences. These included the
Wellington monument in Phoenix Park, the British embassy, the British
ambassador's residence and the First World War memorial at
Islandbridge.[118] These kinds of measures were used by the press to indicate the tension created by the commemoration and to illustrate the fear
that it would be used as a focus for those who wanted to make emphatic
political points. In Northern Ireland Terence O'Neill had noted on the

pressures in that jurisdiction that 'in an age of mass communication . . . [a] bombing or a gimmicky demonstration provides a better headline or a more dramatic picture than the dignified expression of moderate opinion'.[119] In May the republican movement issued a statement distancing itself from this and other incidents:

> From 1954 . . . the Republican Movement has not concerned itself
> in the slightest way with the destruction of monuments of foreign
> origin, nor has the movement aided implicitly or explicitly such
> demolitions. We have refused to settle for the destruction of the
> symbols of domination; we are interested in the destruction of the
> domination itself.[120]

An Phoblacht described the statement as itself a spectacle, 'to see self-styled revolutionaries frantically protesting against any notion that they are responsible for ridding our Capital of that monstrosity erected to perpetuate the memory of an English cut-throat, and an adulterer to boot'.[121] No one was ever charged with the blowing up of the pillar, but in 2001, Liam Sutcliffe, a member of the IRA in Dublin, admitted to the bombing.[122]

The *Northern Standard* chose to interpret the blowing up of the pillar as an indictment of the recent budget in the Republic. Nelson, who, it was suggested, 'must often have had the suspicion that he wasn't exactly the most popular man in Ireland', was nevertheless owed a 'small debt of gratitude for so explosively expressing the feelings of many people with regard to the latest release from Jack [Lynch] and the Moneygrabbers'.[123] John Grigg, in the *Guardian*, described the destruction of the pillar as an insensate act which brought to mind a Biblical blindness. His piece caused some upset, as it opened with the view that 'Nearly everything that is worth looking at in Ireland was made by God or the English.'[124] A letter of rebuttal suggested instead that there should be delight and admiration for the superb timing and efficiency of the pillar's removal, during which nothing had been hurt except John Grigg's feelings. The letter ended by suggesting that a 'serious lesson' may be learned from the operation: 'If an "illegal organisation" could be formed to run Dublin Airport, complete the new Abbey Theatre, and make a start in the Kennedy Concert Hall, all under the cover of darkness, this sort of work might also be accomplished quickly and efficiently.'[125]

The army removed what remained of the pillar with explosives at 3.30 am on 14 March. Thousands of people congregated in O'Connell Street in the hours before the blasts and were reported to be singing and dancing as they waited for the countdown. The pillar fell to claps and cheers.[126] The group 'Go Lucky Four' quickly released their song 'Up Went Nelson', sung to the tune of the 'Battle Hymn of the Republic', which stayed at the top of the Irish charts for eight consecutive weeks. It included the lines, 'The Irish population came from miles around,/ To see the English hero lying on the ground./ The Dublin Corporation had no funds to have it done,/ with the Pillar blew to pieces by the tonne, tonne, tonne'. The popular response to the blowing up of the pillar could be interpreted as delight in seeing the end of a symbol of British rule in Ireland. However, the symbolism was not straightforward. On one level it was clear that Dubliners had responded to the sheer spectacle and to the idea of the slaying of imperial power. However, the blowing up of Nelson represented a challenge to authority that was not limited to empire. The unofficial strike became a means through which all authority could be mocked. The credibility of the state was shaken by the act of violence at the heart of the capital city and the fallen pillar was used to ridicule the inefficiencies of the government and the unpopularity of its financial policies.

James Connolly and Discourses of the Left

The labour movement in Ireland had been increasingly politicised in the decade before the Easter Rising. Leaders of the calibre of James Larkin and James Connolly had helped to organise a significant political force in Irish politics.[127] Labour's importance, however, did not survive the aftermath of the Rising. This created a difficulty for those on the left during the fiftieth-anniversary commemoration. They had to find a way to write their strands back into the story without conceding that the Rising itself may have been a moment when the bourgeois nation state saw off its ideological rivals. Moreover, they had to assert their connection to the Rising if they were going to challenge the government's right to 'own' the commemoration. Michael O'Riordan warned, 'Subtle attempts are being made, not without a degree of success, to convince the people that we will be commemorating the "achievement" of what the '16 men died for; and an attempt to depict them as "the founders of the modern Irish State"'.[128] The republican movement had an important tradition of left-wing thought and this was enjoying a revival in the 1960s. Therefore, for those on the left the commemoration offered the opportunity to reassert their own place within the Irish nationalist canon, challenge Fianna Fáil's place within that canon and participate in the debate on the future direction of the republican movement.

To address the first issue it was essential that the Rising be presented as a high point rather than an end point. The betrayal of the struggle for economic and cultural independence was seen to have come later, therefore; and the figure of Arthur Griffith acted as a lightning rod for much of the frustration of disappointment.[129] George Gilmore, who wrote a series of articles for the *United Irishman*, saw as pivotal the period after the Rising, during which the national question dominated and Labour was told to wait: 'Labour waited – and that was the great failure of our generation. I do not think it is too much to say that it was the determining factor in causing the collapse of the independence movement.'[130] Desmond Greaves, writing in *Marxism Today*, noted that the foot soldiers of the Citizen Army and the Volunteers were largely working class (with officers who came from the artisan and lower professional classes). The bourgeoisie, Greaves argued, had stood aloof in 1916 and had been on the sidelines during the revolutionary period but had, nevertheless, been the sole beneficiary of the sacrifices of the common people.[131] For the editor of the *Irish Socialist*, two currents had always existed in the struggle for independence: those who wanted a limited amount of independence and those who wanted a complete break with Britain. Behind the former group lay class interests which saw the imperial connection as essential for their development and against them stood the workers, the small businessmen and the intellectuals. The temporary alliance carved between these two groups had ended with the Treaty and the coming to power of Cumann na Gaedheal, which had made no serious attempt to change the economic relationship with Britain.[132]

Members of the broad labour movement joined everyone else in attempting to claim or reclaim the Rising. James Connolly and the Citizen Army were central to this process. Brendan Corish, leader of the Labour Party, responding to a speech by Lemass in Tullamore in which he suggested that Fianna Fáil were the sole heirs of the Rising, said that the contribution of the Citizen Army and the leadership of James Connolly 'alone should prevent him [Lemass] from making this attempt to "take over" 1916 for the electoral purposes of Fianna Fáil'.[133] However, for the Labour Party there continued to be a discomfort in using the language of Connolly rather than in merely invoking his name.[134] Connolly had become the national and social movements incarnate and was the linchpin in any act of reclamation. However, the Citizen Army was also a significant bridge between a rebellion by workers and a rebellion by nationalists. It was described as representing 'the most vital link of the many that forever joins the two climacteric years of Irish history – 1913 and 1916'.[135] The Dublin Lockout of 1913 had been a practical failure which was understood as a moral victory but, unlike the Easter Rising, had stopped short of being reframed as a triumph. However, it was argued by Joseph Deasy, the lines of demarcation that divided the various political and social groups during the Lockout and the revolution that followed were remarkably similar. James Connolly was one of the few who understood the alignment of forces merging to challenge the imperialist set-up. That failure of understanding, Deasy asserted, led to the defeat of progressive forces in 1921 and 1922, leaving 'capitulation to capitalism' as official policy.[136]

Connolly's popularity during the jubilee stemmed from the perception both of his personality and his politics. Desmond Ryan had written of him that 'Connolly within a few years [of his death] was buried in a shroud of words, both by his enemies and by his friends . . .'[137] Out of this, however, he emerged as a figure who was seen as more human and much less remote than some of the other signatories of the Proclamation. Hugh Leonard said that Connolly had been his favourite figure to portray in the Telefís Éireann drama *Insurrection*[138] and, in general, the sense that he was 'down to earth and rough tongued'[139] appeared to suit the mood of the time. Waverley Records released an album entitled *His Name was Connolly*, which contained a variety of songs telling tales of Connolly's life and death. One reviewer described them as being delivered in 'a Behanesque rollicking roar, the songs have considerable impact, some of them are touching'.[140] Connolly's life, as well as his death, had a hard edge to it which resonated with those whose lives were hard in the 1960s. It was in the context of economic problems and strike action that Bernardine Truden, who chronicled the jubilee commemoration for the *Boston Globe*, noted that, marking the trend of the times, at Tomás MacAnna's pageant in Croke Park,

> the greatest cheers came, not for any of the marching men, but for the strikers of 1913, when they burst onto the field with their placards. And the loudest boos were not for the redcoats, with their muskets and their cannons, but for the baton charge by the police that helped to break the strike![141]

At the unveiling of a plaque to Connolly in Mallow by his daughter, the local TD, Patrick McAuliffe, noted that the freedom for which the rebel had died included the freedom to demand a just wage and the right of free men to strike in support of that demand.[142]

Connolly had faced hardship, emigration and life in the Dublin slums, so as a figure he was firmly located in the world of realists rather than dreamers. Aspects of his life were retold in the many profiles of the leaders of the Easter Rising produced during the commemoration and Joseph Deasy reproduced a short record of Connolly's life and works.[143] Most commonly Connolly was depicted alongside Pearse as one of the two most significant leaders of the Rising. *An tÓglac*, the newspaper of the Old IRA, had described Connolly as 'the greatest of our revolution-aries', with Pearse as the 'idealist', and in many ways this is how their reputations stood in 1966.[144] Pearse, depicted as the poet-dreamer, had become an other-worldly icon of the revolution, while Connolly repre-sented its pragmatic resolution. They had a symbiotic relationship in the unfolding events: Pearse had written the Proclamation but Connolly's influence had been crucial in rooting it in social as well as national justice. A.V. Sellwood opened his account of the Rising published in 1966 with the observation from one Dubliner, 'Them two together, Padraic Pearse and Connolly! Did you ever see the like? Oil and water will mix better than the Volunteers and Connolly's bunch of reds.'[145]

This mixing of oil and water had been an important element of the Rising. Sellwood himself had noted, 'whatever their wide and sincerely-held divergences in politics, each of these men was, for the time being at least, dependent on the other.'[146] However, for those within the labour movement in 1966, it was important that this was not seen as an alliance of convenience or of opposites. Connolly was not only important to the left because of his prolific and robust writings and contribution to the cause of the worker. He was their link to the national movement and much of what was written in 1966 underlined the fact that Connolly's 'socialism, nationalism and trade union struggles were all complemen-tary', as Deasy wrote, 'one being incomplete without the other and that all constituted not different worlds, but made up his one world'.[147] Desmond Ryan asserted that 'Connolly was a man who belonged to, and worked in two worlds: the world of international socialism and the world of militant nationalism.'[148] And, for Desmond Greaves, Connolly had recognised that it was impossible to counterpose socialism and nationalism within Ireland: 'the two were very different aspects of one democratic movement.'[149]

The labour movement, therefore, linked itself through Connolly to a long tradition of republicanism going back to the United Irishmen, who had initiated a rebellion with 'something approaching a rudimentary General Strike'.[150] The lineage of labour struggles could be further traced through Robert Emmet, John Mitchel and Fintan Lalor.[151] The aim of the left in 1966 was not to debunk the story of Irish nationalism prior to the Rising: it was to embrace it with a different emphasis. All groups wanted to say that the tradition that produced the Easter Rising was their tradition. Moreover, it was seen as important that criticism of the government did not become a wholesale rejection of Irish history and society so that 'Wolfe Tone and Pearse are thrown out of the window along with Lemass and E.A. McGuire'.[152]

However, the aim was not just a matter of staking a claim or marking the bona fides of socialists by linking them to Connolly and Pearse. The fiftieth-anniversary commemoration also offered an opportunity to challenge Fianna Fáil's historical and contemporary position. Lemass and de Valera used the rhetoric of freedom during the jubilee and clearly positioned themselves and the government as the product of a tradition of Irish republicanism dating back to the 1790s. However, within the discourses of the left, it was argued that the struggle for freedom had been abandoned by those who had eventually won out: Griffith and those whose interests were served by the Free State. Greaves articulated the frustration of those who saw the betrayal of the Rising in its immediate aftermath: 'One would almost be led to believe that the Easter Rising was what put into power the class and government who are in power today. Thus has the bourgeoisie torn away the banner of the common people to make trappings for itself.'[153]

The signing of the Free Trade Agreement with Britain in January 1966 – which the *United Irishman* described as the 'recent Act of Union' – represented the sharpest sign to his critics that Lemass had abandoned a policy of independence. Economic dependence on Britain was seen to represent also an end of the struggle for political and cultural independence; so that the commemoration of the Easter Rising had become 'an occasion for mild embarrassment rather than one for rejoicing'.[154] Lemass's policy of relying on foreign capital had led to a position in which he 'in fact repudiates the policy of 1916, while honouring it as a sentimental memory'.[155] As a response to the political establishment for whom 1916 was to be celebrated 'merely as a dead, heroic gesture', the Executive Committee of the IWP affirmed that the objectives of 1916 and the teachings of Pearse and Connolly were as relevant in 1966 as they had been fifty years previously. It called on the working class to challenge those who had abandoned the policies of 1916.[156]

There was a very significant investment in the period 1913–21 which offered a counter to the more usual nationalist 'four glorious years' of 1916–20. For both nationalists and socialists, although elements of the story had to be jettisoned in order to allow the ideological narrative to flow, the Easter Rising was sacrosanct. Lenin had recognised it as a result of the crisis of imperialism in evidence across Europe and this could be used as evidence that Connolly's decision to join the Rising was the right one.[157] In presenting the Lockout in Dublin and the Rising as inextricably bound, the North could also be given a different place in the story. Larkin had led the dockers' and carters' strike in Belfast in 1907 and Connolly had taken up residence in the city in 1911.[158] In the pamphlet published by the Belfast branch of the National Graves Association, *1916–1966: Belfast and Nineteen Sixteen*, Connolly was the figure most discussed and the leader (along with Casement) to whom Belfast felt most connected.[159] Rather than the north-east representing the place of precedents in terms of the formation of the Ulster Volunteers and the signing of the Covenant, it could also be presented as the place in which the strike of 1907 signalled the way for that in Dublin in 1913.

The call in 1966 by those on the left was for a return to the values of Connolly and a rebuilding of the labour movement in order to work towards a social republic rather than a commercial republic.[160] It was noted that the proportion of industrial to agricultural workers had risen enormously and therefore it was never more important to spread the consciousness of its own power throughout the working class.[161] Raftery declared that the 'working-class remain as the "incorruptible inheritors" of 1916'. He argued that, by recapturing Connolly's vision of the unity of the national and social struggles, the working class could give leadership to all who suffered 'from the repudiation of the heritage which was asserted in arms 50 years ago'.[162]

The Hunger Strike

The Irish-language group Misneach expressed its non-participation in the official jubilee through the form of a hunger strike, which involved thirteen people taking nothing but water for a week. The strikers stayed in a back room in a tenement house off Parnell Street in Dublin. They were reported to be sleeping on mattresses laid on the floor in a room heated by an open fire.[163] The *United Irishman* reported that, for the duration of the strike, the premises occupied by Misneach 'became a place of pilgrimage for all the Gaeilgeoirí of the city. The support received was far in excess of that anticipated by the organisers.'[164]

The strike began on Easter Monday and was in protest at the commemoration because 'the ideals of the 1916 men have not been realised and we have nothing to celebrate'. Many of the members belonged to Cumann Chiuain Ard, a branch of the Gaelic League. They pledged to think, speak, write and read only in Irish during the strike period.[165] The writer Máirtín Ó Caidhain said that the hunger strike was an effort to prove 'that there was something left in Ireland which those "celebrating huxters" could not sell, some little spark that might someday light the road to the Republic which Tone, Pearse, Connolly and countless others died to obtain'.[166] The strikers argued that Connolly and Pearse did not die

> to have their death celebrated, but that their aims be achieved: neither intellectual, economic nor physical independence has been gained; nor is any conscious effort being made to move in the direction of the Republic; the opposite is the Truth as the White Paper on the Irish language and the recent Free Trade Agreement with England demonstrate.[167]

The campaign was in tune with language protest movements in Wales, Süd-Tirol, Belgium and elsewhere in Europe.[168] However, the hunger strike was also an effective symbolic vehicle as it resonated in the Irish historical imagination and had the ability to steal headlines at home and abroad. The Irish ambassador in Berne reported that the *Neue Zurcher Zeitung* had published two photographs: one showing the hoisting of the flag in the Garden of Remembrance and the other (bigger one) showing 'the demonstration of partisans of the Irish nationalistic Misneach – [the] movement for an Ireland comprising the whole of the island'.[169] Inevitably, therefore, the hunger strike gained a disproportionate degree of attention and demonstrated that small sacrifices can sometimes carry a reverberation more newsworthy than large celebrations.

Whither Women?

In the period leading up to the Easter Rising, Constance Markievicz identified three significant movements in Ireland: the national movement, the labour movement and the women's movement.[170] Remembrance of the Rising provided an opportunity to revisit the ideals of the period and to inject energy into a discussion of issues that had been central to these movements. Republicans and socialists used the commemoration as means of reconnecting to the original event and assailing the government for the failures and lost opportunities of the intervening years. However, discourses on Irish feminism were not a prominent part of the commemoration. Certain women were clearly visible and vocal during the jubilee, but the historical position of women during the Easter Rising was not used as a way of forcing a debate on the position of women in the 1960s.

The second wave of Irish feminism is traditionally dated from 1968, when the Irish Housewives Association and the Association of Business and Professional Women established an ad hoc committee to call on the government to establish a National Commission on the Status of Women. This eventually led to the setting up of the Council for the Status of Women in 1972.[171] Individual women's groups and networks did exist in the mid-1960s and were on the verge of becoming more systematic in their approach. However, the commemoration of the Easter Rising did not operate as a springboard for the increased radicalisation of feminist debate. There were few female journalists – mostly foreign correspondents – and the content of their copy differed little from that of their male counterparts.

Pockets of feminist critique did exist. Marion Jeffares, writing in the *Irish Socialist* commemorative supplement, looked to the period leading up to and including the Rising as 'the Golden Age of Irish womanhood' and asked, 'What would Markiewicz or Maud Gonne think of the position occupied by women in the Ireland of 1966?' Jeffares noted that, fifty years after the Rising, women still did not have equal pay for equal work, women civil servants were still compelled to give up their jobs when they married and very few women had jobs in politics or public life. She argued that women still qualified for Connolly's description of them in a capitalist society: 'the slave of the slaves'.[172] Nevertheless, in general, 1966 discourses on freedom were concerned with the national question and with economic inequalities and were not translated into gender issues.

During the jubilee of the Easter Rising, prominent women linked by blood or marriage to the dead of Easter Week understood that the anniversary offered them an opportunity to exert their influence by threatening to embarrass the government. Kathleen Clarke was furious that her husband Tom's position as first president of the Republic was being usurped by Pearse and threatened to go public;[173] the sisters of Seán Mac Diarmada made clear their disdain for the 26-county state and Margaret Pearse, the sister of Patrick and Willie, gave an interview to *The Irish Times* in March 1966 saying that she had decided to leave St Enda's school to a religious order rather than to the nation as 'conditions ha[d] changed a lot' since her mother's bequest thirty-three years previously.[174] The threat was made largely to ensure that the government undertook its proper responsibilities towards the maintenance of the former school. The property was, in fact, secured for the state the following year.[175]

The emotional authority of the female relatives looked the state's authority firmly in the eye and was clearly something that Lemass wanted to neutralise. Kathleen Clarke had been an important figure in the preservation of the memory of the republican dead, having been a founder member of the National Graves Association and a trustee of the Wolfe Tone Memorial Fund. However, her offer to serve on the commemoration committee had been declined by the taoiseach as, he wrote, 'the main theme of the celebrations was the honouring of the memory of these leaders, and the association of their close relatives with the preparatory arrangements might be thought to detract rather than add to the impressiveness of the national tribute to them which is envisaged.'[176] Some women did serve on the committee: Phillis Uí Cheallaigh and Máire Bhreathnach (of the Department of Finance) were formidable presences.

Women had played crucial roles in the maintenance and transmission of republican ideals through organisations like Cumann na mBan and the National Graves Association. Historically they often represented uncompromising positions and were themselves significant republicans. However, this did not necessarily mean that they were uncompromising feminists. Cumann na mBan, as the primary organisation of nationalist women, had always seen itself, Margaret Ward has argued, as guardians of the republican conscience rather than a representative of the interests of women.[177] Second-wave feminism in Ireland, as elsewhere, organised itself around the politics of the individual body, much of its early activism concerning female fertility. For certain prominent republican women the stock they traded was dead male bodies rather than those of living females. These women of the Irish political aristocracy increasingly depended upon channelling their dead relatives as a way of asserting political voices. Like Antigone, they became watchers of the respect afforded their deceased brothers and husbands and might have acted to counter the moral power of the state. However, their authority, in general, was used to maintain rather than reshape the masculine heroic ideal and radicalisation of the feminist debate did not take place around the remembrance of the Easter Rising.

Conclusion

In May 1966, once 'all the ballyhoo' had ended, the *United Irishman* considered the events of the previous month. It stated that clearly there had been nothing to celebrate and said instead that the jubilee had revealed a level of disillusionment in Ireland. It noted that at quieter commemorations throughout the country 'Republican speakers plainly exposed the fallacy of the Jubilee celebrations and showed how empty the utterances and rhetoric of the Fianna Fail "patriots" really were.'[178]

The republican movement, along with those of the left, challenged the government's right to the legacy of the Rising and acted to reclaim its tradition for themselves. They were also, however, taking part in their own processes of stocktaking. The fiftieth-anniversary commemoration of Easter Week occurred within the flow of change in Ireland and became a form through which those changes could become manifest. The republican movement was negotiating its own new departure, which incorporated those from the left and which put pressure on its internal unity. In 1966, although republicans had not abandoned physical force as a principle, their approach to bringing about change in Ireland was as heavily textual as it was military. In this new departure the production of long treatises on economics was as much a part of the commitment to republicanism as night-time drilling.

Despite this shift and the fact that the ending of the border campaign had demoralised republicans, there was still a general sense of anticipation that the IRA would do something dramatic to mark the anniversary. In the Republic, the government's fear was that the IRA would derail the commemoration and in Northern Ireland the fear was much more connected to actions that might derail the state. Such was the tension created in the months before the jubilee that the *United Irishman* said a level of hysteria had been created until 'practically every ordinary citizen expected to be assassinated in bed'.[179] Individuals did some dramatic and some minor things to mark the anniversary but as a movement republicans peacefully protested against the official message of the state through their alternative commemorations.

The government in the Republic had the capacity to roll out a spectacle much larger than that employed by republicans and their supporters on the left. Most citizens had no appetite to differentiate between the Rising and the state and were happy to congregate to celebrate their shared history and their independence, whatever that meant. However, not everyone in Ireland accepted the official version of events and, in 1966, this minority gathered and articulated their sustained opposition to the way in which Ireland had been governed in the decades after the Rising.

CHAPTER THREE

'The Other Place'
Commemoration in Northern Ireland

In September 1966, assessing his achievements in office, the prime minister of Northern Ireland, Terence O'Neill, expressed his belief that Ulster was 'with it' and forging ahead towards the 1970s.[1] The language of modernisation, however awkward, was present north of the border as well as in the Republic of Ireland. However, in Northern Ireland too, the past and the present nestled side by side under the same tree. In 1965, while arguing for a progressive unionism, O'Neill had felt it necessary to assert that the Ulster of Carson and Craig was not dead. It was the idea rather than the reality to which he appealed – a nostalgia for the certainties of the earlier century during which Ulster unionism appeared to stand united against its opponents.[2] But myths can be appropriated by all sides and references to violent histories run their own risk.

As the great iconic representative of Ulstermen, Edward Carson's birth in Dublin had not overly troubled unionists. He was central to the origin myth of Northern Ireland. The MP Joseph Burns, speaking in Stormont in March 1966, asserted that 'I would not be here today, you, Mr. Speaker, would not be here today, this building would not be here today, Northern Ireland would not be here today if it were not for the late Lord Carson.' He added, 'This man was the greatest Ulsterman, in my opinion, who ever lived.'[3] The leaders of the Easter Rising had left widows, sisters and nieces who perpetuated the cause but could not perpetuate the name. Carson, in having a son, demonstrated the ill wisdom in having a name without a cause.

The younger Edward Carson had become embroiled in the controversy over the naming of a new bridge over the Lagan in February 1966 and had come under the influence of the Rev. Ian Paisley, who saw this as an opportunity to embarrass O'Neill. The prime minister appeared to be behind the Governor, Lord Erskine's 'unconstitutional' intervention urging that the bridge be named 'Queen Elizabeth' rather than 'Carson' and the former leader's progeny had expressed outrage at the interference.[4] Nat Minford, the Unionist MP for Antrim, had been moved by reports of events at a meeting in the Ulster Hall (organised by Paisley and attended by Carson Jr) to implore Carson's son, who was based in England, 'For God's sake you go and never come back.'[5] The following morning, as a result of this outburst, Minford received several abusive phone calls to his home, the last of which he described as unrepeatable but from a caller he assumed had read *Fanny Hill*.[6] He expanded on his view of Carson's son:

> I think it is highly unfortunate that this young person from Great Britain should be brought over here and paraded almost like a Guy Fawkes guy, because in my opinion he is not *compos mentis* . . . I sincerely hope that I will read in tonight's paper that he has taken the first boat home from Belfast.[7]

The flirtation between Carson's son and politics in Northern Ireland was short-lived but nevertheless underlined the benefit to those in government of Edward Carson remaining dead. Homage to former leaders and commemorative events appear to bring the past to life when in reality they are a celebration of the fact that the past is history. It is this conjunction that supplies the tools for the making of myths.

The unwelcome manifestation of an actual Edward Carson in Northern Ireland in 1966 occurred around the same time as the re-emergence of the Ulster Volunteer Force (UVF). The original incarnation of this paramilitary group had been formed in 1913 as a channel for anti-home rule agitation. For the unionist leadership, its significance rested in the threat rather than in the hope of violence and the arrival of 25,000 rifles and three million rounds of ammunition off the north-east coast in April 1914 had made Carson more mindful of the consequences of the rhetoric of incitement.[8] The contradictions between the unionist elite and the more militant among their followers had been obscured in 1914 by the outbreak of the First World War as paramilitaries traded their uniforms for those of the British Army. The contradictions could not be obscured in 1966. The UVF was re-formed, it was claimed, in anticipation of the fiftieth anniversary of the Easter Rising and the following year, on 21 May 1966, 'Captain William Johnston' issued a declaration of war by the UVF 'against the IRA and its splinter groups'. In June the shooting dead of John Patrick Scullion in the Clonard area of Belfast and of Peter Ward in Malvern Street, off the Shankill Road, led Brian

McConnell, the minister of home affairs, to declare the UVF an unlawful organisation. O'Neill, who had flown back from France where he had been honouring the men of the 36th (Ulster) Division – many of whom had been members of the UVF – who had died at the Somme, declared, 'Let no one imagine that there is any connection whatever between these two bodies: between men who were ready to die for their country on the Fields of France and a sordid conspiracy of criminals prepared to take up arms against unprotected fellow-citizens.'[9] The phantasmic legacy of unionism in the early twentieth century reappeared in 1966 and complicated life for Terence O'Neill. Nationalist ghosts added more fuel to the mix.

Representation and Reality

As with the Republic, the government in Northern Ireland attempted to use commemoration to stabilise its past in order to provide an anchor for its present. However, efforts to create a shared history and culture in Northern Ireland were made much more difficult by the presence of a large minority which could not be incorporated into official depictions of the state and its people as both unionist and Protestant.[10] History and demography had made things much easier for the Republic. When Seán Lemass was asked to consider appointing some 'representatives from what was previously known as the Unionist or Protestant Section'[11] on the commemoration committee for the fiftieth anniversary of the Easter Rising, he barely understood the question. He responded, 'I do not know how we could secure the participation of persons who would be regarded as representatives of the old "Unionist" element, and it is at least very doubtful if persons who would be considered to be so representative would desire this association.'[12] The government in the Republic had a heightened sensitivity as to how disunity at home would tarnish Ireland's reputation abroad, but this could barely hold a candle to the defensiveness of the government in Northern Ireland. The constitutional position of the Republic of Ireland was secure in 1966. Its most vociferous opponents from within wanted to see the territory of the state extended, not demolished. In Northern Ireland, insecurity – real and imagined – regarding its constitutional position continued to be written into the fabric of the place. So much so that the unionist government 'saw unity among protestants – even when that was merely superficial – as the only way in which the state could survive'.[13]

One of the difficulties of constructing an 'imagined community' in Northern Ireland – fundamental in the creation of a shared sense of nationhood – was that many within and without conceived of the Northern Irish nation itself as imaginary. Nations are conceptual entities and can exist only when they are believed to be real. Prior to the meeting between Seán Lemass and Terence O'Neill in 1965, the prime minister had said that such a meeting would not be possible because the taoiseach did not believe that he (O'Neill) existed, since the Republic failed to acknowledge the existence of Northern Ireland. Lemass dismissed this bid for constitutional recognition as a 'gimmick' and, while neither acknowledging the 'absurdity' that the six counties were part of 'Britain' nor denying the 'impossibility' of abandoning hopes for Irish unity, did recognise that 'the Government and Parliament there [in Northern Ireland] exist with the support of the majority in the Six-County area – artificial though that area is . . . Recognition of the realities of the situation has never been a problem with us.'[14]

The perception that Northern Ireland was an artificial reality had been reflected in the inability of many in the Republic to utter its name. Terms such as the 'Six-Counties', the 'Six-County Prime Minister', the 'Stormont Government', the 'North' and (as Lemass demonstrated in the speech quoted above), when all else failed, 'there', were used as alternatives in the official lexicon. Alienation from the Republic was expressed in Northern Ireland by the use of the term Éire, as low-level verbal abuses were traded over (and because of) the border.[15] Throughout the 1960s, however, Lemass had been attempting to retreat from the official position. In May 1960 he wrote to Vivian de Valera regarding the fact that when reprinting an interview Lemass had given to the *Guardian*, the *Irish Press* had changed 'Northern Ireland Government' to 'Stormont Government' throughout the text. Lemass explained:

> I used the term 'Government of Northern Ireland' very deliberately and have, indeed, resorted to it with increasing frequency in Dáil statements. In my view the practice of substituting alternative terms like 'Belfast Government', 'Stormont Government', 'Belfast author-ities' has been the outcome of woolly thinking on the Partition issue. As you know our proposals for the political organisation of a united Ireland have, since 1921, involved the continuation of a Parliament in Belfast with subordinate powers. If these proposals had been accepted at that time or since some name for the subordinate Northern Parliament and Government would have had to be accepted, and it seems clear that the united Dáil of 1921 would not have dissented to the retention of the name 'Government of Northern Ireland' which is, indeed, nearly as good as any other. Our conditioned reluctance to use this title, in the conditions now pre-

vailing, seems to me to serve no national purpose and it is of course advanced in the North as evidence that our proposals in this regard are not seriously meant, or are only a trap.[16]

Terminology was also problematic in Northern Ireland itself. If, for many in the Republic, the naming of the place conferred or withdrew legitimacy, in the North, for some, the official name of the place conceded that it was indeed in Ireland. In 1959 Eric Montgomery had produced a discussion document for the Cabinet Publicity Committee entitled 'Nomenclature: Are we Irish, Northern Irish or Ulster?' which argued that the term 'Northern Ireland' appeared to concede the essential 'Irishness' of the place and that its use allowed people in Great Britain and abroad to 'think of the partition of Ireland as an artificial, ephemeral thing'.[17] The use of 'Ulster' circumvented this problem but created another. Many outside the island had no clear idea where Ulster was located. Little local disagreements took on international dimensions when the attraction of tourists was involved.[18] In 1965, the decision to co-operate with the Republic in joint tourist literature again raised the question of how Northern Ireland should be defined. Cabinet discussions in the North had concluded that any map of the island must make Northern Ireland's position clear, 'both pictorially and textually'.[19] Difficulties had arisen out of Dublin representatives having put forward variations which suggested an impermanence for the constitution of Northern Ireland. The minister of commerce reported that:

> It was intended that the map should be headed 'Ireland'; that the border should be clearly shown; that the Six Counties should be labelled 'Northern Ireland'; that the territory of the Republic should not be labelled. These aspects were satisfactory, but the text of the caption was another matter. In no circumstances could there be any ambiguity about this, and if the co-operative venture were to break down on this point, the onus would clearly lie upon the Republic for attempting to impose its political outlook.[20]

In accepting this formulation, Northern Ireland had conceded the normative position to the Republic and placed the six counties as an internal variation. However, the minister of commerce saw difficulties over the form of words used on the map as a necessary test of 'the Republic's willingness to recognise the constitutional "facts of life"'.[21] The final wording indicated that Northern Ireland was part of the United Kingdom and this was satisfactory to the cabinet. The naming of the border provided another issue. Cabinet Conclusions recorded:

The Chief Whip observed that the words 'customs boundary' were not very strong. If a Free Trade Area came into being, there might not be a customs boundary. He would prefer the term 'frontier'. The Minister of Commerce explained that his Ministry's last proposal had indeed used the words 'land frontier', but that in coming back with the form 'customs boundary' the Department in Dublin had adopted a form put forward at an earlier stage from the Northern Ireland side.[22]

The prime minister commented that the ordinary reader would be interested in the map rather than the footnote but both were clearly important.[23] As a space, the contested nature of Northern Ireland was expressed through the way in which it was mapped, described and divided. Eternal vigilance in asserting that Northern Ireland was a permanent reality underlined the importance of the symbolic and the actual; the pictorial, the textual and the annotation. It was not enough that Northern Ireland existed; it had to be seen to be real.

Nationalist commemorations refused the reality. They looked to an all-Ireland history and identity and employed Irish symbols and traditions to perform their difference. The anniversary of the Easter Rising was particularly significant because the event being commemorated had been pivotal in the process of gaining independence for the twenty-six counties and its remembrance drew on the imagery and rhetoric of Irish unity (therefore nationalist commemorations in the North rejected both the reality of Northern Ireland and the 26-county Republic and demonstrated a determination not to be excluded from the Irish nation)[24]. Moreover, the Easter Rising had taken place during the First World War and its commemoration appeared in direct opposition to that of the Somme.[25] In Northern Ireland, remembering the Rising was not simply an assertion of the politics of independence, it was a rejection of the origin myth of the devolved state. For many in the North it was axiomatic that to glorify the events of Easter Week 1916 was to desecrate the memory of the First World War dead: in order to remember the Rising it was necessary to forget the sacrifice of the Somme.

Unlike the battles of the First World War, the Easter Rising was a short-lived event which had bequeathed named political martyrs rather than unknowing victims of extraordinary carnage. The Rising was a revolutionary strike relayed as a romantic gesture and framed as poetic destiny. Its significance for those who commemorated it was emotional as well as political and, in Northern Ireland, this allowed militant and moderate nationalists to feel connected to it for a complexity of reasons. The confection of politics that the Rising and its aftermath represented also allowed it to become an instrument of myriad political views which pertained in the North in the 1960s, from community activism to the demolition of the border.[26] The forms of commemoration in Northern Ireland were similar to those in the Republic – parades, masses, concerts, speeches – but were given different meaning by a context in which expressions of Catholicism and nationalism were overtly political and oppositional, rather than genuflections to the official history of the state.[27]

Nationalist commemorations in Northern Ireland had always been unofficial. Issues of inclusion and exclusion, therefore, made the naming of public buildings – more permanent memorials – extremely contentious. In March 1966 the Republican Labour MP (in both Stormont and Westminster) for West Belfast, Gerry Fitt, raised the issue of the naming of blocks of flats to be built in his constituency as part of a programme of slum clearance. Fitt acknowledged the worthy nature of the enterprise but objected to the decision of Belfast Corporation's Housing Committee to name each of the buildings after famous British field-marshals, a decision Fitt said the committee knew would antagonise the residents. One building was called Auchinleck House, which, Fitt noted, was a difficult enough name to say when sober.[28] He also observed that the 'only thing the nationally minded people found in the naming of these blocks of flats was that they had casement windows'.[29] With some humour, Fitt demonstrated the way in which nationalists in Northern Ireland found ways to insert their own historical memory into the crevices of the dominant commemorative culture.

In January 1966 a directorate consisting largely of veteran republicans was appointed to oversee the commemorative programme across Northern Ireland.[30] Over two hundred people attended the initial meeting in Dungannon and Larry Bateson, in the chair, explained that it had been judged necessary to set up a separate committee in the North 'because of the different atmospheres under which Celebrations in the Six Counties and Twenty-Six Counties would be held'.[31] In the Republic, the Sinn Féin-organised Golden Jubilee Commemoration Committee had limited success in organising an alternative programme of events, never really managing to dislodge the elaborate offerings of the state. In Northern Ireland republican politics were cast into sharper relief and the context made them immediately more subversive. As a result, Sinn Féin focused its attention on the North and effectively 'construct[ed] Belfast as their capital for 1966'.[32] Their aim was to use the commemoration to re-politicise the population in the North.[33] Republican Liam McMillen, organising secretary on the commemoration committee, judged later that 'although no great material benefit accrued to the IRA from this stirring among the people, there was general satisfaction that progress had been made in dispelling the deadening apathy that had immobilised the people for so many years'.[34] The Nationalist Party had a minimal role in the commemorations in Northern Ireland and the party's leader, Eddie McAteer, made clear that his primary focus in 1966 was the March Westminster elections rather than the 1916 commemorations.[35] However, the broad nationalist community supported the organised events, expressing both high and low levels of politicisation and all expressing a desire for national unity.[36]

Commemorative events took place across Northern Ireland and were concentrated in nationalist areas such as Toomebridge, Coalisland, Newry, Derry, Strabane and Dungiven. In Belfast, the annual parade on Easter Sunday (10 April) to commemorate the Rising took place as usual and approximately 30,000 spectators watched as it proceeded from Beechmount to Milltown cemetery. However, the signature event of the northern commemorations took place in Belfast the following Sunday on 17 April, at which 70,000 people watched a large parade move along the Falls Road to Casement Park led by a colour party bearing the tricolour, the Fianna and Citizen Army flags. *The Irish Times* reported that 'There were more Tricolours to be seen than at any time in Dublin during the week, but the police took no notice.'[37] Betty Sinclair, president of Belfast Trades Council and a leading member of the Communist Party, had been due to speak but agreed to stand down due to pressure from the GAA which threatened to withdraw the use of Casement Park if she did not pull out.[38] The Rev. Ian Paisley had organised a counter-march through Belfast city centre which began with a service in the Ulster Hall, offered in thanksgiving for the defeat of the 1916 Rising. A large police presence kept the marchers apart but there were several skirmishes and six people were detained by the police.[39] Originally the Ulster Hall had been booked for a 1916 commemorative concert but it had been banned by Belfast Corporation's Estates and Markets Committee on the grounds that it would lead to a breach of the peace. Paisley's counter-demonstration was intended to express ownership of the public spaces within Northern Ireland and to perform the 'legitimacy' of those loyal to the Union.[40]

'A Different Cup of Tea'

Commemorations of the Easter Rising had taken place in Northern Ireland prior to 1966 but had consistently attracted more legal controls than any other event or assembly. Individual Easter commemorations had been banned under Section 4 of the Special Powers Act since 1926, with the number prohibited increasing until an outright ban was imposed on commemorations across Northern Ireland during Easter week in 1936.[41] This ban was renewed annually until 1949, when commemorations were assessed on an individual basis as, H.C. Montgomery had argued in the Ministry of Home Affairs, 'undue publicity [was] given to "the anniversary" by the Publication of the Prohibition Order'.[42] Despite the slight shift towards liberalisation, the commemoration of the Rising continued to be contentious in Northern Ireland. The lack of general support for Sinn Féin and the IRA meant that the Easter anniversary had become a central part of public expressions of republicanism.[43] Therefore that which was being paraded in commemorations of the Easter Rising was much more overtly political than the cultural and religious identities being expressed by nationalists on holy days such as St Patrick's Day or the Feast of the Assumption.

Although there were precedents for commemorations of the Easter Rising in Northern Ireland, the prospect of the fiftieth-anniversary celebrations had created a sense of alarm and anticipation (depending on political allegiance) because of its expected scale. The Unionist MP Joseph Burns noted that 'the 1916 celebrations are a very different thing altogether. This is a very different cup of tea from the ordinary celebrations that we have here year after year.'[44] The real significance of the fiftieth-anniversary commemoration in Northern Ireland, however, was not the substance but the context. It occurred at a point at which boundaries were being pushed on all sides of the society and all were being asked, not for toleration, but what it was they were prepared to tolerate. In the comic tragedy of Northern Ireland, timing is everything.

Terence O'Neill, as prime minister, had been attempting a greater accommodation of Catholic sensibilities and his response to the prospect of the golden jubilee of the Easter Rising was determined by a number of pressures. The Wilson government, strengthened by the Westminster election of March 1966, was perceived to be more open to the possibility of intervening in Northern Irish affairs than previous British administrations, so O'Neill was particularly keen that the commemoration should not lead to a breakdown of law and order across Northern Ireland.[45] The concern that the IRA might use the Easter Rising anniversary to reignite its campaign of violence was coupled with the anxiety that a heavy-handed response from the government regarding nationalist parades would heighten tensions and create increased support for republicans. An awareness of British opinion also made it almost impossible for the O'Neill government to ban nationalist commemorative parades outright.[46]

The politics of fear had been usefully exploited by the Unionist Party throughout its history as a way of maintaining Protestant unity. The political emergence of the Rev. Ian Paisley, however, meant that the energies released by the language of sectarianism and menace could be less easily controlled by the unionist elite. The upcoming anniversary of the Easter Rising had provided a heightened backdrop for the Westminster elections in March 1966, and it had been convenient for unionists to talk up the threat of trouble for electioneering purposes. However, they assumed, it has been argued,

> that the spectral genie [of the 1916 celebrations] could be put back in the bottle when the elections no longer required standard unionist horror-tales. Ian Paisley was, however, to demonstrate that the Unionist Party leadership no longer had a monopoly on such tales, nor was their duration and potency at the leadership's command.[47]

By the summer of 1966 RUC intelligence reports assessed the threat from 'extremist Protestant groups' to be greater than that of the IRA.[48] O'Neill was caught in a dilemma which was, in part, of his party's own making (a consequence of thinking there was a difference between responsible sectarianism and irresponsible sectarianism). If he banned nationalist commemorations, he risked civil unrest and censure from Britain. If he did not ban nationalist commemorations, he risked civil unrest and censure from fellow unionists.[49]

Among parts of the broader unionist community there also existed an awareness that the minority population should have the right to some free expression. The concession was couched in qualifications aimed to make clear that allowing the commemoration was not the same as supporting the event being commemorated. Walter Scott, Unionist MP for Belfast Bloomfield, despite believing that the Easter Rising should not be celebrated in Northern Ireland 'as it was a rebellion against the things which were held very dear and at a very inopportune moment in the history of the United Kingdom', nevertheless argued that 'if there is a fraction of this province which feels it has a right to cheer about this incident in past history we as a responsible party should allow freedom of speech, so long as it does not conflict with law and order'.[50] Nat Minford also stated, 'I object strongly to any celebrations of a Rising that is abhorrent to me,' but 'I would still fight for the right of these people to hold their celebrations provided they do it peaceably and in a sensible manner.'[51] In a letter to the Grand Orange Lodge of Ireland, Terence O'Neill opened with the assurance, 'Let me say at the outset that the sentiments behind the 1916 celebrations are repugnant to me and my colleagues in the Government – as indeed they are to the majority of our citizens.'[52] Brian McConnell, minister of home affairs, made a statement to Stormont on 2 March 1966 that encapsulated this position:

> The events which are being celebrated do not commend themselves to the people of Northern Ireland as a whole. It is the duty of the Government to ensure that any celebrations taking place within Northern Ireland do not offend our citizens, and that they should not be held in such places and in such circumstances as are likely to lead to a breach of the peace.[53]

The idea that nationalists were not part of the citizenry of Northern Ireland was implicit in McConnell's remarks. The minister's statement provided rich pickings for his critics among both unionists and nationalists. Harry Diamond, the Republican Labour MP for the Falls, responded by drawing the minister's attention to the fact that there were other commemorations and celebrations held each year which were not universally approved of by the people and that McConnell's statement served no other purpose but the creation of a state of tension.[54] Diamond concluded:

> The real reason for this is obviously to build up a case for the banning of these commemorations simply because if they are held throughout Southern Ireland and throughout Northern Ireland it is a declaration of unity of the Irish people. That is something which this Government obviously resent[s], particularly its effect on outside opinion, owing to the propaganda that has been laid down so far as Northern Ireland is concerned that we are all one way of thinking and have finally accepted the partition of this country as something permanent.[55]

Diamond's assertion touched on a reality beyond its rhetorical puff. The border in Northern Ireland represented a physical, political and conceptual marker of space. Nationalists and unionists had very different relationships with their locality and conceived of it differently. For nationalists, the space could be understood only as part of the whole island, while for unionists the six counties within Northern Ireland represented a separate political and cultural jurisdiction with a different past. Something of this is indicated in Terence O'Neill's reflections on why things had gone wrong for him after the 1965 election: 'The short answer is the following year, in 1966. Moreover the cause, though deeply Irish, had little or nothing to do with Northern Ireland itself.'[56] The contested nature of the border meant that it could always be perceived as both dominant and vulnerable. Its defining position within the history of Northern Ireland meant that it shaped the way in which civic space was perceived across the whole jurisdiction.

Border Politics

Much of the heightened sense of tension in the build-up to the fiftieth-anniversary commemoration of the Easter Rising focused on activities around the border. In February 1966 the *Belfast Telegraph* reported that police authorities in the Republic had begun strengthening stations on the border in anticipation of IRA activity during the Easter celebrations, adding, 'Many of the stations are being re-equipped with radio transmission sets of the kind used during the last campaign of violence by the IRA in Northern Ireland [1956–62], and nearer Easter it is understood that the forces in the border stations will be increased.'[57] Wildly exaggerated reports of the numbers of those expected to travel from the Republic for the commemorations in Belfast – with figures reaching 30,000[58] – added to the sense of alarm.

Brian McConnell also decided to 'seal'[59] the border – by banning North–South rail travel for almost twenty-four hours – to prevent disruptive groups arriving from the Republic during the weekend of the main commemoration in Northern Ireland on 16–17 April. New powers also allowed for the banning of any traffic on the A1 road between Belfast and Dublin perceived to be prejudicial to the maintenance of peace in Northern Ireland. McConnell stated that he would 'not permit the peace of Northern Ireland to be disturbed by provocative incursions of hostile elements'.[60] *The Irish Times* noted that the first reaction in Dublin to the announcement was that 'the measures proposed were melodramatic and even provocative'. It argued that, as the announcement was broadcast in the Republic in a bulletin on Telefís Éireann immediately after midnight on 15 April, and that train services were not to be stopped until 9.30pm the following day, 'intending gunmen or demonstrators would still be able to travel north by train today or most of the day tomorrow. They could also travel by road or could enter the North easily by travelling to Britain and then to Belfast by sea or air.'[61] The Northern Ireland administration wanted to be seen to be doing something to control the commemoration and it was also encouraging the idea that the border – rather than being porous – was capable of being sealed and secured.

The Irish Times was of the view that the move represented a definite setback to the friendliness between Ireland's two governments and that, rather than lessen tension surrounding the jubilee, 'could well start off some real trouble'.[62] The government in the Republic had been taken by surprise by McConnell's decision. Three departments consulted on how best to respond. The Department of Transport and Power decided that it should be treated as a political rather than a commercial decision; the Department of Justice confirmed that, although confidential talks had been held in Dublin at a high police level on 13 April (which had included a police representative from the North), 'no specific information which might justify the Six-County action was mentioned' and the Department of External Affairs was undecided about how best to respond. All therefore instructed the Government Information Bureau to answer enquiries with 'no comment'.[63] A personal message was conveyed from O'Neill to Lemass on 16 April through civil service channels which indicated that the authorities in Northern Ireland had thought it better not to inform the government in the Republic in advance of their decision in order to 'save [it] from embarrassment'.[64]

The government in the Republic of Ireland had already quietly quashed a request put to the Irish Rail Company, Córas Iompair Éireann (CIÉ) by the Golden Jubilee Commemoration Committee (the alternative committee organised by republican groups) in February to organise a special train to take their members to Belfast on 17 April for commemorative events. It was also requested that CIÉ overprint the tickets with the words 'Freedom Train 1966'.[65] Erskine Childers had been approached by CIÉ and the taoiseach, tánaiste and minister for justice were all consulted on how best to respond.[66] The Office of the Minister for Justice advised that:

> In the Minister's view the plans for the IRA/Sinn Féin group to hire a special train from Dublin on the 17 April in order to have a parade in Belfast and an oration in the cemetery is for IRA organisational purposes. Furthermore the Committee's suggestion to CIE that the rail tickets should be overprinted with the slogan 'Freedom Train 1966' appears to be for the purpose of cocking a snook at the Six-County authorities and it would probably give rise to feelings of resentment in Belfast.[67]

Lemass therefore communicated to Childers the view of the Garda authorities that, were such a train to be provided, there would be a strong likelihood 'of trouble in Belfast and of a serious danger to the rolling-stock along the railway line in the Six Counties'. He advised his minister, therefore, to 'so inform CIE and if, in the circumstances, they decide not to provide the train, request them to do so without giving this as the reason, or indicating that they have sought the Government's advice in the matter'.[68] The politics of the border provided opportunities for all political groups to make symbolic gestures, privately and publicly. The railway connection between Dublin and Belfast made possible a constant traffic between the two jurisdictions on the island.[69] The ease with which this could take place created unease among certain sections of Northern Ireland, not just because of the actuality of the passengers but because of what their presence represented. In the event, the number of those who travelled north for the commemorations was small.[70]

Unionist Objections to the Commemoration

Unionist organisations across Northern Ireland made clear their objections to proposed commemorations of the Easter Rising by nationalists. These generally conformed to three central concerns: that groups would travel from the Republic; that the Irish tricolour would be flown along the public highways of Northern Ireland; and that there would be a breakdown of order in an otherwise peaceful place. While the government had sympathy with these objections, it largely adopted the advice of the RUC, which monitored the situation across Northern Ireland and, in terms of the decision to ban any parade, recommended a policy of 'wait and see'.[71]

An early communication in December 1965 from the Inspector General of the RUC to the Ministry of Home Affairs outlined what was known of the upcoming commemorations. It was known that committees had been formed in Belfast, Derry and in other centres to co-ordinate the efforts of local organisers and to raise money by weekly collections. It was reported that organisers hoped that most nationalist areas would be decorated with flags and bunting and that in many cases a person in each street would be asked to take charge of the decorations and the running of céilithe, concerts and other cultural events. Furthermore, nationalist and other organisations known to have been approached included the Irish National Foresters, the Ancient Order of Hibernians, the Pre-Truce IRA and the Gaelic Athletic Association. The report stated that, although commemorations were to take place all over

Ireland, it was known that IRA leaders hoped that as many as possible would attend the principal ceremonies in Belfast.[72] The report concluded:

> It is impossible to forecast the precautions the police will find it necessary to take, or the recommendations which may be made to the Minister as each event in Northern Ireland will have to be dealt with on its own merits. It must be borne in mind, however, that there is every possibility of the IRA or a splinter group attempting to mark the occasion with some spectacular and publicity winning coup.
>
> This will be a period of extreme tension in the Province and any action by the IRA in the interim would make the situation explosive. It is to be hoped that good sense will prevail with extremists on both sides of the community and that they will neither by word nor deed set alight passions which could so easily start political and sectarian troubles in Northern Ireland.[73]

Press reports of planned commemorations had led local groups to lodge their complaints. Six months before the anniversary, a resolution was passed by the East and Mid (part of) Tyrone Unionist Association which stated that 'A serious view is taken of the fact that preparations are in hand, by our political enemies, to have large scale celebrations . . . We fear that these celebrations could disturb the present peaceful state of Northern Ireland and lead to grave breaches of the peace.'[74] A letter to the county inspector in Armagh from the Primatial Black District Chapter No. 4 noted that there had been ' a spirit of tolerance and goodwill prevailing here for a considerable number of years and it would be a retrograde step to allow the good relationship to be disrupted by rebels'.[75] The Unionist Association of Mid-Armagh expressed grave apprehension about the upcoming celebrations, as they were convinced that 'they will be largely used to provoke the loyalists'.[76] The County Londonderry Grand Orange Lodge also wrote to McConnell asking that a proposed parade through the town of Kilrea should be looked into and, if necessary, banned due to the likelihood of trouble.[77]

The concern, therefore, was that visible demonstrations of Irish nationalism in Northern Ireland would disrupt the equilibrium of that place and provoke a response from loyalists. It was believed by some that the actual aim of the Easter Rising commemorations in Northern Ireland was not just a celebration of one identity but an assault on another. In Armagh it was argued that 'the real purpose of a parade through the principal streets . . . especially those streets where the majority of the inhabitants are strenuously opposed to the celebrations, will be to inflame passions which will probably end in violence and bloodshed'.[78] Norman Porter, writing on behalf of the Evangelical Protestant Society, noted, 'we believe these Easter Rising Celebrations are for propaganda to the outside world against Ulster.'[79] Parades and commemorations are ways through which identities are demonstrated and therefore the audience is central. Across Northern Ireland, unionists, understanding well the significance of such events in the marking of territory, objected to becoming the witnesses of an opposing identity.

Despite the objections, however, only one parade was banned in Northern Ireland during the Easter Rising commemorations in 1966, in The Loup, County Derry. The issue was first raised by James Chichester-Clarke, MP for South Derry, who wrote to Brian McConnell in March stating that he was 'especially concerned about the celebration which is proposed for The Loop [sic], Moneymore and which will, I fear, give great offence and which may well be openly resisted by our loyalists'.[80] This was confirmed by a special meeting of The Loup Branch South Derry Unionist Association which stated 'emphatically' that they would not tolerate

> any flag waving or coat trailing by the planned large influx of rebels from Eire which we feel would in reality be purely jubilation over the brutal murder of three members of the RUC at Ballyronan in 1922. We feel we owe these men better than to allow their memory to be sullied or trampled over at this time.

> We would point out that although the man [Seán Larkin] responsible for this foul deed is buried in Loup Cemetery, he was executed in Eire under the Tricolour, by the Cosgrave regime in 1923, therefore we feel there is no grounds for any parades, etc., at Loup, which would definately [sic] lead to a breach of the peace, and destroy the good relations which now exist in Loup district.[81]

A deputation comprising of 'one very extensive contractor and eight farmers of similar standing in and around the area' met with the district inspector of the RUC and with Chichester-Clarke on separate occasions in March to press their case.[82] All members of the deputation stated that, if the forthcoming republican commemoration were allowed to take place on Easter Sunday, 'there would be strong intervention by loyalists at the time, probably resulting in the use of firearms'.[83] A compromise was explored in which the commemoration would be confined to the cemetery grounds and banned from public roads. However, this was not acceptable to the deputation and the district inspector concluded, 'I am convinced beyond all doubt that they are prepared, if necessary, to use sufficient physical force in order to prevent these celebrations taking place.' Compromise, therefore, was not forthcoming from loyalists and, the report noted, 'We cannot enter into any negotiations with the organisers of the event as our action would give the Republican Party all the propaganda they needed during the election campaign.'[84] Furthermore, were the RUC in a position to negotiate with republicans, it was not believed that a voluntary cancellation of the parade was likely and a complete ban was therefore recommended.[85] However, two county inspectors and a district inspector concurred with the advice that 'the Ministerial decision on the banning, or otherwise, of this parade should not be disclosed until after the Election'.[86] McConnell announced that he was banning the march under the Public Order Act, 1951 on 6 April. Dermot Devlin of the South Derry Commemoration Committee countered that the route of the parade had been carefully selected 'to make sure that it would cause no offence to anyone. There is only one Protestant house along the route and this house is not near the public road. It was absolutely ridiculous for the Minister to say there would be public disorder if the parade took place.'[87] An estimated five hundred people gathered at St Patrick's cemetery in protest at the ban. There was no parade on the public road but the tricolour was carried from the gates of the cemetery to the grave of Seán Larkin. There was one arrest for having a tricolour but the police did not raise any objections to the gathering.[88]

In fact arrests in Northern Ireland during the Easter weekend were minimal. Six men were summonsed in Derry for organising the parade in that city without giving the regulation 48-hour notice and two members of the Belfast Battalion of the IRA were jailed for three months for their part in organising the commemoration.[89]

The Irish Tricolour

The flying of the Irish tricolour in Northern Ireland had long been the subject of regulation and prosecution.[90] The significance of flags, of course, is not in the actual but in the symbolic. They are used to mark territory and as a statement of power and allegiance. The appearance of a tricolour in the Sinn Féin offices on Divis Street in 1964 had become the fulcrum for serious violent exchanges. In Northern Ireland, flags were seen literally to give sustenance to political groupings. Eddie McAteer's assertion in 1966 that 'nothing can be gained by stuffing flags down one another's throat' was widely quoted and promptly ignored. John Hume's later intervention that 'you can't eat a flag' was also widely quoted, treated as a revelation and promptly ignored. The Flags and

Emblems (Display) Act (Northern Ireland) of 1954 had been designed to protect the Union flag by making it an offence to interfere with its display, and gave the police the power to have removed or remove any non-Union flag judged to threaten the maintenance of peace. The failure to remove an offending flag, once directed, was an offence that could lead to prosecution. The act pivoted on the word 'display', as it was not within the power of the devolved government in Northern Ireland to ban a foreign flag outright. The Flags and Emblems Act concerned itself with what was acceptable in the public spaces of Northern Ireland and this, as always, was couched in the language of what might lead to a breach of the peace. Unionist and Orange associations across Northern Ireland maintained a watchful correspondence with the government which charted sightings of the Irish flag in the North.[91]

In the months before the 1966 commemoration of the Easter Rising these communications made it clear that the flying of the Irish tricolour would be one of the most contentious aspects of the jubilee. The Loyal Orange Lodge in Magherafelt passed a resolution stating that, while they had no desire to oppose peaceful and limited celebrations in the district, they did wish 'to place on record our determination to oppose the flying of the Tricolour or provocative parades headed by the Tricolour, during the Easter Rising (1916) celebrations'.[92] The Belfast Committee of the Apprentice Boys had also protested against the fact that

> a certain section of the people whom we class as Rebels should be permitted to come from the Republic of Ireland and be permitted to associate with those of their kind in the Six Counties to celebrate the 1916 Rising, and to carry their Tricolour in parades and demonstrations which might excite Her Majesty's Loyal Subjects.[93]

The IRA in Belfast saw the commemoration as 'a golden opportunity to drive a coach and four' through the Flags and Emblems Act and from January until April had devoted all their energies to preparing for the commemorations.[94] Liam McMillen recalled that the services of every member of Cumann na mBan and dozens of other women were enlisted to make thousands of tricolour flags and bunting which were distributed throughout all the nationalist areas of Belfast.[95] As a result these areas were festooned in green, white and orange and the Flags and Emblems Act was virtually unenforceable.

Reports in the local press revealed the way in which the flag resonated with nationalists. At a meeting of the Golden Jubilee Committee in Armagh, two members spoke against the carrying of the tricolour 'until the Free State Government gave assurances that it would not be interfered with'.[96] The chairman had asked the meeting to consider whether or not the flag should be carried in the evening parade on Easter Sunday, adding that, if it was to be carried, it should not be abused in any way. One member suggested that the greatest honour to the men of 1916 would be the carrying of the Irish flag through the thirty-two counties without interference from the RUC, adding, 'I don't want to see it whipped from under someone's coat and flaunted before a crowd. When Lemass came down and shook hands with O'Neill then the time has come when the flag can be flown with honour.'[97] Tensions between the police and the nationalist population were also expressed concerning disappointment that some organisations had not attended the committee meeting. The press reported that the chairman, Mr S. Trainor, felt that intimidation was keeping many away: '"The vast majority of people in the North are still Nationalist minded but if you even breathe Nationalist there is a danger of the RUC lifting you and putting you in for a time. This country is almost as bad as Russia," he commentated, bringing laughter from the members.'[98]

In fact, much depended on the views of the police and it was often local representatives of the RUC who encouraged compromise on the issue of the commemorations. In Coalisland, objections were raised over the flying of the tricolour and it was requested that the parade be banned 'along Church Road which is the loyalist part of the town and where the Parish Church is situated. Easter services will be conducted in this Protestant church during the time of the IRA parade.'[99] The Ministry of Home Affairs contacted the inspector general of the RUC concerning their information that there 'was considerable local resentment in the Coalisland and Dungannon area' and asking that enquiries be made at a local level.[100] The county inspector began his report by stating, 'I do not agree that there is any considerable amount of resentment', and stated that the general population did not think the holding of the parade unreasonable.[101] Indeed it was felt that resentment was confined to 'the militant Paisley type Unionist' and that the demonstrations were being held against the wishes of nationalists 'of a more moderate tendency'.[102] The report continued:

> Regarding the suggestion that the alleged situation would be eased if the Tricolour is not flown in Coalisland on Easter Sunday I can only say that in my opinion this is completely unrealistic ... If the carrying or display of the flag is prohibited by Order then I anticipate that it will take a force of police much greater in numbers than is likely to be available from all sources to enforce the order.[103]

The report concurred that the parade should not progress along the Church Road and, as the route had not at that point been decided upon, the inspector had taken steps to ensure that, when the matter came up for discussion among the organisers, 'objections to the Church Road route will be brought up by one of them'.[104] Furthermore, it was believed that, as the time of the parade had not yet been fixed, it was the intention of Rev. J.W. Beamish, minister of the Parish Church on Church Road, 'to organise his service to coincide with the parade whether morning or afternoon', as he had a history of trying to stir up public resentment over the display of the tricolour in Coalisland.[105] Given the position of the RUC, a compromise was reached in the area and objections to the flying of the Irish flag were withdrawn.[106]

The tricolour was also an issue in the correspondence of the Evangelical Protestant Society, which urged that the main parade to Casement Park be banned in view of 'the growing resentment throughout Ulster at the permission granted to the free flying of the Eire Tricolour' and due to the fact that such a parade was likely 'to cause a breach of the peace and it is an unnecessary act of Sabbath desecration'.[107] McConnell provided a lengthy explanation of the government's position on the flying of the Irish flag:

> It is not correct to say that permission was granted for the free flying of the Tricolour as no such permission is necessary: indeed there seems to be considerable confusion about the legality of flying this flag. It is not illegal to do so and it would not be competent for the Parliament of Northern Ireland to make unlawful the flying of the Tricolour as under the Government of Ireland Act all matters relating to foreign countries, including the flying of their flags, are reserved to the United Kingdom Parliament. The Northern Ireland Government has, however, by virtue of the Flags and Emblems (Display) Act of 1954, been given more powers whereby the police may order the removal of any flag or emblem (which, in practice, most often is the Tricolour) the display of which is likely to cause a breach of the peace.[108]

The commemorations in Northern Ireland represented a celebration across the border of an all-Ireland history, identity and population and this was crystallised in the carrying of a flag. The government in Northern Ireland may have attempted to place distance between itself and the issue but the devil was in the discretion. It found itself in a more peculiar situation regarding another emblem of republicanism, the Easter lily.

The Easter Lily

In the Republic of Ireland, the Easter lily had become not only a symbol but also an instrument of republican agitation. The lily had been adopted as a badge of the Rising by Cumann na mBan in the 1920s. It had become a symbol of resistance to the 26-county settlement and represented for some republicans the national emblem of Ireland.[109] The Easter lily was seen as a less compromised symbol than the tricolour, which had been debased by its association with the partitioned state. Cumann na mBan publicity material explained that the men of 1916 had 'raised the banner of complete separation from England, and the wisdom of their demand united all the people of Ireland. That banner has been basely lowered. In the Easter Lily it is raised again.'[110] The lily became a political issue of a more marked political inflection in the Republic following the passing of the Street and House to House Collections Act (1962), which required that vendors obtain a permit from the chief superintendent of the locality. The refusal of republicans to apply for permits (from a state they did not recognise) meant that the government could have those who sold the Easter lily arrested without having banned the sale of the lily itself.

Intelligence sources understood that, in the years surrounding the jubilee of the Rising, financial support from the public for the IRA had been very limited and had consisted mainly of private collections, door-to-door collections and the sale of Easter lilies, all of which had been restricted by the act since 1962.[111] What they may have lost financially republicans compensated for in publicity. Court appearances were accompanied by protests and banners such as 'They did not seek a permit to win freedom. We do not seek a permit to honour them.'[112] Arrests for selling the lily without permit were followed, in cases such as that of Richard Behal in Kilkenny, by hunger strike in protest at not being treated as a political prisoner.[113] Proinsias Mac Aonghusa, writing in the *Sunday Independent* in March 1964, urged the government not to repeat the mistakes of the previous year through which young men in various parts of the country had been arrested for selling the Easter lily. He warned, 'The public does not support the physical force movement: it gives less support to efforts to harass Republicans on minor matters.'[114] Nevertheless during Easter 1966 the Gardaí reported that, 'as directed', they had taken action 'throughout the country to prevent the unauthorised sales and distributions of Easter Lilies by IRA/SF members'.[115] This resulted in five incidents including 'a slight scuffle', 'a general melee' and subsequent proceedings for common assault in Middleton, County Cork and Urlingford, County Kilkenny, and charges of assault and riotous behaviour in Birr, County Offaly.[116]

The government in the Republic of Ireland had attempted to devise a new logo for the Easter Rising in 1966 and had run a competition for the design of a commemorative badge. The winning motif, 'An Claidheamh Soluis' (the Sword of Light), was designed by Mrs Una Watters and bore quite a resemblance to a stylised lily. The image had been chosen because it symbolised 'intuitive knowledge, education and progress'.[117] Intuitively, many rejected this attempt to rebrand the Rising. The sisters and niece of Seán Mac Diarmada, in refusing to attend the official commemoration for their brother and uncle to be held in his home town of Kiltyclogher, explained in a letter to the Minister for Defence:

> We believe that it is hypocritical for that Government to attempt to do honour to Sean Mac Diarmada while at the same time announcing a ban on the historic Easter Lily, the emblem of Easter week 1916. Sean died for a 32-County republic which has yet to be achieved.[118]

Therefore, in the Republic, the lily continued as a potent symbol of the sense of betrayal in the compromise state. On the day of the official commemorative parade down O'Connell Street, 10 April 1966, the *New York Times* reported that for most it was a proud day, but that in side streets supporters of the 'outlawed Irish Republican Army sold their Easter Lily badges, officially banned but tolerated today. They passed out leaflets reminding the public that some members of their group were in jail for attempting to carry on the old struggle against the British in the six counties of the North.'[119]

The situation in Northern Ireland was somewhat different. In March 1966 the prime minister's secretary had made enquiries regarding reports that the Easter lily had been banned in the Republic of Ireland. The Ministry of Home Affairs clarified the position and reported:

> The Easter Lily is really the symbol of the Easter Week Rebellion and is usually worn by people attending a commemoration service such as those held every year at Milltown Cemetery and at other towns in the North. Under our law if they wish to take up street collections they would require a permit under the Street Collection Regulations (Northern Ireland) 1927 and the Police of course would refuse such permits. However, the house-to-house collections only refer in Northern Ireland to house-to-house charitable collections and if the organizers here wish to hold house-to-house collections they would not be committing any offence.

> The police are, of course, watching this position but they do not
> anticipate any difficulty as most of such collections, which are held,
> are taken up on private property, in chapel grounds, etc.[120]

Officially, therefore, in the Republic of Ireland it was not illegal to
wear an Easter lily but it was against the law to sell one without a permit.
In Northern Ireland it was not illegal to sell the Easter lily door-to-door
but wearing one was rather more complicated. The idea of banning the
lily as an emblem of republicanism had been considered by the
Northern Ireland government in 1928 but a draft order was abandoned
due to the difficulty in defining the emblem the government intended to
prohibit.[121] Nevertheless it was made clear that the public sale, distribution or wearing of the lily was prejudicial to the preservation of the
peace and the police had the authority to remove offending items.[122]
Again, the emphasis was on removing republican insignia from public
view. Incidents of unrest in Belfast during the Easter commemoration in
1966 were linked to the public display of lilies and other emblems. One
young man had to be rescued by police when he was attacked by crowds
waiting for Paisley's parade to pass. He was reported to have been
wearing a tricolour ribbon and an Easter lily on his coat. It was reported
that he was

> set upon by a crowd of women who battered him with their
> umbrellas and several men tried to pull him to the ground. The
> police officer pulled him free and ran with him up Howard street.
> When the officer realised he was being followed by a large section of
> the crowd some of whom were crying 'Kill him, kill him' he turned
> and ran back through the crowd dragging the young man with him
> into the safe neutrality of a Chinese restaurant.[123]

Three young girls, also wearing tricolour emblems, were chased by a
crowd attending the Paisley march and the windows were stoned and
shattered in the house in which one girl sought refuge. In another incident, it was reported that a Belfast Corporation bus had been chased
and stopped when a passenger was seen wearing a tricolour rosette.
Police took him off the bus and escorted him to safety.[124] In all, the
RUC listed six incidents in Belfast in a statement released once the
parades had finished.[125]

The Easter lily represented a political position that was threatening to
both Northern Ireland and the Republic. The tiny emblem signified a
level of continuity with the Rising that sat uneasily with the new
realities. In a final twist, it would also become the symbol of the IRA
split in 1969. Allegiance would be conveyed by the simple act of

attaching the lily to the lapel by adhesive or a pin. 'Stickies', as the nickname for the Official IRA, would prove more robust than 'Pinheads' for the Provisionals.

Breaching the Peace

Writing to the Grand Orange Lodge in February 1967, William Craig, as Minister of home affairs, noted that

> the most significant fact, [regarding the fiftieth-anniversary commemoration of the Easter Rising], not only in Northern Ireland but in a wider sphere, is that the calm and good sense of the Ulster Loyalists enabled these offensive celebrations to pass off without a serious breach of the peace, which might have developed well-nigh to a state of civil war.[126]

He defended the government's decision not to ban the Easter celebrations outright and offered the assurance that 'as Minister of Home Affairs I shall scrutinise with great care every activity of the Nationalist and Republican enemies of Northern Ireland and as far as possible I shall try to ensure that they do not endanger the security, well-being and good name of Northern Ireland'.[127]

Nationalist parades were provocative and created the circumstances in which a breach of the peace might occur. However, the actual threat of disturbance – outlined in multiple correspondences – was from the loyalist population. A central concern, therefore, was not that nationalist parades would be unruly but that they would provoke an unruly response. The Unionist MP Joseph Burns explained where he saw the responsibility to lie:

> Nobody wants difficulty or trouble. It is the last thing we want. But at the same time there is not much sense in men flaunting certain things, realising what is going to happen, really asking for it and then crying wolf, saying, 'We are very good boys, the other fellows are bad boys'. Then the trouble starts. We must realise that the people who do this flaunting are the instigators. This should be understood.[128]

Any incursion of nationalist activity in communal public spaces represented a threat to the unionist hegemony within Northern Ireland. On 24 March 1966 Brian McConnell expressed the hope that

> sense and discretion will be the solution to this problem [of Easter commemorations]. I trust that anyone contemplating a meeting of this kind will have listened to the words of the hon. Member for

> Mourne (Mr. O'Reilly) and that they will have it in such a place
> and in such circumstances that they are not likely to give offence
> and there is not likely to be any trouble.[129]

Therefore nationalist commemorations could be tolerated as long as they could not be seen by unionists.

Nationalists responded by accusing unionists of provoking tension. In November 1965 the commemoration committee in Belfast issued a press release charging the government with portraying the upcoming celebrations as an IRA plot and argued that

> this is an insidious prefabrication to cloak their obvious intention of
> preventing a lawful public display by the people of the North, that
> the spirit of freedom and the desire for communal and national
> unity are very much alive despite all attempts at oppression and
> Divis Street type police brutality and intimidation.[130]

Republicans continued to deny that they were responsible for the build-up in tension and the head of the IRA, Tomás Mac Giolla, told the *New York Times* that British security forces were deliberately fostering tension 'to divide the Catholics and Protestants and to provoke the IRA into premature actions'.[131] In February 1966 the Stormont MP Henry Diamond accused the prime minister and the minister of home affairs of artificially creating tensions around the upcoming jubilee. He argued that their intention was to create a situation in which 'the measure of tolerance that exists within the community will be destroyed and the right of people to hold peaceful commemorations or celebrations of any kind will be prohibited'.[132]

In the aftermath of the jubilee O'Neill explained that 'always at the back of our minds was the knowledge that the IRA was waiting and hoping for a situation which they could exploit'.[133] When talking to their own constituency, unionists placed responsibility for tension on republicans, but the threat from within Protestantism was an equally significant pressure. A scheduled meeting between Ian Paisley, as chairman of the Ulster Constitution Defence Committee (UCDC), and Brian McConnell in April 1966 was cancelled by the latter, prompting the secretary of the UCDC to explain in a telephone conversation that 'his Chairman had certain plans for Easter about which he wanted to tell the Minister but, as the Minister would not see him, he [the Minister] must be held responsible for the consequences'.[134] In Northern Ireland in 1966, all were warning about possible trouble and no one would take responsibility.

Henry Diamond accused the prime minister of being in the business of perpetual scare-mongering, suggesting that 'when the present scare has subsided, he [O'Neill] may well tell us that next year will be the anniversary of the Fenian Rising and that that will create an emotional state throughout the island'. He continued, 'One could go on indefinitely creating scares and tension. Of course, these have the camouflage effect of distracting people's attention from other more important problems. There is a major communal problem here in the North.'[135] The following year, when the centenary of the Fenian Rising of 1867 became an issue, the minister of home affairs prohibited the holding of all public processions and meetings that did not have the specific permission of the RUC for one month from 13 March. He argued that, as even history books sympathetic to the Fenian cause conceded the rising was premature, abortive and never really got under way, there was no good reason to commemorate it in Northern Ireland. Furthermore, Craig stated that, while it was customary to hold celebrations of the Easter Rebellion in Northern Ireland, in the previous year the Rising commemorations had been specifically highlighted, 'heightening the offence given and resulting in a much increased tension which has not yet completely subsided'.[136]

Indeed the tension did not subside. The fiftieth-anniversary commemoration of the Easter Rising cannot be held responsible for the outbreak of the conflict in Northern Ireland in the years that followed. However, the tension generated around the commemoration placed it within a series of events that exacerbated fault lines within the society and contributed to the growing sense of division.[137]

Conclusion

Nationalists in Northern Ireland used the jubilee of the Easter Rising to reassert their aspiration for Irish unity. There were no official events north of the border and unofficial parades and pageants commemorated an event which, many argued, had in fact hardened existing divisions on the island between nationalists and unionists. Through its fiftieth-anniversary commemoration, the Easter Rising has also been held responsible for polarising political positions and the 'orgy of self-congratulation'[138] continues to be seen, by some, to have contributed to the outbreak of the conflict in Northern Ireland.

Commemorative events are not innocent acts of remembrance. However, when that which is being commemorated rhymes with the official history of the state, they can provide the opportunity for both celebration and critical reflection. In divided societies, commemorations can do more than expose the contested nature of historical memory; they can be used to assert and reject the legitimacy of the state. The same event was being commemorated in two jurisdictions in Ireland in April 1966. However, the context altered the meaning of the commemorations and the consequences were very different. In the Republic of Ireland, the main battle over the jubilee commemorations involved ownership of the legacy of the Easter Rising. In the North, the main battle involved ownership of Northern Ireland. Unionists linked the maintenance of peace with the protection of the status quo; eventually both collapsed under the pressure for change.

CHAPTER FOUR

Calling Up the Dead
Pageants and Performance

Ferdia MacAnna, writing of his part in the pageant at Croke Park, scripted and directed by his father Tomás, recalled the issue of payment for boys who had minor roles: 'we made representations to the management . . . At one stage there was talk of a strike: there would be no new nation at the end of the show, we warned, unless financial terms were agreed.' Payment for the nation's youth came in the form of a limited-edition souvenir ten-shilling piece which bore the image of P.H. Pearse. Mac Anna held on to his coin for longer that most others, who traded them for treats. One day, however, he walked into a shop and swapped his coin for ten 64-page comics, that week's editions of the *Victor* and the *Valiant*, a box of Aero chocolate bars and a plastic German paratrooper's helmet. 'For years afterwards,' he wrote, 'I felt like a traitor.'[1]

The schoolboys of the Croke Park pageant were not the only ones who were trading in the image of Pearse for material advantage. The idealism of the 1916 leaders was being repackaged in the service of the economic development of 'modern' Ireland. Like the event it commemorated, the jubilee of Easter Week concealed the advent of change behind the rhetoric of continuity. The commemoration provided an opportunity to assure the Irish population that the legacy of the patriot dead would be fulfilled through economic achievement rather than in the isolated dignity of frugal comfort. It offered confirmation that Irishness would not be diminished by free trade agreements or membership of the European Economic Community. The victory of new over old would have its own monument in the towers of Ballymun named for the signatories of the Proclamation. These buildings demonstrated crude, concrete confidence in the modern and were the only memorials to the signatories of the Rising built by the government in Dublin in 1966.

In April that year, the *Tablet* reported that some twenty people had been injured on the night Nelson had been blown off his pillar in the heart of Dublin. The injuries had come at the airport where 'a mob of youngsters had gathered . . . to welcome home the hero of the hour, Dickie Rock', who had just been placed fourth in the Eurovision Song Contest in Luxembourg.[2] The *Tablet*'s correspondent speculated that the 'pop-song hysteria' had been motivated either by the desire for escape from 'an over-rich dosage of heritage and national identity, from a native language which the natives did not speak and an idealism that bore no evident relation to the search for a job or the lure of the building sites of Britain'. Alternatively the young fans were framed as cosmopolitans groping to become part of a world that was bigger than the little island on which they lived.

Both explanations offered by the *Tablet* suggested that heightened interest in the Eurovision song contest represented a rejection of the little island. It positioned the theme of the Rising as having been set by the poets and dreamers of its number which had created a maelstrom at the heart of Irish society in which the 'death-wish had lived on long after it had served its purpose'. The dilemma for the Republic, therefore, fifty years on, was 'a hankering to keep the dream as long as it [did] not impinge on the reality'. The *Tablet*'s Dublin correspondent concluded:

> Whether we are perilously perched between two stools or crossing the hump between one era and another remains to be seen. Explosions in the night remind us of our past and make us apprehensive. Pressing needs in education, industrial relations and living costs deter us from philosophising about the future.[3]

Modernity

The golden jubilee of the Rising was in fact part of the process through which the Republic crossed over the hump. The memory of the dead was being used to navigate the country through the uncertainty of accelerated modernisation. Throughout the commemoration the government's favoured emphasis on the needs and achievements of 'modern' Ireland was, to some extent, understood in its literal sense, from the Latin *modo* – 'just now'. However, the term is also clearly imbued with a comparative aspect through which that which precedes the modern suffers from its apparent backwardness. Within colonial conditions, the modern was more often associated with foreignness and therefore was not easily naturalised in the process of social and economic development.[4] In Ireland, modernisation had been associated with Anglicisation, and nationalists had fashioned Irishness as traditional, ancient and therefore, theoretically at least, culturally resistant to the forces of modernity. The difficulty in the 1950s and 1960s was in creating a new rhetorical position in which 'modern' connoted progress and was fully naturalised within the national imagination so that modernisation and patriotism became inseparable.

Conceptions of modernity, however, typically suggest an 'epochal rupture' – a point at which the pre-modern ends and the modern begins. This dislocation creates a conflicted relationship with the immediate past, which must be ejected or negated due to the necessity to signal the new order.[5] This rupture is often negotiated with reference to a more distant past. The Irish trajectory of progress, however, had been bound to the story of the national struggle for independence. It had gained its momentum from a cyclical as well as a linear narrative which could absorb failure and reinvent it as part of a greater success. The generational cycle had been clearly articulated by Pearse in the Proclamation and also shaped Seán Lemass's thinking. At a press conference to announce his retirement as taoiseach in November 1966, Lemass said:

> I believe . . . that it is right that the representatives of the newer generation should now take over . . . The 1916 celebrations marked the ending of a chapter in our history and a new chapter has now to begin. As one of the 1916 generation this marked the end of the road for me also.[6]

The handing over of power was an implicit but underlying aspect of the jubilee. However, power would be handed over on the condition that young Ireland understood the wherefore of its birth. If modernity requires a rejection of the immediate past what constitutes the past becomes critical. For those who had not been born in 1916, the past was the Easter Rising. For those who *had* been born, the Rising was part of the living present. The guarantee of the living link was Éamon de Valera and, despite his own plans to retire, Lemass spent the summer campaigning for de Valera's continued presidency.

Pageantry

Bord Fáilte offered the suggestion that there should be more audience participation in the military parade that opened the commemorative week.[7] The result of this was a people's parade that followed the army contingent down O'Connell Street for the opening ceremony. The government committee's initial idea was to provide a spectacle upon which the public could look and applaud. It was clear, however, that ownership of the event would not be the government's alone. Pageantry – literally empty spectacle – would not be the whole of the jubilee. Rather there would be *pageants*, held up and down the country, including two in Croke Park in March and April 1966. They had the specific advantage of involving large local casts.

Pageants had been popular in Europe at the turn of the century. Stephen McKenna – sometime editor of *An Claidheamh Soluis* – had noted the revival of the medieval dramatic form in an article in the *Freeman's Journal* in 1909 which Patrick Pearse republished in the Christmas edition of *An Macaomh*. McKenna praised the pageant for its ability to combine great intensity of emotion with 'lyric poetry' and 'the ornate prose of solemn discourses'. He argued that the pageant as a cultural form could 'gather together the broken threads of our own national history'.[8] Pearse had overseen many pageants at St Enda's and, in 1913, an account of the slaying of Ferdia by Cúchulainn had been performed in the public grounds at Jones's Road, now Croke Park. Pageants of this period across Europe had generally celebrated various forms of heroic masculinity.[9]

The central heroic figure in St Enda's was of course Cúchulainn, and Elaine Sisson has explored in her work the way in which Christian themes were mapped on to bardic heroic deeds so that, as Stephen McKenna suggested, Pearse's ideal Irishman would have been 'Cúchulainn baptised'.[10] Sisson has also argued that while the St Enda's boys looked to the vibrant youth of Cúchulainn before 1916, in the aftermath of the Rising it was the hero's sacrificial death that defined his legend in the popular imagination. This aspect of the Cúchulainn saga in turn became inextricably linked to the death of Pearse.[11] True heroism therefore was cast retrospectively on to life only once it had ended in martyrdom. This was certainly not a new convention for Irish nationalism and yet Pearse's own writing had given the link a poignant articulation and, across Europe during the First World War, heroism rested with young men who were dead.

This forced a reconfiguration of the existing image of youth which had imbued childhood with nostalgia for a more innocent past. Declan Kiberd has noted, in the short stories of Pearse, the 'redemptive strangeness' of the child, who bore to 'fallen adults messages from another world'.[12] After the Rising and the War of Independence, it was those who had fallen in battle who bore the messages from that other world and in whose actions the potential for redemption lay. The young were seen as increasingly detached from knowing the nation. Pearse had offered his death for the sake of future generations but by 1966 his sacrifice had become their burden. Walter Benjamin wrote about that secret agreement between past generations and the present one: 'Our coming was expected on this earth. Like every generation that preceded us, we have been endowed with a *weak* Messianic power, a power to which the past has a claim. That claim cannot be settled cheaply.'[13] A reluctance to recognise the expectations of the past meant that in 1966 the young represented destabilising presences that threatened the redemptive acts which were now the preserve of old veterans and the dead. A major gap to be bridged during the jubilee, therefore, was between the old and the young. The major challenge was to turn an event which had death at its centre into a living example.

Bryan MacMahon, author of the GAA pageant in Croke Park, had been commissioned to write four plays for Telefís Éireann in the weeks leading up to the jubilee. One, 'The Boy at the Train', drew from MacMahon's own experience. He told the *RTV Guide*, 'I was only a scrap of a lad at the time, yet I clearly recall going to the local railway station every evening of Easter Week in 1916 to ask the passengers how the fighting was faring in Dublin.' His more recent memory was of standing in O'Connell Street at the end of the previous February (for the filming of a reunion) and watching a cluster of elderly men gathered at the pillars of the GPO who wore their medals proudly and chatted like children. He recalled:

> As I watched them from mid-road my mind went back over the years. I closed my eyes: again I was a boy waiting for the train to enter the station.
>
> And these men, too, were young, eager, vital and filled with the great adventure of serving a people whose devotion to freedom has scarcely been surpassed in the human story.[14]

For those who were alive during the Rising, its memory suspended them in the vitality of youth. Their difficulty was not only in conveying this to the young in 1966 but in conceding youth to them. This cross-generational relationship is pivotal in the transference of personal or family stories into a more general social memory that can then be expressed in history, fiction, exhibitions, museums and pilgrimages.[15] Memories are enhanced by retelling or re-enactment – either privately or publicly – facilitating the transmission from the embodied or living memory into cultural memory. The latter is used to describe the type of memory that survives through stories and practices once eye-witnesses and participants have died.[16] The fiftieth anniversary of an event is particularly charged, as it occurs at the point at which the living memory is visibly dying, making it imperative that younger generations accept their responsibility to remember.[17]

Seachtar Fear, Seacht Lá

MacMahon addressed this tension between young and old in his pageant, which had been commissioned by the GAA, in which he allowed the young to question the dead. Resolution was only achieved once the seven signatories had given an account of themselves and their actions. *Seachtar Fear, Seacht Lá – Seven Men, Seven Days* was held in Croke Park on 17, 18 and 19 March with a further performance by the full Dublin cast in Casement Park, Belfast. The cast of almost four hundred included the Artane Boys' Band, two pipe bands, 150 boys from the Dublin County Board of the GAA and 100 girls from the Dublin Camogie Board.[18] The pageant used the imagery available from the Easter resurrection of a nation and wove the words of the signatories into the unfolding spectacle.

In a simple design, an ornamental dais with a public address system stood in the centre of the field in Croke Park. It was flanked by those representing Fianna Éireann and Cumann na mBan. Into this scene marched the narrator, dressed in a white shirt and trousers, accompanied by four attendants in similar dress, but with shirts the colours of the four provinces. They were followed by a young man and a young woman. Stage directions indicated that both of these would be 'attired in dress that suggests the Ireland of to-day (Aran ganseys perhaps) but which does not conflict with the ceremonial occasion'.[19] The narrator opened with the lines:

> I am the narrator Over and Above . . .
> I am the caller-up of the dead
> The Challenger of the living
> The Inspirer of the Unborn
> And if to-day I seek to call and challenge and inspire
> I do so with this over-riding purpose in my mind
> That when we have adequately honoured those I call
> We honour them in all the long to-morrows of our land
> In every action of the passing day
> By justice, labour and a deep integrity.[20]

The doubts of youth were then addressed. The young man and the young woman took alternate lines:

YW: It was so long and long ago – ere we were born.
YM: Ere we were born. And yet, 'tis said that they were young like
      us.
YW: They say it was for us they died. I do not know.
YM: I know them by the poetry they wrote
      And yet I am not certain that I know.[21]

In reality the executed leaders had not been young: Pearse was thirty-six, Connolly forty-eight, and Tom Clarke fifty-nine. They had, in fact, been absorbed retrospectively into the more general European memory of the First World War dead.

The narrator filled the possible gap between the young audience and their past with a short ten-line history of Ireland from Cúchulainn through the Normans, ending with the lines:

I was the shaft of sunlight in the cell of Tone
I saw the Fenians stumble in the snow
And I was a bystander in O'Connell Street
When, fifty years ago to-day,
Seven men in seven days.[22]

The voice of Pearse read from the Proclamation. And the young man and the young woman replied:

YW: There is renewal in the air.
      The drums are good: their rhythm bites into the blood.
YW: Even my woman's body answers the drums.
YM: And yet, I am resolved to question those who died.
YW: To find the why and wherefore of their dying.
YM: To see them as men of flesh and blood, not effigies of history.
YW: They must be seen and questioned.[23]

MacMahon linked the young figures to the signatories through a primitive tribal beat, but this did not deny the need for the past to live in order to be questioned. To the soft tapping of drums the narrator intoned:

N: Truths that are clear to age, to adolescence seem unclear.
     The young know not the night of slavery when only the
     pulse-beat of the heart
     Vouched that the dream of centuries still lived.[24]

Here is the reversal of the idea that truth lies with the innocence of youth. In fact Irishness, rather than resting in its purest form in the child, is much more securely tied to those who had to struggle for its survival. The narrator called each signatory in turn to 'speak to Ireland's youth on this, your jubilee of blood'.

On the arrival of Pearse at the podium, young men and women appeared from all parts of the field, some of them in traditional costume and others dressed in 'bright modern dress (slacks etc.)'. They danced forward so that, as the stage directions indicate, 'the whole effect is that of a ballet with undertones of traditional dancing which is light-hearted and impromptu'.[25] As the pageant progressed, each signatory appeared, accompanied by an attendant group of witnesses: Pearse with young men and women; Tom Clarke with the Fenians; Joseph Plunkett with monks; Éamon Ceannt with pipers; Seán Mac Diarmada with transport groups (air, sea and sky); Thomas MacDonagh with singers; and James Connolly with workers. Rather than being represented by their participation in a single event, the signatories were used to express different aspects of Irish life. MacDonagh said:

> I was a Transport man and so from men and women too who man
>   the Transport of our Irish earth and sea and sky
> I call my witnesses . . . Let them come forth
> And vouch for Irish accuracy and zeal
> And, in this fashion, honour Easter week and me.

He was then joined by Irish sailors, airmen, air hostesses and transport workers in uniform. The leaders were brought forward not just to give an account of themselves, but to pay tribute to modern Ireland. The figure of James Connolly decried:

> Call up the workers once again to testify
> How much of dignity they've gained in fifty years
> The slums no more!
> Health not the sole province of the privileged
> And those who grovelled on their knees are erect.[26]

In conveying the vitality of the signatories, *Seachtar Fear, Seacht Lá* attempted to demonstrate that they were a vital part of contemporary Ireland. Ian Hamilton noted in the *Sunday Telegraph*, 'When youth remains a relative condition rather than a virtue and human beings are not consigned to the scrapheap, old men keep their youthfulness.'[27] In April 1966 old men in Dublin had never seemed younger, to everyone but the young. John Jordan complained in *Hibernia* in January 1966 of how the young generation would forget the lessons of the Rising because 'they are asked to admire abstractions', not acquaint themselves with real personalities.[28]

An attempt to resuscitate the participants of the Rising as individuals was a central device used in the two dramatisations most popular with young people during the commemoration: *Seachtar Fear, Seacht Lá* and Telefís Éireann's production of *Insurrection*. The latter series of eight half-hour programmes was written by Hugh Leonard, whose script was an adaptation of Max Caulfield's *The Easter Rebellion*. Caulfield's book was dedicated to his father Malachy, 'who remembers it all', and drew on the testimonies of 125 eye-witnesses.[29] Caulfield created a tribute to the lived experience of his father which, through the technology of television, became a significant shared event in 1966.

Commemoration and the National Broadcaster

Insurrection, which the national broadcaster RTÉ described as 'undoubtedly the most difficult and ambitious project ever attempted by Irish television', was the story of Easter Week as it might have been seen by an Irish news crew at the time.[30] The format borrowed from the example of *Culloden*, a successful British drama, which was broadcast in 1964.[31] The central device used on-the-spot reporters, camera crews at a variety of locations and a studio news anchor, providing a depiction of the coverage of the events of the Rising which was not only impossible in 1916 but also well beyond the means of Telefís Éireann in 1966. Louis Lentin produced *Insurrection* and Michael Garvey directed the film sequences. Dr Kevin B. Nowlan of University College Dublin had been employed as the historical adviser on all television and radio programmes. His brief included 'consultation with survivors of 1916 and responsibility for sifting and evaluating the advice and information thus gathered into terms of programming reference' and *Insurrection* was one of his chief projects.[32] The production involved 93 speaking roles, the services of 300 members of the defence forces and over 200 extras.[33]

Insurrection was part of a comprehensive schedule by RTÉ which included thirty hours of radio programmes and the television broadcast of four series, six individual programmes and outside broadcasting coverage for thirteen public events.[34] An estimated cost of £116,000 for the television programmes was approved by the Radio Éireann Authority in October 1965, some of which would be funded by the cancellation of existing dramas.[35] The eventual cost came in £6,000 under budget.[36] Nevertheless the pressure on RTÉ's resources was considerable. The *Monthly Report* for March 1966 noted that it was the busiest period since the opening of the station. The completion of *Insurrection* and *On Behalf of the Provisional Government* had 'involved a considerable amount of editing and presented many operational problems never before encountered, and necessitated a considerable amount of work overnight'.[37] Editing rooms had to be hired in London to cope with the overflow and the RÉ Authority anticipated hiring forty additional staff on a temporary basis to cope with the commemorative schedule, at a cost of £22,000.[38]

The commemoration naturally raised political questions for RTÉ, and, as a member of the authority, T.W. Moody expressed his concern that in presenting the programmes 'all aspects of the Rising should be taken into account, and it was agreed [by the authority] that in presenting the clash of idealism and emotions, the programmes should be as balanced as possible'.[39] Taoiseach Seán Lemass had written to Joseph Brennan, the minister for posts and telegraphs, in July 1965 expressing the anxiety of the commemoration committee that no radio and television schedule for the jubilee should be finalised without the committee's approval. Lemass concluded, 'I should like you to take this matter up with the [Radio Éireann] Authority both for the purpose of getting their ideas formulated and submitted soon, and to ensure that these programmes will be suitable. (This means in particular no O'Casey).'[40]

The authority minutes recorded that, while it agreed that close communication should be maintained, 'it could not submit its programmes to the Committee for prior approval'. Rather, the director general undertook to impress upon the committee the importance of making *their* plans known well in advance in order that appropriate broadcasting coverage could be mounted.[41] The Abbey Theatre had also been advised that 'an O'Casey play during the period of the celebrations would not be in keeping with the spirit of the occasion'.[42] Both institutions responded by including the *Plough and the Stars* in their schedules later in the year.

In designing an 'appropriate' schedule, broadcasters had to take into account both how best to honour the event and how best to serve their audiences. Jack White, the assistant controller of programmes on television, explained:

> In devising our own programmes for the week we have had to bear in mind that we are dealing with two generations. We are fortunate enough to have among us still a good many of the men and women who asserted Ireland's right to independence on that Easter Monday, fifty years ago. They are the first-hand witnesses: it is natural that we should want to hear them, and that they should want to be heard.
>
> On the other hand, as programme planners we are aware that the great bulk of our audience consists of men and women who were not even born or were in their infancy in 1916. Many of them have no clear idea of the events of Easter Week, and no deep understanding of the men who created the Rising. Our problem was to bring home to them some sense of the heroic drama of that week.[43]

Roibeárd Ó Faracháin, controller of programmes on Radio Éireann, was also attuned to the dual audience. 'Radio, as it happens, has been commemorating the Rising for most of its forty years of existence,' he wrote, but during the fiftieth anniversary 'those of us who saw the clashing of arms and uniforms as men or as children looking through the keyhole, pay our Golden Jubilee tribute in common with the generations who had not yet been born'.[44] Ó Faracháin's assertion illuminates the complex position of 1916 in the Republic of Ireland. There was a sense in which modern Ireland itself was a perpetual tribute to the Easter Rising. Moreover the existence of a national broadcaster – through which a separate Irish culture could be described and defined – might also be seen to represent a continual memorial to the aspirations of the leaders of Easter Week. Therefore, in one sense, the Easter Rising was part of the very fabric of the independent state and in another sense its significance continually receded in the decreasing circles of experience: the soldiers', to that of the child at the keyhole, to the generations not yet born.

On radio, Ó Faracháin anticipated that the 'most evocative' programme would be *The Voice of the Rising*, for which Bryan MacMahon had written a script compiled of songs, ballads, poems and the words of nationalist leaders.[45] The Features Department of Radio Éireann (which had responsibility for the production) described it as 'the ghost at the feast . . . a stealthy intrusion on the note of celebration which we sound for 1916'. It continued:

> It is hot and cold, as history is hot and cold; hot with the memory and taste of idealism; cold with remembered suffering and death. It transcends time and place. 1916 blends with '98 with '47 and with '67. The sense of national personality and continuity is overwhelming. Is anything worse than war? The old question is answered in the old way. Slavery is worse than war . . . Dishonour is worse than war.

The *Voice of the Rising* offered a version of Irish history in which 1916 represented all time, and the experiences of the individual were subsumed into the greater personality of the nation. However, the resilience of narrative lies in its ability to function at the levels of both the abstract and the specific, and the story of 'the struggle for Irish freedom' was populated with heroic individuals – both allegorical and real – who personified the cause. The *Voice of the Rising* ended with the words of Thomas MacDonagh from what was believed to be his address to the court martial in May 1916:

The forms of heroes flit before my vision, and there is one, the star
whose destiny sways my own . . . The seed he sowed fructifies to this
day in God's Church. Take me away, and let my blood bedew the
sacred soil of Ireland. I die in the certainty that once more the seed
will fructify.

MacMahon had himself said of the programme that much of his
inspiration had come from listening to men like Liam Ó Briain and
Éamonn de hÓir of Limerick: 'One still finds in these men the granitic
core that inspired them of old,' he wrote.[46] Both MacDonagh and
MacMahon looked to heroic shapes which were more solid than flick-
ering and this attention to individual characters continued as a central
feature of the most successful dramatisation of the jubilee.

Indigenous television in the Republic had been launched on New
Year's Eve, 1961. By the end of April 1966 the network provided coverage for 98 per cent of the country. The Irish TAM (Television Audience
Measurement) survey for the end of that year estimated that 55 per cent
of homes in the country had television (77 per cent in urban areas and 37
per cent in rural areas). The increase in the number of television sets by
24,000 during the 1966 calendar year marked a decrease compared to
50,000 in 1965.[47] Therefore the jubilee itself was not a significant catalyst
for the acquisition of televisions in Ireland. A critical element in determining the possession of sets was the presence of children in the
household. A sample survey carried out for RTÉ in March 1966 recorded
that 69 per cent of homes that did not have television were also childless.
Surveys taken throughout successive years confirmed that households
with children accounted for the fastest growth in the spread of television
ownership.[48] This demographic information was collected for advertisers
but clearly had influence over the design of television schedules.

Insurrection

Insurrection was the most popular programme on Telefís Éireann during
the commemoration. Viewing figures for the week ending 17 April 1966
showed that the drama appeared five times in the top ten programmes. It
was a lavish production accompanied by widespread pre-publicity. *The
Times* of London reported in January that

The British soldier of today may think himself lucky that he serves
in the army of a nation less historically minded than the Irish. The
gallant troops of the Republic are reported to be up in arms,
metaphorically speaking, because they have been conscripted as film

actors and are not getting the overtime, subsistence, and travel allowances to which they think they are entitled.

Their role, according to the army, included patrolling the streets of Dublin into the small hours in an attempt to capture the drama of the Easter Rising.[49] Closer to home, John Healy quipped in the *Western People* in February that programmes on Telefís Éireann were 'dying like British soldiers, gobbled up by the demands on studio facilities by 1916 . . . and before it is all over I'll swear that there'll be more people involved in re-creating 1916 than there was in the original affair'.[50]

The *RTV Guide* for the week carried high-quality colour photographs from the *Insurrection* set and descriptive pieces from the major figures involved in the production. Hugh Leonard described it as 'a near-as-dammit, full scale reconstruction of the Rising, involving months of filming and weeks of studio work . . . At the beginning,' he said, 'the entire project seemed as gallant and as doomed as the Rising itself.' Leonard's favourite character was James Connolly – 'Bow-legged, fiery, an unquenchable optimist; cheering his men on with "Courage, boys, we are winning!" while the GPO roof blazed overhead', while figures like Pearse and Plunkett remained aloof and unknowable. To remedy this, Leonard argued that 'one dare not *invent* – merely select'; and to this end he used incidents that showed the insurgent leaders 'not as haloed demigods, but as clerks, teachers, weavers, trade unionists and poets, who overnight turned into revolutionaries fighting a doomed war'. 'It was their ordinariness,' he said, 'which made them and the Rising something to be commemorated after fifty years.'[51]

Pre-publicity set the scene for the viewer before a moment of *Insurrection* had been aired. The audience could anticipate that what they were about to see was 'as near-as-dammit' real. Leonard's claim that his role had been to select rather than invent overlooked the fact that the entire enterprise was an invention masquerading as hard news. Indeed Louis Lentin recalled that, while they were filming, a large number of the gathered onlookers 'were certain that it didn't happen like that at all, and said so!'[52] *Insurrection* opened with footage of the sixty-fourth day of the Battle of Verdun. The voice-over noted that casualty figures had not been released, but were believed to be high on both sides, adding, 'French High Command continues to be optimistic about the chances of an offensive on the Somme no later than late June.'[53] Archival footage has often been employed in cinema, 'used in part to explore the boundaries of both the imaginary and the real'.[54] In *Insurrection* there was a blurring of these boundaries as the viewer navigated actual footage,

reportage and re-enactment. Genres were also crossed and cross-refer-
enced so that what unfolded was part documentary, part drama, part
tragedy and part thriller.

However, the genre most associated with *Insurrection* was the western.
The 1916 drama shared its place in the top ten most-watched programmes of the week with, among others, *The Riordans*, *Tolka Row* and
The Virginian.[55] Leonard's drama was broadcast nightly at 9.15pm
through the commemorative week. The most watched episode was
broadcast on Friday 15 April: 'Do You Think We'll Win?' which dealt
with the arrival of General Maxwell and the eventual evacuation of the
GPO. It was preceded at 7.45 pm by *The Virginian*. The programmes in
the schedule bled into each other so that *Insurrection* would live on in
the popular imagination as an Irish equivalent of cowboys and indians.
Fintan O'Toole would write later that for quite a while he confused the
Seven Leaders with the Magnificent Seven – having seen the film in the
commemorative year – so that 'Yul Pearse and Patrick Brynner became
one'.[56] Peter Taylor opens his book *Provos* with reference to the television drama and the recollection of a member of the IRA who was eight
in 1966: 'Each evening we would be sitting riveted to granny's television
watching what was going on. Then we were straight out the following
morning and, instead of playing Cowboys and Indians or Cops and
Robbers, we would immediately engage in our own version of Easter
Week.'[57] The imagery is also juxtaposed in the most recent work on
dramatisations of the Rising, which asserts that Leonard and Nowlan
'were alarmed that their programme inspired children to play "Rebels
and Brits" where once they had played "Cowboys and Indians".[58]

Insurrection has passed into the popular memory as a programme
which, in dramatising the Rising, glamorised its violence.[59] Telefís
Éireann showed its very expensive drama twice in 1966 and it has never
been shown since. For many of those who were young during the
jubilee, *Insurrection* is remembered as the most vivid representation of the
events being commemorated. It has therefore developed its own
mythology: too explosive to be seen again, a recruitment programme for
the IRA and untransmittable after the outbreak of the conflict in the
North. The more mundane reason for its burial in the RTÉ archives is
the effort involved in tracing and paying the actors, who had not waived
their right to repeat fees.[60] More recent academic work by James Moran
and Harvey O'Brien has attempted to move beyond the myths of
Insurrection by placing it in the context of theatrical depictions of the
Rising and documentary film in Ireland and has revealed the series to be

more nuanced and challenging than is popularly imagined.[61] However, the radical message of *Insurrection* should not be over-stated.

Television dramas provide an artificial thrill that is enjoyed by the viewer who, understanding the convention, in fact always knows how things will end, so 'tension is but superficially maintained'.[62] This was true twice over in the case of *Insurrection*. The viewers were both literate in the conventions of cinema and television drama and they knew the events of the Rising: the 'false ending' of the executions leading to the happier conclusion of the independent state. Even within the innovative framework of *Insurrection* the audience essentially felt protected by their prior knowledge.

Insurrection utilised the possibilities of a medium new to the Republic of Ireland. The viewer watched as events unfolded as if in real time. Disbelief and knowledge were both suspended so that, despite the programme's title, the narrator and the audience conspired in their apparent innocence of outcomes. The opening archival footage of the Western Front was followed by the fictional news programme. News anchorman Ray McAnally held up Eoin MacNeill's countermanding order and said into camera:

> What is the connection between this newspaper item and certain startling events off the Kerry coast? This evening we take a close look at Sinn Féin and we ask ourselves what is this organisation? Who are its leaders? And why have the Government not taken action against them for treasonable activities? Parades, marches and so-called manoeuvres are one thing but consorting and planning with the Germans is quite another. Strong words? Well, we shall see.[63]

This false naivety not only created a dramatic opening, it immediately introduced certain elements to the story that disrupted a straightforward heroic narrative. The Somme was mentioned within the first minutes of the series, which itself opened with images of the First World War. The 'startling events in Kerry' were the discovery of guns and ammunition on Banna Strand and the arrest of a man, claiming to be Richard Morton, who was in possession of five sovereigns, eleven shillings and correspondence in a foreign language (which local police instinctively surmised was suspicious). The capture of Roger Casement – because of course it was he – was accompanied by the discovery of three revolvers on the strand by the young daughter of a man who had been visiting a holy well to mark the fact that it was Good Friday. The juxtaposition of the innocent child with the guns signalled that the rebels were a disruptive, potentially dangerous intrusion into the domestic lives of Ireland.[64]

Moreover, as the realisation dawned on the newsroom that there would be a rising, McAnally asked, 'What sort of man will knowingly strike a blow at his lawful rulers undeterred by the knowledge that he cannot win, and that his life is almost certain to be forfeited in exchange for a futile gesture?'[65] This may be ironic innocence, but the point was still made that the actions of the rebels were not easily comprehensible to many of their compatriots.

The use of reporters 'on the spot' was often awkward and sometimes comedic. St Enda's school was door stepped (Pearse would not be drawn into an interview) and it was a Telefís Éireann reporter who first drew Tom Clarke's attention to MacNeill's countermanding order (to which Clarke responded, 'I don't believe it. I knew that MacNeill was . . . but why would he do a thing like that. The blaggard. The dirty blaggard.').[66] However, the device also provided a way of introducing multiple voices. James Moran has pointed to the influence of *The Plough and the Stars* on Leonard's script which reprises Bessie Burgess as 'the citizen of Dublin' whose husband is 'out in the trenches fighting for King and country' and breaks into 'God Save the King' and a Fluther figure, the 'comic drunk' who tries to articulate support for the rebels.[67] McAnally's commentary also drew attention to the suffering of the Dublin poor caused by the Rising, again in tune with the politics of O'Casey:

> In central areas [of Dublin] the plight of the civilian population grows more acute by the hour . . . In many back streets the dead have been lying for days unburied. Food is virtually unobtainable in the poorer districts where hundreds of families are believed to be starving. The threat of a typhoid epidemic looms over the entire city. And yet on the outskirts, the holiday atmosphere of Spring Show Week still prevails. Workers whose offices and factories have been closed by the Rising are crowding onto the beaches.[68]

Moreover, the European context of the Rising was not lost, even in the very local Battle of Northumberland Road. The on-the-scene reporter declared it an incredible sight, British troops taking cover in front gardens, in doorways and behind trees: 'Most of these men are raw recruits and it seems strange they should be getting their first taste of action, not in Flanders mud but in Dublin on a spring day.'[69] An interview with General Lowe, commander of the British forces in Dublin (who had taken time out of the fighting to join Ray McAnally in the studio), was a reminder that foot soldiers in the British Army were themselves victims of the insatiable demands of the First World War and could be mobilised as cannon fodder on whichever front they were required.

With the battle under way, the general described the position as 'highly satisfactory' and the exchange unfolded:

R. McA.: But the battle has been raging for hours in Northumberland Road.

G.L.: I shouldn't call it a battle exactly. More of an extended incident.

R. McA.: The latest reports say that at least one hundred of the Sherwood Foresters have already been killed.

G.L.: There are plenty more where they came from. The rebels will soon find that out.[70]

The heroic focus was not Pearse, whom Leonard had admitted finding a difficult character to realise. The commander-in-chief appeared out of touch — assuring the rebels in the GPO that assistance was on its way from the country — and self-involved: 'If we lose it will mean the end of everything. People will blame us and condemn us. Perhaps in a few years they'll see what we were trying to do.' 'Oh God did anyone ever suffer like this for his country,' was James Connolly's response as he lay wounded, in agony, and clearly beloved of the men and women who tended him.[71] The choice of heroic emphasis was questioned by Ruairí Brugha, as a member of the Radio Éireann Authority. He anticipated criticism of the programme for its failure to feature President de Valera and for featuring Michael Collins in six episodes.[72] He also objected to 'an uncomplimentary reference' to Eoin MacNeill and asked if the veracity of this reference could be checked.[73] (In fact Caulfield records Tom Clarke's response to MacNeill, which the former confided to his bodyguard: 'MacNeill has ruined everything — all our plans. I feel like going away to cry.')[74] Brugha could not, however, have objected to the depiction of his father.

Cathal Brugha emerged as the most dramatic hero of the South Dublin Union. In the re-enactment of the legendary story, Telefís Éireann's correspondent reported that Éamon Ceannt's men were 'defeated, demoralised, waiting for capture or worse'. As the camera panned their broken faces the strains of someone singing 'God Save Ireland' could be heard in the near distance. A young man asked Ceannt, 'What happens when the military gets here?' To which he replied, 'We won't surrender now. We'll fight all the way. To the last man. We'll say a decade of the Rosary lads and then anyone who wants to smoke can do so.' The men recited an Our Father and a Hail Mary in Irish before being interrupted by a young rebel who burst in with the news that Brugha was still alive and was, in fact, the singer. The men, transformed by the news, immediately wanted to fight on, only to discover that the British had left the building, worn down by the single-handed heroism of Cathal Brugha.[75]

The story of the Easter Rising clearly lent itself well to dramatic reconstruction. The impact of *Insurrection*, however, was threefold: it exploited the potential of a new medium in Ireland; it placed the Irish themselves at the centre of a heroic narrative; and it appeared to reinvent the national story. Central to conceptions of Irish nationalism was the idea that independence fulfilled the nation's destiny. The longer-term difficulty with this was that the achievement of freedom might come to be seen as rather unexciting in its inevitability. *Insurrection* used the artificial suspense of television drama to underline the historical reality that the events and outcomes of Easter 1916 were not necessarily predestined. In depicting the unpredictable, sometimes chaotic nature of events, Leonard underlined the heroic intervention necessary to bring the independent state into existence. It was in this way that the national story was reanimated.

Insurrection did attempt to complicate the politics of the Rising and might in some sense be seen as Telefís Éireann slipping O'Casey in through the back door. However, both the medium and the form determined the way in which the message was transmitted. The decision to re-enact the Rising in a television drama allowed the audience to indulge in the temporary illusion of surprise while simultaneously confirming their belief in the destiny of the Irish nation. Hindsight was the key to much of the drama in *Insurrection*. The opening episode ended with Eoin MacNeill saying into camera, 'There will be no Rising.' This worked as a cliff-hanger only because the audience knew he was wrong. Moreover, the internal chaos of the drama was enfolded within the context of the subsequent independent Irish state. The fictional drama ended after the surrender of the rebels; the external reality in April 1966, displayed in multiple public spaces, was the ultimate victory of their insurrection. The version of history in which the continuous struggle for freedom had moved inexorably towards the triumph of the modern Ireland (however it stumbled) was played out in pageants and concerts throughout the country and was confirmed in the adjoining radio and television schedules.

Insurrection received critical and popular acclaim in Ireland and abroad. By 12 May RTÉ could confirm that the full eight-hour series had been shown by BBC2[76] in the UK and by ABC in Australia. A shorter, one-hour special edition had also been shown in Canada,

Finland, Norway, Denmark, Belgium and Sweden.[77] Foreign sales provided a net income for the station of £8,500 and congratulations were extended to the director general of RTÉ by the Radio Éireann Authority and by the director of BBC Television.[78] However, the factual *On Behalf of the Provisional Government* won the Jacob's Television Award for 'the most outstanding contribution to the Easter commemorative programmes' and Telefís Éireann's production of *The Plough and the Stars*, broadcast in September 1966, won the drama award.[79]

Conclusion

The performances marking the 1916 anniversary commemoration which are remembered most vividly – the GAA pageant and *Insurrection* – were acts of translation through which the meaning of the Rising was made contemporary. Both attempted to convey the story in a way in which a generation brought up on the *Victor* and the *Valiant* and German paratroopers could understand. Cultural memory exists in acts of reconstruction so that 'it is fixed in immovable figures of memory and stores of knowledge, but every contemporary context relates to these differently, sometimes by appropriation, sometimes by criticism, sometimes by preservation or transformation'.[80] Group identity develops through the perception of shared axioms and experiences and nations also exist through the assumption of shared values which (though not clearly defined) are groped towards through acts of repetition or commemoration: looking to the past for their co-ordinates and anticipating the future in a constellation of anniversaries. Thus commemorative events become part of the shared memory of a nation and each re-enactment alters the way in which the original event is experienced and understood.

Both *Seachtar Fear, Seacht Lá* and *Insurrection* attempted to remind the audience that those who participated in the Easter Rising had once been mortal, flawed heroes in order that they might flash vividly in the imaginations of those who had not been alive at the time. This emphasis also allowed for a degree of implicit criticism of the leaders which might serve to inoculate the viewer from a more emphatic dissent in the belief of their heroism. 'To their [the Rebels'] memory', Leonard wrote, 'had been fashioned a memorial by people who could not paint or sculpt.'[81] The memorial was a dual tribute to the Easter leaders and to 1960s Ireland. In making the immortal mortal, the living become taller.

Chapter Five

Where Nelson's Pillar was Not
The Memorial Sites
of the Jubilee

When commissioned to design the central sculpture for the Garden of Remembrance, Oisín Kelly was concerned about the 'general difficulty of expressing the heroic in our time'. He intended in his design to create a new nationalist iconography. 'There is no tradition on which to build,' he wrote, 'except harps and shamrocks and Lady Lavery and that bloody stone volunteer shooting splendidly into Bearna Baogail.'[1] The final image encapsulated a sense in which nationalist imagery projected itself into a 'violent gap' or void, replete with an unknown or unspecified danger. In Irish symbolism, the absences often resonate more clearly than the physically present. During the official golden jubilee of the Rising, no monuments to the event or its leaders were unveiled. Instead Easter Week was the implicit omnipresence in images borrowed from other aspects of the nationalist canon. In April 1966 statues were unveiled to Thomas Davis and Robert Emmet and the Garden of Remembrance and Kilmainham Gaol were ceremoniously opened. None of these memorials had been commissioned for the jubilee; delay rather than design involved them in the commemoration. The explicit act of revolution in 1916 was blurred in the events of 1966 into a more vague anniversary of independence. The renaming of streets and railway stations was designed to mark the maturation of the Republic and the appropriation of public spaces underlined the legitimacy of the state. The story of national freedom nudged out the presence of other histories on the Dublin landscape which was overlaid with new meanings.[2] However, the problematic triumph of that long struggle for freedom, which was referenced around the capital city, found its iconic moment not in monument but anti-monument. The most dramatic reconfiguring of the nation's capital – an actual violent gap – came not from the government's hand but from those of maverick republicans.

Nelson's Pillar

In 1964, *The Irish Times* was advised that the Transport Workers' Union of America had offered 'cheerfully to finance the removal of Lord Nelson' from O'Connell Street. The union president, Michael J. Quill, originally from Kerry, argued that visitors to Dublin were left with the impression that Nelson's Pillar meant to the Irish people what the Statue of Liberty meant to Americans and suggested that it should be transported to Buckingham Palace where Nelson was 'respected and loved for his many and victorious battles on behalf of the British Crown'.[3] Quill was not alone in advocating the removal of Nelson; the pillar had long seemed incongruous. The Patrician year of 1961 gave a boost to those who argued the case for the national apostle as a suitable replacement for the admiral and assassination increased the lobby for John F. Kennedy. While the more general view that 'it is about time such a monstrosity was replaced by one of our great patriots'[4] left only the question of which of those most popularly nominated – Pearse, Connolly and Collins – would triumph.

The foundation stone of Nelson's Pillar had been laid amid great ceremony in 1808, and while for some it had become a source of irritation, for many – detached from historical association – it had become a central landmark by which to map the capital city. When asked to comment on the pillar in 1923, W.B. Yeats responded that it represented the feeling of Protestant Ireland for a man who had helped to break the power of Napoleon. 'The life and work of the people who erected it is part of our tradition,' he said. 'We should accept the past of this nation, and not pick and choose.'[5] Monuments to individuals are particularly vulnerable to shifts in political power, after which the heroism they once personified can be reread as grandiloquent hubris. The textured memory Yeats had advocated was exploded in March 1966 by a republican bomb.

The explosion in O'Connell Street underlined certain difficulties faced by the government during the jubilee year. The removal of Nelson had never easily been in its gift. The pillar was maintained by trustees and the over-writing of their responsibility would have required a special Act of the Oireachtas.[6] However, the dramatic toppling of Nelson was contrasted in popular song with the bureaucratic indecision of political power.[7] The state's plans for the jubilee were under threat of usurpation both by dissenting groups and by dissent within groups. The government, which had viewed Nelson more prosaically than his detractors as a potential traffic hazard, was now faced with the problem of how to remove the severed pillar's stump. A report from the Department of

Defence warned that damage to adjoining property was likely to be greater than from the original explosion as the charge would be placed closer to the ground. The report concluded, 'It must also be considered that if we are directed to do this work, no matter what happens, the public will make invidious comparisons with our work and the previous effort.'[8] The superior engineering skills of the IRA would indeed become part of the mythology of the pillar's demise.[9]

Despite the government's efforts to create a choreography for the commemoration that would present Ireland as a modern and harmonious nation, it was unable to control the popular response. The image promoted to an international audience was of a confident nation celebrating its independence, without drawing too clearly the British connection or disconnection. The carnival atmosphere that greeted the transportation of Nelson's head down O'Connell Street, however, gave a lie to this image. The promotion of Ireland as a tourist destination was also jeopardised by the whiff of impending trouble. The Irish ambassador to Canada reported that he had been advised by Irish International Airlines that the 'incident of the Pillar' had 'dramatically altered' the plans of passengers who had intended to go to Dublin for the Easter period, particularly given the subsequent publicity suggesting that 'The Pillar is only the first of many such incidents that are anticipated.'[10]

The state wanted a commemoration that remembered the actions of Easter Week without celebrating the violence at their heart. It attempted to embrace the heroic ideal of the 1916 leaders while simultaneously transforming it. The blowing up of Nelson's Pillar represented the most literal commemorative act of 1966. Symbolically, it re-enacted the toppling of empire and physically it reproduced rubble on O'Connell Street. Nations do not need to re-create in order to remember, but the blowing up of Nelson's Pillar threatened to upstage the government's plans to mark the anniversary of the Rising. The state would find it difficult to offer a single event which would be so instant and iconic/iconoclastic. The hope of Lemass that the memory of the Rising could be harnessed to the needs of practical patriotism was always in danger of unleashing a populist republican moment in 1966. The banning of 'rebel songs' on sponsored programmes on Radio Éireann during the jubilee period was an attempt to set – but would not necessarily control – the tone of the commemoration.

The condition of Northern Ireland added a more serious note to an outpouring of nationalist sentiment. United States Congressman Robert

Sweeney of Ohio, speaking in the House of Representatives, noted that 'the program of urban renewal in Dublin City' should 'serve as a reminder to all of us that the problem of a divided Ireland still exists in a troubled world, and this once free and independent nation is still arbitrarily and unnaturally partitioned by the will of Great Britain'.[11] Irish diplomatic correspondence in the United States could present the Congressman as an 'amiable, if somewhat over-enthusiastic, well-wisher of ours', and the *Washington Post* might feel that he would be better employed concerning himself with problems in Ohio, but the link made by the Congressman was one that would resonate.[12]

The site of the Cyclops on O'Connell Street acted as a receptacle for the selectivity (one-eyedness) of Irish history. Those who cast a blow at the pillar rejected the place of the Anglo-Irish in Ireland's past. However, it was not Nelson himself but the tradition of those who erected the pillar that Yeats wanted to be remembered. Nelson as hero and the authority of the Anglo-Irish had both been problematic. Further selectivity was present in the government's attempt to frame the Rising as an isolated act of military sacrifice with no contemporary echo. But, as Congressman Sweeney articulated, some would see the proxy toppling of empire on O'Connell Street as a reminder of the British presence in the North. Therefore the blowing up of Nelson's Pillar threatened to expose the partial nature of many competing views surrounding the commemoration, as well as to destabilise the event itself.

Lord Nelson had become a symbol of the past which held no mystical presence. The body of the hero is a site on which the aspirations of the nation can be placed. A.J. Lerner, in assessing nineteenth-century statuary in France, sees in monuments to Napoleon a continuation of the public circulation of the mystical body of Christ. The doctrinal shift of the twelfth century in which the consecrated host became the *corpus Christi* rather than the *corpus mysticum* transferred the latter status on to the church so that the host became the sacrament of the collective.[13] The nation, as mystical body, has a relationship to the heroic body that is equally dependent. The individual provides the sacrifice and service through which he or she becomes an embodiment of the nation. Therefore the procession of monuments throughout the city acts as a demonstration of faith in the nation just as the Corpus Christi procession acted as a demonstration of faith in the church. As Lerner also points out, in constructions of nationalism heroes of the past must continue to live in the afterlife of the nation and it is through the monument that the living might commune with the dead.[14]

For Tom Hennigan, writing of the jubilee commemoration in the *Evening Herald*, the veterans of the Rising occupied a space somewhere between life and afterlife. While watching them he was reminded of the lines from Yeats's *Countess Cathleen*: 'The years like great black oxen tread the earth/And I am broken by their passing feet.'[15] He animated the narrative of their parade through the city centre with reference to the inanimate, so that:

> They advanced on the GPO from many points, marching past stout Dan O'Connell confronting the centuries, secure of his place in them. [. . .] Through College Green came the old men . . . watched by the ghosts of Smith O'Brien, Gavan Duffy, Thomas Davis and poor wasted Clarence Mangan, babbling of his Dark Rosaleen.
>
> Waiting for the marchers was the GPO . . . As it waited for them once before. Now, we seemed to be seeing the Ionic portico of Portland stone with the six fluted columns for the first time.
>
> For the first time too, the grave, impassive figures of Hibernia, Mercury and Fidelity on the roof.[16]

In this version, the commemorative march breathes heroic life, not simply into old men and dead men but also into the Post Office building which both anticipated and facilitated the Rising. However, without the attendant commemorative reminders monuments can slip out of view. Rev. Dom Bernard O'Dea, addressing Muintir na Tíre in February 1966, asked:

> Can we find no other way to perpetuate greatness than with a dickied-up tombstone . . . There are few things that so glorify the people who set them up, and torment the people who come later, as monuments. They become the accepted wart in the local face; all see them but nobody notices.[17]

As an example O'Dea cited the best view of the upcoming Easter Sunday national celebrations which would be had 'by a chap who will look down with a one-eyed sailor's grin – the fellow who saw it all, and is still around – looking askance. Monuments my eye!'[18]

Although the procession of statues in the urban landscape can underwrite the historical journey of the nation, their presence can also be problematic. Monuments can be seen to stabilise time and narrative and, as James Young has pointed out, bring events into some cognitive order by placing them in a 'topographical matrix that orients the rememberer and creates meaning in both the land and our recollection'.[19] Nelson disrupted the national narrative as it was constructed on O'Connell Street, which flowed from the Liberator and Parnell. The pillar overshadowed the GPO which was situated at the confluence of the nineteenth-century traditions. Katherine Verdery, in her study of the political lives of dead bodies in postsocialist countries, concurs with Lerner in seeing the transubstantive quality of monumental figures in which 'statues are dead people cast in bronze'. By arresting the process of the individual's bodily decay, she contends, a statue moves that person into the realm of the timeless or sacred. Within the statue, time is frozen at the moment of the individual's historical importance, suggesting the continuation of the values he or she personified. The destruction of a monument reveals the hero as mortal and symbolically destroys the temporal and spatial conceptions the figure represented.[20] This is why the removal of statues is so common after a change to the ruling structure. But, as Verdery also points out, the destruction of monuments may in fact be more important for regimes differing little from what has gone before. In which case legitimisation requires an even greater need to stress discontinuity through the decapitated monument.[21]

Nelson altered the landscape of O'Connell Street. A climb to the top of the pillar afforded an aerial viewpoint that provided a certain detachment through which the capital city could be read in a way that diminished the individual activities of urban existence. Those who climbed to the top became voyeurs of Dublin life as well as participants in that life. This view from above, which has been associated with both the colonial and global gaze, casts those beneath in miniature and reduces the sense of local. Nelson, on O'Connell Street, was often depicted as all-seeing and all-hearing. One of the winning entries in the schools essay competition organised as part of the jubilee commemoration of the Rising told the recent history of Ireland through the eyes of the admiral. 'I see everything that goes on in Dublin and I hear everything that goes on outside it,' the statue told the fictional narrator. 'And don't be misled by people telling you I am English. I may bear a resemblance to that British admiral . . . but inside I am only Leinster granite of fine old Dublin stock, and Irish to the core.'[22]

The pillar's demise allowed the subsequent state commemorative parade to pass down O'Connell Street unencumbered by Nelson's physical or historical presence and, in his absence, Dubliners would have to find different co-ordinates with which to map out their city and by which to orientate themselves. The debate over who should best tower over the capital was reconfigured, as was the gaze the pillar afforded. In the view of the *Church of Ireland Gazette*, there was little to be gained from arguments on the architectural, sentimental or utilitarian rights and wrongs of the affair: 'The Pillar has gone and nothing will bring it back.'[23] The *Gazette* argued that the presence of those who had the means to carry out a major act of sabotage in the capital had been swept, with Nelson's remains, 'under the carpet with a ruthless efficiency . . . No doubt the broken column would have been too rude a reminder to be allowed to remain.'[24] A half-Nelson, as the *Vancouver Washington Columbian* referred to it, would indeed have held a different meaning and, the *Guardian* in London suggested, would have required little politicking to change it from a relic of imperialism into a new national monument. Gerard Fay recalled an old street ballad sung when he was a boy:

> Lord Nelson was an Englishman
> A man of great renown
> But when Ireland gets her freedom
> We shall pull his Pillar down.[25]

Thomas Davis

Successive governments had understood the importance of populating the landscape with memorials that underlined the history of the state and reflected party political positions. Monuments to Collins and Griffith, Cúchulainn and the First World War dead had all courted a certain controversy.[26] Seán Lemass was open to the idea of investing in the nation's past and, in 1962, he expressed his interest in a proposal by Donogh O'Malley for the creation of a National Monuments Board. He wrote to the minister for finance, Jim Ryan:

> Because I think we, as the first generation of Irishmen which has power to do something effective about it, have defaulted in our obligation to preserve and, if possible, to restore these relics of our national past, I am very interested in these proposals.
>
> There is a danger that they may be pushed aside in your Department because of pre-occupation with more urgent business, unless you take an interest in them which I urge you to do.

Ryan did not disagree with the sentiments, but warned that 'colossal increases' in some of the Estimates for the coming year made it difficult to see how they could be met.[27] Nevertheless, the approaching jubilee of the Rising gave an added sense of urgency for the completion of projects such as the Thomas Davis statue, the Garden of Remembrance and the

Kilmainham Gaol Museum, the last of which was being undertaken by voluntary effort.

The Thomas Davis statue in College Green had been beset with bureaucratic difficulties. A proposed statue had been approved by Dublin Corporation in 1945 to commemorate the centenary of Davis's death and instructions had 'been issued for the removal of the air raid shelters from College Green in ample time for the event'.[28] The original plan had been to approach Albert Power to create a sculpture, but his death was followed by a competition which did not elicit suitable alternatives and it was not until 1962 that a maquette from Edward Delaney was approved by the Arts Council.[29] However, on seeing Delaney's plans, the cabinet held the unanimous view that, while the general design of the memorial was suitable, the model of the statue of Davis himself was quite unsuitable.[30] The minister for finance, Jim Ryan, was charged with the task of informing the sculptor and asking him to produce one or more alternatives, 'showing a more acceptable representation of Davis in the traditional rather than the modernistic style'.[31] More specifically, the problems with the statue proposed by Delaney were that it bore no facial resemblance to Davis, the head was too small, the body and arms too long and the legs too squat.[32] Judith Hill has noted that, for Delaney, Davis was a source of inspiration for his art rather than a form whose specific requirements be met.[33] An artistic compromise and political solution between the artist and politicians were found in the agreement that the sculptor's concept would be freely based on the Hogan statue of Davis in City Hall.[34]

For government ministers, the body of Thomas Davis was not an appropriate site for modernistic expression and the statue, when it was unveiled, was not generally popular. *The Irish Times* 'Irishman's Diary' found it impossible 'to reconcile oneself to the penguin effect of the lower part of the figure', and the *Donegal People's Press* opined that

> Davis was an intellectual. His statue does not give any suggestion of that intellectuality. Davis was a man who inspired thousands of Irishmen by his writings. The statue does not represent a man who had sensitivity in his nature. It is square and solid, heavy in its treatment and, all in all, greatly disappointing.[35]

Indeed the structure of the Davis statue is visually elaborate while the figure itself lacks emphatic detail, is anonymous and, more significantly, static.

The Office of Public Works reported that the statue of Thomas Davis would be completed by the end of 1965, and it was decided that the erection and unveiling of the work should be held over to form part of the official jubilee commemoration ceremonies.[36] The Thomas Davis statue had not been commissioned for the jubilee yet he suited the occasion. Davis the patriot had remained a less controversial Young Irelander than contemporaries who had lived to be old. His place in College Green opposite Trinity College and the series of lectures run by Radio Éireann under his name clearly linked Davis with the struggle for freedom through education. College Green was also a significant location, as de Valera noted at the statue's unveiling: 'home of the old Parliament for which Grattan, Flood and the Volunteers won independence from the British Parliament until Pitt, by bribery and corruption, got a majority to vote it away'.[37] The delay in building the Davis statue meant that its home was not entirely glorious. The Office of Public Works had expressed concern that altered traffic conditions left the original site less suitable than it had been and, when another site could not be agreed, a taxi rank had to be removed to facilitate the effectiveness of the design.[38] However, the site of the statue in front of Trinity College did allow de Valera to echo Davis's address to his fellow students, 'Gentlemen you have a country,' and to hope that 'the statue of Davis would remind students that they were Irish students, that this country was their country . . . that the nation was only too happy to have them without any consideration of any differences whatsoever'.[39] The nod to inclusivity was somewhat shaken by the late realisation that no Protestant schools had been asked to participate in the children's choir, which sang 'A Nation Once Again' at the end of the ceremony.[40]

In the final design, the 10-foot figure of Davis overlooks a fountain pool by which four bronze figures – heralds of the four provinces – blow sprays of water through trumpets. Six granite tablets with bronze reliefs surround the pool. Five of these reliefs depict poems written by Thomas Davis. Here, set in stone and bronze, is the traditional view of the position of the Young Irelander in Irish history. The series begins with a depiction of 'The Penal Days'. The ballad recalls a time 'When Ireland hopelessly complained . . . When godless persecution reigned'. It concludes:

> Let all unite
> For Ireland's right,
> And drown our griefs in freedom's song;
> Time shall veil in twilight haze,
> The memory of those penal days.[41]

The conflict within Davis's own position was well illustrated in the recasting of his ballad in bronze. Davis's attempts to create nationhood for Ireland masked the socio-political reality. In his construction sectarianism was a division that could be overcome by an appeal to an inclusive Irish identity. The inclusiveness, however, depended on an exclusion of Englishness. Because of this it has been suggested that Davis 'was, in a sense, asking Irish society to stand still, perhaps even to go into reverse, and retreat from modernisation and Anglicanism'.[42] However, this is to see modernity as resting solely with Englishness. In fact Davis used the tools of that modern society – literacy, newspapers, industry – to argue for his alternative. The contradictions inherent in the state's position (and indeed in the concept of modernity itself) during the jubilee were also present in the statue's design. Irishness was presented in a traditional form while the government also attempted to reformulate the country's image as modern. Again, as in the writings of Davis, an appeal to nationhood was used to obscure the structural inequalities in Irish society.

The sequence of bronze reliefs was also illustrative of the version of Irish history that underpinned the jubilee celebrations. The reliefs move from 'The Penal Days' through 'Tone's Grave' to 'The Burial', which was written on the funeral of Rev. P.J. Tyrell who had been indicted with O'Connell in 1843 during the Repeal campaign. The tributes to Davis's balladry are completed with depictions of 'A Nation Once Again' and 'We Shall Not Fail', both rallying cries for independence. The final relief imports into the series the history of the Famine, which Davis's death prevented him from committing to verse. Its inclusion reconfigures the others so that within this context the penal days are referenced, not as a distant memory but as part of a larger sequence of memories of oppression which explain the continuous struggle for independence ending in the validated state.

In his review of T.P. O'Neill's essay in *Cuimhneachán* (the official souvenir booklet of the commemoration), the historian F.X. Martin had noted that although O'Neill criticised the Proclamation of the Republic as an 'over-simplification of Irish history', he was himself guilty of a similar fault. O'Neill 'identifies Thomas Davis's political aim with that of Wolfe Tone', Martin wrote, '[t]his makes flapdoodle of the historical facts. Davis was a high-minded patriot but he was no Republican.'[43] Martin used more academic language to interrogate the Pearse myth the following year. He started from the view of Augustine Birrell on 30 April 1916: 'It is not an Irish Rebellion – it would be a pity if *ex post facto* it became one, and was added to the long and melancholy list of Irish Rebellions.' Martin argued that in the Proclamation Pearse had sonorously yet clearly expressed the declaration that the insurgents acting in the names of Tone, Emmet, Davis, Mitchell and O'Donovan Rossa represented the political aspirations of an oppressed Irish people. At the very outset of the Rising, therefore, the pitch was being queered for the historians. The proclamation of the republic was presenting them with an interpretation of the past in order to explain the present.[44]

In his memorial statue, Davis's balladry is also used as an interpretative tool for the past which is present-centred. The omission of his well-known 'Orange and Green Will Carry the Day', sung to the air of 'The Protestant Boys', would also have been illustrative of Davis's writings. An extension of his work beyond the ballad would have facilitated a round tower motif or a shelf of books.

The choice of ballads rather than prose has further significance. Luke Gibbons has contrasted the official memory incorporated in public monuments with those memories of the vanquished, 'which attach themselves to fugitive and endangered cultural forms such as the street ballad'.[45] For Gibbons, the power of the ballad in Ireland suggests an alternative formation of national consciousness which eschews the centralising impulse of European nationalism, now understood in its relation to print culture and more specifically (through Benedict Anderson)[46] the newspaper. In contrast, Ireland's national identity existed in unstable images and the fractured, fluid power of allegory and the oral tradition. However, in responding to the mechanisms of British imperialism, Gibbons argues, Irish nationalism was in fact weakened by accepting a unified sense of national consciousness that mimicked (but could never mirror) the centralised European model.[47]

Thomas Davis was part of this process. Along with Gavin Duffy, he recognised the power of street ballads to create significant moments of resistance. Through the *Nation* newspaper, the Young Irelanders sought to harness the ballad to their aim of creating an Irish nationality. They attempted to take popular ballads and broadsides which have been described as 'a popular commentary from below' and turn them into commentaries of a different nature. In appropriating the ballad into the *Nation* the Young Irelanders took a mobile form of communication that preceded the newspaper and formalised it as an adjunct to that medium.[48]

This process takes another step in Davis's statue, in which the ballad is further solidified. Rather than being a form which is open and oppositional, it is incorporated into an official public monument. The meaning is conscribed within a teleological sequence which legitimises the new centralised Irish state. It denotes a shift in Irish nationalism from nationhood to statehood. Through this process the ballad is in some ways divested of its power – which rested in its informal status and encoded meaning – by being formalised. The difference in the ballad as song and ballad as official art was well reflected in Radio Éireann's 'exercising of editorial control' regarding the playing of rebel songs during programmes broadcast as part of the jubilee commemoration of the Easter Rising.

Robert Emmet

All history is a queered pitch. Irish leaders well understood this and some were expert in defining their own legacy. The role of Robert Emmet as head of a 'two-hour rebellion' had been given historical gravitas by his quite brilliant speech from the dock. Emmet's unwritten epitaph hung in the air as the great unanswered challenge of Irish history. From the grave, Emmet passed judgement on the partition of the island, an unknown concept during his life. Two statues to Emmet were unveiled as part of the official jubilee celebrations: one at Iveagh House, with President Éamon de Valera in attendance, and one in Washington, DC (the 'Smithsonian' statue), as the centrepiece of the Irish embassy's commemoration in the United States. The latter, sculpted by Jerome Connor, had been presented to the National Gallery of Art in Washington in 1917. A replica of this statue was presented in Dublin in 1966.

The original 'Smithsonian' statue was to be handed over to the National Park Service for public display on Dupont Circle at Massachusetts Avenue and 24th Street. William Fay, the Irish ambassador in Washington, reported that (apart from a commemorative mass organised by the Irish American Social Club) the 'only special event of importance connected with the Jubilee celebration which took place in the Washington area was the rededication of the statue of Robert Emmet'. The accompanying ceremony, he wrote, 'was a worthy commemoration of this great event in our history. It would be impossible to think of a more appropriate means of commemorating 1916 than by dedicating a statue to the patriot who inspired the men of 1916 – Robert Emmet.' The ambassador continued:

> The statue had, moreover, the great advantage of being aesthetically a fine one, indeed, quite outstanding among the statuary on public display in Washington, and the fact that it was sponsored by the Congress of the United States through the Speaker of the House of Representatives and by the attendance of members of the Cabinet

and the Judiciary, showed that this was a truly national tribute to Ireland's independence by the government and the people of the United States.

A Marino band was present at the rededication ceremony to play 'those melodies of Thomas Moore which [had] particular relevance to Emmet'. In his remarks from the platform, the ambassador emphasised that relations with England were no longer those that had obtained either in Emmet's day or in 1916. This emphasis Fay had thought to be appropriate due to the fact that misreporting in the American press had tended to exaggerate and over-dramatise the various 'minor incidents of a violent character' that had taken place in Ireland during the jubilee period. Moreover, the Emmet statue had been unveiled within a relatively short time after a statue to Winston Churchill had been erected outside the British embassy further up Massachusetts Avenue ('a gift from the English-speaking Union, but of poor artistic quality')[49]. Fay reported that this had been 'seized upon by journalists to found a completely baseless suggestion' that the Emmet ceremony was 'intended in some way as a counter-blast to Sir Winston'.[50] The ambassador insisted that those involved with the Emmet statue had been ignorant of the plans for Churchill until a relatively short time before their own dedication.[51]

The statue in Iveagh House was presented to the people of Ireland by a group of US Congressmen on behalf of its owners, Mr and Mrs Francis Kane. A replica had originally been commissioned by the US government in 1922 for this purpose but had not been presented. The discovery forty later years that the statue had indeed been cast prompted Seán Dowling to argue for its inclusion in the commemoration ceremonies in a way that would give the American friends of Ireland an official part in the proceedings.[52]

At the statue's unveiling, *The Irish Times* reported that de Valera made his first public reference to partition during the official commemoration. In what was described as a quietly spoken, spontaneous reference to Emmet's speech from the dock, the president said that, while the patriot's motives had been vindicated in the hearts of the Irish people and while Ireland's name was well known among the nations of the world, Emmet's epitaph could not be written 'because the Ireland he wished for, the Ireland that Tone wished for, that Lord Edward Fitzgerald wished for, the Ireland in which differences between sections of our people would have been forgotten – that day has not yet arrived'. He continued:

> And it is only when that day has arrived that anyone can truly write
> the epitaph of Emmet. We all hope that day will come soon. We

know that in a democratically elected government the great majority of the Irish people hold safe in their hands the trustees of our nationhood and that with prudence and patience and time all those sections that Tone wished to unite in a united Ireland will come together and that it will achieve the august destiny which the men who wrote the Proclamation of 1916 predicted for it.[53]

The failure to end partition was much easier to concede than other failures within the Republic. Disappointment was cushioned in an optimism that the trustees of nationhood would in time, with patience and prudence, secure that which was Ireland's destiny. The nation might stumble but it would prevail. But the ghosts of dead martyrs could chastise as well as inspire. Rev. O'Dea's address to Muintir na Tíre (which was widely reported) argued that Pearse did not die so that Ireland could dispossess her own and force emigration on those rural communities which 'had weathered the Famine but not the Freedom'.[54] He indicted the nation with the view that Emmet's epitaph was closer to being written in 1916 than it was in 1966. O'Dea subverted the idea of the nation progressing through time, a notion central to nationalist thinking.

The epitaph was also part of that sense of movement towards a complete future which underpinned the psyche of the still young and 'incomplete' state. Marianne Elliott has pointed out that the building of a memorial to Emmet had become firmly associated with the writing of his epitaph.[55] The fact that the martyr's burial place was unknown meant that 'The island [was] his monument/Of him the hills [were] eloquent',[56] giving an even greater sense of connection between Emmet's uninscribed tomb and the history of the nation. The use of an existing statue which had been sculpted in a time innocent of the reality of partition navigated this problem. The work had not been commissioned by the state – which would have been tantamount to admitting the national struggle was at an end – but was a gift and gesture of brotherhood from the United States. The statue in Washington bore the inscriptions 'I wished to procure for my country the guarantee which Washington procured for America . . .' 'I have parted from everything that was dear to me in this life for my country's cause . . .' and 'When my country takes her place among the nations of the earth, then, and not till then let my epitaph be written.' In this way any suggestion that a final statement on the life and death of Robert Emmet had been written underneath his image was denied by his own injunction.

The ambassador, Fay, had not immediately arrived at the idea that Emmet represented the most fitting memorial to the 1916 dead. In the year before the jubilee he had suggested an exhibition of early Irish art in the National Gallery in Washington to mark the occasion, and that a more permanent commemoration for Ireland's 'national independence day' should take the form of the re-establishment of the Ministry for Arts.[57] However, Emmet was not unfitting. Not simply because of his influence over Romantic nationalism and the template he set for the actions of Patrick Pearse, but also because of that sense of forward motion his legend lent to the national story. The appeal of Connor's statue was that it too appeared to be in motion. Fay had considered whether or not it would be in better taste to leave the plinth of the Emmet statue in Washington without an inscription beyond the patriot's name, but concluded that since the speech from the dock had been the principal statement on the man's character and motives, some extracts would be appropriate. Along with the famous last sentence, he suggested 'My country was my idol' because, according to Fay, the 'youthful figure exemplified in the statue almost looks as if he were saying this'.[58] Máirín Allen, in a series of articles on the work of Jerome Connor for the *Capuchin Annual*, spoke of the lightness and fluidity of the bronze Emmet. Noting that the statue was unique in Connor's *oeuvre*, Allen speculated that perhaps there was no moment in Irish history quite like that in which the work was brought forth, indeed that even as he prepared the full-size model for casting, the sculptor could have read of the Kilmainham executions. 'If it were not so simply sculptural in its inner architecture,' Allen wrote, 'this figure might recall the tension, the baroque elegance, of an el Greco saint. There is aristocracy in the nervous, refined head.'[59] Previously, she argued, the artist's best work had stressed stability, but with Emmet movement flowed out of the mind and body, 'spontaneously, as it seems, in the speaking gesture of the hands . . . appealing beyond the judges to posterity'.[60]

Connor's Emmet had been cloned once before. De Valera had spoken at the unveiling of a replica in San Francisco in 1919. The likeness in the statue was inspired by a combination of Petrie's death mask of the patriot and the face of the actor Brandon Tynan. In 1916 the *New York Morning Telegraph* reported that a young actor would pose for Connor and that, thirteen years previously,

> at the age of 21, Brandon Tynan, who is now appearing in 'The Melody of Youth' at the Fulton Theatre, portrayed the title role of Robert Emmet, a play from his own pen. At the time, the young actor's resemblance to the great Irish patriot was so close as to cause widespread comment.[61]

This despite the fact that Emmet's actual appearance was almost as unknowable as his final resting place. The statue which had been 'brought forth' at the time of the Rising and had been dedicated by de Valera before the civil war was to be unveiled anew in 1966, giving Emmet a dual presence in the Rising commemoration. The patriot who Pearse said had died 'that his people might live, even as Christ died' was to be reborn in the commemorative act of Easter 1916 and in its commemoration fifty years later. The statue of Emmet, the redeemer and prophet, represented earlier memories of hope and redemption and it was this hope that those involved in the official commemoration sought to re-gather in 1966.

The Garden of Remembrance

The remaining memorials unveiled during the official jubilee derived their importance from the way in which they reconfigured the spaces they occupied. The Garden of Remembrance excavated a place for itself in the capital city and the Museum at Kilmainham Gaol reordered the meaning of the prison. The idea of creating a public park by the Rotunda Hospital was first suggested in 1935 by the Dublin Brigade Council of the Old IRA. It was on this site that the Irish Volunteers had been founded in 1913. The sculptor Oisín Kelly thought the site ill-advised. He wrote to the Office of Public Works' chief architect, Raymond McGrath, in 1959, 'Parnell Square has already been profaned by buildings which have no consonance whatsoever with the existing Square.'[62] Feeling that the garden would further break up the space, Kelly argued strongly 'that if we are in earnest that such a Memorial should exist, we must have a site where it does not compete with so many discordant voices. I am not suggesting that we must think big but rather that we must think whole.'[63] McGrath also doubted the desirability of the site for a national monument due to its 'vulgarisation' by signboards, mess, snack bars and dance halls.[64]

The space occupied by the Garden of Remembrance demonstrated Ferdinand Leon's description of how the montage of time in the modern city infiltrates the mind of even the most casual visitor: 'If we step from an eighteenth century house into one from the sixteenth century, we tumble down the slope of time . . . Whosoever sets foot in a city feels caught up in a web of dreams, where the most remote past is linked to the events of today.'[65] Nelson's Pillar had shown that monuments alter landscapes but do not necessarily transcend altered political circumstances. The Thomas Davis statue, with its long gestation, situated a traditional view of Irish history among the taxi rank and urban traffic of modern Dublin. The Garden of Remembrance would attempt to place references to ancient Ireland among the snack bars and dance halls and organise the slope of time within and without as a tumbling resistance to the values of the Victorian and Georgian landscape. At the opening of the Garden of Remembrance, on 11 April 1966, as at the unveiling of the Davis statue, de Valera ignored the discordance of the surroundings. He said the site in Parnell Square was in every way suitable due to its proximity to the Rotunda, which had held meetings of the Gaelic League, the IRB and the Irish Parliamentary Party. On the north side of the garden, Coláiste Mhuire held the library in which Tom Clarke and leaders of the IRB had met in September 1914 and come to the 'far-reaching decision that whatever the fortunes of the war might be, there must be an Irish Uprising before it came to an end'.[66]

The architect Dáithí Hanly's design of the garden proposed to create a certain intimacy between the memorial garden and passers-by and to provide a space in which those sitting in the garden should feel both secluded and inspired with respect for the patriot dead.[67] The juxtaposition of symbols from different points of history was an attempt to place them in a sequence that facilitated quiet reflection on all those who gave their lives for Irish freedom, to whom the memorial was dedicated. It suggested a continued line of Irish heroism from ancient to modern.[68] At the official opening de Valera stated:

> the whole design of the Garden is symbolic. It represents faith, hope, peace, resurgence and is a challenge to all the generations that come, to make Ireland of their day worthy of the Ireland of the past. All who enter here, or who pass this Garden by, will, I hope, as they murmur a prayer for the departed, pray also that God may preserve this old nation of ours, and have it always in his keeping.[69]

The garden takes the form of a cross – symbolic of the dead – and is surrounded by a raised lawn. It is laid out as a basilica but with a western-facing apse within which an elevated platform accommodates the symbols of state rather than church. The raised area was designed to facilitate the army guard of honour during ceremonies and is flanked by the national flag and those of the four provinces. The garden's reflecting pool is also cruciform and contains a mosaic of six groups of weapons, taken from Ireland's heroic age, which are broken, symbolising peace. The peace motif is further explored in the protective railings of the garden in which the central panel of the Irish state harp is inset with an olive branch interlinked with the Ballinderry Sword, pointing downwards. A limestone column at the eastern entrance of the garden is decorated with a broken chain, symbolising release from bondage.[70] As a memorial it is not appended on to the landscape in the form of a cenotaph or obelisk but has been sunk into it. The choice of symbols suggests an archaeological integrity for the site, as it unearths beneath Georgian Dublin artefacts of a more ancient Ireland.

In designing the sculptural centrepiece of the Garden of Remembrance, Oisín Kelly saw the architecture as the setting for a sculpture that would give the garden its meaning and enable it to function spiritually as well as physically: 'I cannot overemphasise that the sculpture is not an ornament . . . as something added to increase the beauty of an object. [. . .] In this case the sculpture signifies the purpose, the serious and unique purpose of this garden.'[71] Given the weight of the project and the pressure of other commitments, Kelly had taken some time to produce his report on the central feature, which he admitted on submission 'has been hanging over me so long I shall almost miss it'.[72] His anxiety came from the desire to create a new nationalist iconography which, he felt, would require a poet, 'and I have not the grace for poetry'.[73] The lack of an indigenous cultural language was evidenced in existing memorials which were, he said, 'a conglomeration of foreign elements, Irish in nomenclature and detail but alien in spirit'. For the sculptor, the only exception was Cúchulainn at the GPO, which was too small in scale for its position but in which the theme was 'universal, simple, and part of the popular imagination'.[74] Kelly's research had consisted of reading poetry and Irish mythology and resulted in his choice of the transformation of the Children of Lir into swans, illustrating the line from that fable, 'Once we were men, now we are epochs.' He suggested that the theme was of enough grandeur to illustrate the function of the park and that it was 'both national and universal, and would be easily comprehensible while being of a nature to permit the use of modern idioms, as this sculpture must be contemporary as there is no alternative'.[75]

Kelly's idea for the sculpture had replaced the original plan of the architect for a representation of Éire and the four provinces. The more challenging design was disliked by tánaiste Seán MacEntee for its pagan subject matter. Lemass had asked the tánaiste to interest himself in the design 'with a view to getting more rapid progress' in the matter so that the memorial would be completed for the jubilee. In November 1963 the taoiseach considered that it was now better to leave the settlement of the design entirely to the Office of Public Works with the understanding

that the government would have the opportunity to approve any proposals.[76] The Children of Lir design was officially rejected in 1964 and it
was not until Jim Gibbons, as the new parliamentary secretary to the
minister for finance, suggested to Lemass that the Arts Council be consulted on the design that the life of the sculpture was revived the
following year.[77]

The Arts Council unanimously endorsed Kelly's design, arguing that
'it promises to be one of the masterpieces of Irish sculpture in this
century and that its non-acceptance would be a national catastrophe'.
The report from the Arts Council continued:

> No representational image, however much it might initially win
> facile acceptance, could hope to have such a lasting effect on our
> people's deepest and finest instincts. With sureness of vision Oisín
> Kelly has realised that the longest series of sacrifices that have gone
> to the making of a free Ireland could only be adequately expressed
> sculpturally through some great 'myth'. History cannot be carved;
> the thousands of mouldering long-forgotten historical statues in
> every land give sad proof of the fact.
>
> For the Garden of Remembrance Oisín Kelly's theme of utter trans-
> formation is superbly appropriate. It makes use of a true not a bogus
> Romanticism that befits the type of men and the quality of people
> who are being remembered. Superbly appropriate also is that this
> should be so brilliantly done through the use of one of the country's
> greatest stories, which is at once unmistakably Irish and of course
> almost blatantly Christian.[78]

The government accepted the recommendation and issued a press statement acknowledging the advice of the Arts Council and the
recommendation that the theme was at once national and universal and
made use of a true Romanticism. Reference to bogus Romanticism was
quietly dropped. The statement also addressed the relevance of the sculptural figures, swans being the 'generally-accepted image of resurgence,
triumph and perfection, with undertones of regal sadness and isolation'.[79]

The sculpture did in some sense both clarify and elaborate the
meaning of its surroundings. Within the highly structured space it also
offered a moment of movement and iconographic imagination. Kelly's
design looked to an ancient legend from Ulster for its symbolic reference
in keeping with the gestures to history in the surrounding architecture.
The garden and reflecting pool were designed in the shape of a cross:
symbol not just of the dead but of transformation from life to death to
eternal life. This cycle of metamorphosis was central to the sculpture.

Kelly's influence, 'Once we were men, now we are epochs', revealed those to whom the garden was dedicated as part of a great moment in history and also in that moment made great. The mythical nature of the subject matter of the sculpture underlined the grandeur of the heroic sacrifice. The fusion of the understanding of legend and myth underlined the timelessness of both the symbolic and actual Irish nation.

However, the sculpture of the Children of Lir also shifted the meaning of the garden, which had a sense of resolution within its symbolism. The *Connaght Sentinel* in assessing the plans for a shrine, 'apparently, in memory of all who died for Ireland from 1169 to 1921', recognised a general acceptance for the Children of Lir as the centrepiece, 'which would probably be the best and safest symbolism in the circumstances'.[80] Noting that the country had become quite sensitive about these matters, it concluded, 'There appears to be no objection to memorials to those who died for Ireland provided they are not presented as representing finality or the consummation of the age-old ideal.'[81] The Children of Lir, who McGrath had argued 'are a symbol of the long Irish struggle for freedom',[82] were depicted in Kelly's statue at the point of transition from children to swans, not from swans to adults. The swans stretch skyward, reaching towards a Utopian future, but there is a tension as the eye is pulled earthward towards the crouching human figures. Kelly does not depict the end of the legend but the middle. He sculpts the transitory moment between the 'childhood' of the nation made infantile by the imperial gaze and before the 'adulthood' of full independence. A recognition of this restraint was contained in the government press statement, which juxtaposed the imagery of swans as resurgent, triumphant and perfect with undertones of regal sadness and isolation.

The *Kerryman*, commenting on the delay in approving the statue, remarked that official thinking appeared to be that 'after three hundred years on the waters of the Moy, three hundred years on Lough Foyle, and three hundred years somewhere else, the swans won't mind waiting another three hundred years or so in the Office of the Board of Works'.[83] The span of the period during which the children were swans also suggested itself as a fitting analogy for the long years of Irish history which followed its 'golden age'. The statue was not unveiled until July 1971 on the fiftieth anniversary of the Anglo-Irish truce, but against the background of the conflict in the North. The theme of Irish freedom as an ongoing project became therefore much more explicitly political. At the statue's unveiling Jack Lynch, as taoiseach, made a call to the British government to declare their interest in the unity of Ireland. He returned to the theme three years later when in opposition. In a Dáil debate he had tabled on events in Northern Ireland following the breakdown of the Sunningdale Executive, Lynch accused the taoiseach, Liam Cosgrave, of having lost focus on Irish unity and concluded with the words of the poet John Hewitt:

> This is our fate: eight hundred years' disaster,
> Crazily tangled as the Book of Kells,
> The dream's distortion and the land's division,
> The midnight raiders and the prison cells.
> Yet like Lir's children banished to the waters
> Our hearts still listen for the landward bells.[84]

The statue of the Children of Lir managed to convey an extreme sense of both hope and sorrow. Kelly produced a challenge to existing nationalist iconography but did not succeed in replacing it. The imagery, unlike Cúchulainn, did not have Pearse's imprimatur and lacked the instant gratification of a dead body cast in bronze. However, McGrath wrote, while arguing the case for the statue against MacEntee's objections:

> What the sculptor has done, and this particular sculptor is as much a poet as a sculptor, is simply to use the idea of metamorphosis as a theme for a feature with the universal significance – 'once we were men, now we are epochs'. I think even a simple person is as likely to grasp this imagery as he is that of Heaven and Hell, unless he gets befogged in the details of the Lir legend.[85]

Kilmainham Gaol

The idea of restoring the gaol at Kilmainham as a historical museum was the initiative of Lorcan Leonard, an engineer from Dublin. His interest in the site became urgent on learning that the Office of Public Works intended to invite tenders for the demolition of the prison. Leonard was also frustrated by the limit of Irish imagery and saw plans to level Kilmainham Gaol as 'the last act of the philistines who had already provided a rash of "Mother Eire's" [sic] and celtic crosses from one end of the country to the other to prove, I suppose, the respectable and Catholic character of the "four glorious" years'. In 1958, along with Paddy Stephenson,[86] Leonard decided to call a meeting of people who might be interested and 'who by their "records" would add weight' to the eventual petition to the government. There followed the circulation of information to men known to the organisers as having been closely identified with the republican movement at one time or another, in order to expand the base of volunteers.[87] The committee therefore comprised representatives of the Old IRA Literary and Debating Society, the Old Dublin Society, the Old Citizen Army and the Old Fianna. In February 1960 the government approved a scheme leasing the property to the Kilmainham Jail Restoration Committee for five years at a nominal rent of 1d a year. If their operation failed, the jail would revert to being the property of the Commissioners for Public Works.[88] It was at the inaugural meeting of the newly empowered committee that Brendan Behan famously proposed to put 'the split' at the top of the agenda.[89]

It was Leonard's intention to 'elevate that weed-grown, debris-strewn yard . . . to the most holy spot in Ireland'.[90] The task was difficult, as years of neglect had left the prison in a state of dangerous disrepair. The Restoration Committee cleared the idea of voluntary recruitment with the trade unions and over two hundred volunteers began the process of reclamation. Restoration sub-committees were set up in London, Cork and New York and industrialists and businessmen were asked to donate the price of restoring one cell each at 100 guineas.[91] The money-raising efforts were more difficult than expected. The committee in London, which was made up of members of various Irish organisations in Britain, gained publicity from the donation of £2 2s 0d to their fund from the Irish ambassador in London, Hugh McCann. They received £10 donations from the GAA, the Anti-Partition League of Ireland and the Irish Club London and £20 from the Gresham Ballroom, Highgate, but fundraising events were poorly attended. McCann reported, 'Although I set a headline by making a personal contribution to the fund – which was mentioned in the press . . . the appeal for the fund met with very limited success in London.'[92] Nevertheless the extensive programme of volunteering and fundraising in Ireland progressed sufficiently to allow for the opening of the museum within the jail to be incorporated in the jubilee commemoration of the Rising.

In an editorial for the *Dublin Historical Record*, Paddy Stephenson had said of Kilmainham:

> Grey, gaunt, old and sadly battered it stands like a fortress on the south west approach to the City, symbolic of the power that erected it, as if still defending the usurpers in their wrongful possessions and resisting the attempts of the rightful owners outside to make violent incursion to regain their heritage . . . It still stands, but broken and showing the marks as of a defeated warrior with cloven head gaping to the sky. But these marks of defeat were not gained in heroic combat, to our shame, they are marks of indifference and . . . Neglect

of this generation to acknowledge the debt it owes to those who agonised within its grey walls for our sake.[93]

Kilmainham Gaol, like the GPO, had come to be seen as an almost living participant in the history of Ireland. Built in 1796, as an extension of the existing jail on the gallows hill, it was finally closed to inmates in 1924. The opening of the new jail in the eighteenth century had coincided with the emergence of the United Irishmen and throughout its history had been home to a majority of the leaders of the Irish nationalist cause. The jail had been dubbed the 'Irish Bastille' by Charles Teeling, a contemporary of the 1798 rebellion and Kilmainham inmate. The term did more than link Irish republicanism with the ideals of the French Revolution. It encapsulated an understanding of the building as representing both oppression and liberty. It was this combined meaning that gave the building such significance. In a historical booklet issued to raise funds for the restoration project it was noted that the 'fabric itself is a museum piece, a document in stone illustrating the social conscience of the eighteenth and nineteenth centuries'.[94]

Kilmainham Gaol had come to represent the continued presence of its occupants. 'If ghosts can walk again the stones of Kilmainham must re-echo to the footsteps of the countless dead who suffered here for Ireland,' the Restoration Society suggested.[95] These ghosts were not simply those of renown who were documented in official histories or who were present in the known nationalist narrative. The society noted the failure of historians to chronicle the struggle of Irish people in the first half of the nineteenth century, the silence of poets to sing their praise. But the dungeons of Kilmainham had not been 'untenanted in those dark and evil days'. Moreover the Invincibles, whose memory in particular Leonard had wanted to perpetuate and who, it was felt, had often been omitted from the nation's story, had been held in Kilmainham: Tim Kelly sang songs throughout the night before his execution, ending with 'The Memory of the Past' before he 'lay down to sleep for the last time'.[96] For those who restored it, the power of Kilmainham as a memorial lay in its relationship with the inmates. It was felt that they had given the building importance and it could not deny them.

Behan had not been wrong to table the split. The early meetings on restoration had been assured that 'in order to preserve unity of purpose nothing relating to the events after 1921 would be introduced into any activity, publicity or statements in connection with Kilmainham'.[97] The attempt to limit possible divisions by jettisoning the civil war demarcated the jail as a less contested site in Irish history and underlined its place of importance in the struggle against British authority. The narrative arc incorporated in Kilmainham appeared to reach its end at the opening of the museum when the former prisoner, Éamon de Valera, returned as president of Ireland. 'I am not strange to this place,' he told those assembled, 'I have been here before, but it was not as bright then as it is now.'[98] However, the story of Kilmainham was much more complicated. De Valera had indeed been there before; the last time in 1924, imprisoned by his former comrades.

Kilmainham Gaol, like Lord Nelson, was depicted as an all-seeing, all-hearing witness to Irish life. The east wing of the prison had been built in 1861 and, although an imperfect panopticon, had been designed in the spirit of that disciplinary gaze. The restoration of the prison therefore reclaimed it from its imperial associations and reconstituted it as an integral part of the nationalist narrative. The privileging of this story meant that, in fact, the jail would be used as a selective witness. The stories of non-political prisoners would not be incorporated into the history of Kilmainham until several years into the life of the museum. Rather, the lives of those prisoners who had resisted the reforming mechanism of the prison, designed to control minds as well as bodies, conformed to an alternative order of things. The panoptic prison system operated differently to that older system of punishment in which public flogging or execution was intended to offer an example and deterrent to the rest of society. The nineteenth-century penal system was concerned instead with the impact of punishment on the individual. The restoration of Kilmainham returned the suffering of the prisoners to the public's gaze and the prisoners' lives, displayed as spectacle, were intended as a moral reminder of the brutality of the British system and the virtue of the Irish struggle for independence.

Conclusion

The memorials unveiled during the official commemoration of 1966 did not encapsulate in a single figure the revolutionary action of the Easter Rising. However, through the ritual of their unveiling they were interpreted as different parts of the same struggle. A struggle that was given legitimacy by subsequent events and that gave legitimacy to Pearse's understanding of his place in history as set out in the Proclamation. Through his speeches at the memorial sites, de Valera offered them as compasses by which the landscape of the city could be navigated in its relation to the journey towards freedom.

The commemoration in 1966 had two competing realities at its heart: the achievement of independence and the failures of freedom. The former was nominally celebrated in monument around the capital city. Fifty years after the event, the Rising straddled the generations of those for whom it was a lived experience and those for whom it was part of the normative culture. Those who had been rebels in 1916 now had the power to formalise their memory in symbol and narrative and ultimately to oversee the casting of the collected memory of the nation in monument. Pierre Nora's view of collective memory sheds light on the process at work: 'The less memory is experienced from inside the more it exists through its exterior scaffolding and outward signs.'[99] Or, as Young has clarified, 'once we assign monumental form to our memory, we have to some degree divested ourselves of the obligation to remember. In shouldering the memory work, monuments may relieve viewers of their memory burden.'[100] Thus Lemass, in requesting that the relics of the national past be restored, was in some sense delegating to the monuments the responsibility for remembering. In having achieved almost forty years of unbroken statehood in the Republic, and having marked this moment with statues, the Irish nation in that jurisdiction was being released from the burden of having to remember its own history. Indeed it is possible to argue that the commemorative moment of 1966 was part of a longer process of forgetting, leading to the silence that surrounded the seventy-fifth anniversary of the Rising in 1991.

However, there was a compelling pull from that other reality in 1966. The failures of freedom were in abundant evidence: partition, the status of the Irish language and emigration. A sense of the nation's lack of completion was present in the statue of the Children of Lir, in the inability of the Kilmainham Museum to deal with the civil war and in Emmet, who was memorialised but not epitaphed. So it was in the absences (of pillar, epitaph and aged Children of Lir) that the commemoration was defined. And it was the anti-monument (which most clearly symbolised the hybrid state of free and unfree) that provided the iconic moment of the golden jubilee.

CHAPTER SIX

From History
into Art

Writing of Constance Markievicz in the *Daily Express* Donald Seaman described her as tailor-made for Hollywood films:

> What a cracker! She went to war in a gorgeous, high-necked, tight-fitting, bottle green uniform made to her own design. Over it she wore a matching green hat topped with a great green feather that clashed with her flowing auburn hair. At the time of the Rising she was a sensational 42.[1]

Markievicz had caused similar reactions among her contemporaries, encouraged, not least, by her posing for a series of stylised photographs in military uniform. In a week of articles under the heading 'Six Days that Changed History', the *Daily Express* promised 'Beginning in Intimate and Fascinating Detail, the Story of an Armed Revolt that Shook Britain and Led to the Birth of a Free Nation'. Seaman narrated the story of the Rising with sensationalist ease and concluded, 'We are friends again now. Principally because of the preposterous, foolish, bungled, costly, brave Easter Rebellion of 1916.'[2]

It is not possible to represent violence without conceding or conveying an aesthetic. The act, in being described, is moved from the actual to the abstract; is given an external form. It was inevitable therefore that the Easter Rising, in being commemorated, would become aestheticised. However, it was also an event that had been given poetic form even before it had taken place. Pearse, Plunkett and MacDonagh had all committed their thoughts to verse and indeed Roger Casement (though more famous and infamous for his prose) had written the occasional poem. Pearse, Connolly and MacDonagh had each written plays and were alert to the theatrical and dramatic potential of what they were about to undertake. The boundary between life and art had been blurred further during Easter Week 1916 when Máire Nic Shiubhlaigh, a main actor at the Abbey Theatre who often played Cathleen Ní Houlihan in Yeats's play of that name (which was playing at the National Theatre at the time), joined the fighting in Jacob's Factory.[3]

Therefore the Easter Rising in Ireland has been particularly susceptible to readings that emphasise the poetic and theatrical above the military. A year after the fiftieth-anniversary commemoration William T. Thompson published *The Imagination of an Insurrection*, in which he approached the history of the period with 'literary eyes' and suggested that the leaders of the Rising had 'lived as if they were in a work of art, and this inability to tell the difference between sober reality and the realm of imagination is perhaps one very important characteristic of the revolutionary'.[4] The tragic heroism of the rebels existed in an imaginative space but, Thompson argued, 'when brought into the light and perceived with historical objectivity, they become incompetent, irrational, pretentious, and ridiculous'.[5] This demonstrates well the complexity of the relationship between the actual lives of the rebels and what those lives came to represent. The originary moment of the independent state required a tragic grandeur that may well have been absent in the Rising when set against the scale of the tragedy of the First World War. It has at times therefore been dissected as if it were a text to be read rather than a failed insurrection during which over four hundred people died. The importance of the symbolic is not in dispute here, except when it increasingly obscures that which it has been put in place to symbolise.

That Ireland was the kind of place in which even revolutions were poetic was a commonplace that sat uneasily with some of its citizens in 1966, not least those who were themselves poets and artists. In a special issue of the *Dublin Magazine* in spring 1966 the editorial argued, 'If we are prepared to confront realities, we must surely admit that from a cultural point of view Ireland is a disgrace.' It described as 'humiliating' the fact that the Northern Ireland Arts Council should receive approximately twice as large a grant as that of the Republic, which had to serve almost twice the population, concluding, 'Now that the North, long derided as merely commercial, is showing more recognition than we of the value of the arts, perhaps we will be driven into seriously taking stock of our situation.'[6] The failure of the Irish state to provide a robust infrastructure for the arts was evidenced by the pitiable state of the Municipal Gallery; the absence of a proper concert hall; the tearing down of even the very best of Georgian Dublin; and the Irish theatre which 'lay down and died some years ago, and the Theatre Festival is no more than an annual exhibition of its dead body'.[7] The poet's revolution, it seemed, had not ushered in a state that gave sustenance to the arts. In the same issue of the *Dublin Magazine*, the poet Eavan Boland said of Pearse that, fifty years later, 'if his plans have gone awry, it is because later generations seized the form of his message without the spirit'.[8] During the jubilee the government commissioned several artistic works which suggested that it understood the importance of form in terms of commemoration even if, beyond this, it had often felt it could not afford – financially or morally – to allow complete freedom of the artistic spirit.

The difficult relationship between art and commemoration was apparent in the contradictions in a speech in April 1966 by George Colley, minister for education, at the opening of the exhibition at the National Gallery organised to mark the jubilee of the Easter Rising. Colley stated that the aim of the exhibition was to show how the arts in a general sense had been

> used to transmit the ideas of those dreamers of great dreams who, century after century, in spite of overwhelming opposition, kept alive the concept of freedom. It must be remembered that while such great idealists and poets as Pearse, MacDonagh and Plunkett were so gifted that they could create their own visions and bring them to reality, the ordinary man and woman have to be stimulated into realising their potentials . . . The whole Exhibition is in fact a practical example of the place that art should hold in our lives – to preserve whatever of the past is great and beautiful and, in this case, to make us more conscious of the heights of heroism of which man is capable.

Colley moved from seeing art as visionary – that which can create new realities – to that which monumentalises the past. This easy slippage from one to another reveals much about the relationship between the state and the arts in the Republic. Declan Kiberd has argued that the rebels 'sought a dream of which they could not directly speak: they could only speak of having sought it'.[9] Once this dream could be spoken, it ceased to be visionary. The state could celebrate the arts as the source of the destruction of the imperial bond but could not tolerate them as a source of destabilisation in independent Ireland. Artists from the past might be lauded for the courage of their invention but, once established, the state could not be invented again, only reinvented from within. Emphasis on the Rising as an artistic endeavour might serve to blunt the message of violence in its aftermath but it also created the double bind that, once such power had been conceded, art could never be seen as a political innocent. The commonplace in Ireland fifty years after the Rising was, in fact, that freedom did not extend to artistic expression. When John McGahern was sacked from his teaching job in 1966 for the publication of his novel *The Dark*, which appeared on the list of banned books, his entreaty to have the reason for his dismissal explained in writing received the response from the school manager, 'Mr McGahern is well aware of the reason for his dismissal.'[10] The need for censorship went without saying.

The technology of art – its form, structure, machinery of communication or craft – is different from the technique, which Seamus Heaney has described as, in part, 'the watermarking of your essential patterns of perception . . . it is that whole creative effort of the mind's and body's resources to bring the meaning of experience within the jurisdiction of form'.[11] For Heaney, 'Words themselves are doors; Janus is to a certain extent their deity, looking back to a ramification of roots and associations and forward to a clarification of sense and meaning.'[12] In this sense, words are also commemorative acts. Different forms of art provided different 'doors' or spaces in which to present history and they framed the way in which the past would be represented. However, the watermarking of art – the singular voice of the artist – produces multiple meanings and makes stability something of an illusion.

In 1966 the commemoration committee commissioned work in several art forms – including film and music – and employed existing work to convey something of the meaning of the Rising. Poetry, as the most established art form connected to Easter Week, was referenced throughout the commemoration in official literature, journalistic reportage and commentary. The familiarity of the medium allowed it to disrupt a simple or linear national narrative during the jubilee and it was through the poetic voice that the history of the First World War was included in the commemoration. The reception of other forms of art also, often unintentionally, exposed contradictions within the commemorative message, as art always has the potential to subvert as well as to serve authority.

The Politics of Poetry

In 1966 Seamus Heaney wrote a sonnet to mark the fiftieth anniversary of the Easter Rising, 'Requiem for the Croppies'. Heaney's commemorative reflection recalled the failed uprising of the United Irishmen of 1798. The Easter Rising is present only by inference, as the poem ends with an image of re-growth from the graves of the rebels. The poem was published three years later in 1969, two months before violence would become widespread in Belfast, and Heaney would later observe, 'From that moment the problems of poetry moved from being simply a matter of achieving the satisfactory verbal icon to being a search for images and symbols adequate to our predicament.'[13] In the political context of 1966 it was possible to view poetry of and about the Easter Rising as providing a 'verbal icon'. Icons replace memory and can appear to provide safe spaces through which to explore ideas. It was in this sense that poetry provided a medium through which the Rising could be located within the context of the First World War. However, in being emblematic of the event itself, poetry also raised as well as resolved certain ambiguities and resisted stable readings of the past and present.

The Rising as a poet's rebellion was an image happily promoted by the Department of External Affairs and enjoyed by foreign audiences. The ambassador in Canberra noted that a piece by Patrick O'Donovan in the *Bulletin* had been the subject of much favourable comment among the Irish community there.[14] For O'Donovan the Easter Rising (which 'trailed its failure like a long robe of honor') had been brought about by men of great purity who were 'preoccupied by death and the wild legends and the black history of their people . . . They were not interested in getting rich. They were passionately in love – with an idea of Ireland.'[15] In the *Sunday Star*, Washington, Mary McGrory described the Rising (a 'unique and glorious fiasco') as the only one in history to have been fermented and fought by poets. Pearse and his fellows-in-arms were depicted as children of the Celtic literary revival who had their minds full of Gaelic fairytales and folklore and memories of Ireland's past wrongs and glories.[16] The *New York Times*, which eschewed a romantic notion of the Rising, nevertheless noted that the Proclamation had been read in 1916 by a poet, accompanied by a professor of English, a theatre director, a labour leader and several journalists.[17] The *San Francisco Examiner* drew parallels between the poet-leaders of the Rising and 'another Irish son', John F. Kennedy, whose words were quoted: 'When power leads man towards arrogance, poetry reminds him of his limitations. When power narrows the areas of man's concern, poetry reminds him of the richness and diversity of his existence. When power corrupts, poetry cleanses.' The *Examiner* journalist Donald Stanley, who had characterised the Irish as 'natural propagandists', had himself conceded a version of the Rising in which poetry rather than bloodshed had become the source of purification.[18]

W.B. Yeats

Mary McGrory had written that 'it was the luck of the Irish to produce for this supreme moment William Butler Yeats, who is widely regarded as the finest poet of the Twentieth century'.[19] Yeats's connection with the culture of the revolutionary period meant that few in the journalistic world dwelt too long on his poetic ambiguities. The final line of his response to the Rising in 'Easter 1916' was quoted liberally in the international press without much sense that 'a terrible beauty' was anything more than a rhetorical flourish. It became an easy way to convey support for the Rising with all the necessary qualifications.

Yeats had become an important part of the Irish brand. The film *Yeats Country* (1965) was directed by Patrick Carey and partly sponsored by the Department of External Affairs. The film received widespread international recognition and was requested for screening by the embassies in Lagos and Lisbon during the commemoration.[20] More significantly, a large number of the newspaper stories of the jubilee carried a photograph of Yeats, often with only a loose connection to the text. Therefore if, as John Wilson Foster has argued, 'Easter 1916' was 'a formidable attempt at appropriation', one in which the poem offered 'a canonical image of the Rising that establishes the importance as much of Yeats to the Rising as of the Rising to Yeats', the poet had succeeded, in some quarters, in placing his imprint on an event in which he took no part.[21] Yeats was useful abroad as an acknowledged literary giant but less needed in Ireland as anointer of the dead and less welcome as an uneasy respondent in verse. In Ireland his ambivalence spoke primarily to those who sought to complicate the process of commemoration.

Maud Gonne is reported to have thought 'Easter 1916' 'wholly inadequate to the occasion'[22] and Yeats's political nerve was inadequate to early publication.[23] This ambivalence meant that in 1966 Yeats was not automatically the laureate of the Rising for his fellow countrymen. His work was certainly not absent in Ireland during the jubilee commemoration but neither was it omnipresent. Erskine Childers, the minister for transport and power, had anticipated that Yeats's famous refrain would be quoted throughout the celebrations and wrote to several cabinet colleagues, including Seán Lemass, advocating instead 'Green Branches' by James Stephens, which he described as 'the best romantic poem of 1916' and 'much more useful than "A Terrible Beauty is Born" [*sic*] by W.B.

Yeats'. Childers urged Michael Hilliard, the minister for defence, to get a copy of 'Green Branches' photostatted from the National Library and suggested that it be used for a declamation in public and for radio and television broadcasts.[24]

'Green Branches' referred to a section of Stephens's poem 'Spring – 1916' which links the green innocence of youth with the fertile green graves and memory of the dead:

> Be green upon their graves, O happy Spring!
> For they were young and eager who are dead!
> Of all things that are young, and quivering
> With eager life, be they rememberéd!
> They move not here! They have gone to the clay!
> They cannot die again for liberty!
> Be they remembered for their land of aye!
> Green be their graves, and green their memory![25]

Stephens's politics were more palatable to the organisers of the commemoration than the more tortured position of the Anglo-Irish Yeats. A third edition of Stephens's classic account of the Rising, *The Insurrection in Dublin*, had been published in time for the jubilee. Stephens, unlike Yeats, had been in Dublin during the Rising and had recorded his response and published it in the same year. He drew a portrait of an insurrection being fought, among antipathetic Dubliners, in deadly silence and led by good men: 'men, that is, who willed no evil, and whose movements of body or brain were unselfish and healthy'.[26] Stephens was a supporter of Irish independence but he also argued vigorously in the last chapter of *The Insurrection in Dublin* that before Ireland could be called a nation it should be made a nation. This meant proper engagement with Ulster so that 'anything that smells, however distantly, of hatred for England will be a true menace to Ulster. We must swallow England if Ulster is to swallow us.'[27] Stephens's final plea was for a political future that focused on the local and on getting Irish affairs in order. *The Insurrection in Dublin* concluded with a line that would, in fact, have been the perfect declamation for the 1966 commemoration: 'From this day a great adventure opens for Ireland. The Volunteers are dead, and the call is now for volunteers.'[28]

Stephens's poem is closer in sentiment and style to early First World War poetry (as is that of Pearse) than that of Yeats. Again, the framing of the rebels as young and eager belies the reality of many of those who died. Unlike 'Easter 1916' there is no mention of the former lives of the rebels such as 'a drunken, vainglorious lout', John McBride, who could be transformed only by his death and remains untransformed in the poem. Instead there is a celebratory tribute to the sacrifice of the rebels which does not rely overtly on the memorialising of the poet.

Yeats was also being chastised for his early pessimism by the popularity in 1966 of the American poet Joyce Kilmer, who had enlisted in the United States Army in 1917 and was killed by a sniper during the Second Battle of the Marne the following year. Kilmer's poem 'Easter Week' had been dedicated to the memory of Joseph Mary Plunkett and opened with Yeats's lines from 'September 1913' followed by a retort:

> 'Romantic Ireland's dead and gone,
> It's with O'Leary in the grave.'
> Then, Yeats, what gave that Easter dawn
> A hue so radiantly brave?

The poem, which mentions the nationalist figures Lord Edward Fitzgerald, Patrick Sarsfield, Robert Emmet and P.H. Pearse, includes the stanza:

> Romantic Ireland never dies!
> O'Leary lies in fertile ground,
> And songs and spears throughout the years
> Rise up where patriot graves are found.[29]

Kilmer's poem had been a staple of Irish-American commemorations and in 1966 found its way into a variety of publications[30] and appeared in souvenir brochures for the jubilee, including that of Mallow, County Cork, which noted that, as a poet, Kilmer was able to 'appreciate [the leaders'] objectives, to admire their ideals'.[31]

Poetry and the First World War

'Easter Week' was also reproduced in *Éire-Ireland: Weekly Bulletin of the Department of External Affairs*, which noted that Kilmer had 'flung back at Yeats his own earlier words'.[32] Kilmer had the advantage over Yeats of being a soldier as well as a poet, and of having died in battle. Those who had appreciated the importance of the Easter Rising, despite being positioned at the Western Front, were welcome reminders that not all who fought in the First World War had been opposed to the insurrection. In 1966 this poetry took on an added significance as it could be used to introduce the broader context of the war into the nationalist commemoration. The thousands of Irishmen who volunteered to fight in the First World War had been given no place in a dominant narrative that shaped history into a long sequence of events which culminated in the creation of the independent state. Nevertheless Seán Lemass had referred earlier in the year to the war in which 'tens of thousands of generous young Irishmen, responding to the call of their Parliamentary leaders, had volunteered enthusiastically to fight, as they believed, for the liberty of Belgium'. He continued:

> In later years it was common – and I also was guilty in this respect – to question the motives of those men who joined the new British armies formed at the outbreak of the war, but it must, in their honour and in fairness to their memory, be said that they were motivated by the highest purpose, and died in their tens of thousands in Flanders and Gallipoli believing they were giving their lives in the cause of human liberty everywhere, not excluding Ireland.[33]

In attempting magnanimity Lemass exposed his own ideological boundaries. For many in the Republic the First World War did not represent a radical break with the past as it did for other European countries. Instead it was understood as part of the longer struggle for independence. Rather than seeing the period of 1914–18 as one that represented loss, fighting (for and against Britain) was offered as the surety that those enterprises and projects that had begun before the war would be completed.[34] Attempts to accommodate nationalists who fought in the First World War into this schema cast them as victims who had been misled into acting prematurely and had become involved in the wrong war.[35] The idea was perpetuated not only by the taoiseach, but in popular literature and journal essays. *The Scorching Wind*, Walter Macken's historical novel, follows two brothers through the period from 1916 to the civil war. Their father, an old Fenian, on hearing of the Rising in Dublin, says of his son Dualta, who has enlisted in the British Army: 'He was in the wrong war. You hear that. The wrong war. Oh, Dualta why didn't you wait?'[36] For his son, realisation began to dawn on the fields of battle: 'I was out in the mud . . . What for? I wondered. I thought of my father. He was right. Why was I there? I was deceived.' However, on returning to Dublin he reflected, 'When I saw the burned city, tattered tricolours, and the executions, how they died, I thought, out there, I had no cause, just an amateur mercenary. Now there is a cause. You see?'[37]

The non-fictional son of the 1916 rebel Desmond Fitzgerald returned to his father's words fifty years later and characterised him and the other Volunteers as men who, faced with widespread support for Britain's war effort, 'suddenly found themselves convinced . . . that the final end of the Irish nation was at hand, unless they acted dramatically to call back the nation's soul from the very shadow of death'.[38] For Garrett FitzGerald, writing in 1966, the violence of the Rising was not an unproblematic moral issue. However, he sought to remind the public of his father's view that:

> For centuries England had held Ireland materially. But now [through the First World War] it seemed that she held her in a new and utterly complete way. Our national identity was obliterated not only politically, but also in our own minds. The Irish people had recognised themselves as part of England.[39]

FitzGerald did not want the war to be written out of Irish history 'in a misguided effort to develop the patriotism of our children' because, '[i]n an attempt to portray an unbroken Irish tradition of armed resistance to British rule, history – as it is taught – diminishes and renders meaningless the Rising of 1916'.[40] For FitzGerald the war made sense of Easter Week because it made critical the need for radical action. Equally, the view was general in the Republic of Ireland that, without Easter Week, the First World War would have made no sense at all. This reading dominated in allusions to the First World War during the jubilee of the Rising.

Seán Lemass also drew on the experience of his father to give shape to the change the Rising brought forth. In a speech which attempted to speak to the memory of those who had enlisted to fight in the First World War, he had begun by 'recounting a personal experience':

> My father had been a stalwart of the Irish Parliamentary Party who trusted John Redmond beyond argument, and who indeed resented any questioning of his leadership. I returned home after the Rising on a Saturday night – alone, because my brother who had been wounded in the fighting was still in hospital – wondering what family arguments our participation in it might involve, but on the following Sunday morning my father entered my bedroom with a large celluloid tri-colour button in the lapel of his coat. At first I thought this to be a demonstration of solidarity with his sons and perhaps an act of defiance of those of his own friends who were finding fault with us, but in the days following I found out how deeply he had been moved and how much the change in him reflected the change which had taken place amongst the Irish people as a whole. It was then I understood that the Easter Rising was not just an isolated incident in Irish history but something much more profound . . . not only an end but a beginning.[41]

This represented several concessions by Lemass. He very rarely spoke of his personal experience of this period – his contributions during the jubilee were minimal and restrained – and he never spoke of his older brother with whom he had been very close. Noel Lemass had been killed after the Civil War ceasefire of May 1923 and his body dumped in the Dublin mountains. Furthermore, Lemass prefaced his remarks about those who had responded 'to the call of their Parliamentary leaders' with the information that his father too had 'trusted John Redmond beyond argument'. These recollections of his private past had been offered to underline the sincerity of his inclusion of the First World War dead in official Irish memory. This was certainly how it was understood in the press at the time. It was described by one commentator as 'the best tribute of all, even if it comes a little late'.[42] However, while attempting to defend the motives of those who joined the British armies during the war, Lemass repeated the qualification that the soldiers fought, 'as they believed' and 'believing they were giving their lives' for freedom; exposing his own belief that while the motives of these soldiers should not be questioned, they were mistaken.

Irish Soldier Poets

Much of the poetry by Irishmen serving in the British Army during the First World War contained elements of ambiguity and ambivalence. Therefore, while the inclusion of this poetry in official literature during the commemoration appeared to be inclusive of the European war experience, it also reinforced a nationalist understanding of that war. The poetry of Francis Ledwidge and Tom Kettle – both of whom enlisted in the British Army during the First World War – provides similar confirmation of this point of view and was featured in official and unofficial poetry collections during the jubilee of the Rising. In 'The Dead Kings', written in January 1917, Ledwidge is lost in a reverie with Ireland's past only to awake and find himself in France. *Éire-Ireland: Weekly Bulletin of the Department of External Affairs* noted that Ledwidge 'had put on khaki in the belief that he was fighting for Ireland's cause' and that the poem, written in the Gaelic metre, told of 'the tragedy and power inherent in the revolution of his fellow poets in Ireland'.[43] Quoting from Ledwidge in his contribution to the Edwards and Pyle edited collection on the Rising, Major Henry Harris noted, 'not all poets were on the side of the Rising'.[44] However, it has been argued that Ledwidge was consumed by the Rising rather than the war in which he fought and produced over twenty poems on the former and none of equal standing on the latter.[45]

Tom Kettle was equally difficult to place. He had been a Home Rule MP who joined the British Army and is reported to have recognised immediately that the rebels would 'go down in history as heroes and martyrs, and I will go down – if I go down at all – as a bloody British officer'.[46] Kettle sustained a belief in constitutional nationalism until his death at the Somme in September 1916. His poetry made several appearances during the jubilee including in an address by the minister for education, George Colley, at the presentation of historical items by Captain de Courcy-Wheeler to the National Museum. Colley opened with Kettle's words, 'We keep the past for pride' and noted that in this poem the poet had 'envisaged an ending to "the bitter years", a happy ending after which the English and Irish, all passion spent, would meet in close friendship and wish only to recall the deeds of valour or chivalry that had occurred during their long struggle'.[47] In quoting briefly from Kettle's poem 'Reason in Rhyme' Colley gestured towards the way in which this poet had become a bridging figure between two strands of nationalist tradition in Ireland.

For Brian Boydell, who had been commissioned by Radio Éireann to compose a cantata for the commemoration, Kettle represented more generally the sincerity of belief and tragic loss of all those who had died in war in 1916. Boydell recorded that he thought the invitation to him for the composition was particularly interesting and 'a tremendous sign of the coming maturity in the country that an Anglo-Irishman should be invited to do this, rather than someone who was known to be, shall we say, an ardent Gael. Secondly, I happen to have been president of the Irish Pacifist Movement.'[48] Radio Éireann had specified that the music should contain settings of 1916 poems and Boydell worked with Tomás Ó Suilleabháin on constructing a text. The cantata, 'A Terrible Beauty is Born', was performed at the Gaiety Theatre in Dublin on 11 April 1966.[49]

While disagreeing with the violence of the Easter Rising, Boydell came to view the commission as an opportunity to contemplate the fundamental ideals of those who had taken part, 'because there is no doubt that those ideals were sincere – bound up, I think, in the ideal of freedom of the individual, which is tremendously important'.[50] As its title suggests, the composition opened and closed with words from Yeats's 'Easter 1916'. The last line of the poem, which had given Boydell his title, had recommended itself because it was shot through with innuendo. The composer did not see the fiftieth anniversary of the Rising simply as an occasion to 'wave flags and say hurrah about everything without thinking about certain question marks which are left in the air . . . in some ways the whole work aims at a question mark'. For Boydell, the ambiguity was a necessary tempering of complacent celebration because 'there are still many things left to be done – in fact the really important things are left to be done' in order to make the best possible use of the freedom gained by the actions of 1916.[51]

Yeats's poem punctuates seven others in the composition, including 'Renunciation' by Pearse, 'In Memoriam' by Thomas MacDonagh and 'Sixteen Dead Men' by Dora Sigerson.[52] The final poem is Kettle's 'Reason in Rhyme'. Boydell lists this in the score as 'Cancel the Past' and opens the extract from the poem with the lines 'Cancel the past! Why yes!/We too have thought/Of conflict crowned and drowned in olives of peace.' He explained the importance of the sentiment by saying, 'it is high time that we in Ireland stopped and thought more about the future than living in the past and nursing past grudges . . . That does not mean that we deny the past in any sense, but that we cancel the grudges and hates of the past.'[53] Boydell's reading is more emphatic than the poem may allow. Kettle had written 'Reason in Rhyme' as a response to the English poet William Watson, who was a champion of English imperialism. Earlier in the poem he writes:

> We Irish, to be brief are nowise grievers for the sake of grief.
> I pray you, dry those sympathetic tears,
> They rust the will; and, Will, your nation's sin
> Is no dead shame, meet to be covered in,
> But a live fact that sears.
>
> Cancel the past? Soothly when it befalls
> That ye amend the present, and are just,
> Go knock your head on Dublin Castle Walls:
> Are they irrelevant historic dust.
> Or a hard present tense?[54]

Clearly Dublin Castle had ceased to be central to British administration by 1966. However, Kettle problematises the relationship between the past and present and, rather than endorse the call that the past be cancelled, addresses those interests which are served by this demand. Kettle confronts the power relationship between England and Ireland: 'And when you make your banquet, and we come,/Soldier with equal soldier must we sit,/Closing the battle, not forgetting it.'[55] Kettle – as an Irish nationalist who fought in the First World War – may have appeared to be the ideal symbol for a tentative reconciliation of the various military traditions of all those who died in 1916, but he had written too much during his life to be appropriated in silence. His 'political testimony' had been published in the *Freeman's Journal* in August 1916 and asked 'by the seal of the blood given in the last two years' that Ireland be given colonial home rule, 'a thing essential in itself and essential as a prologue to the reconstruction of the Empire'.[56] Therefore Kettle had to be quoted carefully and sparingly. For Boydell, the call to cancel the past had been most appealing whereas, for Colley, Kettle had sanctioned keeping the past for pride. This central dilemma reverberated throughout the jubilee commemoration. In fact the poet advocated neither cancellation nor preservation without consideration and qualification.

The poetic turn given to the Easter Rising elevated it beyond the prosaic reality of military and political happenings. Fifty years later poetry could again be used to obscure those realities through both elision and misrepresentation. The lines of the Easter leaders were used liberally to authorise all manner of political points; however, rebels were not the only soldier poets of the period. In Ireland the body of work by those who fought in the First World War is limited by both its quantity and quality. Nevertheless poetry provided a lingua franca through which the traditions of soldier with equal soldier might speak. However, the different historical trajectories on the island made such equality extremely difficult. The moves in the Republic to acknowledge those who fought in the First World War were significant, if limited. The weakness in these attempts was not in the failure to understand the point of the war: Irish nationalists were not alone in seeing it as an unfathomable waste of human life. Rather it was in the denial that there were some who fought not for Belgium or the freedom of Ireland but for the British Empire.

History in Museums and Galleries

An effective national narrative conforms to the three 'C's' of rhetorical discourse by being credible, convincing and compelling.[57] And so it is with the narrative of the nation. However, credibility depends upon concealing the narrative element (the selection, plotting and characterisation) and presenting it as straightforward historical fact. This is more easily achieved in spaces in which authority has already been established: buildings, institutions, academic books or news programmes. The official commemoration of the Easter Rising contained four expositions of Irish history expressed in the authoritative spaces of the museum, the gallery and the documentary film: Cuimhneachán 1916 at the National Gallery, a historical exhibition at the National Museum, a documentary film, *An Tine Bheo*, and a commemorative film, *The Irish Rising*.

Museums are used to contain art in the sense of both housing the artefact and constraining the message. Paintings and exhibits are situated within narratives plotted by textual explanation and spatial organisation. The layout and sequence of museums and galleries are intentional and never objective. Nevertheless, until the late 1960s and 1970s, as Neil Harris has argued, museums were treated 'not as places where knowledge was disputed or contested, but as sanctuaries where it was secure'.[58] This is hardly surprising given their function as the archival resource of national and imperial epistemologies. Thomas Richards has pointed out that the administrative core of the British Empire was built around knowledge, producing institutions like the British Museum.[59] The empire, having been extended beyond what was physically practical, left British civil servants to organise it into manageable pieces. They became the acquirers not of land but of information, which was collated and classified so that, as Richards suggests, 'They pared the Empire down to file-cabinet size.'[60] The British collected vast quantities of information from across the globe: 'They surveyed and they mapped. They took censuses, produced statistics. They made vast lists of birds.'[61] Museums housed and displayed this imperial knowledge and placed order on the world therein contained, arranging it into nations, groups, types and periods. The 'scientific' basis for the arrangement of these facts and artefacts meant that it was seen not only to be above dispute but also to be above politics.

National museums also organise information in such a way that it underpins the existence of the nation. The National Museum in Dublin[62] had been an extension of Victorian acquisitiveness and the Republic of Ireland was not alone among post-independent states in perpetuating a version of what Benedict Anderson calls 'political museumizing'.[63] This was clearly evident in two exhibitions held at the National Gallery and the National Museum in April 1966. The catalogue of the National Gallery exhibition *Cuimhneachán 1916: Commemorative Exhibition of the Irish Rebellion 1916* explained in its prelude:

> According to historians, the Irish race has the oldest traditions of any European people. These are epitomised in the pre-christian and early christian objects in the National Museum. In the painting of the marriage of Eva and Strongbow [the opening painting in the exhibition], Daniel Maclise includes a number of these precious celtic objects as possessions of the defeated Irish. The picture therefore serves to symbolise the end of the era of a free Celtic people and the beginning of the series of invasions and persecutions which held this race captive until nearly fifty years ago.[64]

In being reproduced, solid objects became shifting symbols both of the continuity of the Celtic tradition and the assault on that tradition. The exhibition had been arranged, the catalogue explained, 'to enable the character and force of the indomitable body of men and women who died or lived for Ireland in 1916 to be seen through the eyes of the artist'.[65] It did not attempt to record aspects of Irish society 'other than those battles which took place in the slow 300 years of resurgence before 1916 and which were clear armed manifestations of Ireland's nationality'.[66] Through the sequence of paintings in the exhibition Ireland's nationality was both legitimised and naturalised, as was the tradition of physical force.

At the opening of the historical exhibition at the National Museum, Patrick Hillery, minister for industry and commerce, said:

> The Greeks were wont to erect a trophy at the spot where the tide of battle had turned in their favour. Our own ancestors erected a cairn where a great man was buried; and to it the passers-by contributed each a stone. This day we in our turn are putting a stone in the cairn of those great men of our people who sacrificed themselves in that 'Easter watch and resurrection' of fifty years ago which, in almost the last words of Pearse, 'redeemed Dublin from many shames'.[67]

Hillery subtly linked Irish antiquity with that of Greek civilisation. The imagery of placing a stone in the cairn added weight to the act of commemoration and, in its simplicity, made it seem both natural and innocent. Consciously or subconsciously, the imagery also loosened the imperial connection by turning the site from a museum, set up under British jurisdiction, into a Celtic cairn. Retrieval from British connections was, of course, generally fanciful in this context; the site was not being reconstituted in a similar way to that of Kilmainham Gaol. The museum in Kilmainham had upturned the authority of the jail whereas the National Museum utilised the authority established in the site under the British administration and applied it to underwriting the authority of the Irish state. Encased in the exhibition were what Hillery described as 'the personal relics of the men and women who had become part of Irish history: the casual ordinary things they wore and used in their daily life'.[68] These 'casual ordinary things' were given significance because of to whom they had once belonged and these individuals were in turn significant because of their place in the narrative of Irish history laid out in the museum, from the foundation of the Gaelic League in 1893 until 1921 (the cut-off point was not explained, only articulated as a date).[69]

Pearse was represented by his barrister's wig and gown; his brother Willie by a jacket and vest of a Gaelic costume; Tom Clarke by a flag of the United States taken from his house and a certificate of United States citizenship and Thomas Ashe by handcuffs he had worn.[70]

Glass cases within the exhibition divided the history of the period into discrete sections and, more importantly, ascribed individuals to their proper place. The death mask of Arthur Griffith was placed with a newspaper and pamphlets belonging to Sinn Féin and the greatcoat and cap of Michael Collins were placed in their own case within the sequence of the Anglo-Irish war. Collins's death mask was contained within a case entitled 'Dáil Éireann' alongside the death mask of Cathal Brugha.[71] Individuals were suspended in time, safely contained within the history of the struggle for independence. The incongruity of having such vivid references to their deaths – Collins and Brugha had died violently while fighting on different sides during the Civil War – raised and resolved the division that followed the Treaty. Both men were placed securely within a historical sequence which led ultimately (and in this case implicitly) to the 26-county state. The only possible cut-off date for any historical exhibition is the present. Therefore Collins and Brugha could be framed in such a way that they shared in the victory of the modern-day Republic of Ireland.

An Tine Bheo

The past cannot be reproduced. How it is represented depends upon the organisation of time within specific spaces. The documentary film – like the museum and the gallery – requires that the viewer believes in the authenticity of the images presented. It addresses the world in which we live, rather than the world imagined by the film maker. This is what differentiates documentary from the genres of fiction.[72] The non-fictional status suggests a degree of objectivity, reliability and credibility.[73] Archival footage provides proxy relics of the past and underlines the authenticity of the documentary form. The editorial process also differs from that of fiction and, as Bill Nichols has argued, often displays

> a wider array of disparate shots and scenes than fiction, an array yoked together less by a narrative organised around a central character than by a rhetoric organised around a controlling logic or argument. Characters, or social actors, may come and go, offering information, giving testimony, providing evidence. Places and things may appear and disappear as they are brought forward in support of

the film's point of view or perspective. A logic of implication bridges these leaps from one person or place to another.[74]

Nichols describes this type of editing as *evidentiary* and differentiates it from the continuity editing of cinema.[75] This process can be seen to differing degrees in the two documentaries commissioned for the commemoration of the Easter Rising. Images are juxtaposed to demonstrate the link between 1916 and 1966. The underlying logic is that modern-day Ireland represents the ultimate victory of the Rising. The ideals of the leaders of 1916 and the economic success of 1960s Ireland are mutually vindicating.

An Tine Bheo ('The Living Flame'), a film by Gael Linn, was commissioned by the government's commemoration committee. In their proposal for the project Gael Linn explained that their film would not only commemorate the Rising, 'it would also relate that event to the modern lives of the audience who are its heirs'. The proposal outlined the theme of the film:

> A people is not a mere collection of individuals, but an entity with a common past. In this past there are certain soaring peaks of national achievement, yet, in the bustle of everyday life it is natural that such distant events should but hover in the dim background. At an anniversary, however, they leap into prominence and are recognised as a living reality. The Easter Rising is for us such an event, and it is the constant reality of 1916 running through our lives today that we wish to express. This is a theme to enrich the audience with an insight into themselves and a glimpse of their significance in the perspective of their history.[76]

The commission for the film was agreed in principle by a meeting of the commemoration committee on 30 April 1965 and a small sub-committee was formed to liaise with Gael Linn. It included Phillis Uí Cheallaigh, Máire Bhreathnach, Frank Coffey and Frank Thornton.[77] A script outline was agreed and further development was conducted in accordance with this and in consultation with the sponsor.[78] Gael Linn had urged a speedy decision on the commission, arguing that 'it will be only by great effort that a film of quality can be completed by next Easter',[79] and External Affairs warned the commemoration committee that, 'In view of this Department's experience with Gael-Linn in the matter of film-making, you will, I think, need to keep after them to ensure that there is no delay.'[80] Within a year of its commission the film was ready for its première, hosted by Frank Aiken, at the Savoy Cinema in Dublin on 10 April 1966, for a budget of £1,459 10s 7d.[81]

An Tine Bheo was directed by Louis Marcus, with Robert Monks as the chief cameraman and a script by Brendan Ó hEithir and Eoin Ó Suilleabháin. Throughout the 45-minute film, which was shot in 35 mm and in colour, images of contemporary Ireland are merged with reminiscences of veterans and memorials to the dead. The narration is read in Irish and the words of veterans and nationalist leaders are read in English. The film opens at Arbour Hill, the burial ground of fifteen of the sixteen men executed for their part in the Easter Rising. The words of six veterans reflect the confluence of time and history:

Veteran 1: I remember Easter Week as vividly as [if] it only happened last year.

Veteran 2: I can visualise all the positions again as if I was in them tonight.

Veteran 3: I feel it's a part of my life, and a lasting memory.

Veteran 4: Oh, it's unforgettable – at times I think it's only a few years ago.

Veteran 5: I lived through the experience many times during the past fifty years.

Veteran 6: It's indelibly impressed on my memory – every detail of it.[82]

The film moves to images of Dublin Castle which, one veteran explains, was regarded as the centre of British authority in Ireland; after which voiceovers and commentary are used to plot the history of resistance to that authority from the rebellion in 1798 until that of Easter 1916. The sense of Irish history as a repetitive, commemorative sequence of uprisings indicates the way in which time and ideological difference were collapsed in the nationalist imagination so that 1798, 1916 and 1966 were inextricably knotted. The position of the United Irishmen was also significant in the longer rope of rebellions as the first articulation of republican thought in Ireland. Throughout the fiftieth-anniversary commemoration of the Easter Rising 1798 was used as the starting date in pageants and programme narratives throughout the country and it often appeared as the beginning of time. It was not just a nationalist trajectory that was being acknowledged in this historical ordering. It was also a celebration of the modern.

Gael Linn was alert to the potential of cinema to bring different elements together 'so that new meaning emerges from the contrast; picture reacts upon picture, and the visuals as a whole react with the sound-track to give the subject fresh significance'.[83] Bernadette Truden wrote in the *Boston Globe* that *An Tine Bheo* 'contrasts the harsh events of fifty years ago and the placid exterior of life today. This is the main theme, the way in which the present enshrines the past and the ghost-like presence of history lives on as a background to everyday life.'[84]

The landscape of 1960s Ireland emerged as the subject of most significance. Over images of St Stephen's Green, the commentary explains: 'Today's sunshine and serenity is a far cry from the violence of that week, 50 years ago. A free generation strolls through the Green which was a battlefield.'[85] A long cinematic salute to Liberty Hall is accompanied by 'A Nation Once Again' on the soundtrack. There is no continuity of image or action throughout the film and the commentary segues from Pearse to the GAA to asking whether socialism had been the pertinent question. However, for those familiar with the story, the sense of seamlessness and continuity in Irish history is clearly in evidence. A photograph of the capture of Éamon de Valera in 1916 melts into footage of him in Áras an Uachtaráin and is explained with the commentary:

> The irony of history. A prisoner once sentenced to death becomes President. Among the bills he signs is one which removes the death penalty. His residence is where visiting Kings used to stay. The wheel has turned full circle, but it's more than symbolic. Freedom was never merely a case of a change of flags over the Castle.[86]

What freedom is, or whether indeed socialism had been the pertinent question, are issues raised and never answered by *An Tine Bheo*. References to the 1913 Lockout, James Larkin and James Connolly are immediately assumed into the broader nationalist story, with the implication that the struggle for workers' rights and the struggle for freedom are things past. Reference to blood on Dublin streets during the Lockout is used as a way of introducing the Irish Citizen Army and its contribution to the armed tradition. The behemoth of nationalism had swallowed the labour movement in 1916 and, fifty years later, it was being paraded once more to quell disputes in industrial relations. History has many ironies and not all were being alluded to in *An Tine Bheo*. Lemass himself described the Easter Rising as having 'released forces which had been moving deep but almost unsuspected in the Irish soul'. These forces, he argued, 'had been disturbed by the labour struggles of 1913, by the Ulster Volunteer movement and by the impact of the world war'.[87] In this version of history, the Lockout was a misguided disruption. In *An Tine Bheo* labour disputes were being given a more assured recognition in the past while being rendered invisible in the present.

The opening voice of the film is that of the narrator: 'They rose up at Easter, a small group of armed men who had a dream.' Veterans of the Rising, who bore witness to the event as the film unfolded, were framed as those who 'connect one generation to the next'. These men offered visible evidence of the 'living reality of the Easter Rising' and also, by their presence, sanctioned the idea that freedom had been gained. Later in *An Tine Bheo*, the narrator asserts that 'every generation is tied to the previous one. However not every generation changes the course of history.'[88] The cautionary note is sounded: the task of the present generation is to honour and remember, not to revolutionise.

The film was not received with great approval by the commemoration committee. A letter from External Affairs to all missions stated, 'Whilst a definitive appraisal cannot, of course, be made until the completed film has been seen, it appears that "An Tine Bheo" (which some members of the Committee thought was unimaginative and somewhat too long drawn out) will not be of great interest to other than Irish audiences.' This, coupled with a reduction in the provision for the purchase of films by External Affairs, meant that there was no plan to order copies of the film for the use of diplomatic centres abroad.[89] Despite such a discouraging pitch, *An Tine Bheo* was requested by agencies serving large Irish populations such as London and San Francisco and the film was shown non-commercially to some groups abroad.[90]

At its première in Dublin *An Tine Bheo* was shown alongside Gael Linn's ground-breaking film of 1959, *Mise Éire*, and could barely survive the comparison. Though overlong, *An Tine Bheo* is not an uninteresting film. It is, however, a hybrid creature which attempts to salute the achievements of 1960s Ireland with a format that was technologically traditional for this time. Piaras Mac Lochlainn, the secretary of the commemoration committee, had written to Gael Linn asking for their co-operation in ensuring that the film receive a wide distribution in Ireland. The correspondence was written in English, 'as you [Gael Linn] may wish to show it to people in the cinema trade who are not fully fluent in Irish'.[91] *An Tine Bheo* was shown in commercial cinemas in Ireland but shared its place in the programmes with, among others, *Reptilicus* ('What was this beast born fifty million years out of time?') at the Carlton; *The Flight of the Phoenix* ('One of the most startling twists of fate you have ever experienced in a motion picture!') at the Capitol; *Blindfold* ('Living dangerously . . . and loving every minute of it!') at the Savoy and, at the Fine Arts, Tony Richardson's *The Loneliness of the Long Distance Runner*. In its own way *An Tine Bheo* was a beast born a few years out of time and had neither the dramatic excitement to be a commercial success nor the artistic merit to be taken up by art house cinemas internationally.

The Irish Rising

George Morrison (who had directed *Mise Éire*) fared no better than Louis Marcus in his commemorative film *The Irish Rising*, which had been commissioned by the Department of External Affairs in November 1965. There had been little enthusiasm among civil servants on the commemoration committee regarding the making of the film, as expenditure for the jubilee was already higher than expected and there was a feeling that Telefís Éireann's output would suffice for transmission on foreign television stations.[92] However, Frank Aiken, as minister for external affairs, had taken a particular interest in the project in anticipation of widespread international attention for the fiftieth anniversary of the Rising. It was explained to Piaras Mac Lochlainn that 'there is always the danger that if this country does not provide material, foreign stations will be tempted to use British or other material which would not present the Rising in a favourable light'.[93] It was further argued that the telecasting of a suitable film would 'not only help to correct erroneous views of the Irish struggle for independence but by including some material on the Dublin of today, will also assist in disseminating abroad a more accurate picture of modern Ireland'.[94] The commission was for a 16 mm film, 'two-thirds composed of actuality material of the Rising, the remaining one-third to be devoted to the Dublin of today'.[95] To this end it was suggested to Morrison that he include shots of contemporary Ireland, including the ESB (electricity) station at Ringsend, Telefís Éireann headquarters in Donnybrook, the ESB transformer and the Unidare factory in Finglas.[96]

Despite the hope that the film would provide a showcase for the technological accomplishments of Ireland in the 1960s, budgetary constraints meant that *The Irish Rising* would be a modest undertaking. Costs were pared from the outset by the decision that the film would be confined to ten minutes (although Morrison's commission was eventually for a fifteen-minute film).[97] As the film (unlike *An Tine Bheo*) was intended for television distribution, it was decided that 'the use of colour (which would be a good deal more costly than a black and white film) should be excluded. Colour television is now becoming increasingly popular in the United States but at present is available only in a minority of homes.' The film, which reproduced much of the footage Morrison had used in *Mise Éire* and reused some of Seán Ó Riada's music, was accompanied by a script that could be read by 'a commentator with a local accent' or translated in non-English-speaking countries.[98] The eventual cost of *The Irish Rising* was £2,700.[99]

The introductory note to Morrison's film described the Easter Rising as 'the end of one phase of Irish history and the beginning of another' and the body of the work rehearsed a standard narrative of the history of the event. The final section of the film, however, provides images of modern Dublin as requested, beginning with shots from along the Liffey, including, as the script indicates, 'Aston Quay with heavy traffic' and 'Liffey looking down stream with modern buildings'. The camera also lingers long over the electricity generating station in Ringsend, showing the switchboard and operating controls, before moving to the trans-former station in Finglas. A shot of the Telefís Éireann building is followed by a sequence showing the filming of *Insurrection*, the much more successful television portrayal of the Rising. The concluding shots include those of schoolchildren and the artist Patrick Scott at work. Over these images, which last just over one and a half minutes, the sup-plied commentary reads:

> Dublin today.
> The seat of the independent Government of Ireland, it is also the commercial and cultural capital of the country . . .
> Power for the city –
> – for the country and for entertainment.
> Irish television prepares a dramatisation of the 1916 Rising to bring it alive –
> – for the new generation . . .
> Independence has meant social and economic progress;
> and inspiration for the artist.
> Pearse, a poet, a teacher, as well as a revolutionary, foresaw the future Ireland:
> 'What if the dream come true? And if millions unborn shall dwell in the house that I shaped in my heart, the noble house of my thought?'[100]

Once *The Irish Rising* had been made, External Affairs was anxious that it be shown as widely as possible and copies were sent to eighty television networks and independent stations in North America, Western Europe and Australia. It was shown in the United States (by CBS), Canada (in Regina and Ottawa), Luxembourg, Portugal, Switzerland, Italy and New Zealand, but set no pulses racing. The most positive comment came from the consulate in San Francisco, which reported that reaction had been favourable and that those in charge of the programme at the television studio had been very pleased with it.[101] The embassy in Brussels also found it served a useful purpose, as the French-language network in

Belgium had used excerpts from *The Irish Rising* in a longer serialised history programme, *The War 1914–1918*. This included a contribution from Professor Gorielli of the University of Brussels, which offered a defence of Casement's actions in the Congo. Gorielli discussed the Easter Rising in general and Casement in particular and 'briefly examined the meaning of loyalty and showed how the men of 1916 had been right in giving their first loyalty to Ireland'. The correspondence concluded, 'The footage you supplied could not in fact have been put to better use.'[102] German and French television networks in Switzerland also made use of edited versions of the film. Both, however chose to omit the scenes of modern Dublin.[103]

Elsewhere, *The Irish Rising* was either shelved or rejected. In Germany, plans to add a German soundtrack for broadcasting were abandoned as it was decided the film would not be of general interest to the audience, and the embassy in The Hague reported that the Catholic Television Service KRO had decided against showing the film as, 'having seen it, they consider it lacks action'. Further enquiries by the embassy 'endeavouring to ascertain what film they [KRO] had seen and which they considered lacking in action (they actually said "dull and lacking in action")' suggested that perhaps they were confusing it with the Gael Linn film.[104] Most critical was the response from the embassy in Lisbon, which reported that the day after it was shown a TV critic had judged *The Irish Rising* 'the poorest item on the programme for that evening'. The chargé d'affaires had seen a preview of the film the morning before and had been filled with misgivings about the desirability of having it shown in public at all. In view of official approval he had not ventured to suppress it but felt that 'showing it not only could add nothing to our national prestige, but would almost certainly detract therefrom'. The report concluded:

> I have no pretensions to be a cinema critic but the whole show appeared to me – and to such of my friends who have seen it – to be ill conceived, technically third rate, incoherent and disjointed and altogether amateurish. I think it is a thousand pities that it was ever shown abroad as it just made us look silly and naïve. Compared with the efforts in other countries in the same field our effort was humiliating.[105]

An Tine Bheo and *The Irish Rising* were not intended as fictional films and yet they had, to some extent, been engaged in depicting the fantasy of 'modern' Ireland. Reality, however, had overwhelmed the fantasy and the lack of technological sophistication in both films revealed 1960s

Ireland as falling somewhere short of its ambition and expectation. In commissioning these films, the government had shown itself to be trying too hard to emphasise the economic progress made in Ireland since independence and also, of course, it had not tried hard enough. The commissions had elicited work from some of the most talented practitioners in Ireland, yet the limits of time, budget and rubric resulted in films that did not stand the test of screening, never mind the test of time.

The ordering of information in galleries and documentaries indicated certain fissures in representations of the present in 1960s Ireland. In the exhibitions in the National Museum and the National Gallery the arrangement of artefacts referred to the past and the present was embodied in the viewer. The sequence of information conveyed the idea of the resilience, struggle and authenticity of the Irish nation for which an independent state was the natural ending. The success and integrity of the state were implicit, not explicitly articulated. The documentary films commissioned for the commemoration attempted to say something specific about the virtues of 1960s Ireland and this was much more problematic. The key to an authoritative narrative structure is that it is unobtrusive, so that what is contained within seems to be self-evident. In *An Tine Bheo* and *The Irish Rising* there existed a contradiction between what was being suggested and what was being shown. References to the technological progress of modern Ireland were compromised by the poor technological quality of the films. Creating an ordered representation of the past did not necessarily translate into a convincing representation of the present.

Conclusion

Ireland on the Go, a tourism promotional film made in 1966, opened with the observation that Ireland was a 'country well on its way into the future but with one foot in the past she cherishes so much'.[106] How this past should be cherished was a central question being asked of artists and practitioners during the fiftieth anniversary of the Easter Rising. The branding of Ireland to tourists involved a retention of the idea that Ireland was a poetic and mystical place, and the Easter Rising could be provided as evidence of the power of Ireland's poets and dreamers to dislodge an empire. Given this common characterisation of the Rising, it was fitting that the commemoration committee would draw attention to artistic expressions during the jubilee in 1966.

Art appeared to offer vehicles through which the mythic nature of the Rising could be expressed and made meaningful. The elasticity of artistic expression also appeared to provide space in which the subplots and subtexts of Irish history could be accommodated within the over-arching and overwhelming narrative of Irish nationhood. The divisions caused by the Lockout, the First World War, the Treaty and partition had not ceased to exist in Irish society in the 1960s. Poetry, paintings and films could be used to address these divisions. However, the way in which art was used and organised precluded any understanding that did not conform to the nationalist ideological position of the Republic of Ireland. Nevertheless, art cannot be so easily conscripted into a single vision and, during the jubilee, it continued to offer pockets of ambiguity and ambivalence that tilted at the official message.

CHAPTER SEVEN

'What to Do with their Lovely Past?'
Promoting the Commemoration
Abroad

'They dream their lives away casually here,' Jimmy Breslin wrote of Ireland in the *New York Herald Tribune* in 1966, 'but at the same time the dreaming is what makes them. Dreaming of sex comes out far better than sex.' The wise man might riddle what dream had come true fifty years after the Easter Rising. Breslin laced his coverage of the commemoration with stories of poverty, pubs, poetry and a propensity to believe in leprechauns in a way that the government in Dublin found distasteful and irreverent. But Breslin's view of Ireland was not intended as a critical onslaught. He was more concerned with the new enemy in Ireland: the worship of the car. 'If there is anything that can kill the romance and the lilt of a place it is a good auto salesman with a full showroom,' he wrote. He deplored the mechanical culture of the United States in which their idea of a good poet was Robert Lowell, a man for whom it should be a felony to give a sheet of paper.[1]

Breslin's coverage highlighted what Seán O'Faoláin described as the dominating problem for all Irish politicians: what to do with their lovely past. 'For while everybody in Ireland wanted efficiency and modernisation', O'Faoláin wrote, 'everybody also wanted to preserve the old folk-ways and the old folk-values that had been our laws of life for centuries.'[2] The end of economic protectionism meant that Ireland in the 1960s had to convince those outside that it was modern but different. Future economic development relied on a presentation of the Republic as happy in the embrace of modern technology while maintaining the romance and lilt that attracted tourists to the place. 'Money talks,' said one Irish commentator. 'It is the one language that we have most effectually revived.'[3] The jubilee of the Rising provided an opportunity for politicians to project the image of Irishness at home and abroad as that which could carry its lovely past into a prosperous future.

One effective response from nations burdened by their pasts is to commemorate themselves into a state of forgetfulness. The ritual replaces memory and facilitates selectivity. Therefore the commemoration in 1966 offered an effective vehicle through which to unveil a reinvented Ireland. It both signalled Ireland's uniqueness and, through the pomp and pageantry, provided the props for a well-designed set to present to the broader world. The jubilee attempted to assert a confident national narrative in a new Ireland that was simultaneously honouring the old.

Images and Reflections

Coverage of the visit of President John F. Kennedy three years earlier had provided a technological and emotional rehearsal for the golden jubilee of the Rising. The recent arrival of a national television broadcaster in Ireland meant that both events would be experienced differently at home and witnessed more widely abroad. Basil Payne had described watching, 'or rather participating in' Kennedy's speech on television as a unique experience for any Irishman. He wrote in the *Capuchin Annual* of 1964, 'Here was a moment "in and out of time", a moment of living history when one was able to assess and cherish one's own position in time and tradition; a moment when one could look outwards, inwards and upwards simultaneously.' Kennedy reflected the Irish back to themselves in confident and positive terms. W.R. Dale, writing in the *New Statesman*, noted that an 'eminent and cosmopolitan' Irishman had said the president's visit had meant, 'Simply this. I'm an Irishman and a Catholic, and from now on I feel I am not a second-class citizen.'[4] The Republic of Ireland appeared no longer to examine its reflection in the crack'd mirror; however, there was always the danger of stepping through another looking glass into a wonderland of lazy imagery. Payne reviewed some of the coverage of the president's visit in the foreign press:

> 'Begorra! It's Himself,' said the headlines in the *Wall Street Journal*, content to churn out a jaded cliché, calculated to coincide with the popular misconception of rustic Ireland still so prevalent in America. And *Newsweek*'s correspondent, writing presumably through pre-selected green-tinted spectacles, reported that 'Dublin festooned itself with shamrocks, papier-mache green derbies, souvenir shille-laghs and other exotic paraphernalia associated with Irishmen in New York and Boston (but never, well seldom, in Ireland).'

Payne's sense of Kennedy's visit as a moment of multi-dimensional self-reflection was reflected back as 'rustic' farce. Britain provided the more positive image:

> The 'quality' British newspapers generally served us fairly and well. Patrick O'Donovan [an Australian of Irish descent], in the *Observer*, described Mr. Kennedy's visit as 'a civilised and beautiful gesture', adding with a mixture of astringent good sense and genuine admiration that 'in Irish history, this was the first wholly satisfactory act of nationhood; all the others, even to the gaining of independence, have been compromises and less than the best that was possible. This, with a Catholic President from the Irish diaspora singing her praises and taking time off from the brutalities of power, was the real thing . . . Ireland never showed herself to better advantage, never demonstrated more clearly her individuality and maturity, and there was not a trace of shamrockery in sight.'[5]

The 1916 jubilee also offered the possibility of looking outwards, inwards and upwards simultaneously; a moment in time and tradition when history could be re-lived as well as lived. O'Donovan (a third-generation emigrant) understood the desire in Ireland for that satisfactory act of nationhood which would be viewed seriously from the outside. Kennedy's visit underlined the importance of the Irish nation abroad. The jubilee tested the Republic's ability to generate a moment of celebration from within.[6] Yet self-belief was tentative in Ireland. The response to President Kennedy exposed a lack of confidence rather than confidence itself. Payne's *Capuchin Annual* article referenced the Bord Fáilte annual report of 1963, which had discussed the need to replace Ireland's still rather hazy image abroad and suggested, 'There also seems to be a case for projecting a positive image inwards, to ourselves.'[7]

The visit of Prince Rainier and Princess Grace of Monaco in 1961 had also given a fillip to favourable publicity for Ireland, especially in Europe and the United States.[8] Endorsement from famous Irish-Americans complemented the efforts of Bord Fáilte, which had undergone strengthening and reorganisation in 1956 and had been part of the process of offsetting the decline in income from tourism in the years after 1949.[9] In commenting on its wide-ranging efforts to improve the image of Ireland abroad, Bord Fáilte noted that 'some countries have a conflict between the national picture presented for political and economic reasons, and that intended to attract tourists'. It continued:

> It must be stressed that a satisfactory tourism picture need not necessarily conflict with that desired by a modern, progressive State

anxious to develop its industrial activities. Broadly speaking, we present Ireland as a tranquil, unspoiled country with a richness of historical treasures, and a friendly intelligent people; but to succeed in attracting visitors we must also convey a picture of a good standard of living, reflected in shops and services, and a modern infrastructure of well run hotels, efficient transport and good roads.[10]

In 1966 the tourist industry was worth an estimated £78 million to the Irish economy so image was integral to economic reality.[11] In March 1965 correspondence to all diplomatic missions from the Department of External Affairs reported that the taoiseach placed particular stress on the desirability of publicising the commemoration of the Rising abroad and of encouraging persons of Irish descent to visit Ireland during the celebrations.[12] There was also a link between the vision projected outwards and the mirror in which the Irish saw themselves. Éamon de Valera's St Patrick's Day broadcasts had become an important part of this dual process and have been described as a vehicle through which to 'project mental images of Ireland for public consumption [abroad] . . . a metaphorical shop window'.[13] The most famous of these broadcasts, the 'dream speech' of 1943, had been aired only in Ireland because of the Second World War and demonstrated that an idealised form of Irishness spoke loudly to the audience at home as well as abroad.[14]

St Patrick's Day had long been an important part of the international expression of Irish culture. By the 1950s its focus in Dublin had become an industrial pageant. However, abroad – particularly in the United States – the Irish government could not control the way in which the national day was celebrated. The New York parade had been televised live since 1949 and in 1965 Aer Lingus sponsored the broadcast and screened advertisements promoting Ireland as a tourist destination.[15] However, the increased commercialisation, the changing socio-economic circumstances of the Irish diaspora and the broadening appeal of St Patrick's Day to the non-Irish meant that the event became associated with a simplistic, commodified Irishness that seemed increasingly detached from Ireland itself. An *Irish Times* editorial in 1963 noted that 'the shenanigans attending St Patrick's Day abroad have become more and more embarrassing to the mother country'. The New York parade in particular, the newspaper argued, could be described at best as expressing 'the sentimentality and condescension usually saved for poor relations or chronic drunks'.[16]

The effort to jettison the burden of the caricatured 'stage Irishman', who was poor, chronically drunk and bereft of intellectual sophistication, would not be met with immediate rewards. This was in part because the Irish themselves had conspired in the marketing of their culture with gauche abbreviations such as the leprechaun and the shillelagh and the broader pool of alternative cultural references was rather shallow. The fiftieth anniversary of the Easter Rising was one in a longer list of events which, it was hoped, would help to promote a more positive image of Ireland abroad. The An Tóstal festival, which first took place in 1953, had been conceived in an effort to attract those of Irish descent back to Ireland. The three-week event began at Easter and incorporated commemorations of the Rising in its programme. The idea of the festival had been generated by Pan American Airlines, which advised the government that the festival would serve the dual purpose of 'drawing the Irish world more closely together with the mother country, and secondly, of developing visitor traffic to Ireland among these people who are most receptive to such an appeal'.[17] The festival has been described as a combination of 'Catholicism, nationalism, nostalgia, and sporting events in a representative cocktail of Irish culture', as 'politics lurked in the wings'.[18] However, the ideas spawned during the conception of this festival created an influential template for marketing Ireland to tourists in the subsequent decades in a bid to encourage those of Irish descent to open their wallets.[19] It proved difficult to find the imaginative shift that would create a challenge to well-established commodities and social expressions.

The anticipated homecoming of the diaspora did not materialise for the fiftieth anniversary of the Easter Rising any more than it had for An Tóstal. The Irish ambassador in Canberra reported that there was 'not much prospect of attracting people from Australia to go to Ireland for April'.[20] The Irish Society in Ottawa had organised its charter flight, which catered for 150 people, to coincide with the commemoration, though the organiser reported that the group would 'not include any particularly important or notable personalities'.[21] In England the trend was to hold local events to mark the 1916 jubilee rather than to travel to Ireland.[22] Irish societies in the United States did charter flights, including a Columbus Tour group, 'The Irish Freedom Trail', led by Brendan Malin of the *Boston Globe*. Four flights left New York: organised by the National Graves Association in association with the Irish Institute, which had 137 passengers; the Casement-Monteith Memorial Group with 30 passengers; the National Board, Ancient Order of Hibernians, including 137 passengers; and the Jersey City Group, which was led by Thomas J. Whelan, the mayor of Jersey City, and included 177 passengers.[23] In fact the Bord Fáilte report for the year ending

March 1967 noted that it was the first year in a decade in which tourist revenue had not increased.[24]

Nevertheless promotion of the commemoration did prompt those outside the country to cast an eye over Ireland, its history and current state. Excluding Britain, newspapers that sent dedicated news reporters to Ireland included ten from the United States, two from Canada, two from France and two from Germany.[25] The majority of international print media, however, relied on reports from the Associated Press. Despite suggestions in September 1965 that a press office 'should be established, no immediate action was taken and the infrastructure was poor. Less than a month before the commemoration a memorandum from Frank Coffey in External Affairs noted that, following intervention from the tánaiste, the taoiseach had directed that a press office should be set up in central Dublin. However, he warned that on the question of telephones the Post Office had advised that they 'could not guarantee early installation of the four lines we required owing to difficulty with the Union'.[26] Nevertheless, although the jubilee did not provide a financial boost through tourism, it operated as part of that longer-term strategy of propagating a particular version of Irish history and of the character of independent Ireland.

The Politics of Promoting the Rising

The central message to convey to an international audience during the fiftieth anniversary of the Easter Rising was that Ireland was a modern, forward-looking nation. This took a degree of management during an event which purported to be celebrating a moment from the past which represented an attack on Britain during the First World War. Moreover, within certain readings of history, the Easter Rising could be viewed as an act of rejection of the modernity associated with the British Empire and confirmation, in fact, of Ireland's backwardness. It was important, therefore, that the event be promoted as a positive act of independence rather than as a negative assault on Britain. It was also important that the Republic of the 1960s could be offered in evidence of the ultimate success of the Rising.

Early planning for the commemoration had had to confront the problematic nature of promoting the Rising abroad. An approach to President Johnson of the United States to contribute a message to the *Easter Commemoration Digest* for the 1916 jubilee year had prompted an informal intervention from Nathan Glazer of the State Department to Noel Dorr of the Irish embassy in Washington.[27] In conversation Glazer 'appeared to take it for granted that it would be out of the question for the White House to send a message – not because of the standing of the magazine but because of the event to be commemorated'.[28] The difficulty lay in the relationship between the United States and Britain, with Glazer noting that certain officials in the British embassy in Washington had on occasion displayed some lingering bitterness about the 1916 Rising, 'although it had occurred before they were born'. Glazer further attested that 'we have already been able to choke off several approaches made by the various Irish societies through Congressmen, asking the President to designate official U.S. representatives to attend the celebrations'. Dorr responded by depicting the commemoration 'from one viewpoint as marking a half century of achievement by an independent Ireland, rather than solely as a remembrance of an anti-British event' with parallels with the Fourth of July, which emphasised the positive, American – rather than the negative, anti-British – aspect of the occasion.[29]

The ambassador, William Fay, in forwarding the information to External Affairs, noted the 'Anglophile tendencies of the upper echelons of the State Department', but 'having regard to our good relations with England at present, and also with Northern Ireland, I do not feel that there is any justification for the State Department's attitude as thus revealed'. Furthermore Fay was of the view that, provided the giving of offence was carefully avoided, 'I cannot see why we should be expected not to celebrate in a worthy way such an important event in our history, merely as a gesture of friendship to our former enemy.'[30] Fay revisited his idea of setting up a National Commission of the Fine Arts as a permanent memorial to the men of Easter Week. Pointing out that the taoiseach had emphasised the aspect of reconciliation in the celebration, Fay wrote, 'There will always be Anglophiles, both at home and abroad, who will grumble about "re-opening old wounds". I can imagine nothing better calculated to still such criticism than that a commemoration of our insurrection should show, once again, that we give primacy to the spiritual.' Fay had opened his remarks by mentioning that, as a matter of protocol, invitations to the embassy's reception would be issued '"To commemorate the Fiftieth Anniversary of the Proclamation of Irish Independence". It would be inadvisable to refer to the Easter Rising, as this would not normally be known here as such.'[31] The Rising was framed in a way which would minimise any difficult connections. A violent and divisive event was being repackaged as one representing the beginning of modern Ireland. Nevertheless, the general tone in advice to diplomatic outposts was one of sensitivity regarding the politics of the commemoration without becoming too defensive. Correspondence to all missions in January 1966 suggested that, where possible, commemoration of the Rising should be combined with the traditional St Patrick's Day reception. This arrangement, it was argued, would have 'the double advantage of avoiding to a great extent special additional expenditure, for which no extra funds will be available, and it would help to meet the susceptibilities of persons who might hesitate to attend a function solely to commemorate the rebellion against Great Britain'. However, the advice continued:

> On this latter point . . . the Minister feels that Missions need not be too sensitive about any embarrassment which an invitation to attend a commemoration of the Rising might cause in official, or indeed other quarters. It is quite normal for countries which have very recently achieved their independence to mark the anniversary by a reception without giving offence to anybody.[32]

Beyond the diaspora, response to the commemoration was in general muted where it was not ambivalent. In Belgium the embassy felt that it had to work to counter 'the usual Belgian line on the Easter Rising, to the effect that it weakened the Allied War effort in Europe'. Its association with Roger Casement added further to the lack of support for the Rising in that country.[33] Throughout Britain, the commemoration gave rise to extensive coverage in the media which was often sympathetic to the events of Easter Week. However, officially there could be no clear association with the 1916 jubilee. Roy Hattersley MP, who had agreed to accompany members from the Sparkbrook Labour group to Ireland for the event, had been informed that the Foreign Office was 'anxious that no British Member of Parliament should be at the "celebrations" and [he] responded to the pressure'.[34] Diplomacy also attended the return from Britain of the flag of the Irish Republic which had hung over the GPO in April 1916. The choreography of the event reflected the concerns of the British ambassador as recorded by Hugh McCann in External Affairs:

> He informed me that Whitehall are naturally anxious to obtain some favourable publicity from the gesture, and he was asked whether he considered that he should make a formal presentation of the flag.
>
> The Ambassador informed me that he was anxious to avoid the type of criticism that arose when he walked behind the remains of Roger Casement on their return to Ireland. He made a passing reference to possible protests and resignations (presumably from the British Legion). For this reason he was inclined to recommend against a

formal handing-over ceremony with photographs. He wondered whether it would not be better for him to deliver the flag quietly to the National Museum here – the return to be subsequently announced in a Press statement.[35]

Initial concern over whether or not the correct flag had been nominated for return was overcome[36] and it was handed over privately to J.G. Molloy, the Irish ambassador in London. The taoiseach then received the flag on behalf of the Irish people and passed it to the custodianship of the National Museum.[37]

The Department of External Affairs noted that the number of messages of congratulation from foreign heads of state was few (United States, India, Germany, Spain, Monaco and Pakistan) and caused only one surprise – sincere wishes from the Soviet Union.[38] The government was only keen to receive recognition for the jubilee of the Rising provided the attention conformed to the image it was trying to convey.[39] The decision to confine the official commemoration to a domestic guest list with an audience supplied by the Irish at home and from abroad signalled a fear of both rejection and association. External Affairs advised the secretary of the commemoration committee in December 1965 of its concern that the attendance of Breton nationalist groups at the ceremonies would cause 'embarrassment with the French Government'. It was thus anxious that any participation by the Bretons 'should be discreet, orderly and unprovocative'. It had been decided that the general public, through voluntary organisations and public representatives, should be able to take part in the jubilee parade and there was a concern that this decision would cede control of the politics of the event:

> The Bretons, and indeed such Scottish and Welsh Nationalist groups as come to Dublin, may well wish to take part in the parade but we feel that we should now take a definite decision that participation in the parade is confined to Irish bodies and to representatives of Irish societies abroad. You will appreciate that Heads of Mission accredited to Dublin will probably be invited to the reviewing stand at the GPO, to Arbour Hill, the Garden of Remembrance and to the other places where commemoration will take place. It is imperative that we should avoid causing any embarrassment to the French or British representatives by allowing the Bretons, Scots and Welsh to avail themselves of these opportunities of making anti-French or anti-English propaganda.[40]

The Irish ambassador in Paris advised that Breton political activities were regarded as of little importance in France. He noted that frequent

Breton cultural displays were of a purely cultural kind 'even though they may well be infused with vague political longings'. He suggested raising the issue with the French Foreign Office to avoid any misunderstanding.[41] Equally, the Irish ambassador in Brussels advised that Flemish nationalist groups should not be accorded any recognition:

> The character and objectives of an essentially domestic political movement in Belgium are not, of course, a matter for the Irish government even if they claim to draw inspiration from Irish nationalism. On the other hand, it is equally not in our interests even to appear to give countenance in any way to such a movement, particularly one which arouses such controversy and emotion in this country. To do so would obviously leave us open to the charge of taking sides in a Belgian internal quarrel and could prove highly embarrassing for our relations with the Belgian government.[42]

The government's response to other nationalist groups exposed its own contradictory position. The Republic of Ireland would take credit for striking a decisive blow at the British Empire, but by the 1960s it had, like many small nations, a vested interest in the promotion of international law and in international stability. Having attained statehood through violence, the Republic of Ireland now wanted to uphold the power of sovereign states rather than the nations remaining within such states. This all sat uneasily, given its own constitutional claims on Northern Ireland.

Images of Irishness

Ireland had positioned itself, by the 1960s, as a good international citizen in the realm of foreign affairs but there continued to be a residual sense of insecurity regarding the image of Irishness abroad. Since the jubilee of the Easter Rising was seen as an opportunity to showcase the modernity of Ireland, it was inevitable that the commemoration would become a form of audit or stocktaking. From the outset, therefore, the meaning of the commemoration was expanded beyond a narrow concern with Easter Week and instead came to embrace the trinity of the Rising, independence and the fruits of that independence in modern Ireland. The three strands merged into an indivisible unity so that criticisms of any aspect of the commemoration were seen as a reflection on the whole enterprise.

The 1916 jubilee thus represented an opportunity to celebrate the legitimacy of the state and to assert the good character of its citizens.

The government saw in the commemoration the possibility of redrawing the image of Ireland, but the mere repetition of the word 'modern' would not in itself be enough to convince outsiders that Ireland really belonged to the modern world. Moreover, as a new aesthetic, this Ireland of the factories was much less attractive visually and also less specifically Irish. The difficulty for those attempting to forge a new image of Ireland lay in the fact that the country's reputed uniqueness in the world rested in a series of clichés which, whatever their latent poetry, could hardly be seen as progressive. Coverage of the commemoration exposed Ireland or Irishness to depictions of itself which, although easily recognisable by a foreign (particularly Anglophone) audience, imprisoned its image within a non-modern landscape and did nothing to excite confidence at home.

John Vachon, writing in *Look Magazine*, noted that Ireland was 'a somber, enigmatic land with sudden brightnesses of green and gold. It rains softly here.' The twentieth century, he remarked, was seeping in slowly: 'There are smokestacks, cocktail lounges, great jet-busy airports, glass brick, and even urban renewal. But it is easy to travel the country and never see any of them at all.'[43] In attempting to characterise Irish society for their readerships, journalists often resorted to stereotype. 'The Irish, a romantic, musical, quick tempered people, are better at stimulating sympathy than rewarding it,' chided Donald Stanley in the *San Francisco Examiner and News*. Stanley excelled at regurgitating stereotypes: 'That the Irish are indefatigable is a positive and proven quality of the race. (The Gaelic granny of one of my wife's friends, for example, was the principal at three wakes. At two of them she revived and popped up in the midst of the activities.)'[44] The *Vancouver Washington Columbian* was also given to summary judgments: 'Two strange things about the Irish: They have a way of acting prematurely, and they never seem to give up.'[45] The London *Daily Express* reported that in Easter Week 'salvation for the British came undeservedly, because this was an Irish rebellion and had been bungled'.[46] Elsewhere, G.K. Chesterton's observation about the Irish – that all their wars are merry and all their songs are sad – prefaced a description of the 'Emerald Isle' for Americans as 'awash with a fortnight of ceremonies dedicated to that merry and sad abortion, the Easter rebellion of 1916'.[47]

Sloan Wilson, writing in *Fact Magazine*, had gone to Ireland some years previously with the rooted belief that it was a land of emerald-green lawns where most girls looked like Maureen O'Hara and everyone was full of witty remarks and vast earthy laughter. As a divorcé, he had been greeted instead with disapproval by his fiancée's Protestant relatives. Wilson had become 'morbidly' fascinated by the Irish and their loss of population. A people who had spent centuries fighting British rule now 'committed national suicide by failing to reproduce themselves in their homeland and emigrating'.[48] The impossibility of divorce and contraception, Wilson argued, had resulted in the Irish de-sexualising themselves to the point that they had become in a real way sexless. In Ireland fighting was considered far less sinful than kissing, Wilson wrote, and drunkenness was thought to be preferable to physical love: 'I never saw lovers in Irish parks, but I saw alcoholics slumped on many a bench.'[49] The killing of sex had led to an unproductive nation with low output in both agriculture and industry. The phrase 'the Irish of it' was used to describe all acts of ignorance, clumsiness and shiftlessness. Wilson conceded a charm in the politeness and sense of community that continued in Ireland but had been lost in America. Yet, after spending only a few weeks in the country, he was overcome by boredom:

> Nothing ever changes in Ireland, not even the weather . . . The rich stay rich, the poor stay poor, and the engaged couples stay engaged, year in and year out. Streets under construction remain under construction, apparently forever. The miniscule menus in hotels never change . . . Nothing is seasoned and everything is overcooked. Even talking isn't much fun in Ireland . . . Serious talk about money, sex, religion, or politics is much too explosive there to be allowed in polite circles. One can't even talk about books because all the good ones have been banned.[50]

The editor of *Fact Magazine*, Warren Boroson, asked Lemass in a letter for a response to the 'picture of a nation that has castrated itself, using the Catholic church as a kind of weapon'. The taoiseach's office advised, 'Take no action on this nonsense.'[51]

The fiftieth anniversary of the Easter Rising posed many questions for Ireland and prompted the further question of how best to respond to critical coverage. The issue was more pressing regarding articles that had a wide readership or where members of the Irish diaspora looked for a reply. Responses were often determined by the degree of vulnerability felt by the Irish in the location of publication. Jimmy Breslin's articles in the *New York Herald Tribune*, which the American ambassador had regarded as 'would-be humorous' and of a quality best treated by silence, caused more upset when reproduced in Canada. Breslin described the veterans who had appeared on O'Connell Street as 'craggy and creased . . . they sat in dark overcoats, and they all wore drab hats old enough to have British bullet holes in them'.[52] He took up his position in the Raven Pub, where he was soon joined by an old soldier from the reviewing platform who ordered a whiskey. 'The barkeep pushed a half of Paddys at him,' Breslin recounted. '"Good *Healt*", the Captain said. "*Tank* you and God bless you," one of the mob now in the pub called out.' Outside, children came running through the smoke arising from soft coal and wood that hung in the air, and they importuned strangers for money:

> The kids on Sheriff St. and the blocks and alleys around it live in houses that have overflowing garbage cans inside the front doors and no baths inside the flats. Once a week everybody on the block goes to Tara St. public baths a couple of blocks away. Last year a movie with Richard Burton in it was filmed on Sheriff St. The set was of a public bath. When the kids looked out the windows and saw it, they streamed out of their filthy houses with towels over their arms and ran at the doors in the set and knocked it over.[53]

When the article appeared in the *Toronto Star*, it led to complaints to J.A. Belton, the Irish ambassador in Canada, from several Irish citizens. The embassy there decided not to make a formal complaint; instead, Belton planned to contact the editor in an effort to change his attitude towards Ireland. 'I realise this will not be easy,' the ambassador admitted, 'since the paper has long been known for militant "Orangeism" as well as sensationalism.'[54]

The Politics of Exile

Challenges to a positive image of Irishness oscillated between lazy stereotypes and acute observations by journalists. Moreover, the Irish abroad could not always be trusted to conform to the official political impulse to reinvent the revolutionary period as one shaped by a combination of dreaming and determination. A certain exasperation was expressed in less than diplomatic language in the correspondence from Irish consulates and embassies which underlined the gap between the economic and social backgrounds of these officials and the communities they were in place to serve. Irish culture had itself often survived through kitsch representations, religious rituals and the exuberant physicality of parades. The weaknesses of such representations were recognised by the Fianna Fáil executive, which adopted a resolution at the 1965 Ard Fheis of the party asking that the government improve the quality standards for souvenirs of Ireland, particularly in view of the upcoming jubilee.[55]

The most elaborate souvenir of the commemoration was the booklet *Cuimhneachán*, which detailed the events that had taken place in Ireland during the week of celebration.[56] Exhaustive attempts to encourage members of the Irish diaspora to buy a copy in order to recoup the costs tested the commitment of both Irish citizens abroad and embassy officials. In London an internal memo recorded that the booklet had been offered to the managers of over four hundred bookstalls in Catholic churches across Britain, resulting in requests for only twenty copies. The attaché Tom Feehan had been in touch with various Irish societies by letter, telephone and special visits to meetings, and 'after much pressure' distribution had been successful.[57] In 1967, however, the Cheltenham Irish Association reported that, since it had sold only five copies, it would raffle the remainder at social events, as 'people are more likely to buy a sixpenny draw ticket than spending fifteen shillings on a book.'[58]

The Irish embassy in Australia had to rely for distribution in New Zealand on a contractor who was viewed as a bit of a 'chancer' and had 'a habit of operating rather close to the margin of the law', because he was deemed one of the few people prepared to expend the required energy.[59] The individual in question was described as a single man in his thirties who lived in a caravan, had low living costs, and neither drank nor smoked. He claimed to be the Australasian agent for Waterford Crystal, Irish Linens, Irish Tweeds and the Irish Souvenir and Novelty lines. His claim was disputed by the listed companies, but it did seem that he was the New Zealand agent for the Irish Hospitals Sweepstake, for which he placed tickets in a network of eight hundred hairdressers' shops.[60]

The foot soldiers disseminating Irish culture and Irish goods reflected the depressed economic circumstances of many of the Irish abroad. There was the further problem of the politics of these groupings. Domestic Irish politics were being redirected towards a practical acceptance of the Northern Irish state. But wholesale rejection of partition was a significant part of Irish political identity overseas. As with the commemoration at home, there was a concern in official circles that memories of the Rising would heighten radical republican sentiments. Most commemorations abroad where there was a sizeable Irish community included mass, a parade, Gaelic games and some kind of cultural event, such as a concert or céilí. Banquets organised by specific Irish groups were particularly popular in the United States. But the politics of the twentieth century could not easily be elided in certain areas. In London early discussions of preparations for the commemoration elicited from the Irish embassy the view that it would be necessary to 'discourage effectively arrangements which would be lacking in dignity or would have objectionable political undertones'. It was decided that the embassy should encourage the formation of a committee that could be trusted to act 'with imagination and discretion', and with which the embassy could 'establish a degree of liaison and quiet control'.[61]

The committee in London was made up of members of the Gaelic League, the United Irish League, the Old IRA and the Council of Irish County Associations, with a chairman who was an Irish dentist. Suggestions for the London commemoration included mass in Westminster Abbey and a concert in the Royal Albert Hall. Despite little enthusiasm for a parade to Trafalgar Square, there was also a general feeling among members of the committee that some form of meeting should be held there, 'since not to do so would be to surrender the tradition of such meetings to organisations such as Clann na hÉireann or the Connolly Association'.[62] The political position of the aforementioned groups was problematic for the committee in the event that they should wish to be associated with the commemoration. It was decided that no great consideration should be paid to groups that did not recognise the Irish government, though their members should be 'treated with courtesy' and allowed to take part in the celebrations as individuals. Officials in London were anxious to be kept informed of planned events in Dublin because, as the embassy reported, 'word of the [government] committee's work is reaching individuals in London through other sources, and their superior knowledge can be not only embarrassing but dangerous if we wish to maintain our influence on the committee here so that they keep on the rails.'[63] In the event, Clann na hÉireann[64] achieved a measure of association with committees in London, Birmingham and Glasgow. The London committee agreed on condition that the group guaranteed its 'good behaviour'; it was argued that this arrangement 'enables us [embassy staff] to control to some extent Clann na hÉireann's activities on 1916 in London, and it also keeps the present committee together, which might otherwise split on the issue'.[65]

In Sydney the commemoration involved a traditional march led by the Irish National Association – which the ambassador, Eoin MacWhite, had described as 'one of the crosses I have to bear'.[66] The main ceremony took place at the tomb of Michael Dwyer, the famous County Wicklow rebel of 1798 and later who had ended his days as a high constable in Sydney in 1815. The association had approached the embassy six months before the commemoration (unusually), asking for permission to participate and seeking suggestions as to how the event should be marked. The ambassador, however, viewing the organisation as 'pretty incompetent', was 'not anxious to acquire, in any way, the blame for the almost inevitable failure'.[67] A 'fiery oration' was delivered to a crowd of five hundred people by Peter McLoughlin, a builder who had left Ireland in 1947. He urged unification with the six northern counties. 'The task of these men we remember today,' he declared, 'has still not been finished.'[68] In Melbourne a gathering at the tomb of the father of Terence MacSwiney, the lord mayor of Cork who had died after a 74-day hunger strike in 1920, was reportedly 'taken over by the Connolly Club and certain organisations of extremist republican sympathies'.[69] In New York, Clan na Gael and the IRA Veterans Club held a commemoration which included mass, followed by a concert and a social in the Manhattan Ballroom. They were considered to be 'a potentially rather extreme group' able to 'muster a negligible number of adherents'; they were the only organisation of this kind not participating in the main commemorative ceremonies directed by the Easter Week committee in that city.[70]

Domestic politics in the host nations were also an issue. Two thousand people attended the commemoration sponsored by the Irish National Association in Canberra; this event at Waverley cemetery included six survivors of the Rising and several members of the Australian parliament. It was described by the Irish embassy as 'very much a Labour Party show'.[71] In San Francisco plans to hold an outdoor concert or pageant were abandoned on the advice of the mayor and the chief of police, who 'feared that such an event, in commemoration of an insurrection, would attract troublemakers, particularly those who oppose American involvement in Vietnam'. Nevertheless, a 'Golden Jubilee Concert' (not organised by the commemoration committee), given by the Clancy Brothers and Tommy Makem, attracted three to four thousand people.[72]

Despite official anxiety, cultural and political strands were woven together without causing disturbances. The Irish Freedom League organised a commemorative dinner at the Hibernian Hall in San Francisco. The sponsors embraced resolutions critical of the Irish government, but an invitation was extended to the Irish consul, who agreed 'to pay a short visit "at the coffee stage"'. He reported that there were about twenty people present ('mostly elderly'), and that

> one man from the Six Counties made some remarks which came close to being critical of government policy in dealing with illegal organisations, but no harm was done, as he was immediately followed

by a visiting priest, who made a special point of welcoming the official representative of the government of Ireland.[73]

Republican sympathisers were also well contained in Birmingham, England, where a large crowd gathered to watch a parade of several hundred families; the turnout was reportedly less than that for a normal St Patrick's Day. The procession was described in the local newspaper as including 'a sprinkling of patriotic banners with Gaelic words'; it was followed by a message from the IRA asserting the need for Irish reunification, which received applause that 'was more polite than enthusiastic'. The commemoration concluded with a special mass later in the evening and a céilí in Birmingham Town Hall the following night.[74]

Despite tentative moves towards ecumenism at home, there was no sense that the Irish community abroad was anything other than Catholic. In New York branches of the Ancient Order of Hibernians organised masses and communion breakfasts in Queens and Manhattan.[75] A commemorative service also took place at St Ignatius Church in San Francisco on 24 April 1966; the attendance was described as 'not as many as one might have expected in a city with such a large Irish and Irish-American population'. But other priests in San Francisco recited special masses at the request of the Old IRA Men's Association in St Patrick's Church and at the behest of the Central Council of Irish Republican Clubs in St Finbar's Church.[76] In Cleveland, Ohio, the Irish consular representative attended a communion breakfast after mass and was asked one loaded question, which he 'replied to privately', concerning the possible transfer to the Dáil of powers held by the Westminster parliament.[77] In Boston a majority of the local Irish societies sent representatives to the special mass that was celebrated in Holy Cross Cathedral. A mass in the Russian Byzantine rite, together with a memorial service for those who had given their lives in 1916, was held later in the week at the Church of Our Lady of Kazan in Boston.[78] The special mass in Canberra drew the ambassador and the secretary of the Irish embassy, along with a numerous local congregation.[79] There were even stirrings in Africa and South America. An archbishop presided over a commemorative mass in Lagos, Nigeria, where the Irish missionary presence was strong; and the visiting chancellor of the Roman Curia took charge of the commemorative service on Easter Sunday in Buenos Aires, Argentina. Gracing the latter event were the aide-de-camp of President Arturo Illia of Argentina, representatives of the government and diplomatic corps, and members of the Irish colony.[80]

The fiftieth anniversary of the 1916 Rising was also marked in India. In New Delhi appropriate prayers were said at the Anglican Cathedral of the Redemption, which the Irish ambassador (a Protestant) normally attended, but the official service was held at the Catholic Cathedral of the Sacred Heart, where 'there was almost a full attendance of the Irish colony'.[81] The ambassador reported that this official service had the advantage that the Irish nuns in Delhi could participate: 'The nuns are not at the moment allowed to attend receptions or such worldly functions, though I understand from the archbishop that the existing rigid regulations may eventually be relaxed.'[82] The sermon was delivered by the Jesuit priest Fr Charles Gerald Lenaghan from Belfast, who spoke at length about the parliamentary tradition in Irish politics, but also compared the partition of Ireland to the division of Judea from Samaria. Fr Lenaghan suggested that the Samaritans had feared the Jews as much as Protestant Orangemen in the North currently feared his fellow-countrymen in the South. He argued that the Orangemen must be won over by charity and an extra measure of tolerance: 'Southerners may say: "We have had a Jewish lord mayor of Dublin, a Protestant president, and a Protestant ambassador; we are tolerant!" But that is merely justice, and not tolerance.'[83]

In Italy, the fiftieth anniversary of the Easter Rising passed off quietly. It proved impossible to hold a specific religious service during Holy Week, and the commemoration was marked by a radio programme that veiled the political story behind a narrative of the history of Irish music. The text, supplied by the Irish embassy in Rome, joined the cultural and political through such statements as: 'The abolition of the Irish parliament in 1800 exactly coincides with the fall of Dublin as a musical centre'; and 'It is against this background of freedom and independence attained, of nationalist fervour, of renewal and broadening of horizons, that one must see the work of the new generations of Irish composers like Gerard Victory, Frederick May, George Bodley, and many others.'[84]

Traditional St Patrick's Day celebrations were a focus for embassies where the Irish community was small or less organised. In Denmark the Irish colony was judged to include fewer than fifty people, only half of whom traditionally attended the reception at the embassy for St Patrick's Day. It was therefore decided to hold a joint function in March that would also commemorate the anniversary of the Rising.[85] In Buenos Aires, on the other hand, the celebrations comprised a month of events that began with the annual St Patrick's Day banquet and were given extra momentum by the dedication of a bust of General José de San Martin to the people of Ireland. Dr José Richards, the president of the Federation of Irish Argentine Societies, flew to Dublin with the bust, which was received by Seán Lemass at Iveagh House on 14 April as part of the official commemoration ceremonies in Ireland. Lemass noted that Argentina was celebrating the 150th anniversary of its own independence, and that it was the country with the greatest Irish emigrant stream in Latin America.[86] The Irish ambassador in Buenos Aires reported that press coverage was exceptionally good, and that 'Ireland has been continuously in the news here for nearly two months'. In asserting that the celebrations could not have been more successful, he noted, 'Indeed, the position was well summed up by "La Nación," a leading daily, which said that St. Patrick's Day is now celebrated in Buenos Aires as if it were an Argentine national holiday.'[87]

The commemoration was a cultural as well as a political phenomenon. In Boston, with its large and long-established Irish community, a central but autonomous feature of the commemoration was the second Modern Irish Arts Festival at the Massachusetts Institute of Technology. The two-week programme of events was directed by Mary Manning, a close relative of Erskine Childers, son of the executed republican and minister for transport and power in Lemass's government. Childers wrote to de Valera on her behalf, asking that the president send a message of goodwill and congratulations to the organising committee. A letter from de Valera duly arrived, expressing the hope that the enterprise would be 'an outstanding success'.[88] The organisers did not want their programme to be 'diminished by the inclusion of partisan or popular patriotic material'; it was therefore staged separately from the religious ceremonies, sporting events, parades, exhibitions and lectures conducted by local Irish-American societies.[89] Nevertheless, financial assistance for the festival was secured from a list of sponsors that included the Éire Society, the Irish Heritage Society, speaker of the House of Representatives John McCormack and Senator Edward M. Kennedy.[90] While support from the Boston Irish community was not as strong as the sponsors had hoped, the festival attracted a 'large and influential section of the non-Irish community in Boston and New England'. The Irish consulate in Boston was of the opinion that the festival had served 'in no small measure to correct an adverse impression of Irish culture which is still too prevalent'. Indeed, the festival prompted 'one widely read columnist of Irish extraction to write, "And to think that once we only had the St. Patrick's Day parade in South Boston"'.[91]

Despite the optimism of this particular columnist, the fiftieth anniversary of the Easter Rising offered little in the way of original expressions of Irish culture and continued the fixation with religious services and parades. In many ways the very feature that made Ireland unique in the world was its violent struggle for independence (including the Easter Rising), but this was also the aspect of Ireland's twentieth-century history that made the government most uncomfortable. It wanted, ideally, an apolitical commemoration of a political event, and the achievement of this objective was always going to be problematic. St Patrick's Day had already commodified Irish culture, and the 1966 commemoration was also largely understood as a vehicle through which 'Ireland' could be marketed abroad. The brochure accompanying a commemorative concert in the Royal Albert Hall on Sunday 10 April 1966 carried the word 'TRADITION' on its opening page, followed by the description: 'Oral communication from age to age. Thus a feeling developed from past successes, a respect for proven accomplishments. A very important word to the people of Navan Carpets.'[92] Advertisements for Cork Dry Gin, Erin Foods and Aer Lingus sat alongside extensive essays on the 1916 leaders in brochures, pamphlets and programmes – all amounting to one extended advertisement for the Republic of Ireland.

Conclusion

The reinvention and marketing of Ireland as a modern nation during the fiftieth anniversary of the Easter Rising was not an easy process. Nevertheless, against the images of an Ireland locked in the past were set certain representations of a country easing its way out of poverty and making slow but discernible economic progress. The *New York Times* judged that, after a long struggle, 'Ireland seems to have managed to have overcome the handicap of having lost its industrial northern counties, and has begun to develop a balanced economy.'[93] The *Oregon Journal*, based in Portland, noted that Ireland had 'built steadily day by day, year by year, on [the] standards of freedom, and gradually improved her economic position – retaining her reputation as a fresh and friendly land'.[94] Patrick O'Donovan, writing in the Australian *Bulletin*, also noted that the society 'whose awareness of the past is probably the most vivid and tragic on earth, is stepping into the modern world'. He pointed out that

> the Irish have strained to modernise their meagre resources. They encourage foreign capital. They build free ports and link them with light industrial estates. They use computers as much as any country

in Europe. They have elaborate managerial training schools. They carefully nurture their growing hotel industry, since tourism is their new source of wealth. They are trying to wean their cooks away from the frying pan and the kettle, which still dominate Irish cuisine. The dreadful air of poverty has lifted.[95]

In the *Weekend Telegraph* in London, Ian Hamilton acknowledged that Lemass's economic policies had helped to bring about 'the dispersion of that air of decay which was appreciated more by romantic tourists than by the natives'.[96] The journalistic endorsements were certainly not over-whelming, but they did suggest some success for the government's attempt to showcase the achievements of the independent state.

Official correspondence concerning the fiftieth anniversary of the Easter Rising underlines the sense in which the commemoration was not so much about celebration and self-congratulation as it was an exercise in control and communication. Although determined to mark the occasion and urging Irish diplomatic officials around the world not to be intimidated by the politics of the event, politicians and civil servants were keen that it not be celebrated as an anti-British action. Neither did they want its example to give succour to contemporary nationalist groups who were shaking their fists at old imperial powers. Through this process it was apparent that the Irish cringe was as colonial as it was cultural. The context of the 1916 Rising had given that event heroic grandeur: a romantic (rather than pragmatic) military action by a small, would-be nation against a world power. But it was also the historical context – a world war, a contentious treaty with Britain in 1921, and a civil war – which was most uncomfortable politically. Therefore, instead of conveying the complexity of the event, the Irish political and diplomatic elite found it easier to present the Rising as a moment of clarity (or modernity) that had ushered in a new era in Irish history.

Towards 2016

Writing in *Irish Spotlight* in May 1966, Seán Lemass noted that 'Now indeed is the time to seek answers to the question: "What sort of a nation do we wish to be in fifty years hence?"' and argued:

> Our hopes for the future rest on our confidence in ourselves, and on the final dying out of the old slave spirit which, in the past, bedevilled our efforts to get the nation reorganised for progress, and which still influences the behaviour of some individuals. In the next half-century we will no longer be able to find in history an excuse for our failure in any field of activity, if we should fail.[1]

Throughout its commemorative history the Easter Rising has been an event around which the failures of the southern state are held up for scrutiny even while the state itself is celebrating its independence. This role, as a moment of Irish stocktaking, was consolidated for the Rising by the elaborate official commemoration of its fiftieth anniversary. The Easter Rising was seen not just as part of the long struggle for independence but also as part of a story of Irish modernity, which had its beginnings in the 1798 rebellion and was heavily promoted in 1966. This had implications for subsequent commemorations of the Rising, including the seventy-fifth anniversary in 1991, which was noted for its muted nature. There were, in fact, two tensions being played out in the twenty-five years following the jubilee commemoration: one generated in the north of the island and the other in the south.

The generic myth of the Easter Rising transmits a story of heroism and ethnic identity; the images of the leaders of Easter Week became emblematic of the sacrifice that had brought about the independence of the state. By 1966, veterans of the Rising had become president and taoiseach of the Irish Republic and it was in their interests to minimise the focus on militarism and emphasise the 'new patriotism' which was a practical form of social responsibility designed to domesticate the battle-field lessons of the Rising. However, in 1968 developments north of the border made it impossible to gloss the violence at the heart of the Republic's origins.

The conflict in Northern Ireland made official commemorations of the Rising difficult for several reasons. The way in which Easter Week had been monumentalised, in the Nietzschean sense, so that it acted as a force of inspiration to future generations, had required that it must be 'wrenched into a general shape, with all its sharp corners and angles broken off'.[2] This meant that, despite its proximity in chronological terms, the leaders of the Rising had become further and further removed from the actuality of their lives and had become symbolic of an ideal. The outbreak of violence in Northern Ireland, and the clear belief by republicans that they acted in the tradition of the men and women of 1916, meant that it was very difficult for there to be a free-standing myth of the Rising. The northern conflict, in effect, grounded the Rising in the reality of its historical past: it reinstated the sharp corners and angles.

The struggle between the government and republicans over ownership of the Rising was as old as the independent state. However, the northern Troubles raised the stakes to an unprecedented level. The Irish state and its citizens had shown considerable ambivalence towards republican violence throughout the 1970s and 1980s. Jack Lynch, as taoiseach when the Troubles began, was completely unprepared for the violent developments and his impassioned rhetoric in August 1969 had encouraged many to believe that the Irish Army would become involved in the fight. Charles Haughey, who was taoiseach during the subdued seventy-fifth anniversary of the Rising, had been sacked from office and tried in 1970 over allega-tions of his involvement in illegally importing arms for Northern Ireland. Haughey played the northern card, with varying degrees of success, throughout his political career but, in reality, his stance was modified on becoming taoiseach for the first time in 1979. He was therefore in no position to undertake an elaborate commemoration in 1991.

There continued to be no simple answer to the question of who owned 1916. The Irish government did not want to be seen to concede legitimacy to republicans by honouring Ireland's past martyrs and there was a concern that highlighting the historical fight for independence would enhance the emotional connection felt by Irish people towards the aims of the Provisional IRA. Paramilitary violence was condemned by Irish governments but the contradiction inherent in condemning violence while also commemorating an act of violent rebellion became difficult to sustain and it became more prudent to play down the significance of the Rising in Ireland's past. Moreover, the commonly held, if erroneous, view that the fiftieth-anniversary commemoration of the Easter Rising caused the outbreak of conflict in Northern Ireland meant that subsequent commemorations were viewed as potentially very dangerous.[3]

The specific myth of the Rising being promoted in 1966 – of Irish modernisation – also had implications for the way in which 1916 anniversaries were commemorated in the years that followed. Modernisation had failed to deliver the promised prosperity. The rhetoric of the fiftieth anniversary had urged the country to unite in its efforts to serve the economy. The commemoration of 1966 emphasised that freedom was an ongoing process rather than an endpoint. It was difficult to continue to argue to a generation born long after the foundation of the state that the country would thrive as a result of hard work and sacrifice. Moreover, during the years of conflict in Northern Ireland an influential group of intellectuals in the Republic rejected the links which had been made in the 1960s between patriotism and modernity and argued instead for a scepticism which had no accommodation for nationalism. Adherence to the narrative of history that privileged the Easter Rising was seen to be at the very least backward and at the very worst extremely harmful.

Therefore, by its seventy-fifth anniversary in 1991 the visibility of the memory of the Easter Rising in public spaces had become extremely problematic. The publication of a book of essays, *Revising the Rising*, demonstrated the way in which interpretations of the legacy of Easter 1916 had become bitterly contested in the years since 1966 (and indicated ways in which the Rising was understood as part of an economic as well as a political ideological battle). Declan Kiberd's essay 'The Elephant of Revolutionary Forgetfulness' lambasted the 'new orthodoxy' which promoted the kind of modernity that had little room for nationalism and none at all for nuance: 'the real problem is that the designer-Stalinists who control so many Irish debates can deal with only one idea at a time: for them it must always be a simple choice between tradition or modernity, nationalism or social progress, soccer or Gaelic football.' Those who tried to combine elements of both, Kiberd argued, represented an insupportable ambivalence and so were targeted for vicious attack.[4] Edna Longley compared sanctified histories [such as that of the Easter Rising] to Ireland's equivalent of Marxist-Leninism: 'all the more insidious because their roots go deeper. The deconsecration of Irish memory is overdue – and underway.'[5] What is noticeable about *Revising the Rising* compared to the edited volumes published to mark the fiftieth anniversary of 1916 is the focus not on fact but on meaning. Gearóid Ó Crualaoich's essay addressed this directly. He revisited a call from F.X. Martin for an institute for the study of the Rising, and suggested instead one to examine 'how the Rising did and does and could – as mythic-historical event and as cultural resource – interact with and influence current affairs'.[6]

By the 1990s the memory of the Rising was being used by some commentators to offset the effects of the modernity it had been used to promote in the 1960s. For Ó Crualaoich it represented a vehicle for the kinds of cultural production that counter-balanced mass-produced disposable modern goods (such as fast food and pop music) that are driven by business interests and consumed passively.[7] For this to happen, Ó Crualaoich argued, the Easter Rising had to be detached from its historical moorings and 'come to life ... as a proper myth', that would serve to elucidate and valorise various aspects of society, a resource that would build and reinforce their sense of individual freedom, personal self-esteem and true participation in life's affairs.[8] By its seventy-fifth anniversary the Easter Rising was viewed much more comprehensibly by academics as a cultural product as well as a historical event. And it was clear that by 1991 the commemoration of the Rising in 1966 had been demonised for two reasons: it was seen to have been implicated in the beginnings of the northern Troubles and it had become entangled in a much larger debate on Irish modernisation.

By the ninetieth anniversary of the Easter Rising in 2006 circumstances had changed greatly.[9] The Good Friday Agreement, providing a framework for peace in Northern Ireland, had been ratified by a majority of the people on the island in 1998, and the Republic of Ireland was experiencing a high point in economic prosperity, commonly referred to as the Celtic Tiger. Not only was it possible to commemorate the Easter Rising without concerns over the impact this would have on militants, it was seen as essential that the state claim back the legacy of the Rising from peacetime republicans who were now electoral political rivals of the government party Fianna Fáil. The exhumation and state funerals in 2001 of ten Volunteers who had been executed during the War of Independence (the best known of whom was Kevin Barry) was a clear signal that the government intended to reclaim the legacy of the republican dead. Similarly, in 2006 the re-instatement of a military parade on O'Connell Street (suspended since 1972) reflected both confidence in the stability of the northern peace process and an assertion that the army of the Irish state was the true successor of the Easter rebels.[10] Moreover, the confidence born of economic prosperity led to a sense of pride in independence and to a desire to celebrate the achievements of the southern state. As in 1966, the triumph of the Easter Rising was presented as resting in the economic success of the Irish Republic. Where there was critical debate, the emphasis in the commemoration of 2006 was on the commitment contained within the Proclamation to guarantee religious and civil liberty, equal rights and equal opportunities to all Irish citizens.[11] The issue of sovereignty was seen by many to have been resolved and the focus instead was on civil rights rather than national freedom. This change in emphasis also reflected the Irish government's new relationship with Northern Ireland and the removal, in 1998, of any constitutional claim to the six counties in the north of the island.

The collapse of the Irish economy in 2008 redrew the parameters of the debate again. As has been noted, historically anniversaries of the Easter Rising have been shaped, in part, by the economic position of the independent state. Commemorations of 1916 have been used to advance the idea of modern economic development (as in 1966) but have also been characterised as an anti-modern form of nationalism as well as solace from modernity (as in 1991). It was therefore not inevitable that the Proclamation of the Irish Republic would be looked to as a point of noble reference when the economic sky fell in. Nevertheless, when the International Monetary Fund (IMF) was called into the Republic of Ireland in November 2010, it was in no more unlikely a quarter than *The Irish Times* that the leaders of the Easter Rising were invoked as having been dishonoured by the loss of economic sovereignty, in its leader article 'Was it for this?':

> It may seem strange to some that *The Irish Times* would ask whether this is what the men of 1916 died for: a bailout from the German chancellor with a few shillings of sympathy from the British chancellor on the side. There is the shame of it all. Having obtained our political independence from Britain to be masters of our own affairs, we have now surrendered our sovereignty to the European Commission, the European Central Bank, and the International Monetary Fund.[12]

The *Irish Examiner*, also responding to the arrival of the IMF, published a 'Proclamation of Dependence' on its front page. Using the familiar format and wording of the 1916 document, the *Examiner* summoned Irishmen and Irishwomen to the Republic's financial sovereign funeral. It concluded with a play on the closing aspirations of the Proclamation: 'In this supreme hour of failure the Irish nation must, by its memories of valour and discipline and by the readiness of its children to sacrifice their financial futures for the common good of the international money markets, prove itself somehow worthy of the august destiny to which it has now called time on.'[13]

It was clear that, almost a hundred years after it took place, the Easter Rising represented the most powerful available symbol of Irish sovereignty. It was being used as the ultimate expression of Irish nationhood and identity and its power lay in the fact that it represented these things independently of the Irish state. When Queen Elizabeth II visited the Republic of Ireland in 2011 the most compelling symbolic moment of her four-day trip was the observation of silence in the Garden of Remembrance. This is part of the ongoing and shifting significance of dead martyrs in Ireland; their importance by turns recedes and emerges, and at times provides an emotional language beyond the practical imperfections of independence.

Each commemoration of the Easter Rising constructs its own message. The structure of the formal commemoration in 2016 is unlikely to differ much from what has gone before: people will march and the Proclamation will be read. However, it will also represent an opportunity to assess the progress made in Ireland over one hundred years and to consider the benefits and abuses that have resulted from independence. It will operate as a bellwether for the Irish state and nation. The way in which the population responds to the anniversary in 2016 ultimately will be determined by the level of confidence it has in the official messages of the Irish state. The hundredth anniversary of the Easter Rising will be a test of the credibility of those who represent power in Ireland – north and south. It will be a telling indication of Irish citizenry's relationship with authority.

Bibliography

Archive Sources

Bord Fáilte
Annual Reports 1960–1967

Dublin Diocesan Archive
Correspondence with the Department of the Taoiseach
Irish Hierarchy Minutes

Irish Film Institute
Gael Linn Archive
Correspondence relating to *The Irish Rising*

Kilmainham Gaol Archive
Documents relating to the restoration and opening of the gaol

Labour History Museum, Dublin
Seán Dunne Papers

Military Archive, Cathal Brugha Barracks
Ceremonies in Provincial Centres
Pageant at Croke Park

National Archives of Ireland
Department of the Taoiseach
Department of External Affairs
Government Information Bureau
Office of the Secretary to the President

National Graves Association
Minutes 1965–6

Office of Public Works
Garden of Remembrance
Thomas Davis Statue

Public Record Office of Northern Ireland
Cabinet Conclusions
Fiftieth Anniversary of the Easter Rising
Home Affairs

RTÉ Libraries and Archives
Annual Reports
Authority Minutes
Monthly Reports
TAM Surveys

Royal Albert Hall Archive
Commemorative concert

University College Dublin Archive
De Valera Papers
Fianna Fáil Papers

Audio and Visual Sources

Cuimhneacháin 1916 Closing Ceremony, Dir: Burt Budin (Telefís Éireann, 1966)
Discovery: The Ghosts of Kilmainham, Dir: Peter Kennerley (Telefís Éireann, 1966)
Garden of Remembrance Ceremony, Dir: Michael Monaghan (Telefís Éireann, 1966)
Insurrection, Dir: Louis Lenton (Telefís Éireann, 1966)
Ireland On the Go, Dir. Richard Matt (A Mattco Production, 1966)
The Irish Rising, Dir: George Morrison (Department of External Affairs, 1966)
On Behalf of the Provisional Government, Pro: Aindreas Ó Gallchóir (Telefís Éireann, 1966)
This Week: The Ulster Problem, Dir: Peter Robinson (Rediffusion, 1966)
An Tine Bheo, Dir: Louis Marcus (Gael Linn, 1966)
The Voice of the Rising, Pro: Pádraic O'Neill (Radio Éireann, 1966)

Official Documents

Dáil Debates
Northern Ireland Commons Debates

Newspapers and Magazines

Aberdeen Daily World
Anglo-Celt
An Phoblacht
Belfast Newsletter
Belfast Telegraph
Birmingham Post
Boston Globe
Bulletin
Chicago Tribune
Church of Ireland Gazette
Connaght Sentinel
Corkman
Daily Express
Derry Journal
Donegal People's Press
Evening Herald
Fact Magazine
Guardian
Herald Tribune
Hibernia
Irish Catholic
Irish Independent
Irish News
Irish Socialist
The Irish Times
Kerryman
Leinster Leader
Leitrim Observer
Limerick Leader
Longford News
Look Magazine
Los Angeles Times
Marxism Today
Newry Telegraph
New Statesman
New York Herald Tribune
New York Morning Telegraph
New York Times
Northern Standard
Offaly Independent
RTV Guide
San Francisco Chronicle
San Francisco Evening Herald

San Francisco Examiner
Sligo Champion
Sunday Independent
Sunday People
Sunday Press
Sunday Star
Tablet
The Times
Tipperary Star
Ulster Gazette and Armagh Standard
United Irishman
Vancouver Washington Columbian
Washington Post
Weekend Telegraph
Western People

Contemporary Sources

1916–1966: What has Happened? (Dublin: TCD Publishing Company, 1966)
1916 Commemoration Committee of London, *Ireland, 1916–1966* (London: 1916 Commemoration Brochure, 1966)
Boland, Eavan, 'Aspects of Pearse', *Dublin Magazine*, Spring 1966, pp. 46–55
Boydell, Brian, *A Terrible Beauty is Born* (1965)
Caulfield, Max, *The Easter Rebellion* (London: Four Square, 1965)
Deasy, Joseph, *The Teachings of James Connolly (With a Brief Outline of his Life)* (Dublin: New Books, 1966)
Department of Eternal Affairs, *Cuimhneachán 1916–1966: A Record of Ireland's Commemoration of the 1916 Rising* (Dublin: Department of External Affairs, 1966)
Dudley Edwards, Owen and Pyle, Fergus (eds), *1916: The Easter Rising* (London: MacGibbon & Kee, 1968)
Economic Research Institute, 'The Irish Economy in 1966' (Dublin: The Economic Research Institute, 1966)
FitzGerald, Garrett, 'The Significance of 1916', *Studies*, vol. 55, no. 217, Spring 1966, pp. 29–37
Fitzhenry, Edna C. (ed.), *Nineteen-Sixteen: An Anthology* (Dublin: Browne & Nolan, 1966)
Gilmore, George, *Labour and the Republican Movement* (Dublin: Republican Publications, 1966)
Greaves, Desmond, 'Reflections on the Fiftieth Anniversary of the Easter Rising, *Marxism Today*, April 1966, pp. 110–16
Harris, Henry, 'The Other Half Million', in Dudley Edwards and Pyle (eds), *1916: The Easter Rising*, pp. 101–15
Kettle, Tom M., *Poems and Parodies* (Dublin: Talbot Press, 1916)

Kilmainham Jail Restoration Society, *Kilmainham* (Dublin: Kilmainham Jail Restoration Society, 1961)

Leonard, L.C.G., 'The Kilmainham Project as I Dreamt and Lived It', unpublished, Kilmainham Gaol Archive

Mac Anna, Tomás, 'Aiséirí: Glór-Réim na Cásca', unpublished script, 1966

Mac Aonghusa, Proinsias (ed.), *Corish Speaks: Speeches on the National Affairs by the Leader of the Labour Party Brendan Corish* (Dublin: New Century Publications, 1966)

Mac Giolla Choille, Breandán (ed.), *Intelligence Notes, 1913–1916* (Dublin: Oifig an tSoláthair, 1966)

Macken, Walter, *The Scorching Wind* (Basingtoke: Pan, 1988 [1965])

McMahon, Bryan, 'Seachtar Fear, Seacht Lá', unpublished script, 1966

Martin , F.X. (ed.), 'Eoin MacNeill on 1916', *Irish Historical Studies*, vol. 12, no. 47, 1960–1, pp. 226–71

Martin, F.X., '1916 – Myth, Fact and Mystery', *Studia Hibernia*, vol. 7, 1967, pp. 7–126

Martin, F.X. (ed.), *Leaders of Men of the Easter Rising: Dublin 1916* (London and New York: Methuen, 1967)

Morrison, George, 'The Irish Rising 1916', unpublished script, 1966

National Graves Association, Belfast Branch, *1916–1966: Belfast and Nineteen Sixteen* (Belfast: National Graves Association, 1966)

National Gallery of Ireland, *Cuimhneachán 1916: A Commemorative Exhibition of the Irish Rebellion 1916* (Dublin: Dolmen Press Limited, 1966)

Nolan, S. (ed.), *Easter Week 1916–1966* (Dublin: *Irish Socialist*, 1966)

Nowlan, Kevin B. (ed.), *The Making of 1916: Studies in the History of the Rising* (Dublin: The Stationery Office, 1969)

O'Brien, Conor Cruise, 'Embers of Easter 1916–1966', in Dudley Edwards and Pyle, *1916: The Easter Rising*, pp. 225–40

Ó Broin, Leon, *Dublin Castle and the 1916 Rising: The Story of Sir Matthew Nathan* (Dublin: Helicon, 1966)

Ó Dubhghaill, M., *Insurrection Fires at Eastertide: A Golden Jubilee Anthology of the Easter Rising* (Cork: Mercier Press, 1966)

Ó hEithir, Brendan and Ó Suilleabháin, Eoin, 'An Tine Bheo', unpublished script, 1966

O'Neill, Terence, *Ulster at the Crossroads* (London: Faber & Faber, 1969)

Rogers, W.R., 'Ireland and Her Past', *New Statesman*, 8 April 1966

Royal Hibernian Academy of the Arts, *1916–1966: Catalogue of the One Hundred and Thirty-Seventh Exhibition* (Dublin: Dolmen Press Limited, 1966)

Ryan, Desmond, 'James Connolly', in J.W. Boyle (ed.), *Leaders and Workers: The Thomas Davis Lectures* (Cork: Mercier Press, 1966) (Broadcast on Radio Éireann in 1961)

Sellwood, A.V., *The Red Gold Flame* (London: Corgi, 1966)

Shaw, Francis, SJ, 'The Canon of Irish History: A Challenge', *Studies: An Irish Quarterly Review*, Summer 1972, pp. 113–53

Stephens, James, *The Insurrection in Dublin* (Dublin: Scepter Books, [1916]
    [1965])
Thompson, William T., *The Imagination of an Insurrection, Easter 1916: A Study of
    an Ideological Movement* (Oxford: Oxford University Press, 1967)
Truden, Bernardine, Recollections of the 50th Anniversary of the Easter Rising
    of 1916 (Dublin, no publisher, 1966)
Wilson, Sloan, 'Ireland and the Irish (Without the Usual Blarney)', *Fact
    Magazine*, vol. 3, no. 2, March/April 1966, pp. 29–37

Books, Articles and Pamphlets

1912–1962 Ulster Covenant Jubilee Souvenir (Belfast: Alexander Boyd Displays
    Ltd, 1962)
Adams, Gerry, *Politics of Irish Freedom* (Dingle: Brandon Books, 1986)
Adorno, Theodor, *The Culture Industry: Selected Essays on Mass Culture* (London:
    Routledge, 1991)
Allen, Máirín, 'Jerome Connor – Two', *Capuchin Annual*, 1964, pp. 353–69
Anderson, Benedict, *Imagined Communities: Reflections on the Origins and Spread of
    Nationalism* (London and New York: Verso, 1983)
Assmann, Jan, 'Collective Memory and Cultural Identity', *New German Critique*,
    no. 65, 1995, pp. 125–33
Augusteijn, Joost, *Patrick Pearse. The Making of a Revolutionary* (Houdsmills:
    Palgrave, 2010)
Beiner, Guy, 'Negotiations of Memory: Rethinking 1798 Commemorations',
    Irish Review, vol. 26, no. 1, 2000, pp. 60–70.
Beiner, Guy, *Remembering the Year of the French: Irish Folk History and Social
    Memory* (Madison, WI: University of Wisconsin Press, 2007)
Benjamin, Walter, *Illuminations* (London: Pimlico, 1999)
Bhreathnach-Lynch, Síghle, 'Commemorating the Hero in Newly Independent
    Ireland: Expressions of Nationhood in Bronze and Stone', in Lawrence W.
    McBride (ed.), *Images, Icons and the Nationalist Imagination* (Dublin: Four
    Courts Press, 1999), pp. 148–65
Bolger, Dermot (ed.), *Letters from the New Island. 16 on 16: Irish Writers on the
    Easter Rising* (Dublin: Raven Arts Press, 1988)
Bolger, Dermot (ed.), *Letters from the New Island* (Dublin: Raven Arts Press, 1991)
Boyce, D. George, *Nationalism in Ireland* (London: Routledge, 1991)
Boyce, D. George, 'Interpreting the Rising', in D. George Boyce and Alan
    O'Day (eds), *Modern Irish History: Revisionism and the Revisionist Controversy*
    (London: Routledge, 1996), pp. 163–87
Boym, Svetlana, *The Future of Nostalgia* (New York: Basic Books, 2001)
Brady, Ciarán (ed.), *Interpreting Irish History: The Debate on Historical Revisionism*
    (Dublin: Irish Academic Press, 1994)
Brearton, Fran, *The Great War in Irish Poetry: W.B. Yeats to Michael Longley*
    (Oxford: Oxford University Press, 2000)

Brown, Terence, *The Life of W.B.Yeats: A Critical Biography* (Dublin: Gill & Macmillan, 2001)

Bryson, Lucy and McCartney, Clem, *Clashing Symbols: A Report on the Use of Flags, Anthems and other National Symbols in Northern Ireland* (Belfast: Institute of Irish Studies, 1994)

Cleary, Joe, 'Introduction: Ireland and Modernity', in Joe Cleary and Claire Connolly (eds), *The Cambridge Companion to Modern Irish Culture* (Cambridge: Cambridge University Press, 2005), pp. 1–24

Collins, Peter, *Who Fears to Speak of '98? Commemoration and the Continuing Impact of the United Irishmen* (Belfast: Ulster Historical Foundation, 2004)

Conekin, Becky E., *The Autobiography of a Nation: The 1951 Festival of Britain* (Manchester: Manchester University Press, 2003)

Connerton, Paul, *How Modernity Forgets* (Cambridge: Cambridge University Press, 2009)

Connolly, Linda and O'Toole, Tina, *Documenting Irish Feminisms: The Second Wave* (Dublin: Woodfield Press, 2005)

Cronin, Mike and Adair, Daryl, *The Wearing of the Green: A History of St Patrick's Day* (London and New York: Routledge, 2006)

Daly, Mary E., 'Nationalism, Sentiment and Economics: Relations between Ireland and Irish-America in the Postwar Years', *Éire-Ireland*, vol. 37, 2002, pp. 74–92

Daly, Mary E., 'Irish Free State/Éire/Republic of Ireland: "A Country by Any Other Name"?', *Journal of British Studies*, vol. 46, no. 1, January 2007, pp. 72–90

Daly, Mary E., 'Less a Commemoration of the Actual Achievements and More a Commemoration of the Hopes of the Men of 1916', in Mary E. Daly and Margaret O'Callaghan (eds), *1916 in 1966: Commemorating the Easter Rising* (Dublin: Royal Irish Academy), 2007, pp. 18–85.

Daly, Mary. E. and O'Callaghan, Margaret, (eds), *1916 in 1966: Commemorating the Easter Rising* (Dublin: Royal Irish Academy, 2007), pp. 1–17

Davis, Thomas, *National and Historical Ballads, Songs, and Poems* (Dublin: James Duffy, 1869)

Doherty, Gabriel, 'National Identity and the Study of Irish History', *English Historical Review*, vol. 111, no. 441, 1996, pp. 324–49

Doherty, Gabriel and Keogh, Dermot (eds), *1916: The Long Revolution* (Cork: Cork University Press, 2007)

Dolan, Anne, *Commemorating the Irish Civil War: History and Memory, 1923–2000* (Cambridge: Cambridge University Press, 2003)

Donohue, Laura K., 'Regulating Northern Ireland: The Special Powers Acts, 1922–1972', *Historical Journal*, vol. 41, no. 4, 1998, pp. 1089–1120

Dunne, Tom, *Rebellions: Memoir, Memory and 1798* (Dublin: Lilliput Press, 2004)

Edwards, Ruth Dudley, *Patrick Pearse: The Triumph of Failure* (London: Gollancz, 1977)

Elliott, Marianne, *Robert Emmet: The Making of a Legend* (London: Profile Books, 2004)

English, Richard, *Armed Struggle: The History of the IRA* (London: Macmillan, 2003)

Ferriter, Diarmaid, 'Commemorating the Rising, 1922–65: "A Figurative Scramble for the Bones of the Patriot Dead"?', in Daly and O'Callaghan (eds) *1916 in 1966*, pp. 198–218

Fitzpatrick, David, 'Commemoration in the Irish Free State: A Chronicle of Embarrassment', in Ian McBride (ed.), *History and Memory in Modern Ireland* (Cambridge: Cambridge University Press, 2001), pp. 184–203

Foster, John Wilson, *Colonial Consequences: Essays in Irish Literature and Culture* (Dublin: Lilliput Press, 1991)

Foster, R.F., 'Remembering 1798', in *The Irish Story: Telling Tales and Making it up in Ireland* (Oxford: Oxford University Press, 2002)

Foy, Michael and Barton, Brian, *The Easter Rising* (Stroud: The History Press, 1999)

Gibbons, Luke, 'Where Wolfe Tone's Statue Was Not: Joyce, Monuments and Memory', in Ian McBride (ed.), *History and Memory in Modern Ireland* (Cambridge: Cambridge University Press, 2001), pp. 139–59

Gibbons, Luke, 'Narratives of the Nation: Fact, Fiction and Irish Cinema', in Luke Dodd (ed.), *Nationalisms: Visions and Revision* (Dublin: Film Institute of Ireland, 1999)

Gibbons, Luke, *Transformations in Irish Culture* (Cork: Field Day, 1996)

Gillis John R. (ed.), *Commemorations: The Politics of National Identity* (Princeton, NJ: Princeton University Press, 1996)

Hanley, Brian and Millar, Scott, *The Lost Revolution: The Story of the Official IRA and the Workers' Party* (Dublin: Penguin, 2009)

Harris, Neil, 'Museums and Controversy: Some Introductory Reflections', *Journal of American History*, vol. 82, no. 3, December 1995, pp. 1102–10

Hart, Peter, 'The Fenians and the International Revolutionary Tradition', in Fearghal McGarry and James McConnell (eds), *The Black Hand of Republicanism: Fenianism in Modern Ireland* (Dublin: Irish Academic Press, 2000)

Hay, Marnie, *Bulmer Hobson and the Nationalist Movement in Twentieth Century Ireland* (Manchester: Manchester University Press, 2009)

Heaney, Seamus, *Preoccupations: Selected Prose, 1968–1978* (London and Boston: Faber & Faber, 1984)

Hegarty, Shane and O'Toole, Fintan, *The Irish Times Book of the Rising* (Dublin: Gill & Macmillan, 2006)

Hennessey, Thomas, *Northern Ireland: The Origins of the Troubles* (Dublin: Gill & Macmillan, 2005)

Higgins, Roisín, 'The Constant Reality Running through our Lives: Commemorating Easter 1916', in Liam Harte, Yvonne Whelan and Patrick Crotty (eds), *Ireland: Space, Text, Time* (Dublin: Liffey Press, 2005), pp. 45–56.

Higgins, Roisín, Holohan Carole and O'Donnell Catherine, '1966 and All That', *History Ireland*, April 2007, pp. 31–6

Higgins, Roisín, 'I Am the Narrator Over and Above … The Caller up of the Dead: Pageant and Drama in 1966', in Daly and O'Callaghan (eds), *1916 in 1966*, pp. 148–72

Higgins, Roisín, 'Projections and Reflections: Irishness and the Fiftieth Anniversary of the Easter Rising', *Éire–Ireland*, vol. 42, nos 3 & 4, Autumn & Winter 2007, pp. 11–34

Higgins, Roisín, 'Sites of Memory and Memorial', in Daly and O'Callaghan (eds), *1916 in 1966*, pp. 272–302

Higgins, Roisín, 'Remembering and Forgetting P.H. Pearse', in Roisín Higgins and Regina Úi Chollatáin, *The Life and After-Life of P.H. Pearse: Pádraic Mac Piarais: Saol agus Oidhreacht* (Dublin: Irish Academic Press, 2009), pp. 123–40

Higgins, Roisín, 'The Changing Fortunes of National Myths: Commemorating Anzac Day and the Easter Rising', in Katie Holmes and Stuart Ward (eds), *Exhuming Passions: The Pressure of the Past in Ireland and Australia* (Dublin: Irish Academic Press, 2011), pp. 145–62

Higgins, Roisín, 'The *Nation* Reading Rooms', in James Murphy (ed.), *The History of the Irish Book*, vol. IV (Oxford: Oxford University Press, 2011), pp. 262–73

Hill, John, *Cinema and Northern Ireland: Film, Culture and Politics* (London: British Film Institute, 2006)

Hill, Judith, *Irish Public Sculpture: A History* (Dublin: Four Courts Press, 1998)

Holohan, Carole, 'More than a Revival of Memories? 1960s Youth and the 1916 Rising', in Daly and O'Callaghan (eds), *1916 in 1966*, pp. 173–97

Horgan, John, *Seán Lemass: The Enigmatic Patriot* (Dublin: Gill & Macmillan, 1997)

Hunt, Hugh, *The Abbey: Ireland's National Theatre, 1904–1978* (Dublin: Gill & Macmillan, 1979)

Jackson, Alvin, 'Unionist History (i)', *Irish Review*, no. 7, Autumn 1989, pp. 58–66

Jackson, Alvin, 'Unionist Myths 1912–1985', *Past and Present*, vol. 136, no. 1, 1992, pp. 164–85

Jarman, Neil and Bryan, Dominic, 'Green Parades in an Orange State: Nationalist and Republican Commemorations and Demonstrations from Partition to the Troubles, 1920–70', in T.G. Fraser (ed.), *The Irish Parading Tradition: Following the Drum* (Basingstoke: Macmillan, 2000), pp. 95–110

Jarman, Neil, 'Commemorating 1916, Celebrating Difference: Parading and Painting in Belfast', in Adrian Forty and Susanne Küchler (eds), *The Art of Forgetting* (Oxford: Berg, 2001), pp. 171–95

Jeffery, Keith, 'Parades, Police and Governance in Northern Ireland, 1922–69', in Fraser (ed.), *The Irish Parading Tradition*, pp. 78–94

Johnson, Nuala C., *Ireland, the Great War and the Geography of Remembrance* (Cambridge: Cambridge University Press, 2003)

Kiberd, Declan, *Inventing Ireland: The Literature of a Modern Nation* (London: Vintage, 1996)

Kiberd, Declan, 'The Elephant of Revolutionary Forgetfulness', in Máirín Ní Dhonnchadha and Theo Dorgan (eds), *Revising the Rising* (Derry: Field Day, 1991), pp. 1–19

Kildea, Jeff, "'Who fears to Speak of '14–'18?" Remembrance in Ireland and Australia', in Laurence M. Geary and Andrew J. McCarthy (eds), *Ireland, Australia and New Zealand: History, Politics and Culture* (Dublin: Irish Academic Press, 2008)

Laffan, Michael, 'Easter Week and the Historians', in Daly and O'Callaghan (eds), *1916 in 1966*, pp. 323–42

Laffan, Michael, 'The Decade of the Rising: F.X. Martin on 1916', in Howard B. Clarke and J.R.S. Phillips, *Ireland, England and the Continent in the Middle Ages and Beyond: Essays in Memory of a Turbulent Friar, F.X. Martin, O.S.A.* (Dublin: University College Dublin Press, 2006), pp. 325–32

Laffan, Michael, 'Insular Attitudes: The Revisionists and their Critics', in Ní Dhonnchadha and Dorgan (eds), *Revising the Rising*, pp. 106–21

Lane, Jim, *Miscellaneous Notes on Republicanism and Socialism in Cork City, 1954–69* (Cork: Jim Lane, 1997)

Leach, Daniel, '"Repaying a Debt of Gratitude": Foreign Minority Nationalists and the Fiftieth Anniversary of the Easter Rising in 1966', *Éire-Ireland*, vol. 34, nos 3 & 4, Autumn & Winter 2008, pp. 267–89

Leerssen, Joep, 'Monument and Trauma: Varieties of Remembrance', in Ian McBride (ed.), *History and Memory in Modern Ireland* (Cambridge: Cambridge University Press, 2001), pp. 204–22

Lerner, A.J., 'The Nineteenth-Century Monument and the Embodiment of National Time', in M. Ringrose and A.J. Lerner (eds), *Reimagining the Nation* (Buckingham: Open University Press, 1993), pp. 176–96

Lloyd, David, *Ireland After History* (Cork: Field Day, 1999)

Longley, Edna, 'The Rising, the Somme and Irish Memory', in Ní Dhonnchadha and Dorgan (eds), *Revising the Rising*, pp. 223–53

Lynch, Brian, 'Through the Eyes of 1916', *History Ireland*, March/April 2006, pp. 54–7

Lyons, J.B., *The Enigma of Tom Kettle* (Dublin: Glendale Press, 1983)

Macleod, Jenny, *Reconsidering Gallipoli* (Manchester: Manchester University Press, 2004)

Mac Stíofáin, Seán, *Revolutionary in Ireland* (Westmead: Saxon House, 1974)

McBride, Ian, *The Siege of Derry in Ulster Protestant Mythology* (Dublin: Four Courts Press, 1997)

McBride, Ian (ed.), *History and Memory in Modern Ireland* (Cambridge: Cambridge University Press, 2001)

McBride, Lawrence W. (ed.), *Images, Icons and the Nationalist Imagination* (Dublin: Four Courts Press, 1999)

McCarthy, Conor, *Modernisation: Crisis and Culture in Ireland 1969–1992* (Dublin: Four Courts Press, 2000)

McDiarmid, Lucy, *The Irish Art of Controversy* (New York: Cornell, 2005)

McGahern, John, *Memoir* (London: Faber & Faber, 2005)

McGarry, Fearghal, *The Rising: Ireland, Easter 1916* (Oxford: Oxford University Press, 2010)

McIntosh, Gillian, *Forces of Culture: Unionist Identities in Twentieth-Century Ireland* (Cork: Cork University Press, 1999)

McKenna, Mark, 'Anzac Day: How Did it Become Australia's National Day?' in Marilyn Lake and Henry Reynolds (eds), *What's Wrong with Anzac?* (Sydney: New South Wales Press, 2010), pp. 110–34

McKenna, Mark and Ward, Stuart, '"It Was Really Moving, Mate":The Gallipoli Pilgrimage and Sentimental Nationalism in Australia', *Australian Historical Studies*, no. 129, April 2007, pp. 141–51

McKittrick, David, Kelters, Séamus, Feeney, Brian and Thornton, Chris, *Lost Lives: The Stories of the Men, Women and Children who Died as a Result of the Northern Ireland Troubles* (Edinburgh: Mainstream Publishing Company, 1999)

Moloney, Ed, *A Secret History of the IRA* (London: Penguin, 2002)

Moran, James, *Staging the Easter Rising: 1916 as Theatre* (Cork: Cork University Press, 2005)

Morris, Ewan, *Our Own Devices: National Symbols and Political Conflict in Twentieth-Century Ireland* (Dublin: Irish Academic Press, 2005)

Morris, William, *The Water of the Wondrous Isle* (London: Ballantine, 1972)

National Graves Association, *The Last Post* (New York: National Graves Association, 1986)

Nichols, Bill, *Introduction to Documentary* (Bloomington and Indianapolis: Indiana University Press, 2001)

Ní Dhonnchadha, Máirín and Dorgan, Theo (eds), *Revising the Rising* (Derry: Field Day, 1991)

Nolan, Emer, 'Modernism and the Irish Revival', in Cleary and Connolly (eds), *The Cambridge Companion to Modern Irish Culture*, pp. 157–72

Nora, Pierre, 'Between Memory and History: Les Lieux de Mémoire', *Representations*, vol. 26, Spring 1998, pp. 7–25

O'Brien, Conor Cruise, *States of Ireland* (Frogmore: Panther Books, 1974)

O'Brien, Harvey, *The Real Ireland: The Evolution of Ireland in Documentary Film* (Manchester: Manchester University Press, 2004)

O'Callaghan, Margaret and O'Donnell, Catherine, 'The Northern Ireland Government, the "Paisleyite Movement" and Ulster Unionism in 1966', *Irish Political Studies*, vol. 21, no. 2, June 2006, pp. 203–22

O'Callaghan, Margaret, '"From Casement Park to Toombridge": The Commemoration of the Easter Rising in Northern Ireland', in Daly and O'Callaghan, *1916 in 1966*, pp. 86–147

Ó Crualaoich, Gearóid, 'Responding to the Rising', in Ní Dhonnchadha and Dorgan (eds), *Revising the Rising*, pp. 50–68

O'Donnell, Catherine, *Fianna Fáil, Irish Republicanism and the Northern Ireland Troubles, 1968–2005* (Dublin: Irish Academic Press, 2007)

O'Donnell, Catherine, 'Pragmatism Versus Unity: The Stormont Government and the 1966 Easter Commemoration', in Daly and O'Callaghan, *1916 in 1966*, pp. 239–71

O'Donnell, Ruán (ed.), *The Impact of the 1916 Rising: Among the Nations* (Dublin: Irish Academic Press, 2008)

O'Faoláin, Seán, *The Irish* (London: Penguin, 1969, revised edition)

Officer, David, '"For God and Ulster": The Ulsterman on the Somme', in McBride (ed.), *History and Memory in Modern Ireland*, pp. 160–83

Ó h-Agáin, Deasún, *Liam McMillen: Separatist Socialist Republican* (Dublin: REPSOL Pamphlet no. 21, 1976)

O'Neill, Terence, *The Autobiography of Terence O'Neill* (London: Rupert Hart-Davis, 1972)

Patterson, Henry, 'Seán Lemass and the Ulster Question, 1959–65', *Journal of Contemporary History*, vol. 34, no. 1, 1999, pp. 145–59

Payne, Basil, 'Ireland Today: Image and Reality: Some Reflections on President Kennedy's Visit', *Capuchin Annual*, 1964

Puirséil, Niamh, *The Irish Labour Party 1922–73* (Dublin: University College Dublin Press, 2007)

Purdie, Bob, *Politics in the Streets: The Origins of the Civil Rights Movement in Northern Ireland* (Belfast: Blackstaff, 1990)

Richards, Thomas, *The Imperial Archive: Knowledge and the Fantasy of Empire* (London and New York: Verso, 1993)

Rigney, Ann, 'Plenitude, Scarcity and the Circulation of Cultural Memory', *Journal of European Studies*, vol. 35 no. 1, 2005, pp. 209–26

Roche, Anthony, 'Staging 1916 in 1966: Pastiche, Parody and Problems of Representation', in Daly and O'Callaghan (eds), *1916 in 1966*, pp. 303–22

Ryan, Annie, *Witnesses: Inside the Easter Rising* (Dublin: The Liberties Press, 2005)

Savage, Robert J., *Irish Television: The Political and Social Origins* (Cork: Cork University Press, 1996)

Savage, Robert J., *A Loss of Innocence? Television and Irish Society, 1960–72* (Manchester: Manchester University Press, 2010)

Shaw, G.B., 'Preface for Politicians (1906)', *John Bull's Other Island* (London: Penguin, 1984)

Sisson, Elaine, *Pearse's Patriots: St Enda's and the Cult of Boyhood* (Cork: Cork University Press, 2005)

Swan, Seán, *Official Irish Republicanism, 1962–1972* (www.lulu.com, 2007)

Switzer, Catherine, *Unionists and the Great War: Commemoration in the North of Ireland in 1914–1939* (Dublin: Irish Academic Press, 2007)

Taylor, Peter, *Provos: The IRA and Sinn Féin* (London: Bloomsbury, 1997)

Thompson, E.P., *The Making of the English Working Class* (Middlesex: Penguin, 1982)

Tóibín, Colm, *Beauty in a Broken Place* (Dublin: Lilliput Press, 2004)

Townshend, Charles, *Easter 1916: The Irish Rebellion* (London: Penguin Books, 2006)

Treacy, Matt, 'Rethinking the Republic: The Republican Movement and 1966', in O'Donnell (ed.), *The Impact of the 1916 Rising*, pp. 221–40

Trimble, David, *The Easter Rebellion of 1916* (Lurgan: Ulster Society Publications, 1992)

Vance, Jonathan, *Death So Noble: Memory, Meaning and the First World War* (Vancouver: University of British Columbia Press, 2000)

Verdery, Katherine, *The Political Lives of Dead Bodies: Reburial and Postsocialist Change* (New York: University of Columbia Press, 1999)

Ward, Margaret, *Unmanageable Revolutionaries: Women and Irish Nationalism* (Dingle: Brandon, 1983)

Whelan, Yvonne, *Reinventing Modern Dublin: Streetscape, Iconography and the Politics of Identity* (Dublin: University College Dublin Press, 2003)

Wills, Clair, *Dublin 1916: The Siege of the GPO* (London: Profile Books, 2009)

Winter, Jay, *Sites of Memory, Sites of Mourning: The Great War in European Cultural History* (Cambridge: Cambridge University Press, 1995)

Winter, Jay and Sivan, Emmanuel, *War and Remembrance in the Twentieth Century* (Cambridge: Cambridge University Press, 2000)

Winter, Jay, *Remembering War: The Great War Between Memory and History in the Twentieth Century* (New Haven and London: Yale University Press, 2006)

Young, James Edward, *The Texture of Memory: Holocaust Memorials and Meanings* (London and New Haven: Yale University Press, 1993)

Unpublished Theses

Shauna Gilligan, 'Image of a Patriot: The Popular and Scholarly Portrayal of Patrick Pearse, 1916–1991', unpublished MA thesis, National University of Ireland, 1993

Holohan, Carole, 'Every Generation has its Task: Irish Youth in the Sixties', unpublished PhD thesis, University College Dublin, 2009

Mackle, Clodagh, 'The Attitude of the Published Press in Northern Ireland towards the Fiftieth Anniversary of the Easter Rising in 1966', unpublished MA thesis, Queen's University Belfast, 1997

O'Dwyer, Rory, 'The Golden Jubilee of the 1916 Rising', unpublished MA thesis, University College Cork, 1993

Notes and References

INTRODUCTION

1 National Archives of Ireland, Department of the Taoiseach (hereafter cited as NAI DT), 97/6/162, T. Prendergast to Seán Lemass, 10 March 1966.

2 See David McKittrick, Séamus Kelters, Brian Feeney and Chris Thornton, *Lost Lives: The Stories of the Men, Women and Children who Died as a Result of the Northern Ireland Troubles* (Edinburgh: Mainstream Publishing Company, 1999), p. 5.

3 David Trimble, *The Easter Rebellion of 1916* (Lurgan: Ulster Society Publications, 1992), p. 33.

4 Ibid., pp. 33–4.

5 *The Times* (London), 28 April 1967, in Terence O'Neill, *Ulster at the Crossroads* (London: Faber & Faber, 1969), p. 125.

6 Terence O'Neill, *The Autobiography of Terence O'Neill* (London: Rupert Hart-Davis, 1972), pp. 78 and 87.

7 Conor Cruise O'Brien, *States of Ireland* (Frogmore: Panther Books, 1974), p. 144.

8 Michael O'Loughlin in Dermot Bolger (ed.), *Letters from the New Island* (Dublin: Raven Arts Press, 1991), p. 227.

9 This view has been placed under sceptical scrutiny by Declan Kiberd in 'The Elephant of Revolutionary Forgetfulness', in Máirín Ní Dhonnchadha and Theo Dorgan (eds), *Revising the Rising* (Derry: Field Day, 1991), pp. 1–19.

10 University College Dublin Archive, Fianna Fáil Archive (hereafter cited as UCDA FFA), P176/922, publicity pamphlet 'President of the Nation'/'Uachtarán an Náisiúin'; UCDA FFA, P176/922 (11), Notes for Speakers.

11 *Northern Standard,* 11 February 1966.

12 Ibid.

13 UCDA FFA, P176/922, O'Higgins election leaflet.

14 *Northern Standard*, 11 February 1966.

15 Alvin Jackson, 'Unionist History (i), *Irish Review,* Autumn 1989, p. 62.

16 Charles Townshend, *Easter 1916: The Irish Rebellion* (London: Penguin Books, 2006), pp. 153–4.

17 Joost Augusteijn (ed.), *The Memoirs of John M. Regan: A Catholic Officer in the RIC and RUC, 1909–48* (Dublin: Four Courts Press, 2007), p. 92 sited in Fearghal McGarry, *The Rising: Ireland 1916* (Oxford University Press, 2010), p. 132.

18 Townshend, *Easter 1916*, pp. 181–6.

19 McGarry, *The Rising*, p. 41.

20 Ibid., pp. 286–7.

21 Ibid., p. 154.

22 Peter Hart, 'The Fenians and the International Revolutionary Tradition', in Fearghal McGarry and James McConnell (eds.), *The Black Hand of Repubicanism: Fenianism in Modern Ireland* (Dublin: Irish Academic Press, 2000), p. 199; Declan Kiberd, *Inventing Ireland:The Literature of the Modern Nation* (London:Vintage, 1996), p.203.

23 McGarry, *The Rising*, p. 8.

24 Ibid., p. 281.

25 Townshend, *Easter 1916*, p. 355.

26 Conor Cruise O'Brien, 'The Embers of Easter 1916–1966', in Owen Dudley Edwards and Fergus Pyle, *1916: The Easter Rising* (London: MacGibbon & Kee, 1968), p. 238.

27 David Lloyd, *Ireland After History* (Cork: Field Day, 1999), pp. 89–100.

28 Roisín Higgins,'Remembering and Forgetting P.H. Pearse', in Roisín Higgins and Regina Uí Chollatáin, *The Life and After-Life of P.H. Pearse: Pádraic Mac Piarais: Saol agus Oidhreacht* (Dublin: Irish Academic Press, 2009), pp. 123–40.

29 Ibid., p. 129.

30 William Fallon in *The Sunday Press*, 14 April 1963.

31 *Chicago Tribune*, 1 May 1916.

32 F.X. Martin (ed.), 'Eoin MacNeill on 1916', *Irish Historical Studies*, vol. 12, no. 47, 1960–1, pp. 226–71.

33 F.X. Martin, '1916: Myth, Fact, and Mystery', *Studia Hibernia*, vol. 7 (1967), p. 39.

34 F.X. Martin (ed.), *Leaders of Men of the Easter Rising: Dublin 1916* (London and New York: Methuen, 1967), p. xi. For a discussion of Martin's contribution to the historiography of the Easter Rising see Michael Laffan, 'The Decade of the Rising: F.X. Martin on 1916', in Howard B. Clarke and J.R.S. Phillips, *Ireland, England and the Continent in the Middle Ages and Beyond: Essays in Memory of a Turbulent Friar, F.X. Martin, OSA* (Dublin: University College Dublin Press), pp. 325–32.

35 Marnie Hay, *Bulmer Hobson and the Nationalist Movement in Twentieth-Century Ireland* (Manchester: Manchester University Press, 2009), p. 244.

36 Max Caufield's *The Easter Rebellion* (1963) is a readable but uncritical narrative of the Rising, while also continually popular was Brian O'Higgins's *The Soldier's Story of Easter Week* (1925).

37 Leon Ó Broin, *Dublin Castle and the 1916 Rising: The Story of Sir Matthew Nathan* (Dublin: Helicon, 1966); Breandán Mac Giolla Choille (ed.), *Intelligence Notes, 1913–1916* (Dublin: Oifig an tSoláthair, 1966).

38 F.X Martin, *Leaders and Men of the Easter Rising: Dublin 1916* (London: Methuen, 1967).

39 Kevin B. Nowlan (ed.), *The Making of 1916: Studies in the History of the Rising* (Dublin:The Stationery Office, 1969).

40 Maureen Wall, 'The Background to the Rising, from 1914 until the Issue of the Countermanding Order on Easter Saturday 1916' and 'The Plans and the Countermand:The Country and Dublin', in Nowlan, *The Making of 1916*, pp. 157–97 and pp. 201–51.

41 The Irish version, Seán Mac Diarmada, is used throughout the book to describe the 1916 signatory. This is how he was referred to by his sisters during the commemoration, and it is how he signed himself on the Proclamation. Where

monuments and commemorative groups use MacDermott the Anglicised version of the name is adopted.

42 Dudley Edwards and Pyle, *1916: The Easter Rising.*

43 National Archives of Ireland, Department of External Affairs, 2000/14/90, Paul Keating to Seán Ronan, 12 April 1966.

44 Conor Cruise O'Brien, 'The Embers of Easter 1916–1966', in Edwards and Pyle, *1916: The Easter Rising,* p. 226.

45 O'Brien, 'Embers of Easter', p. 231.

46 Ibid., p. 237.

47 Francis Shaw, SJ, 'The Canon of Irish History: A Challenge', *Studies: An Irish Quarterly Review,* Summer 1972, pp. 113–53.

48 Ibid., pp. 118–19.

49 See for example D. George Boyce, 'Interpreting the Rising', in D. George Boyce and Alan O'Day (eds), *Modern Irish History: Revisionism and the Revisionist Controversy* (London: Routledge, 1996), pp. 163–87.

50 Michael Laffan, 'Insular Attitudes: The Revisionists and their Critics', in Ní Dhonnchadha and Dorgan (eds), *Revising the Rising,* pp. 106–21. See also Michael Laffan, 'Easter Week and the Historians', in Mary E. Daly and Margaret O'Callaghan (eds), *1916 in 1966: Commemorating the Easter Rising* (Dublin: Royal Irish Academy, 2007), pp. 323–42.

51 For a flavour of the exchanges see Ciarán Brady (ed.), *Interpreting Irish History: The Debate on Historical Revisionism* (Dublin: Irish Academic Press, 1994).

52 Ruth Dudley Edwards, *Patrick Pearse: The Triumph of Failure* (London: Gollancz, 1977).

53 *The Irish Times,* 18 April 1977.

54 Elaine Sisson, *Pearse's Patriots: St Enda's and the Cult of Boyhood* (Cork: Cork University Press, 2005), p.2.

55 Michael Foy and Brian Barton, *The Easter Rising* (Stroud: The History Press, 1999); Annie Ryan, *Witnesses: Inside the Easter Rising* (Dublin: The Liberties Press, 2005); James Moran, *Staging the Easter Rising: 1916 as Theatre* (Cork, 2005); McGarry, *The Rising.*

56 Gabriel Doherty and Dermot Keogh (eds), *1916: The Long Revolution* (Cork, 2007); Ruán O'Donnell (ed.), *The Impact of the 1916 Rising: Among the Nations* (Dublin: Irish Academic Press, 2008); Joost Augusteijn, *Patrick Pearse: The Making of a Revolutionary* (Houndsmills: Palgrave, 2010).

57 Shane Hegarty and Fintan O'Toole, *The Irish Times Book of the Rising* (Dublin: Gill & Macmillan, 2006).

58 Ní Dhonnchadha and Dorgan (eds), *Revising the Rising.*

59 Ian McBride (ed.), *History and Memory in Modern Ireland* (Cambridge: Cambridge University Press, 2001); *The Siege of Derry in Ulster Protestant Mythology* (Dublin: Four Courts Press, 1997).

60 Anne Dolan, *Commemorating the Irish Civil War: History and Memory, 1923–2000* (Cambridge: Cambridge University Press, 2003).

61 Guy Beiner, 'Negotiations of Memory: Rethinking 1798 Commemorations', *The Irish Review* vol. 26, no. 1, 2000, pp. 60–70; *Remembering the Year of the French: Irish Folk History and Social Memory* (Madison, WI: University of Wisconsin Press, 2007).

62 Thomas Bartlett, 'Sticking to the Past', *Times Literary Supplement,* 25 January 2002; Peter Collins, *Who Fears to Speak of '98? Commemoration and the Continuing Impact of the United Irishmen* (Belfast: Ulster Historical Foundation, 2004); Tom Dunne, *Rebellions: Memoir, Memory and 1798* (Dublin: Lilliput Press, 2004); R.F. Foster,

'Remembering 1798', in *The Irish Story: Telling Tales and Making it up in Ireland* (Oxford: Oxford University Press, 2002), pp. 211–34.

63 Daly and O'Callaghan (eds.), *1916 in 1966.*

64 Clair Wills, *Dublin 1916: The Siege of the GPO* (London: Profile Books, 2009).

65 Ibid., p. 105.

66 Ibid., p. 118.

67 David Fitzpatrick, 'Commemoration in the Irish Free State: A Chronicle of Embarrassment', in McBride, *History and Memory in Modern Ireland*, p.196.

68 Wills, *Dublin 1916*, pp. 146–8. Colm Tóibín has explored these events in his play *Beauty in a Broken Place* (Dublin: Lilliput Press, 2004).

69 Townshend, *Easter 1916*, p. 348. See also James Moran, *Staging the Easter Rising: 1916 as Theatre* (Cork: Cork University Press, 2005), pp. 30–52.

70 Yvonne Whelan, *Reinventing Modern Dublin: Streetscape, Iconography and the Politics of Identity* (Dublin: University College Dublin Press, 2003), pp. 166–7.

71 Fitzpatrick, 'Commemoration in the Irish Free State', pp. 198–202.

72 Rosemary Ryan, 'Commemorating 1916', *Retropsect 4* (1984), pp. 59–62, cited in Diarmaid Ferriter, 'Commemorating the Rising, 1922–65: 'A Figurative Scramble for the Bones of the Dead', in Daly and O'Callaghan, *1916 in 1966*, p. 207.

73 Fitzpatrick, 'Commemoration in the Irish Free State', p. 186.

74 Neil Jarman, 'Commemorating 1916, Celebrating Difference: Parading and Painting in Belfast', in Adrian Forty and Susanne Küchler (eds), *The Art of Forgetting* (Oxford: Berg, 2001), p. 188.

75 Roisín Higgins, 'The Changing Fortunes of National Myths: Commemorating Anzac Day and the Easter Rising', in Katie Holmes and Stuart Ward (eds), *Exhuming Passions: The Pressure of the Past in Ireland and Australia* (Dublin: Irish Academic Press, 2011), pp. 153–8.

76 McGarry, *The Rising*, p. 37.

77 Wills, *Dublin 1916*, pp.179 & 201.

78 'Message from Margaret Pearse to the People of Ireland', *Easter Commemorative Digest*, 1966.

79 Thanks to Mary Daly and Brian Crowley for pointing this out.

80 McGarry, *The Rising*, pp. 272–3.

81 Dermot Bolger (ed.), *Letters from the New Island* (Dublin: Raven Arts Press, 1991), p. 16. For a discussion of history, historians and national identity see Gabriel Doherty, 'National Identity and the Study of Irish History', *The English Historical Review*, vol. 111, no. 441, 1996, pp. 324–49.

82 Jarman, 'Commemorating 1916', p. 188.

83 Ibid., p. 189.

84 Neil Jarman and Dominic Bryan, 'Green Parades in an Orange State: Nationalist and Republican Commemorations and Demonstrations from Partition to the Troubles, 1920–70', in T.G. Fraser (ed.), *The Irish Parading Tradition: Following the Drum* (Basingstoke: Macmillan, 2000), p. 98.

85 The estimated turnout for the official parade was 2,000. *Northern Standard*, 15 April 1966.

86 *The Irish Times*, 11 April 1966.

87 NAI DT, S9815C, Submission to the government from the Minister for Defence, 10 December 1954; Cabinet Minute, 14 January 1955.

88 Paul Connerton, *How Modernity Forgets* (Cambridge: Cambridge University Press, 2009), p. 85.

89 *Longford News*, 16 April 1966.

90   *The Irish Times*, 11 April 1966.

91   Ibid.

92   Carson read the document on 19 September 1912, standing on a stone step outside Craigavon, the residence of James Craig. The stone was preserved and inscribed to commemorate the event. The souvenir brochure of the fiftieth anniversary of the Ulster Covenant in 1962 noted that the step was part of the UVF Hospital, now the Somme Nursing Home. Craigavon House itself is now empty. *1912–1962 Ulster Covenant Jubilee Souvenir* (Belfast: Alexander Boyd Displays Ltd, 1962).

93   A cartoon image of the GPO published in *Dublin Opinion* in 1924 showed steps at the front of the portico, indicating that the idea that Pearse stood on the steps of the GPO and read the Proclamation had already penetrated the public imagination to a significant extent. The GPO has no steps. In Wills, *Dublin 1916*, p. 145.

94   The photograph appeared in the *Daily Sketch*, 10 May 1916.

95   *New Statesman* (London), 8 April 1966.

96   John R. Gillis, 'Memory and Identity', in John R. Gillis (ed.), *Commemorations: The Politics of National Identity* (Princeton, NJ: Princeton University Press, 1996), p. 3.

97   Gillis, 'Memory and Identity', p. 8.

98   E.P. Thompson, *The Making of the English Working Class* (Middlesex: Penguin, 1982), p. 12.

99   See, for example, Joep Leersen, 'Monument and Trauma: Varieties of Remembrance', in McBride (ed.), *History and Memory*, pp. 204–22.

100 Connerton, *How Modernity Forgets*, pp. 8–9.

101 Joe Cleary, 'Introduction: Ireland and Modernity', in Joe Cleary and Claire Connolly (eds), *The Cambridge Companion to Modern Irish Culture* (Cambridge: Cambridge University Press, 2005), p. 2.

102 Connerton, *How Modernity Forgets*, p. 27.

103 *Irish Times*, 11 April 1966.

104 Conor McCarthy, *Modernisation: Crisis and Culture in Ireland, 1969–1992* (Dublin: Four Courts Press, 2000), p. 31.

105 Svetlana Boym, *The Future of Nostalgia* (New York: Basic Books, 2001), p. xvi.

106 Jenny Macleod, *Reconsidering Gallipoli* (Manchester: Manchester University Press, 2004), p. 12.

107 Jeff Kildea, '"Who fears to speak of '14–'18?" Remembrance in Ireland and Australia', in Laurence M. Geary and Andrew J. McCarthy (eds), *Ireland, Australia and New Zealand: History, Politics and Culture* (Dublin: Irish Academic Press, 2008), p.241. Kildea draws on the work on Jenny Macleod, 'The Fall and Rise of Anzac Day: 1965 and 1990 Compared', *War and Society*, no. 20 (May 2002), pp. 149–68.

108 On the latter point, see Mark McKenna 'Anzac Day: How did it Become Australia's National Day?' in Marilyn Lake and Henry Reynolds (eds), *What's Wrong with Anzac?* (Sydney: New South Wales Press, 2010), pp. 114–17; Mark McKenna and Stuart Ward, '"It Was Really Moving, Mate": The Gallipoli Pilgrimage and Sentimental Nationalism in Australia', *Australian Historical Studies*, no. 129 (April 2007), pp. 141–51.

109 *Belfast Newsletter*, 7 July 1916; David Officer, '"For God and Ulster": The Ulsterman on the Somme', in Ian McBride (ed.), *History and Memory in Modern Ireland* (Cambridge: Cambridge University Press, 2001), p. 173.

110 Officer, 'For God and for Ulster', p. 183.

111 Jay Winter, *Remembering War: The Great War Between Memory and History in the Twentieth Century* (New Haven and London: Yale University Press, 2006), p. 41.

112 At least 5,000 men of the Ulster Division did not answer their name at a roll call

the morning after the opening day of battle. At least half of these are believed to have been lying dead on the battlefield. Officer, 'For God and for Ulster', p. 160.

113 Jonathan Vance, *Death So Noble: Memory, Meaning and the First World War* (Vancouver: University of British Columbia Press, 2000), p. 9.

114 Nuala C. Johnson, *Ireland, the Great War and the Geography of Remembrance* (Cambridge: Cambridge University Press, 2003), p. 165.

115 Fran Brearton, *The Great War in Irish Poetry: W.B. Yeats to Michael Longley* (Oxford: Oxford University Press, 2000), p.7.

116 For a very thought-provoking discussion of these issues see Brearton, *The Great War in Irish Poetry*, pp. 3–42.

117 *The Irish Times,* 21 October 1965.

118 Seán Lemass, 'The Use Made of Freedom', *Boston Globe,* January 1966.

119 National Archives of Ireland, Government Information Service (hereafter cited as NAI GIS), Speech by Seán Lemass to the Annual Congress of Muintir na Tíre, 16 August 1966.

120 Becky E. Conekin, *The Autobiography of a Nation: The 1951 Festival of Britain* (Manchester: Manchester University Press, 2003), p. 53.

121 *Irish Catholic,* 10 February 1966.

122 *Offaly Independent,* 9 April 1966.

123 Office of Public Works (hereafter cited as OPW), A/96/6/9/1 (17) (24) Garden of Remembrance, Oisín Kelly to Raymond McGrath, 23 January 1959. The sculpture was not unveiled until 1971.

124 University College Dublin Archives, de Valera Papers, P150/3376. Notes on features of interest in the Garden of Remembrance by Dáithí Hanly.

125 Bolger, *Letters from the New Island*, p. 10.

126 Ibid., p. 225. This was first published in pamphlet form as Dermot Bolger (ed.), *16 on 16: Irish Writers on the Easter Rising* (Dublin: Raven Arts Press, 1988). Bolger collected a series of New Island pamphlets into a single volume in 1991 and wrote an extensive introduction.

127 For a discussion of the presentation of the Rising to a younger generation during the 1966 commemoration see Carole Holohan, 'More than a Revival of Memories? 1960s Youth and the 1916 Rising', in Daly and O'Callaghan, *1916 in 1966*, pp.173–97.

128 NAI DT, 97/6/161, Press conference to launch the commemorative programme, 11 February 1966.

129 Bolger, *Letters from the New Island*, p. 227.

130 Johnson, *Ireland, the Great War*, p. 165.

131 See the *Census of Population of Ireland* for years 1961, 1966, 1971, in Carole Holohan, 'Every Generation has its Task: Irish Youth in the Sixties', unpublished PhD thesis, University College Dublin, 2009, p. 8.

132 Eilis Pearse in an interview with Lucy McDiarmid, 9 July 1965, in Lucy McDiarmid, *The Irish Art of Controversy* (New York: Cornell, 2005), p. 202.

Chapter One

1 *Birmingham Post,* 11 April 1966.

2 National Archives of Ireland, Department of the Taoiseach (hereafter cited as NAI DT), 96/6/193, Notes on the Formal Opening of the Garden of Remembrance, 4 January 1966.

3 NAI DT, 97/6/162, Minutes from the sixth meeting of the commemoration committee, 4 March 1966.

4   Bernadette Truden, who wrote a column for the *Boston Globe* on the commemoration, recorded that 'everyone in Dublin [was] singing it'. 'Recollections of the 50th Anniversary of the Easter Rising of 1916' (Dublin, 1966). Truden's columns were collected in pamphlet form.

5   Eurovision was the international broadcasting network run by the European Broadcasting Union.

6   National Archives of Ireland, Department of External Affairs (hereafter cited as NAI DEA), 2000/14/77, Proposed TV Film to celebrate 'The Irish Rising – 1916'.

7   NAI DEA, Madrid Embassy, I.C. 3/9, External Affairs to All Missions, 31 January 1966.

8   NAI DEA, 2000/14/77, Paul Keating, London Embassy to Frank Coffey, External Affairs, 26 February 1966.

9   NAI DEA, 2000/14/77, Andy O'Rourke, London Embassy to Frank Coffey, External Affairs, 28 January 1966.

10   *The Irish Times*, 11 April 1966.

11   Ibid.

12   For a discussion of the impact of the commemoration on the internal politics of Ulster unionism see Catherine O'Donnell, 'Pragmatism Versus Unity: The Stormont Government and the 1966 Easter Commemoration', in Mary E. Daly and Margaret O'Callaghan, *1916 in 1966: Commemorating the Easter Rising*, (Dublin: Royal Irish Academy, 2007), pp. 239–71.

13   See ibid., pp. 241–2.

14   *The Irish Times*, 8 April 1966.

15   University College Dublin, Fianna Fáil Archive (hereafter cited as UCDA FFA), 176/772, Presidential Address by Seán Lemass to Fianna Fáil Ard Fheis, Dublin, 16 November 1965.

16   NAI GIS, 1/221, Speech by Seán Lemass at the Annual Dinner of West Galway Comhairle Dáil Cheantair of Fianna Fáil, Salthill, 27 January 1966.

17   NAI DT, S 9361k/62, Seán Lemass speaking at the Fianna Fáil Ard Fheis, 16 January 1962.

18   UCDA FFA, 176/772, Presidential Address by Seán Lemass to Fianna Fáil Ard Fheis, Dublin, 16 November 1965.

19   *The Irish Economy in 1966*, The Economic Research Institute, Dublin, July 1966.

20   National Archives of Ireland, Government Information Service (hereafter cited as NAI GIS), 1/221, Speech by Seán Lemass at the Annual Dinner of West Galway Comhairle Dáil Cheantair of Fianna Fáil, Salthill, 27 January 1966.

21   NAI GIS, 1.221, Speech by Seán Lemass to the Annual Congress of Muinitir na Tíre, Gormanstown, County Meath, 16 August 1966.

22   *Northern Standard*, 22 April 1966.

23   *Tipperary Star*, 16 April 1966.

24   NAI DT, 97/6/157, Minutes of the first meeting of the commemoration committee, 19 February 1966. The six government Departments were Finance, External Affairs, Education, Industry and Commerce, Office of Public Works and Defence. The lay members present at the first meeting were Leslie Bean Thomáis de Barra, Harry Colley, Simon Donnelly, Seán Dowling, Éamonn Martin and Frank Thornton.

25   Dáil Éireann Debates (hereafter cited as DED), vol. 215, 6 May 1965.

26   On 16 April 1964 the *Limerick Leader* noted the concerns of opposition deputies that, given that 1966 was potentially a year of elections to the Dáil, the Seanad and the presidency, Fianna Fáil would 'try to make it a year of ultimate triumph' in all

three contests. The concern existed that 'the all-over victory, according to critics, would be so sweeping that the death-blow would be given to all effective Opposition and, indeed, that in future there would be an Opposition only in name, as in the Six Counties'. General elections were held in Northern Ireland and the Republic of Ireland in 1965 returning Unionist and Fianna Fáil governments respectively. The presidential election, held in June 1966, saw Éamon de Valera re-elected with a reduced majority. A general election was also held in the UK in March 1966 which returned a Labour government under Harold Wilson.

27 DED, vol. 208, 12 March 1964.
28 NAI DT, 97/6/158, Minutes of the fourth meeting of the commemoration committee, 23 February 1965.
29 UCDA FFA, P176/348, 9 November 1965, in Mary E. Daly, 'Less a Commemoration of the Actual Achievements and More a Commemoration of the Hopes of the Men of 1916', in Daly and O'Callaghan, (eds), *1916 in 1966*, p. 22.
30 NAI DT, 97/6/157, Minutes of the first meeting of the commemoration committee, 19 February 1966.
31 NAI DT, S9815e/62, Honorary Secretaries of the Federation of the IRA, 1916–21 to Seán Lemass, 7 June 1962; Department of Defence to Seán Lemass, 21 July 1962.
32 NAI DT, S10500 C/63, Seán McEntee to Seán Lemass, August 1962. McEntee raised the issue following a debate in the letters columns of *FOCUS*.
33 NAI DT, 97/6/158, Minutes of the third meeting of the commemoration committee, 30 April 1965.
34 Ibid.
35 This was utilised most effectively by Radio and Telefís Éireann. Programme series such as *Insurrection* on television and *The Week of the Rising* on radio were aired nightly throughout the commemoration and revisited events as they had unfolded daily throughout Easter week 1916.
36 UCDA, de Valera Papers, P150/3369, Message from the President to the People of Ireland, Easter 1966.
37 UCDA FFA, 176/772, Presidential Address by Seán Lemass to Fianna Fáil Ard Fheis, Mansion House Dublin, 16 November 1965.
38 NAI DT, 97/6/158, Minutes of a meeting at the Office of Public Works at which civil servants and representatives of Bord Fáilte Éireann, Telefís Éireann and Radio Éireann were present, 21 May 1965.
39 NAI DT, S9815e/62, Honorary Secretaries of the Federation of the IRA, 1916–21 to Lemass, 7 June 1962.
40 NAI DT, 97/6/157, Minutes of the first meeting of the commemoration committee, 19 February 1966.
41 NAI DT, 97/6/158, Minutes of the third meeting of the commemoration committee, 30 April 1965.
42 Military Archives, Cathal Brugha Barracks, Department of Defence (hereafter cited as MA DDA), 48151/3 (118), Memo from P. Ó Murcada regarding a meeting held with C. Desmond, the Lord Mayor of Cork, 7 September 1965; Waterford National Memorial Committee to Piaras Mac Lochlainn, 13 October 1965.
43 MA DDA, 48151/3 (118), S. Ó Coigligh, Musaem Poiblí Chorcaí, to Ó Murcada, 9 September 1965.
44 *Western People*, 10 April 1966, *Northern Standard*, 22 April 1966.
45 *Cuimhneachán 1916–1966: A Record of Ireland's Commemoration of the 1916 Rising* (Dublin: Department of External Affairs, 1966), p. 23.

46 NAI DT, 97/6/158, Minutes of the third meeting of the commemoration committee, 30 April 1965.
47 *Irish Independent*, 12 April 1966.
48 *New York Times*, 11 April 1966. The *Herald Tribune* put the figure at 250,000, 12 April 1966.
49 *RTV Guide*, 8 April 1966.
50 *Birmingham Post*, 11 April 1966.
51 *Washington Post*, 11 April 1966.
52 *New York Times*, 11 April 1966.
53 *Los Angeles Times*, 11 April 1966.
54 Mass was also said in the Pro Cathedral and a United Service under the auspices of the Dublin Council of Churches was held in St Patrick's Cathedral. On Saturday 16 April a special mass in Irish was said in the Church of the Sacred Heart in Arbour Hill (the burial plot for fourteen of the leaders of the Rising) for the veterans of the Rising and was attended by the president and the taoiseach. A second mass, with full military ceremonial, was also said in Arbour Hill on 24 April. Those present included members of the government, the judiciary, the Oireachtas, veterans and relatives of the leaders of the Rising. Mass was followed by a procession to the 1916 Memorial Plot where the president unveiled a plaque to the memory of those who had died as a result of the Easter Rising. The plaque bore the names of sixty-four members of the Irish Volunteers and Irish Citizen Army. This included sixty-two men who had been killed in action and Thomas Kent and Roger Casement who had been executed. The names did not include those of the fourteen men who were buried in the plot. *Cuimhneachán*, p. 72.
55 *Northern Standard*, 1 April 1966.
56 For a discussion of the government's relationship with religious communities during the jubilee see Daly, 'Less a Commemoration of the Actual Achievements', pp. 44–50.
57 Archbishop of Dublin Archive, Irish Hierarchy Minutes, Quarterly Meeting of the Standing Committee, 27 April 1965.
58 NAI DT, 97/6/159, Jim Gibbons to Lemass, reporting a conversation with Most Reverend Dr Simms, 18 December 1965.
59 *Church of Ireland Gazette*, 4 February 1966.
60 Lemass had written to the archbishop of Dublin, John Charles McQuaid, in May 1965 to say that Jim Gibbons, the parliamentary secretary to the minister for finance, would be overseeing arrangements for the fiftieth-anniversary ceremonies and requesting that the archbishop appoint one of his staff to consult and advise on the role of the church in the commemoration. Archbishop of Dublin Archive, Correspondence with the Department of the Taoiseach, Seán Lemass to John Charles McQuaid, 3 May 1965. McQuaid appointed Rev. Dr MacMahon and the administrator, Father Murray.
61 Dublin Diocesan Archive, Correspondence with the Department of the Taoiseach, Notes of meetings and conversations by James A. MacMahon: Mr O'Dowd and Mr O'Sullivan of the Taoiseach's Office met Fr MacMahon and Fr Houlihan at Archbishop's House, Monday 10 January 1966, 11 am. The record of the meeting in the Taoiseach's Office did not differ significantly: see NAI DT, 96/6/193, Memorandum from O'Sullivan to the Department of the Taoiseach, 10 January 1966
62 NAI DT, 96/6/193, Memorandum by O'Sullivan, 13 January 1966.
63 NAT DT, 96/6/193, Memorandum, Department of the Taoiseach, 3 March 1966.
64 NAI DT, 96/6/193, Samuel Park to Seán Lemass, 1 March 1966.

65 NAI DT, 96/6/193, Isaac Cohen to Seán Lemass, 28 February, 1966.

66 NAI DT, 96/6/193, Winifred Bewley to Seán Lemass, 14 February, 1966.

67 NAI DT, 96/6/193, Memorandum on the formal opening of the Garden of Remembrance, 4 January 1966.

68 NAI DT, 96/6/193, Note from Daithí Hanly on the Garden of Remembrance, 18 February 1966.

69 *Sunday People*, 17 April 1966.

70 *The Irish Times*, 12 April 1966.

71 NAI DT, 97/6/157, Minutes of the first meeting of the commemoration committee, 19 February 1965.

72 NAI DT, 97/6/158, Minutes of the fourth meeting of the commemoration committee, 23 July 1965.

73 NAI DT, 97/6/158, Minutes of the third meeting of the commemoration committee, 30 April 1965.

74 NAI DT, 97/6/158, Minutes of the fourth meeting of the commemoration committee, 23 July 1965. See also Chapter 4 this volume.

75 NAI DT, 97/6/158, Minutes of the fourth meeting of the commemoration committee, 23 July 1965.

76 NAI DT, 97/6/159, Liam Cosgrave to Seán Lemass, 7 September 1965.

77 NAI DT, 97/6/159, Jim Gibbons to Seán Lemass, 29 September 1965.

78 *Western People*, 8 January 1966. The 1965 OECD Report *Investment in Education*, with data showing the levels of inequality in Ireland, provided evidence for the growing number who had been demanding greater access to education. See Daly, 'Less a Commemoration', p. 34.

79 UCDA FFA, National Executive Minutes, 14 June 1965.

80 NAI GIS 1/77, George Colley at the press conference at the Gresham Hotel to announce the award of scholarships by the Educational Building Society to commemorate the 1916 Rising, 25 May 1966.

81 *The Irish Times*, 15 March 1966; *Anglo-Celt*, 26 February 1966; *Kerryman*, 24 September 1966.

82 NAI GIS 1/77, Address by George Colley at a press conference at the Shelbourne Hotel to launch Bolands Limited's Scholarship Scheme in commemoration of Easter Week, 18 February 1966. Scholarships to secondary schools effectively became redundant with the announcement in September 1966 that free secondary schooling and a free school transport system would be introduced the following year. Daly, 'Less a Commemoration' p. 34.

83 *Cuimhneachán*, p. 60.

84 *The Irish Times*, 15 April 1966.

85 *Cuimhneachán*, pp. 82–4.

86 Ibid., p. 32.

87 *The Irish Times*, 16 March 1966. The renamed stations were: Dublin, Westland Row (Pearse), Amiens Street (Connolly), Kingsbridge (Heuston); Cork (Kent); Limerick (Colbert); Dún Laoghaire (Malin); Waterford (Plunkett); Galway (Ceannt); Dundalk (Clarke); Drogheda (MacBride); Sligo (Mac Diarmada); Bray (Daly); Wexford (Ó hAnnracháin); Kilkenny (MacDonagh); and Tralee (Casement). NAI DT, 97/6/160.

88 *Irish Independent*, 13 April 1966.

89 NAI DT, 97/6/138, Memorandum for the government, March 1965.

90 *The Irish Times*, 12 March 1966.

91 Connolly and Clarke (3d) would be used for inland postcards; Ceannt and Mac Diarmada (8d) for overseas surface and airmail to Europe; and MacDonagh and

Plunkett (1s 5d) for overseas airmail letters. NAI DT, 97/6/138, Memorandum for the government, March 1965.

92 NAI DT, 97/6/163 (no date).

93 Tralee Easter Week Commemoration Committee Statement in *The Kerryman*, 12 February 1966.

94 NAI DT, 97/6/157, Minutes of the first meeting of the commemoration committee, 19 February 1965.

95 Ibid.

96 NAI DT, 97/6/163, 'Cuimhneachán 1916 Tubhaile Órga Éirí Amach Sheachtain na Cásca, Clár, 10 go 24 Aibreán 1966'. For a discussion of the parody and pastiche in MacAnna's pageant see Anthony Roche, 'Staging 1916 in 1966: Pastiche, Parody and Problems of Representation', in Daly and O'Callaghan, *1916 in 1966*, pp. 303–22.

97 MA DD, 47969 (3), Report and memorandum from MacAnna, 10 January 1966.

98 NAI DT, 97/6/157, Minutes of the second meeting of the commemoration committee, 19 March 1965; NAI DT, 97/6/158, Minutes of the fourth meeting of the commemoration committee, 23 July 1965.

99 MA DD, 47969 (3), MacAnna to unknown recipient, 23 June 1965.

100 MA DD, 47969 (3), Report and memorandum from MacAnna, 10 January 1966.

101 MA DD, 47969 (3), P.J. Bourke to John Carroll, Department of Defence, 1916 Pageant Committee, 19 January 1966.

102 MA DD, 47969 (3), Alpho O'Reilly, Telefís Éireann to John Carroll, 2 March 1966; List of items borrowed from the Army for Croke Park Pageant, 12 May 1966.

103 MA DD, 47969 (3), Loss of Revolver, Webley, D.P. Ser. No. 2077 – 1916 Pageant, 21 April 1966.

104 MA DD, 47969 (3), Internal note, 19 July 1966.

105 Ferdia MacAnna in Dermot Bolger (ed.), *Letters from the New Island, 16 on 16: Irish Writers on the Easter Rising* (Dublin: Raven Arts Press, 1988), p. 37.

106 Truden, *Recollections of the 50th Anniversary of the Easter Rising of 1916*.

107 MA DD, 47969 (3), Gunnar Rugheimer to Piaras Mac Lochlainn (no date).

108 NAI DT, 97/6/160, Draft of information to be sent to schools.

109 *The Irish Times*, 23 April 1966.

110 NAI DT, 97/6/158, Meeting of commemoration committee civil servants and representatives of Bord Fáilte Éireann, Telefís Éireann and Radio Éireann, 21 May 1965.

111 MA DD, 48151/3 (118), From commemoration committee to the Crawford Municipal School of Art, Cork, 25 March 1965.

112 MA DD, 48151/3 (118), Letters included in the file on Ceremonies at Provincial Centres.

113 MA DD, 48151/3 (118), Seán Lemass to Michael Hilliard, 24 July 1965.

114 MA DD, 48151/3 (118), Memorandum, 18 November 1965.

115 MA DD, 48151/3 (118), From the Department of the Taoiseach to P. Ó Murchu, Department of Defence, 24 January 1966.

116 NAI DT, 97/6/162, Seán Lemass to Frank Aiken, 7 March 1966.

117 MA DD, 48151/3 (118), From Tomás Ó Cléirigh, Waterford to Piaras Mac Lochlainn, 15 June 1966.

118 MA DD, 48151/3 (118), Report from H.L. Ó Broin OIC to Árd Aidiunach Ceanncheathrú an Airm, 18 January 1966.

119 MA DD, 48151/3 (118), From Mary B. Tierney, commemoration committee, Cloughjordan, to Department of the Taoiseach, 11 February 1966.

120 MA DD, 48151/3 (118), From Patrick Duffy, Mayo commemoration committee to the Department of Defence, 19 April 1966.
121 MA DD, 48151/3 (118), Breakdown of expenses for provincial commemorations, Department of Defence, 29 July 1966.
122 MA DD, 48151/3 (118), From the Department of the Taoiseach to P. Ó Murchu, Department of Defence, 24 January 1966.
123 *Anglo-Celt*, 15 January 1966; *Leinster Leader*, 9 April 1966.
124 *Newry Telegraph*, 9 April; *Northern Standard*, 22 April 1966.
125 UCDA de Valera Papers, P150/3400, Souvenir Brochure from Mallow.
126 NAI, Office of the Secretary to the President, 97/7/56, Cuimhneacháin 1916.
127 *Northern Standard*, 18 March 1966; *Anglo-Celt*, 4 April 1966.
128 *Leitrim Observer*, 12 March 1966.
129 *Sligo Champion*, 4 March 1966.
130 *Carloviana: Journal of the Old Carlow Society*, December 1966, p. 26.
131 *Kerryman*, 2 April 1966.
132 *Offaly Independent*, 4 May 1966.
133 *Northern Standard*, 22 April 1966.
134 Ibid., 7 April 1966.
135 *The Midland Tribune, Tipperary Sentinel and Offaly County Vindicator*, Easter 1966.
136 *Corkman*, 2 April 1966.
137 *Derry Journal*, 19 April 1966.
138 *Kerryman*, 14 May 1966; *Limerick Leader*, 11 January 1966.
139 *Kerryman*, 5 March 1966.
140 *Limerick Leader*, 23 May 1966.
141 *Northern Standard*, 18 February 1966.
142 *Corkman*, 29 November 1966.
143 *Northern Standard*, 22 April 1966.
144 *Sligo Champion*, 8 April 1966.
145 See Daly, 'Less a Commemoration' for a discussion of the GAA's role in the commemoration, pp. 50–1.
146 *United Irishman*, February 1966.
147 *Leitrim Observer*, 12 March 1966.
148 *Anglo-Celt*, 5 February 1966.
149 *Western People*, 8 January 1966.
150 *The Irish Times*, 21 March 1966.
151 Ibid., 7 March 1966.
152 *Kerryman*, 12 March 1966.
153 *Sligo Champion*, 18 February 1966.
154 *Western People*, 12 February 1966.
155 Ibid., 5 February 1966.
156 *Irish Socialist*, March 1966.
157 *The Irish Times*, 11 March 1966.
158 Ibid., 25 April 1966.
159 *Leitrim Observer*, 19 March 1966.
160 NAI DT, 97/6/583, Invitation List for Reception in Honour of the 50th Anniversary of the Rising 1916.
161 NAI DT, 97/6/164, Report to Mr Ó Súilleabháin, Secretary, Department of the Taoiseach, on the State Reception at Dublin Castle, 17 April 1966.
162 NAI DT, 97/6/490, Memorandum, 16 May 1966.
163 NAI DT, 97/6/164, Report to Mr Ó Súilleabháin, Secretary, Department of the

Taoiseach, on the State Reception at Dublin Castle, 17 April 1966.

164 *Cuimhneachán*, p. 66.

165 Ibid.

166 The original draft of the speech is available in UCDA de Valera Papers, P150/3381.

167 *Cuimhneachán*, p. 64.

168 Public Record Office of Northern Ireland, HA/32/2/8, (59), Statement by the Prime Minister of Northern Ireland, 18 April 1966.

CHAPTER TWO

1 *Irish Socialist*, June 1966.

2 The most acute critique of the Rising and its legacy was penned by Conor Cruise O'Brien in *The Irish Times* and reprinted as 'Epilogue: The Embers of Easter, 1916–1966', in Owen Dudley Edwards and Fergus Pyle (eds), *1916: The Easter Rising* (London: MacGibbon & Kee, 1968), pp. 223–40.

3 Richard English, *Armed Struggle: The History of the IRA* (London: Macmillan, 2003), p. 84.

4 Liam McMillen's lecture to commemorate the birth of Wolfe Tone, Tailor's Hall, Dublin, June 1972, in Deasún Ó h-Agáin, *Liam McMillen: Separatist Socialist Republican* (Dublin: REPSOL Pamphlet no. 21, 1976), p. 1. I am grateful to Brian Hanley for bringing this pamphlet to my attention.

5 National Archives of Ireland, Department of the Taoiseach (hereafter cited as NAI DT), 98/6/495, 'Review of Unlawful and Allied Organisations: December 1, 1964, to November 21, 1966', Report from the Commissioner, An Garda Síochána, November 1966.

6 Roy Johnston had been a member of the Communist Party of Great Britain and the Connolly Association. Anthony Coughlan was a lecturer at Trinity College Dublin who had been an organiser of the Connolly Association in Britain. English, *Armed Struggle*, pp. 85–6.

7 Matt Treacy, 'Rethinking the Republic: The Republican Movement and 1966', in R. O'Donnell (ed.), *The Impact of the 1916 Rising: Among the Nations* (Dublin: Irish Academic Press, 2008), p. 225.

8 Roy Johnston, 'Liberation', in *1916–1966: What Has Happened?* (Dublin: TCD Publishing Company, 1966), p. 8.

9 Gerry Adams, *Politics of Irish Freedom* (Dingle: Brandon Books, 1986), p. 9.

10 Bob Purdie, *Politics in the Streets: The Origins of the Civil Rights Movement in Northern Ireland* (Belfast: Blackstaff, 1990), p. 130.

11 English, *Armed Struggle*, p. 95.

12 Ibid., p. 84.

13 Adams, *Politics of Irish Freedom*, pp. 8–9. For a discussion of the conflicting views within the IRA in the 1960s see Brian Hanley and Scott Millar, *The Lost Revolution: The Story of the Official IRA and the Workers' Party* (Dublin: Penguin, 2009), pp. 22–51.

14 Ed Moloney, *A Secret History of the IRA* (London: Penguin, 2002), p. 58.

15 *United Irishman*, February 1966.

16 Lane belonged to the breakaway republican group Irish Revolutionary Forces. He has recorded his experiences in 'Miscellaneous Notes on Republicanism and Socialism in Cork City, 1954–69' (unpublished). I am grateful to Brian Hanley for bringing these notes to my attention.

17 *An Phoblacht*, November 1965.

18 Treacy, 'Rethinking the Republic', p. 227.

19 *The Times*, 14 May 1966.

20 Treacy, 'Rethinking the Republic', p. 227.
21 *United Irishman*, May 1966.
22 *New York Times*, 10 April 1966.
23 *San Francisco Chronicle*, 6 April 1966.
24 *Look*, 19 April 1966.
25 *Washington Post*, 10 April 1966.
26 National Archives of Ireland, Department of External Affairs (hereafter cited as NAI DEA), 2001/37/781, Washington Embassy to External Affairs, 2 May 1966; NAI DEA, 2000/14/90, Canberra Embassy to External Affairs, 27 April 1966.
27 *New York Times,* 10 April 1966.
28 Ibid., 8 April 1966.
29 *Washington Post*, 9 April 1966.
30 Ibid., 18 April 1966.
31 NAI DEA, 2000/14/87, Ambassador, Berne, to External Affairs, 13 April 1966.
32 NAI, DT, 98/6/495, 'Review of Unlawful and Allied Organisations'.
33 Treacy, 'Rethinking the Republic', p. 228.
34 *New York Herald Tribune*, 15 April 1966.
35 *Sunday Press*, 16 February 1966.
36 *The Irish Times*, 15 April 1966.
37 NAI DT, 98/6/495, 'Review of Unlawful and Allied Organisations'.
38 Treacy, 'Rethinking the Republic', p. 229.
39 NAI DEA, 2000/14/91, Copy of O'Higgins's report sent to External Affairs, 3 March 1966.
40 NAI DEA, 2001/37/781 P.153 II, From San Francisco Consulate to External Affairs, 6 May 1966.
41 *New Times*, 1 May 1966.
42 *Weekend Telegraph*, 6 April 1966.
43 Ibid., 6 April 1966.
44 NAI DEA, 2000/14/84, Paul Keating, Counsellor, London Embassy, to Frank Coffey, 14 March 1966.
45 NAI DEA, 2000/14/84 (no date).
46 *New York Times*, 9 April 1966.
47 Public Record Office (hereafter cited as PRO) PREM3/980, Wilson to R.F.D. Shuffrey, Home Office, 13 December 1965, in Treacy, 'Rethinking the Republic', p. 232.
48 NAI DEA, 2000/14/90, Paul Keating, London Embassy, to Charles Whelan, External Affairs, 16 May 1966.
49 PRO PREM, 13/980, O'Neill to Soskice, 12 December 1965, in Treacy, 'Rethinking the Republic', p. 232.
50 PRO PREM, 13/980, Jenkins to Wilson, 4 May 1966, in Treacy, 'Rethinking the Republic', p. 233.
51 NAI DT, 98/6/495, 'Review of Unlawful and Allied Organisations'.
52 Ibid.
53 NAI DT, 98/6/495, 'IRA Organisation/Aide memoire', Department of Justice, 9 December 1966.
54 *United Irishman*, January 1966.
55 Ibid., March 1966.
56 *New York Times*, 9 April 1966.
57 *Belfast Telegraph*, 24 February 1966. For a discussion of the claims and counter-claims regarding the build-up of tension see Catherine O'Donnell, 'Pragmatism

Versus Unity: The Stormont Government and the 1966 Easter Commemoration', in Mary E. Daly and Margaret O'Callaghan, (eds), *1916 in 1966: Commemorating the Easter Rising* (Dublin: Royal Irish Academy, 2007), pp. 41–6.

58 NAI DT, 98/6/495, 'Review of Unlawful and Allied Organisations'.

59 Clarke died in 1976 and is buried in Glasnevin cemetery in a grave tended by the National Graves Association. National Graves Association, *The Last Post* (New York: National Graves Association, 1986), p. xxix.

60 *Irish Press*, 9 February 1966.

61 NAI DT, 97/6/161, Office of the Minister for Justice to Seán Lemass, 22 February 1966. The committee consisted of Joseph Clarke (president), Éamonn Mac Thomáis (chairman), Máire Bean Mhic Giolla, Monica Bean Uí Riain, Fintan Smith, Éamonn Sammon, Jack Butler (vice-chairman), Thomas McNeill, Joe Nolan and Larry Bateson.

62 *The Irish Times*, 9 February 1966.

63 *United Irishman*, March 1966.

64 *The Irish Times*, 9 February 1966

65 Ibid., 11 April 1966.

66 NAI DT, 97/6/490, Joseph Clarke to the Taoiseach's Office, 15 April 1966.

67 NAI DT, 97/6/490, Civil Service Memorandum, 21 April 1966.

68 *The Irish Times*, 11 April 1966.

69 Ibid.

70 NAI DT, 97/6/162, Piaras Mac Lochlainn to Department of the Taoiseach, 10 March 1966.

71 *The Irish Times*, 18 April 1966.

72 National Graves Association Minutes, 28 March 1966.

73 Nuala Johnson, *Ireland, the Great War and the Geography of Remembrance* (Cambridge: Cambridge University Press, 2003), pp. 153–61.

74 NAI DT, 97/6/159, Seán Lemass to Jim Gibbons, 2 October 1965.

75 *United Irishman*, February 1966.

76 *The Irish Times*, 6 April 1966.

77 National Graves Association Minutes, 14 April 1966.

78 *The Irish Times*, 19 April 1966.

79 NAI DEA, 2000/14/72, Information received from the Consulate General, New York, 7 March 1966.

80 National Graves Association Minutes, 20 April 1966.

81 Ibid., 14 April 1966.

82 *The Irish Times*, 19 April 1966.

83 Ibid., 25 April 1966.

84 National Graves Association Minutes, 28 March 1966.

85 Hanley and Millar, *The Lost Revolution*, p. 55.

86 *The Irish Times*, 25 April 1966.

87 *United Irishman*, May 1966.

88 *The Irish Times*, 25 April 1966.

89 *Irish Socialist*, June 1966.

90 NAI DT, 98/6/495, 'Review of Unlawful and Allied Organisations'.

91 *The Irish Times*, 25 April 1966

92 Ibid.

93 Military Archives Cathal Brugha Barracks, Department of Defence (hereafter cited as MA DD), 48151/3 (118), Patrick O'Rourke to Lemass, 13 December 1965.

94   MA DD, 48151/3 (118), Report from H.L. Ó Broin OIC to Árd Aidiunach, Ceanncheathrú an Airm, 18 January 1966.
95   MA DD 48151/3 (118), Margaret McDermott (sister), Rose McDermott (sister) and K.B. Keany (niece) to Minister for Defence, 2 April 1966.
96   *Sligo Champion*, 15 April 1966.
97   University College Dublin Archives, Fianna Fáil Archive (hereafter UCDA FFA), P176/342 (6), Fianna Fáil General Files, The Secretary, Monaghan Comhairle Dáil Ceanntair (no signature, no date).
98   MA DD 48151/3 (118), Private memorandum, Department of Defence, 1 February 1966.
99   The estimated turnout for the official parade was 2,000. *Northern Standard*, 15 April 1966.
100   *Northern Standard*, 15 April 1966.
101   *Kerryman*, 26 February 1966.
102   Ibid.
103   *Kerryman*, 16 April 1966.
104   Ibid.
105   *The Irish Times*, 2 February 1966.
106   *Limerick Leader*, 12 February 1966.
107   Ibid., 20 March 1966.
108   Ibid., 16 April 1966.
109   *Derry Journal*, 15 April 1966.
110   *United Irishman*, June 1966.
111   Seán Mac Stíofáin, *Revolutionary in Ireland* (Westmead: Saxon House, 1974), p. 96.
112   Treacy, 'Rethinking the Republic', p. 237.
113   Mac Stíofáin, *Revolutionary in Ireland*, p. 96.
114   Ibid., p. 93.
115   Ibid., p. 99.
116   *The Irish Times*, 8 March 1966.
117   Ibid., 9 March 1966.
118   *Guardian*, 9 March 1966; *Birmingham Post*, 11 April 1966.
119   *Birmingham Post*, 9 April 1966.
120   Republican Publicity Bureau Statement, *United Irishman*, May 1966.
121   *An Phoblacht*, May 1966.
122   Treacy, 'Rethinking the Republic', p. 230.
123   *Northern Standard*, 18 March 1966.
124   *Guardian*, 10 March 1966.
125   Ibid., 14 March 1966.
126   *The Irish Times*, 14 March 1966.
127   D. George Boyce, *Nationalism in Ireland* (London: Routledge, 1995, third edition), p. 305.
128   *Irish Socialist*, March 1966.
129   See, for example, George Gilmore, *Labour and the Republican Movement* (Dublin: Republican Publications, 1966), p. 19; A. Raftery, '1916 Re-examined', in S. Nolan (ed.), *Easter Week 1916–1966*, published by the *Irish Socialist*, Dublin, 1966.
130   Gilmore, *Labour and the Republican Movement*, p. 19.
131   Desmond Greaves, 'Reflections on the Fiftieth Anniversary of the Easter Rising, *Marxism Today*, April 1966, p. 115.
132   Raftery, '1916 Re-examined', p. 4.
133   Proinsias Mac Aonghusa (ed.), *Corish Speaks: Speeches on the National Affairs by the*

Leader of the Labour Party Brendan Corish (Dublin: New Century Publications, 1966), p. 13.

134   Niamh Puirséil, *The Irish Labour Party, 1922–73* (Dublin: University College Dublin Press, 2007), p. 238.

135   Joseph Deasy, '1913–1916: Similar Battle Lines!', in Nolan, *Easter Week 1916–1966*, p. 5.

136   Deasy, '1913–1916', p. 5.

137   Desmond Ryan, 'James Connolly', in J.W. Boyle (ed.), *Leaders and Workers: The Thomas Davis Lectures* (Cork: Mercier Press, 1966; broadcast on Radio Éireann in 1961), p. 67.

138   *RTV Guide*, 8 April 1966. The *Irish Socialist* noted that for once it agreed with the *Sunday Independent* in believing Connolly had emerged as the dominant, most dramatic and most determined figure in the series *Insurrection*. *Irish Socialist*, June 1966.

139   A.V. Sellwood, *The Red Gold Flame* (London: Corgi, 1966), p. 17.

140   *United Irishman*, May 1966.

141   Bernardine Truden, *Recollections of the 50th Anniversary of the Easter Rising of 1916* (Dublin, 1966). This collection of articles was originally published in *The Boston Globe*.

142   *Corkman*, 18 June 1966.

143   Joseph Deasy, *The Teachings of James Connolly (With a Brief Outline of his Life)* (Dublin: New Books, 1966).

144   *An tÓglac*, vol. 1, no. 10, 1965.

145   Sellwood, *The Red Gold Flame*, p. 17.

146   Ibid., p. 18.

147   Deasy, *The Teachings of James Connolly*, p. 3.

148   Ryan, 'James Connolly', p. 67.

149   Greaves, 'Reflections', p. 112.

150   Ibid.

151   Ibid.

152   *Irish Socialist*, June 1966.

153   Greaves, 'Reflections', p. 116.

154   Raftery, '1916 Re-examined', p. 4.

155   Ibid.

156   *Irish Socialist*, April 1966.

157   Michael O'Riordan, 'Lenin Supported the Men of Easter Week', in Nolan, *Easter Week 1916–1966*, p. 20.

158   Betty Sinclair, 'Connolly in Belfast', in Nolan, *Easter Week 1916–1966*, pp. 16–17.

159   National Graves Association, Belfast Branch, *1916–1966: Belfast and Nineteen Sixteen* (Belfast, no date).

160   Michael McInerney, 'Politics', in *1916–1966: What Has Happened?* p. 18.

161   Greaves, 'Reflections', p.116.

162   Raftery, '1916 Re-examined', p. 4.

163   *The Irish Times*, 14 April 1966.

164   *United Irishman*, May 1966.

165   *The Irish Times*, 13 April 1966.

166   *Irish Press*, 11 April 1966, in Mary E. Daly, 'Less a Commemoration of the Actual Achievements and More a Commemoration of the Hopes of the Men of 1916', in Daly and O'Callaghan, *1916 in 1966*, p. 54.

167   *Irish Press*, 11 April 1966 in Daly, 'Less a Commemoration', p. 54.

168   Daly, 'Less a Commemoration', p. 55.

169 NAI DEA, 2000/14/90, Ambassador, Berne, to External Affairs, 21 April 1966.

170 *Irish Citizen*, 22 September 1913.

171 Linda Connolly and Tina O'Toole, *Documenting Irish Feminisms: The Second Wave* (Dublin: Woodfield Press, 2005), p. 16.

172 Marion Jeffares, 'Women and Easter Week', in Nolan, *Easter Week 1916–1966*, p. 24.

173 NAI DT, 97/6/469, Kathleen Clarke to Éamon Martin, 29 March 1965.

174 *The Irish Times*, 10 March 1966.

175 NAI DT, 98/6/8D, Government Information Bureau, 1 February 1967.

176 NAI DT, 97/6/469, Seán Lemass to Kathleen Clarke, 14 May 1965.

177 Margaret Ward, *Unmanageable Revolutionaries: Women and Irish Nationalism* (Dingle: Brandon, 1983), p. 250.

178 *United Irishman*, May 1966.

179 Ibid.

CHAPTER THREE

1 *Belfast Telegraph*, 28 September 1966, in Thomas Hennessey, *Northern Ireland: The Origins of the Troubles* (Dublin: Gill & Macmillan, 2005), p. 61.

2 Alvin Jackson, 'Unionist Myths, 1912–1985', *Past and Present*, vol. 136, issue 1, 1992, pp. 167–9.

3 *Northern Ireland Commons Debates* (hereafter NICD), vol. 62, col. 1551, 2 March 1966.

4 A majority of Unionist councillors on Belfast Corporation had voted to call the new bridge 'Carson'. Lord Erskine had intervened, urging that it be named 'Queen Elizabeth' as the queen was due to open the bridge officially when she visited in July. Resentment centred around the governor's unconstitutional intercession and the suspicion that it had been prompted by O'Neill. Edward Carson had been conscripted to the cause of defending his father's name and denouncing both Erskine and O'Neill. Hennessey, *The Origins of the Troubles*, pp. 44–5.

5 NICD, vol. 62, col. 1527, 1 March 1966.

6 NICD, vol. 62, col. 1545, 2 March 1966. The film version of *Fanny Hill* had come to Belfast in March 1966 amid much publicity and some controversy.

7 NICD, vol. 62, col. 1545, 2 March 1966.

8 Jackson, 'Unionist Myths', pp. 180–1. The fiftieth anniversary of the gun-running in 1964 saw O'Neill and Paisley compete for its legacy, with 1,800 joining the latter in the Ulster Hall and only 500 gathering with O'Neill in Larne. Jackson, 'Unionist Myths', p. 175.

9 Hennessey, *The Origins of the Troubles*, pp. 56–7.

10 For a discussion of unionist cultural identities in Northern Ireland see Gillian McIntosh, *Forces of Culture: Unionist Identities in Twentieth-Century Ireland* (Cork: Cork University Press, 1999).

11 National Archives of Ireland, Department of the Taoiseach (hereafter cited as NAI DT), 97/6/157, Liam O'Doherty (member of the commemoration committee) to Seán Lemass, 27 April 1965.

12 NAI DT, 97/6/157, Seán Lemass to Liam O'Doherty, 28 April 1965.

13 McIntosh, *Forces of Culture*, p. 3.

14 NAI DT, S9361 K/63, Speech by Seán Lemass at a dinner to mark the 40th year in Dáil Éireann of Deputy Thomas McEllistrim, Manhattan Hotel, Tralee, 29 July 1963.

15 For a discussion of Northern Ireland's objections to the use of 'Ireland' as the official title of the Republic see Mary E. Daly, 'Irish Free State/Éire/Republic of

Ireland: "A Country by Any Other Name"?', *Journal of British Studies*, vol. 46, issue 1, January 2007, pp. 72–90.

16   NAI DT, S1957/63, Seán Lemass to Vivian de Valera, Managing Director of the *Irish Press*, 14 May 1960.

17   Public Record Office of Northern Ireland (hereafter cited as PRONI), CAB9F/123/72, 17 April 1959, in John Hill, *Cinema and Northern Ireland: Film, Culture and Politics* (London: British Film Institute, 2006), p. 143.

18   Hill, *Cinema and Northern Ireland*, p. 143.

19   PRONI, CAB 4/1313 (11), 23 August 1965.

20   Ibid.

21   PRONI, CAB 4/1315 (12), 19 October 1965.

22   Ibid.

23   Ibid.

24   Mary E. Daly and Margaret O'Callaghan, 'Introduction: Irish Modernity and "The Patriot Dead" in 1966', in Mary E. Daly and Margaret O'Callaghan (eds), *1916 in 1966: Commemorating the Easter Rising* (Dublin: Royal Irish Academy, 2007), p. 5.

25   See Edna Longley, 'The Rising, the Somme and Irish Memory', in Máirín Ní Dhonnchadha and Theo Dorgan (eds), *Revising the Rising* (Derry: Field Day, 1991), pp. 29–49.

26   Margaret O'Callaghan, '"From Casement Park to Toombridge": The Commemoration of the Easter Rising in Northern Ireland', in Daly and O'Callaghan (eds), *1916 in 1966*, p. 95.

27   For discussion of events that took place across Northern Ireland see O'Callaghan, 'From Casement Park', pp. 86–138.

28   NICD, vol. 62, col. 1556, 2 March 1966.

29   NICD, vol. 62, col. 1553, 2 March 1966.

30   O'Callaghan, 'From Casement Park', p. 100.

31   *United Irishman*, February 1966.

32   O'Callaghan, 'From Casement Park', p.108.

33   Ibid., p.107.

34   Liam McMillen's lecture to commemorate the birth of Wolfe Tone, Tailor's Hall, Dublin, June 1972, in Deasún Ó h-Agáin, *Liam McMillen: Separatist Socialist Republican* (Dublin: REPSOL Pamphlet no. 21, 1976), p. 6.

35   O'Callaghan, 'From Casement Park', p. 92.

36   Roisín Higgins, Carole Holohan and Catherine O'Donnell, '1966 and All That' *History Ireland*, April 2007, pp. 35–6.

37   *The Irish Times*, 18 April 1966.

38   Brian Hanley and Scott Millar, *The Lost Revolution: The Story of the Official IRA and the Workers' Party* (Dublin: Penguin, 2009), p. 55.

39   *The Irish Times*, 18 April 1966.

40   Paisley and Councillor James McCarroll were arrested and charged with unlawful assembly in Belfast on 6 June 1966.

41   Laura K. Donohue, 'Regulating Northern Ireland: The Special Powers Acts, 1922–1972', *Historical Journal*, vol. 41, no. 4 (1998), p. 1096. Under Regulation 4 of the Special Powers Act, meetings, assemblies and processions could be banned by the issuing of a proclamation of prohibition.

42   PRONI, HA/32/1/467, 1 April 1946, memorandum by H.C. Montgomery, assistant secretary in the Ministry of Home Affairs, in Keith Jeffery, 'Parades, Police and Governance in Northern Ireland, 1922–69', in T.G. Fraser (ed.), *The Irish Parading Tradition: Following the Drum* (Basingstoke: Macmillan, 2000), p. 87.

43 Neil Jarman and Dominic Bryan, 'Green Parades in an Orange State: Nationalist and Republican Commemorations and Demonstrations from Partition to the Troubles, 1920–70', in Fraser, *The Irish Parading Tradition*, p. 97.
44 NICD, vol. 62, col. 1550, 2 March 1966.
45 O'Callaghan, 'From Casement Park', p. 99.
46 Ibid., p. 99.
47 Margaret O'Callaghan and Catherine O'Donnell, 'The Northern Ireland Government, the "Paisleyite Movement" and Ulster Unionism in 1966', *Irish Political Studies*, vol. 21, no. 2, June 2006, p. 205.
48 The RUC inspector general wrote to J.E. Greeves at Home Affairs, 22 June 1966:
While there is always the IRA and its splinter groups in the background ready to seize any opportunity to disturb the peace, the fact is that an equal or even greater threat is posed at present by extremist Protestant groups, many of whom are members of loyalist organisations. These are the people whom it may be possible to reach at meetings of the Loyal Orange Order and other similar bodies, and it may be that leaders of Protestant Churches could also play their part before it is too late.
(PRONI, CAB9B/300/1 in O'Callaghan and O'Donnell, 'The Northern Ireland Government', p. 210).
49 An aspect of the problem was conveyed by William Craig to the Grand Orange Lodge of Ireland the following year:
As a member of this [Cabinet Security] Committee I then felt, and still do, that a complete prohibition of these celebrations would have been unwise because undoubtedly the organisers would have flouted the law. Large forces would have had to be kept ready to deal with such breaches and this would have seriously weakened the dominant position of our security forces and would have presented the IRA with invaluable psychological and tactical opportunities to advance their cause whilst our forces were engaged in dealing with illegal processions etc.
(PRONI HA/32/2/8 (77), 9 February 1966).
50 NICD, vol. 62, col. 1559, 2 March 1966.
51 NICD, vol. 63, cols 230–1, 24 March 1966.
52 PRONI, CAB9B/299/1, Terence O'Neill to Sir George Clarke, Grand Orange Lodge of Ireland, as agreed at a meeting of the Security Committee, 4 April 1966 dated 5 April 1966.
53 NICD, vol. 62, col. 1539, 2 March 1966.
54 NICD, vol. 62, col. 1540, 2 March 1966.
55 NICD, vol. 62, cols 1540–1, 2 March 1966.
56 Terence O'Neill, *The Autobiography of Terence O'Neill* (London: Rupert Hart-Davis, 1972), p. 76.
57 *Belfast Telegraph*, 15 February 1966.
58 NICD, vol. 62, col. 1543, 2 March 1966.
59 The headline in *The Irish Times* read: 'North Virtually Seals the Border', 15 April 1966. This phrase was used across the Irish and British media.
60 *Belfast Telegraph*, 15 April 1966, in Catherine O'Donnell, 'Pragmatism Versus Unity: The Stormont Government and the 1966 Easter Commemoration', in Daly and O'Callaghan, *1916 in 1966*, p. 245.
61 *The Irish Times*, 15 April 1966.
62 Ibid.
63 NAI DT, 97/6/164, Memorandum, 15 April 1966.
64 NAI DT, 98/6/495, Memorandum outlining communication between Whitaker (Department of Finance, Republic of Ireland) and Malley (Prime Minister's

Office, Northern Ireland) regarding cross-border trains, 16 April 1966.

65 NAI DT, 97/6/161, F. Lemass, General Manager, Kingsbridge Station to Erskine Childers, Minister for Transport and Power, 18 February 1966.

66 NAI DT, 97/6/161.

67 NAI DT, 97/6/161, Office of the Minister for Justice to Seán Lemass, 22 February 1966.

68 NAI DT, 97/6/161, Seán Lemass to Erskine Childers, 23 February 1966.

69 The railway connection between Dublin and Belfast was operated by CIÉ who paid the transport authorities in Northern Ireland for the use of the permanent way and certain facilities north of the border.

70 *The Irish Times*, 18 April 1966.

71 Regarding objections to a parade in Dungannon/Coalisland, the Ministry of Home Affairs was sent a report from the district inspector which was accompanied by the communication 'The Inspector General agrees that the policy of "wait and see" would seem the proper one at the moment.' PRONI, HA/32/2/8 (11), The Office of the Inspector General to J.E. Greeves, Home Affairs, 9 February 1966.

72 PRONI, HA/32/2/19 (4), The Inspector General of the RUC to the Secretary, Ministry of Home Affairs, 1 December 1965.

73 Ibid.

74 PRONI, HA/32/2/19 (1), East and Mid (part of) Tyrone Unionist Association, Cookstown, to J.O. Bailie, Unionist Headquarters, Glengall Street, 9 October 1965.

75 PRONI, HA/32/2/19 (9), Primatial Black District Chapter No. 4 to W. Sparrow, County Inspector, RUC, 1 March 1966.

76 PRONI, HA/32/2/19 (9), Urban and Corporation Branch of Mid-Armagh Unionist Association to W. Sparrow, County Inspector, RUC station, Armagh, 23 February 1966.

77 PRONI, HA/32/2/19 (25), County Londonderry, Grand Orange Lodge to Brian McConnell, 6 April 1966.

78 PRONI, HA/32/2/19 (9), Primatial Royal Black District Chapter No. 4 to W. Sparrow, County Inspector, RUC, 1 March 1966.

79 PRONI, HA/32/2/19 (28), The Evangelical Protestant Society, Belfast to Brian McConnell, 14 April 1966.

80 PRONI, HA/32/2/8 (17), Major J.D. Chichester-Clark to Brian McConnell.

81 PRONI, HA/32/2/8 (25), Loup Branch South Derry Unionist Association to District Inspector Woods, RUC station, Magherafelt, 14 March 1966.

82 PRONI, HA/32/2/8 (29), Report of the District Inspector, Magherafelt, regarding 'Unionist Objections to the forthcoming Republican Commemoration Celebrations to be held at The Loup, Moneymore, County Londonderry, on Easter Sunday, 10 April, 1966'.

83 PRONI, HA/32/2/8 (29), Report of the District Inspector, Magherafelt, regarding 'Unionist Objections'.

84 Ibid.

85 Ibid.

86 PRONI, HA/32/2/8 (31), County Inspector to Inspector General, RUC, 16 March 1966.

87 *Derry Journal*, 8 April 1966.

88 *The Irish Times*, 11 April 1966.

89 *Derry Journal*, 21 June 1966; McMillen, 'The Role of the IRA', p. 6.

90 In 1933 the government issued a regulation stating that:
Any person who has in his possession, or displays, or causes to be displayed, or assists

in displaying or in causing to be displayed in any public place . . . any emblem, flag or other symbol consisting of three vertical or horizontal stripes coloured respectively green, white and yellow purporting to be an emblem, flag or symbol representing the Irish Republican Army . . . An Irish Republic . . . or . . . any . . . unlawful association shall be guilty of an offence.

(Donohue, 'Regulating Northern Ireland', p. 1107).

91 Donohue, 'Regulating Northern Ireland', p. 1108.
92 PRONI, HA/32/2/8 (16), Magherafelt District Loyal Orange Lodge No. 3 to Brian McConnell, 21 February 1966.
93 PRONI, HA/32/2/19 (11), Apprentice Boys of Derry, Belfast and District Amalgamated Committee to Brian McConnell, 5 March 1966.
94 McMillen, 'The Role of the IRA', p. 6.
95 Ibid.
96 *Ulster Gazette and Armagh Standard*, 10 February 1966.
97 Ibid.
98 Ibid.
99 PRONI, HA/32/2/8 (6), John D. Taylor to Brian McConnell, on behalf of Killyman District Loyal Orange Lodge, 27 January 1966.
100 PRONI, HA/32/2/8 (8), J.E. Greeves to Sir Albert Kennedy, Inspector General, RUC, Belfast, 31 January 1966.
101 PRONI, HA/32/2/8 (9–10), Report of the County Inspector, Tyrone regarding 'Easter Commemoration 1966', 9 February 1966.
102 Ibid.
103 Ibid.
104 Ibid.
105 Ibid.
106 PRONI, HA/32/2/8 (12), J.E. Greeves, Ministry of Home Affairs to S.S. Hopkins, County Inspector, RUC Headquarters, Belfast, 14 February 1966.
107 PRONI, HA/32/2/19 (28), Norman Porter to Brian McConnell, 14 April 1966.
108 PRONI, HA/32/2/19 (29), Brian McConnell to Norman Porter, 15 April 1966.
109 Seán Swan, *Official Irish Republicanism, 1962–1972* (www.lulu.com, 2007), p. 122.
110 *Honesty*, 19 April 1930, sited in Ewan Morris, *Our Own Devices: National Symbols and Political Conflict in Twentieth-Century Ireland* (Dublin: Irish Academic Press, 2005), p. 46.
111 NAI DT, 98/6/495, 'Review of Unlawful and Allied Organisations: December 1, 1964, to November 21, 1966', Report from the Commissioner, An Garda Síochána, November 1966.
112 *Irish Press*, 1 April 1964. Also see Swan, *Official Irish Republicanism*, pp. 122–4.
113 *Sunday Press*, 16 February 1964.
114 *Sunday Independent*, 29 March 1964.
115 NAI DT, 98/6/495, 'Review of Unlawful and Allied Organisations'.
116 Ibid.
117 *Cuimhneachán 1916–1966* (Dublin: Department of External Affairs, 1966), p. 93.
118 Military Archives Cathal Brugha Barracks, Department of Defence, 48151/3 (118), Margaret McDermott, Rose McDermott and K.B. Keany to Minster of Defence, 2 April 1966.
119 *New York Times*, 11 April 1966.
120 PRONI, HA/32/2/19 (24), Ministry of Home Affairs to the Prime Minister's Office, 31 March 1966.
121 Donohue, *Regulating Northern Ireland*, p. 1096.
122 Ibid.

123 *The Irish Times*, 18 April 1966.

124 Ibid.

125 *Belfast Telegraph*, 18 April 1966.

126 PRONI, HA/32/2/8 (77), William Craig to Walter Williams, Grand Secretary, Grand Orange Lodge of Ireland, 9 February 1967.

127 Ibid.

128 NICD, vol. 63, col. 242, 24 March 1966.

129 NICD, vol. 63, col. 245, 24 March 1966. O'Reilly had said:
I do not think there is a great possibility of strife or trouble because of these celebrations. I think in the main they will be held in areas where they will give little or no offence to people with other views. It is certainly the duty of the Government to permit citizens to hold peaceable celebrations. That is their first duty. It is their duty to do everything possible to keep the peace. (NICD, vol. 63, col. 240, 24 March 1966).

130 PRONI, HA/32/2/19 (4), From the Inspector General of the RUC to the Secretary of the Ministry of Home Affairs, 1 December 1965.

131 *New York Times*, 6 April 1966.

132 NICD, vol. 62, cols 1412–13, 24 February 1966.

133 *Belfast Newsletter*, 30 April 1966.

134 PRONI, HA/32/2/8 (55), Memorandum by J.E. Greeves of a telephone conversation with Noel Docherty, 6 April 1966.

135 NICD, vol. 63, col. 1509, 25 May 1966.

136 PRONI, HA/32/2/13, Statement by Minister of Home Affairs, House of Commons, 7 March 1967.

137 For the repercussions for the O'Neill administration see O'Donnell, 'Pragmatism Versus Unity', pp. 261–5.

138 David Trimble, *The Easter Rebellion of 1916* (Lurgan: Ulster Society, 1992), pp. 33–4.

CHAPTER FOUR

1 Dermot Bolger (ed.), *Letters from the New Island: 16 on 16 Irish Writers on the Easter Rising* (Dublin: Raven Arts Press, 1988), pp. 37–8. MacAnna's pageant, *Aiséirí*, was funded by the commemoration committee and was part of the official programme of events.

2 *Tablet*, 9 April 1966.

3 Ibid.

4 Emer Nolan, 'Modernism and the Irish Revival', in Joe Cleary and Claire Connolly, (eds), *The Cambridge Companion to Modern Irish Culture* (Cambridge: Cambridge University Press, 2005), pp. 159–60.

5 Joe Cleary, 'Introduction: Ireland and Modernity', in Cleary and Connolly, *Cambridge Companion*, p. 2.

6 National Archives of Ireland, Government Information Service, 1/222, Preliminary statement by the taoiseach for a press conference, Leinster House, 8 November 1966.

7 National Archives of Ireland, Department of External Affairs, 610/20/5, From External Affairs to All Missions, 22 November 1965.

8 Elaine Sisson, *Pearse's Patriots: St Enda's and the Cult of Boyhood* (Cork: Cork University Press, 2005), p. 91.

9 Ibid., p. 83.

10 Ibid., p. 80.

11 Ibid., p. 98.

12 Declan Kiberd, *Inventing Ireland: The Literature of a Modern Nation* (London:Vintage, 1996), p. 103.

13 Walter Benjamin, *Illuminations* (London: Pimlico, 1999), pp. 245–6.

14 *RTV Guide*, April 1966, p. 28.

15 Jay Winter and Emmanuel Sivan, *War and Remembrance in the Twentieth Century* (Cambridge: Cambridge University Press, 2000), p. 3.

16 Ann Rigney, 'Plenitude, Scarcity and the Circulation of Cultural Memory', *Journal of European Studies*, vol. 35, issue 1, March 2005, p. 14.

17 See Carole Holohan's work on young people and the commemoration, 'More than a Revival of Memories? 1960s Youth and the 1916 Rising', in M.E. Daly and M. O'Callaghan, *1916 in 1966: Commemorating the Easter Rising* (Dublin: Royal Irish Academy, 2007), pp. 173–97.

18 GAA Ard Comhairle, 4 February 1966. I am grateful to Carole Holohan for this reference.

19 Bryan MacMahon, *Seachtar Fear, Seacht Lá*, unpublished script, p. 2.

20 Ibid., pp. 3–4.

21 Ibid., p. 6.

22 Ibid.

23 Ibid., p. 7.

24 Ibid., p. 9.

25 Ibid., p. 15.

26 Ibid., p. 31.

27 *Weekend Telegraph*, 6 April 1966.

28 *Hibernia*, January 1966, p. 15.

29 Max Caulfield, *The Easter Rebellion* (London: Four Square, 1965).

30 *RTV Guide*, 8 April 1966, p. 3.

31 *Culloden*, dir. Peter Watkins (1964), BBC.

32 Radio Telefís Éireann Archives (hereafter cited as RTÉ Archives), 'Radio Éireann Authority, Agenda and Documentation', 22 September 1965. Nowlan had been brought on board by Francis McManus. I am indebted to Prof. Kevin B. Nowlan for giving generously of his time to discuss the 1966 commemoration.

33 *RTÉ Annual Report 1967*, p. 7.

34 Ibid., p. 4.

35 RTÉ Archives, 'Radio Éireann Authority minutes' (hereafter cited as Authority minutes), 20 October 1965. The combined radio and television output was known as Radio Telefís Éireann after 1961, and the broadcasting authority continued under the name Radio Éireann Authority. R.J. Savage, *Irish Television: The Political and Social Origins* (Cork: Cork University Press, 1996), p. 92.

36 RTÉ Archives, Authority minutes, 11 May 1966. The budget for commemorative radio programmes was £3,400 and was exceeded by £1,100.

37 RTÉ Archives, 'RTÉ Monthly Report' (hereafter cited as 'Monthly Report'), March 1966. *On Behalf of the Provisional Government* was a series of half-hour programmes on the seven signatories of the Proclamation which included interviews with relatives and friends. I would like to thank the producer of the programmes, Aindreas Ó Gallchóir, for discussing the programmes with me. This documentary series made a significant impact on its audience and was more critically acclaimed than *Insurrection*. See Brian Lynch, 'Through the Eyes of 1916', *History Ireland*, March/April, 2006, pp. 54–7.

38 RTÉ Archives, 'Monthly Report', March 1966; Authority minutes, 20 October 1965.

39 RTÉ Archives, Authority minutes, 30 July 1965. For a discussion of the internal politics of the RTÉ Authority at this time see Robert J. Savage, *A Loss of Innocence? Television and Irish Society 1960–72* (Manchester: Manchester University Press, 2010), pp. 90–102.

40 National Archives of Ireland, Department of the Taoiseach (hereafter cited as NAI DT), 97/6/158, Seán Lemass to Joseph Brennan, 24 July 1965.

41 RTÉ Archives, Authority minutes, 30 July 1965.

42 NAI DT, 97/6/160, Report from the commemoration committee (no date).

43 *RTV Guide*, 8 April 1966, p. 5.

44 Ibid.

45 *The Voice of the Rising* was broadcast at 6.45 pm on Easter Sunday, 10 April 1966.

46 *RTV Guide*, 8 April 1966, p. 28.

47 *RTÉ Annual Report*, 1967, p. 5.

48 RTÉ Archive, TAM surveys.

49 *The Times*, 17 January 1966.

50 *Western People*, 5 February 1966.

51 *RTV Guide*, 8 April 1966.

52 Ibid.

53 *Insurrection*, dir. Louis Lentin, RTÉ, Episode 1, 'There Will Be No Rising'.

54 Luke Gibbons, 'Narratives of the Nation: Fact, Fiction and Irish Cinema', in Luke Dodd (ed.), *Nationalisms: Visions and Revision* (Dublin: Film Institute of Ireland, 1999), p. 66.

55 *RTV Guide*, 13 May 1966. The TAM ratings for the week ending April 17 1966 showed the top ten television shows to be: (1) *Insurrection*; (2) *The Riordans*; (3) *The Virginian*; (4) *Tolka Row*; (5) *Insurrection*; (6) *The Late Late Show*; (7) *Insurrection*, *Insurrection* and *On Behalf of the Provisional Government*; (10) *Quicksilver, Insurrection* and *School Around the Corner*.

56 Bolger, *16 on 16*, p. 41.

57 Peter Taylor, *Provos: The IRA and Sinn Féin* (London: Bloomsbury, 1997), p. 6.

58 James Moran, *Staging the Easter Rising: 1916 as Theatre* (Cork: Cork University Press, 2005), p. 115. In fact Nowlan's main criticism of *Insurrection* is that the conceit of the news broadcast was rather gauche.

59 For a brief discussion of this see Declan Kiberd, 'The Elephant of Revolutionary Forgetfulness', in Máirín Ní Dhonnchadha and Theo Dorgan (eds), *Revising the Rising* (Derry: Field Day, 1991), p. 2. Peter Taylor makes a direct link between the programme and the desire of a young recruit to join the IRA. Taylor, *Provos*, p.6.

60 Kiberd, 'The Elephant of Forgetfulness', p. 2.

61 Harvey O'Brien, *The Real Ireland: The Evolution of Ireland in Documentary Film* (Manchester: Manchester University Press, 2004).

62 Theodor Adorno, *The Culture Industry: Selected Essays on Mass Culture* (London: Routledge, 1991), p. 161.

63 *Insurrection*, Episode 1.

64 Ibid.

65 *Insurrection*, Episode 2, 'We've Put Emmet in the Shade'.

66 *Insurrection*, Episode 1.

67 Moran, *Staging the Easter Rising*, p. 115.

68 *Insurrection*, Episode 5, 'When We Are All Wiped Out'.

69 *Insurrection*, Episode 4, 'Two Thousand Sherwood Foresters'.

70 Ibid.

71 *Insurrection*, Episode 5.

72 RTÉ Archive, Authority minutes, 30 March 1966. The presence of Collins is certainly exaggerated.
73 RTÉ Archives, Authority minutes, 20 April 1966.
74 Caulfield, *Easter Rebellion*, p. 63.
75 *Insurrection*, Episode 5.
76 BBC2 was still in its infancy and would have been received by only a minority of the population.
77 National Archives of Ireland, Department of External Affairs, 2000/14/106, RTÉ to the Department of External Affairs, 12 May 1966.
78 RTÉ Archives, Authority minutes, 11 May 1966.
79 Lynch, 'Through the Eyes of 1916', p. 57.
80 Jan Assmann, 'Collective Memory and Cultural Identity', *New German Critique*, issue 65, 1995, p. 130.
81 *RTV Guide*, 8 April 1966.

CHAPTER FIVE

1 Office of Public Works (hereafter cited as OPW), A/96/6/9/1 (17) and (24), 'Garden of Remembrance', Oisín Kelly to Raymond McGrath, 13 March 1958 and 23 January 1959. 'Bearna Baogail' translates as the 'violent gap' or 'gap of danger'.
2 See Yvonne Whelan, *Reinventing Modern Dublin: Streetscape, Iconography and the Politics of Identity* (Dublin: University College Dublin Press, 2003).
3 *Irish Times*, 22 January 1964. Michael Quill died suddenly in January 1966 and did not live to see the jubilee.
4 *Sunday Press*, 21 May 1961.
5 Quoted in the *Evening Herald*, 17 January 1961.
6 National Archives of Ireland, Department of the Taoiseach (hereafter cited as NAI DT), S4523C/95, 7 July 1964. Jim Ryan, the minister for finance, had raised, for informal parliamentary discussion, the issue of replacing Nelson with Patrick Pearse for the jubilee commemoration. However, Lemass replied with concerns that such an act would require compensation to the trustees, would be unpopular with traders on O'Connell Street and it was unlikely that a statue would be ready for 1966. He concluded, 'I agree we should look at the question, but I do not think we will find it easy to reach the right answers.'
7 'Up Went Nelson' by the Go-Lucky Four stayed at the top of the Irish charts for eight weeks.
8 NAI DT, 97/6/18, 9 March 1966.
9 In fact a Dáil statement noted that claims for compensation for the first explosion amounted to £18,924 and claims after the second explosion valued £4,180. *Irish Independent*, 8 March 1967.
10 National Archives of Ireland, Department of External Affairs (hereafter cited as NAI DEA), 2000/14/72, Smith McGrath, District Sales Manager, Irish International Airlines, Toronto, to John Belton, 14 March 1966.
11 NAI DEA, Embassy Releases 2003, 2001/37/781, P153 II, *Congressional Record: Proceedings of 89th Congress, Second Session*, 8 March 1966.
12 NAI DEA, Embassy Releases 2003, 2001/37/781 P153 II, P. de Paor, Irish Embassy, Washington, to B. Uas. Ó Ceallaigh, Irish Consulate General, Chicago, 4 April 1966. However, Sweeney was advocating political action, not violence, in his speech.
13 A.J. Lerner, 'The Nineteenth-Century Monument and the Embodiment of National Time', in Marjorie Ringrose and A.J. Lerner (eds), *Reimagining the Nation*

(Buckingham: Open University Press, 1993), p. 180. Lerner draws on the work of E.H. Kantorowicz, *The King's Two Bodies: A Study in Medieval Political Theology* (Princeton, NJ: Princeton University Press, 1957).

14 Lerner, 'The Nineteenth-Century Monument, pp. 177–81.
15 Quoted in the *Evening Herald*, 11 April 1966.
16 Ibid.
17 *Irish Catholic*, 10 February 1966.
18 Ibid.
19 James E.Young, *Holocaust Memorials and Meaning* (New Haven, CT:Yale University Press, 1993), p. 7.
20 Katherine Verdery, *The Political Lives of Dead Bodies: Reburial and Postsocialist Change* (New York: University of Columbia Press, 1999), p. 5.
21 Ibid., p. 6.
22 NAI, Office of the Secretary to the President, 97/7/81 (no date). Essay by Clara Connelly, Convent FCJ, Bunclody, County Wexford, joint runner-up in the under-18 essay competition in English, '1916–2016'.
23 *Church of Ireland Gazette*, 18 March 1966.
24 Ibid.
25 *Vancouver Washington Columbian*, 7 April 1966; *Guardian*, 9 March 1966.
26 See Anne Dolan, *Commemorating the Irish Civil War: History and Memory, 1923–2000* (Cambridge: Cambridge University Press, 2003); Nuala Johnston, *Ireland, the Great War and the Geography of Remembrance* (Cambridge: Cambridge University Press, 2003).
27 NAI DT, S5004E/62, Seán Lemass to Jim Ryan, 21 December 1962; Ryan to Lemass, 31 December 1962.
28 OPW, A99/3/5 (2) 'Thomas Davis statue', Corporation of Dublin to the Department of Defence, 26 July 1945.
29 OPW, A99/3/5 (220) 'Davis', Arts Council to the Office of Public Works, 9 May 1962.
30 NAI DT, S13610D/62, Cabinet Minute, 23 November, 1962.
31 NAI DT, S13610D/62, Cabinet Minute, 27 November, 1962.
32 NAI DT, S13610D/63, Cabinet Minute, 19 February 1963.
33 Judith Hill, *Irish Public Sculpture: A History* (Dublin: Four Courts Press, 1998), p. 202.
34 NAI DT, S13610D/63, Cabinet Minute, 17 April 1963.
35 *Irish Times*, 10 December 1966; *Donegal People's Press*, 29 April 1966.
36 NAI DT, 97/6/158, Minutes of the third meeting of the commemoration committee, 30 April 1965.
37 *Cuimhneachán 1916–1966: A Record of Ireland's Commemoration of the 1916 Rising* (Dublin: Department of External Affairs, 1966), p. 62.
38 OPW, A99/3/5 (153), 'Davis', Supplementary notes for Parliamentary Questions, 14 November 1960; OPW, A99/3/5 (220), 'Davis', Arts Council to the Office of Public Works, 9 May 1962.
39 *Cuimhneachán*, p. 62.
40 OPW, A99/3/33 (63), 'Davis', Memorandum for the Chairman of the Office of Public Works, 16 April 1966.
41 Thomas Davis, *National and Historical Ballads, Songs, and Poems* (Dublin: James Duffy, 1869), p. 147.
42 D.G. Boyce, *Nationalism in Ireland* (London: Routledge, 1991, second edition), p. 164.
43 *RTV Guide*, 16 December 1966.
44 F.X. Martin, '1916: Myth, Fact and Mystery', *Studia Hibernia*, no. 7, 1967, p. 9.

45   Luke Gibbons, *Transformations in Irish Culture* (Cork: Field Day, 1996), pp. 145–6.
46   Anderson's seminal work illustrated ways in which the newspaper incorporated senses of time, space and ritual that were central to the imagined unity that underlines the nation. Benedict Anderson, *Imagined Communities: Reflections on the Origins and Spread of Nationalism* (London and New York: Verso, 1983).
47   Gibbons, *Transformations in Irish Culture*, pp. 145–6.
48   See Roisín Higgins, 'The Nation Reading Rooms', in James Murphy (ed.), *The History of the Irish Book*, vol. IV (Oxford: Oxford University Press, 2011), p. 271.
49   NAI DEA, 2000/14/83, William Fay to Department of External Affairs, 23 June 1966.
50   Ibid.
51   Ibid.
52   NAI DT, 96/9/96, Seán Dowling to Piaras Mac Lochlainn, 27 October 1965. Dowling was an Old IRA man who became chairman of the Restoration Committee of Kilmainham Jail and was one of the original members of the government's commemoration committee for the fiftieth anniversary of the Easter Rising.
53   *Irish Times*, 14 April 1966.
54   *Irish Catholic*, 10 February 1966.
55   Marianne Elliott, *Robert Emmet: The Making of a Legend* (London: Profile, 2004), p. 212.
56   T.D. Sullivan, 'Emmet', *Irish People*, 15 August 1903, in Elliott, *Robert Emmet*, p. 168.
57   NAI DEA, 2000/14/97, Fay to the Department of External Affairs, 9 November 1965; NAI DEA, 2000/14/98, Fay to External Affairs, 19 January 1965.
58   NAI DT, 96/6/96, Fay to the Department of External Affairs, 20 January 1966.
59   Máirín Allen, 'Jerome Connor – Two', *Capuchin Annual*, 1964, p. 364.
60   Ibid.
61   *New York Morning Telegraph*, 6 March 1916.
62   OPW, A/96/6/9/1 (29) 'Garden', Report of Oisín Kelly to the Office of Public Works, 12 May 1959.
63   Ibid.
64   OPW, A/96/6/9/1 (34), 'Garden', Memo from McGrath regarding Kelly's report, 26 May 1959.
65   Quoted in Luke Gibbons, 'Where Wolfe Tone's Statue was Not: Joyce, Monuments and Memory', in Ian McBride (ed.), *History and Memory in Modern Ireland* (Cambridge: Cambridge University Press), p. 141.
66   University College Dublin Archive (hereafter cited as UCDA), de Valera Papers, P150/3376, Copy of de Valera's speech (no date).
67   OPW, A/96/6/9/1 (2), 'Garden', Report accompanying Hanly's original proposal for the architectural competition (no date).
68   For a comparative look at the symbolism of the Garden of Remembrance and the Islandbridge First World War Memorial, see Síghle Bhreathnach-Lynch, 'Commemorating the Hero in Newly Independent Ireland: Expressions of Nationhood in Bronze and Stone', in L.W. McBride (ed.), *Images, Icons and the Nationalist Imagination* (Dublin: Four Courts Press, 1999), pp. 158–63; Whelan, *Reinventing Modern Dublin*, pp. 177–85.
69   UCDA de Valera Papers, P150/3376, Copy of de Valera's speech (no date).
70   UCD de Valera Papers, P150/3376, 'Note on features of interest by the architect Mr Dáithí Hanly' (no date).
71   OPW, A/96/6/9/1, (29), 'Garden', Report from Kelly, 12 May 1966.

72 OPW, A/96/6/9/1 (28), 'Garden', Kelly to McGrath, 12 May 1966.
73 OPW, A/96/6/9/1 (24), 'Garden', Kelly to McGrath, 23 January 1959.
74 OPW, A/96/6/9/1 (30), 'Garden', Report from Kelly, 12 May 1966.
75 Ibid.
76 OPW, A/96/6/9/1 (152), 'Garden', Seán Lemass to Seán MacEntee, 21 November 1963.
77 OPW, A/96/6/9/1 (312), 'Garden', Jim Gibbons to Seán Lemass, 14 July 1965.
78 NAI DT, 96/6/193, Report for the Office of Public Works, 1 November 1965.
79 NAI DT, 96/6/193, Statement issued by the Government Information Service on behalf of the Parliamentary Secretary to the Minister for Finance, 26 February 1966.
80 *Connaght Sentinel*, 16 April 1962.
81 Ibid.
82 OPW, A/96/6/9/1 (52), 'Garden', Memorandum from McGrath, 18 October 1960.
83 *Kerryman*, 8 February 1964.
84 Dáil Debates, vol. 273, 26 June 1974.
85 OPW, A/96/6/9/1 (319), 'Garden', Memorandum by McGrath, 23 September 1965.
86 Paddy Stephenson was a veteran of the Easter Rising and founder of the Old Dublin Society.
87 Kilmainham Gaol Archive (hereafter cited as KGA), Lorcan C.G. Leonard, 'The Kilmainham Project As I Dreamt and Lived It', unpublished, no date, p. 3.
88 NAI DT, S6521D/63, Memorandum for the government from the Minister for Finance, 13 February 1960.
89 *Irish Times*, 19 December 1985.
90 KGA, Leonard to Seán Dowling, 9 June 1958.
91 *Irish Times*, 30 November 1960.
92 NAI DEA, London Embassy, F100/11/8, Hugh McCann to the Department of External Affairs, 5 December 1961.
93 *Dublin Historical Record*, vol. XIV, no. 3, July 1957.
94 The Kilmainham Jail Restoration Society, *Kilmainham* (Dublin: Kilmainham Jail Restoration Society, 1961), p. 19.
95 Ibid.
96 Ibid., pp. 1–13.
97 KGA, Leonard, 'Kilmainham Project', p. 4.
98 *Irish Press*, 11 April 1966.
99 Pierre Nora, 'Between Memory and History: Les Lieux de Mémoire', *Representations*, vol. 26 (Spring, 1989), p. 13.
100 James Edward Young, *The Texture of Memory: Holocaust Memorials and Meanings* (London and New Haven: Yale University Press, 1993), p. 5.

CHAPTER SIX

1 *Daily Express*, 23 March 1966.
2 Ibid., 22 March 1966; 26 March 1966.
3 Other members of the Abbey Company also participated in the Rising and were remembered in a plaque unveiled by Seán Lemass at the opening of the new Abbey Theatre in July 1966. Hugh Hunt, *The Abbey: Ireland's National Theatre, 1904–1978* (Dublin: Gill & Macmillan, 1979), p. 195.
4 William T. Thompson, *The Imagination of an Insurrection, Easter 1916: A Study of an Ideological Movement* (Oxford: Oxford University Press, 1967), p. ix. Thirty years later

Declan Kiberd also described the leaders as having 'offered their lives to the public as works of art' and the Rising as 'street theatre'. Declan Kiberd, *Inventing Ireland: The Literature of the Modern Nation* (London: Vintage, 1996), pp. 201–3.

5   Thompson, *The Imagination of an Insurrection*, p. 75.

6   'Editorial', *Dublin Magazine*, Spring 1966, pp. 5–7.

7   Ibid., p. 6.

8   Eavan Boland, 'Aspects of Pearse', *Dublin Magazine*, Spring 1966, p. 50.

9   Kiberd, *Inventing Ireland*, p. 200.

10   John McGahern, *Memoir* (London: Faber & Faber, 2005), p. 251.

11   Seamus Heaney, *Preoccupations: Selected Prose, 1968–1978* (London and Boston: Faber & Faber, 1984), p. 47.

12   Heaney, *Preoccupations*, p. 52.

13   Ibid., p. 56.

14   National Archives of Ireland, Department of External Affairs (hereafter cited as NAI DEA), 2000/14/90, Ambassador, Canberra, to External Affairs, 27 April 1966.

15   *The Bulletin*, 16 April 1966.

16   *Sunday Star*, 10 April 1966. McGrory's article, described as 'excellent' by the embassy in Washington, was considered of a much higher standard than the coverage of either the *New York Times* or the *Herald Tribune*, NAI DEA, 2001/37/781, William Fay to Department of External Affairs, 2 May 1966.

17   *New York Times*, 11 April 1966.

18   *San Francisco Examiner and News*, 17 April 1966.

19   *Sunday Star*, 10 April 1966.

20   NAI DEA, 2000/14/77, Embassy in Lagos to Department of External Affairs, 25 March 1966. *Rhapsody of a River* (1965) was directed by Louis Marcus and sponsored by Gael Linn and the Department of External Affairs; NAI, DEA, 2000/14/77, Embassy in Lisbon to Department of External Affairs, 9 February 1966. *Yeats Country* won a Golden Bear at the Berlin Film Festival, a diploma of merit at the Edinburgh Film Festival, first prize at the Chicago Film Festival and first prize for best colour short at the Barcelona International Film Festival as well as being nominated for an Oscar. See Harvey O'Brien, *The Real Ireland: The Evolution of Ireland in Documentary Film* (Manchester: Manchester University Press, 2004), p. 145.

21   John Wilson Foster, *Colonial Consequences: Essays in Irish Literature and Culture* (Dublin: Lilliput Press, 1991), p. 133.

22   Joseph Hone, *W.B. Yeats, 1865–1939* (London: Macmillan, 1965), p. 300, quoted in Wilson Foster, *Colonial Consequences*, p. 134.

23   There is no conclusive answer as to why Yeats did not publish 'Easter 1916' until 1920. For a discussion of the issue see Terence Brown, *The Life of W.B. Yeats: A Critical Biography* (Dublin: Gill & Macmillan, 2001), pp. 234–6.

24   NAI DT, 97/6/159, Erskine Childers to Michael Hilliard, 17 August 1965 and Military Archives Cathal Brugha Barracks, Department of Defence, 47969 (3), 10 September 1965, Childers to Hilliard, 10 September 1965.

25   James Stephens, 'Spring – 1916', in Edna C. Fitzhenry (ed.), *Nineteen-Sixteen: An Anthology* (Dublin: Browne & Nolan, 1966), p. 65.

26   James Stephens, *The Insurrection in Dublin* (Dublin: Scepter Books, 1965), p. 78.

27   Ibid., p. 93.

28   Ibid., p. 94.

29   Joyce Kilmer, 'Easter Week', in Fitzhenry, *Nineteen-Sixteen: An Anthology*, pp. 97–8.

30   M. Ó Dubhghaill, *Insurrection Fires at Eastertide: A Golden Jubilee Anthology of the*

Easter Rising (Cork: Mercier Press, 1966), p. vii; Fitzhenry, *Nineteen-Sixteen: An Anthology*, pp. 97–8.

31 University College Dublin Archives (hereafter UCDA), de Valera Papers, P150/3400, Souvenir Brochure, Mallow 1966.

32 *Éire-Ireland: Weekly Bulletin of the Department of External Affairs*, 15 February 1966, no. 729, p. 5.

33 National Archives of Ireland, Government Information Service (hereafter NAI GIS), 1/221, Speech at the inaugural meeting of the Law Students' Debating Society of Ireland, King's Inns, Dublin, 18 February 1966.

34 Fran Brearton has argued that the First World War mattered, and matters, to Ireland, not, as for Churchill or, more generally, English consciousness, because it entailed a break with the past, the destruction of pre-war institutions, but because it played a part in a history whose main themes and 'institutions' existed long before the Great War and continued long after it was over. Fran Brearton, *The Great War in Irish Poetry: W.B. Yeats to Michael Longley* (Oxford: Oxford University Press, 2000), p. 7.

35 For a comprehensive discussion of these issues see ibid., pp. 3–42.

36 Walter Macken, *The Scorching Wind* (Basingtoke: Pan, 1988), p. 42. This novel was first published by Macmillan in 1964 and reissued by Pan (an imprint of Macmillan) in 1966.

37 Ibid., p. 62.

38 Garrett FitzGerald, 'The Significance of 1916', *Studies*, Spring 1966, p. 29.

39 Ibid., p. 31.

40 Ibid.

41 NAI GIS, 1/221, Speech at the inaugural meeting of the Law Students' Debating Society of Ireland, King's Inns, Dublin, 18 February 1966.

42 Henry Harris, 'The Other Half Million', in Owen Dudley Edwards and Fergus Pyle (eds), *1916: The Easter Rising* (London: MacGibbon & Kee, 1968), p. 114.

43 *Éire-Ireland: Weekly Bulletin of the Department of External Affairs*, 15 February 1966, no. 729, p. 6.

44 Harris, 'The Other Half Million', p. 108.

45 Brearton, *The Great War in Irish Poetry*, pp. 20–1.

46 Quoted in J.B. Lyons, *The Enigma of Tom Kettle* (Dublin: Glendale Press, 1983), p. 293.

47 NAI GIS, 1/77, Address by George Colley, National Museum, Dublin, 19 April 1966. The donation of items belonging to Capt. Henry de Courcy (who had served in the British forces during the Rising and had been present when the surrender notice had been received from Pearse) had been agreed with his son after extracts of the captain's diary of the period were serialised in the *Sunday Express*. The newspaper had suggested that he make the gift and had made the arrangements and paid expenses on the condition that it got the exclusive story. The donation included one of the original surrender manifestos by Pearse, Connolly and MacDonagh; several typed orders signed in Connolly's own handwriting; the original hand-written safe-conduct letter from General Lowe to Nurse O'Farrell in return for her assistance; and the Proclamation, posters and war sheets printed or published by both sides. NAI DEA, 2000/14/100, Confidential memorandum by Seán Ronan, Department of External Affairs.

48 *RTV Guide*, 8 April 1966, p. 35.

49 The RTÉ Symphony Orchestra performed the cantata with Our Lady's Choral Society, conducted by Tibor Paul and broadcast live on Radio Éireann with commentary by Terry Wogan.

50 *RTV Guide*, 8 April 1966, p. 35.
51 Ibid.
52 Brian Boydell, *A Terrible Beauty is Born* (1965).
53 *RTV Guide*, 8 April 1966, p. 35.
54 Tom M. Kettle, *Poems and Parodies* (Dublin:Talbot Press, 1916), pp. 62–3.
55 Ibid., p. 65.
56 Quoted in Lyons, *The Enigma of Tom Kettle*, p. 298.
57 Bill Nichols, *Introduction to Documentary* (Bloomington and Indianapolis: Indiana University Press, 2001), p. 51.
58 Neil Harris, 'Museums and Controversy: Some Introductory Reflections', *Journal of American History*, December 1995, p. 1107. I am grateful to Kris Brown for this reference.
59 Thomas Richards, *The Imperial Archive: Knowledge and the Fantasy of Empire* (London and New York:Verso, 1993), p. 4.
60 Ibid., p. 3.
61 Ibid., p. 3.
62 The origins of the National Museum of Ireland lie with the Science and Art Museum Act of 1877 which led to the transfer of buildings and collections of the Royal Dublin Society to state ownership. The building on Kildare Street was the original home of the Dublin Museum of Science and Art, which opened in 1890.
63 Benedict Anderson, *Imagined Communities: Reflections on the Origins and Spread of Nationalism* (London and New York:Verso, 1983), p. 183.
64 National Gallery of Ireland, *Cuimhneachán 1916: A Commemorative Exhibition of the Irish Rebellion 1916* (Dublin: Dolmen Press Limited, 1966), p. 11. This note referred to the painting by Daniel Maclise, *The Marriage of Richard De Clare, Earl of Pembroke, Surnamed Strongbow, with Eva, Daughter of Dermot MacMorrogh, King of Leinster, after the Capture of Waterford in 1170* (first exhibited 1854).
65 National Gallery of Ireland, *Cuimhneachán 1916*, p. 5.
66 Ibid.
67 NAI DEA, 2000/14/87, Address by Patrick Hillery on behalf of the Minister for Education at the 1916 Exhibition in the National Museum, Dublin, 12 April 1966.
68 Ibid.
69 NAI DEA, 2000/14/84, List of cases in the 1916 Exhibition.
70 Ibid.
71 Ibid.
72 Nichols, *Introduction to Documentary*, p. xi.
73 Ibid., p. 22.
74 Ibid., pp. 28–9.
75 Ibid., p. 30.
76 NAI DEA, 2000/14/71, Gael Linn to Department of External Affairs (no name, no date).
77 NAI DT, 97/6/158, Minutes of the third meeting of the commemoration committee, 30 April 1965.
78 Gael Linn Archive [photocopy, Irish Film Institute Archive] (hereafter cited as GLA), Box 78/63, Gael Linn to Department of External Affairs, 1965 (no exact date).
79 Ibid.
80 NAI DEA, 2000/14/71, Frank Cofffey to Piaras Mac Lochlainn, 9 June 1965.
81 GLA, Box 78/59, Budget for *An Tine Bheo*.
82 NAI DEA, 2000/14/71, *An Tine Bheo* script.

83 NAI DEA, 2000/14/71, *An Tine Bheo* script outline.

84 Bernardine Truden, *Recollections of the 50th Anniversary of the Easter Rising of 1916* (Dublin, 1966). This collection of articles was originally published in *The Boston Globe*.

85 *An Tine Bheo*, dir. Gael Linn, 1966 (translation Gael Linn).

86 *An Tine Bheo* (translation Gael Linn).

87 GIS 1/221, Speech by Seán Lemass at the inaugural meeting of the Law Students' Debating Society of Ireland, Kings Inns, Dublin, 18 February 1966.

88 *An Tine Bheo.*

89 NAI DEA, Madrid Embassy, IC 3/9, Department of External Affairs to All Missions, 16 February 1966.

90 For correspondence see NAI DEA, 2000/14/71.

91 GLA, Box 78/65, Pairas Mac Lochlainn to Riobard Mac Gabhrán, 25 November 1965.

92 NAI DEA, 2000/14/77, Frank Coffey to Seán Ronan, 20 October 1965.

93 NAI DEA, 2000/14/77, Frank Coffey to Piaras Mac Lochlainn, 5 November 1965.

94 NAI DEA, Madrid Embassy, IC 3/9, Department of External Affairs to All Missions, 16 January 1965.

95 NAI DEA, 2000/14/77, Frank Coffey to George Morrison, 12 November 1965.

96 NAI DEA, 2000/14/77, Department of External Affairs to George Morrison, 4 February 1966.

97 NAI DEA, 2000/14/77, Frank Coffey to Piaras Mac Lochlainn, 5 November 1965.

98 NAI, DEA, 2000/14/77, Frank Coffey to Piaras Mac Lochlainn, 18 October 1965.

99 IFIA, SOF/9/11, *The Irish Rising.*

100 NAI DEA, 2000/14/77, 'The Irish Rising 1916' (1966), script.

101 NAI DEA, 2000/14/77, Consulate in San Francisco to Department of External Affairs (no date).

102 NAI, DEA, 2000/14/77, Embassy in Brussels to Department of External Affairs, 21 June 1966.

103 NAI DEA, 2000/14/77, Embassy in Berne to Department of External Affairs, 11 July 1966.

104 NAI DEA, 2000/14/77, Embassy in The Hague to Department of External Affairs, 22 March 1966 and 5 April 1966.

105 NAI DEA, 2000/14/77, Embassy in Lisbon to Department of External Affairs, 19 April 1966.

106 *Ireland On the Go*, dir. Richard Matt (A Mattco Production, 1966).

CHAPTER SEVEN

1 *New York Herald Tribune*, 13 April 1966.

2 Seán O'Faoláin, *The Irish* (London, 1969, revised edition), p. 145.

3 Quoted in W.R. Rogers, 'Ireland and Her Past', *New Statesman*, 8 April 1966.

4 Ibid.

5 Basil Payne, 'Ireland Today: Image and Reality: Some Reflections on President Kennedy's Visit', *Capuchin Annual*, 1964, pp. 301–2.

6 The Eucharistic Congress in 1932 was also dependent on an external relationship, with the Catholic Church in Rome.

7 Payne, 'Ireland Today, Image and Reality', pp. 301–5.

8 *Bord Fáilte Éireann* (Annual Report for year ending 31 March 1962), p. 14.

9 *Bord Fáilte Éireann* (Annual Report for the year ending 31 March 1964), p. 7.

10 Ibid., p. 8.

11 *Bord Fáilte Éireann* (Annual Report for the year ending 31 March 1966), p. 7.

12 National Archives of Ireland, Department of External Affairs (hereafter cited as NAI DEA), 610/20/5, Buenos Aires Embassy, Department of External Affairs to All Missions, 5 March 1965.

13 Mike Cronin and Daryl Adair, *The Wearing of the Green: A History of St Patrick's Day* (London and New York: Routledge, 2006), p. 147.

14 Ibid., p. 149.

15 Ibid., p. 167.

16 *Irish Times*, 25 March 1963, in Cronin and Adair, *The Wearing of the Green*, p. 171.

17 National Archives of Ireland, Department of the Taoiseach (hereafter cited as NAI DT) S15297A, An Tóstal, in M.E. Daly, 'Nationalism, Sentiment and Economics: Relations between Ireland and Irish America in the Postwar Years', *Éire-Ireland*, vol. 37, 2002, p. 80.

18 Daly, 'Nationalism, Sentiment and Economics', p. 81.

19 Ibid., pp. 80–1.

20 NAI DEA, 2000/14/72, Ambassador in Canberra to Department of External Affairs, 25 October 1965.

21 NAI DEA, 2000/14/72, Embassy in Ottawa to Department of External Affairs, 28 March 1966.

22 NAI DEA, 2000/14/72, Embassy in London to Department of External Affairs, 26 March 1966.

23 NAI DEA, 2000/14/72, Consulate in New York to Department of External Affairs, 7 March 1966.

24 *Bord Fáilte Éireann* (Annual Report for the year ending 31 March 1967), p. 9.

25 NAI DEA, 2000/14/79, Attendance of Foreign Press and Film Representatives.

26 NAI DEA, 2000/14/96, Memorandum by Frank Coffey, 15 March 1966.

27 The *Easter Commemoration Digest* was not an official publication, but was compared in content with *An Cosantóir*, the journal of the Irish Defence Forces. Its audience was primarily in the United States.

28 NAI DEA, 2000/14/97, Memorandum by Noel Dorr, 26 October 1965.

29 Ibid.

30 NAI DEA, 2000/14/97, William Fay to Hugh McCann, Department of External Affairs, 2 November 1965.

31 Ibid.

32 NAI DT, 97/6/161, Department of External Affairs to All Missions, 31 January 1966.

33 NAI DEA, 2000/14/77, Brendan Dillon, Counsellor, Brussels, to Department of External Affairs, 21 June 1966.

34 Roy Hattersley in a letter to the author, 15 March 2005. The letter continues: 'It was a strange decision for the Foreign Office to take and may have been the initiative of an individual minister. At the time the government was clearly anxious to show its sympathy for Irish nationalism – hence the return of Roger Casement's remains.'

35 NAI DT, 97/6/532, Note from Hugh McCann (recipient not specified), 7 March 1966.

36 NAI DT, 97/6/532. The British Museum had been displaying a tricolour which had, in fact, originated in Limerick. The flag from the GPO had the words 'Irish Republic' on green cloth.

37 *Irish Press*, 13 April 1966.

38 NAI DEA, 2000/14/102, Notes for the Tánaiste in response to a Dáil question

from Oliver J. Flanagan (no date). For greater detail on the content of the messages see Roisín Higgins, 'Projections and Reflections: Irishness and the Fiftieth Anniversary of the Easter Rising', *Éire-Ireland*, vol. 42, nos 3 & 4, Autumn & Winter 2007, pp. 11–34.

39 For a comprehensive discussion of the involvement of foreign minority nationalists in the commemoration see Daniel Leach, '"Repaying a Debt of Gratitude": Foreign Minority Nationalists and the Fiftieth Anniversary of the Easter Rising in 1966', *Éire-Ireland*, vol. 43, nos 3 & 4, Autumn and Winter 2008, pp. 267–89.

40 NAI DEA, 2000/14/78, Department of External Affairs to Piaras Mac Lochlainn (no day), December 1965.

41 NAI DEA, 2000/14/78, Ambassador in Paris to Department of External Affairs, 14 January 1966.

42 NAI DEA, 2000/14/78, Ambassador in Brussels to Department of External Affairs, 2 March 1966.

43 *Look*, 19 April 1966.

44 *San Francisco Evening Herald and News*, 17 April 1966.

45 *Vancouver Washington Columbian*, 7 April 1966.

46 *Daily Express*, 22 March 1966.

47 *Aberdeen Daily World*, 12 April 1966.

48 Sloan Wilson, 'Ireland and the Irish (Without the Usual Blarney)', *Fact Magazine*, vol. 3, no. 2 (March/April 1966), pp. 29–37.

49 Ibid.

50 Ibid.

51 NAI DEA, 98/3/11, Letter to the Taoiseach, 13 April 1966.

52 *New York Herald Tribune*, 12 April 1966.

53 Ibid.

54 NAI DEA, 98/3/10, J.A. Belton, Ambassador in Ottawa, to Department of External Affairs, 24 May 1966.

55 University College Dublin Archives, Fianna Fáil Papers, 176/772, Ard Fheis 1965.

56 *Cuimhneachán 1916–1966: A Record of Ireland's Commemoration of the 1916 Rising* (Dublin: Department of External Affairs, 1966).

57 NAI DEA, London Embassy, L114 /89, Part 2, Internal Memorandum, 10 May 1967.

58 NAI DEA, London Embassy, L114 /89, Part 2, 15 January 1968.

59 NAI DEA, 2000/14/114, Eoin MacWhite, Ambassador in Canberra, to Department of External Affairs, 10 February 1967.

60 Ibid.

61 NAI DEA, L114/89, Embassy in London to Department of External Affairs, 31 May 1965.

62 NAI DEA, L114/89, Embassy in London to Department of External Affairs, 19 July 1965.

63 Ibid.

64 Clann na hÉireann had been formed in 1964 and described itself as 'the only organisation in Britain catering for the Nationally-minded emigrant', *United Irishman*, May 1966. The IRA's assessment of their work noted that 'Their preparations for the Easter Commemorations are progressing favourably – they expect to make a lot of ground among the exiles through the public lectures which they are organising for Easter Week.' NAI DT, 98/6/495, 'Review of Unlawful and Allied Organisations: December 1, 1964, to November 21, 1966', Report from the Commissioner, An Garda Síochána, November 1966.

65 NAI DEA, L114/89, Embassy in London to Department of External Affairs, 16 February 1966.
66 NAI DEA, 2000/14/72, Eoin MacWhite, Ambassador in Canberra, to Department of External Affairs, 25 October 1965.
67 Ibid.
68 *Daily Telegraph* (Sydney), 11 April 1966.
69 NAI DEA, 2000/14/85, Eoin MacWhite to Department of External Affairs, 7 April 1966.
70 NAI DEA, 2000/14/83, Consulate in Boston to Department of External Affairs, 14 March 1966.
71 NAI DEA, 2000/14/83, Consulate in Boston to Department of External Affairs, 13 April 1966.
72 NAI DEA, 2000/14/83, Consulate in San Francisco to Department of External Affairs, 28 April 1966.
73 Ibid.
74 *Birmingham Post*, 11 April 1966.
75 NAI DEA, 2000/14/72, Consulate in New York to Department of External Affairs, 31 January 1966.
76 NAI DEA, 2000/14/83, Consulate in San Francisco to Department of External Affairs, 28 April 1966.
77 NAI DEA, 2000/14/83, Consulate in Chicago to Department of External Affairs, 28 April 1966.
78 NAI DEA, 2000/14/83, Consulate in Boston to Department of External Affairs, 23 June 2006.
79 NAI DEA, 2000/14/85, Embassy in Canberra to Department of External Affairs, 13 April 1966.
80 *Daily Sketch*, 16 April 1966; NAI DEA, 2000/14/85, Embassy in Buenos Aires, 12 April 1966.
81 NAI DEA, 2000/14/85, Embassy in New Delhi to Department of External Affairs, 12 April 1966.
82 NAI DEA, 2000/14/85, Embassy in New Delhi to Department of External Affairs, 12 April 1966.
83 NAI DEA, 2000/14/85, Embassy in New Delhi to Department of External Affairs, 12 April 1966.
84 NAI DEA, 2000/14/92.
85 NAI DEA, 6.25, Embassy in Copenhagen to Department of External Affairs, 15 November 1965.
86 NAI DT, 97/6/164, Speech by Seán Lemass on receiving the bust of General José de San Martín, Iveagh House, Dublin, 14 April 1966.
87 NAI DEA, 2000/14/85, M.L. Skentelbery, Ambassador in Buenos Aires, to Department of External Affairs, 26 April 1966.
88 NAI Office of Secretary to President, 97/7/56, Erskine Childers to Éamon de Valera, 30 March 1966; de Valera to organising committee, MIT, 1 May 1966.
89 NAI DEA, 2000/14/83, Consulate in Boston to Department of External Affairs, 27 October 1965.
90 NAI DEA, 2000/14/83, Consulate in Boston to Department of External Affairs, 23 June 1966.
91 NAI DEA, 2000/14/83, Consulate in Boston to Department of External Affairs, 16 June 1966.
92 Royal Albert Hall Archive, 1916 Commemoration Committee of London, *Ireland,*

1916–1966 (London: 1916 Commemoration Brochure, 1966).

93   *New York Times*, 10 April 1966.

94   *Oregon Journal*, 13 April 1966.

95   *Bulletin* (Australia), 16 April 1966.

96   *Weekend Telegraph* (London), 6 April 1966.

EPILOGUE

1   *Irish Spotlight*, May 1966.

2   Friedrich Nietzsche, *On the Use and Abuse of History for Life* (1873), translated by Ian Johnston 2010, http://records.viu.ca/~johnstoi/nietzsche/history.htm

3   For a more detailed look at the seventy-fifth anniversary commemoration see Roisín Higgins, 'The Changing Fortunes of National Myths: Commemorating Anzac Day and the Easter Rising', in Katie Holmes and Stuart Ward (eds), *Exhuming Passions: The Pressure of the Past in Ireland and Australia* (Dublin: Irish Academic Press, 2011), pp. 153–8.

4   Declan Kiberd, 'The Elephant of Revolutionary Forgetfulness', in Máirín Ní Dhonnchadha and Theo Dorgan (eds), *Revising the Rising* (Derry: Field Day, 1991), p. 15.

5   Edna Longley, 'The Rising, the Somme and Irish Memory', in Ní Dhonnchadha and Dorgan, *Revising the Rising*, p. 49.

6   Gearóid Ó Crualaoich, 'Responding to the Rising', in Ní Dhonnchadha and Dorgan, *Revising the Rising*, p. 68.

7   Ibid., pp. 66–7.

8   Ibid., p. 68.

9   For a discussion of the events surrounding the Rising see Gabriel Doherty, 'The Commemoration of the Ninetieth Anniversary of the Easter Rising', in Gabriel Doherty and Dermot Keogh (eds), *1916: the Long Revolution* (Cork: Mercier Press, 2006), pp. 376–407.

10   Ibid., p.379.

11   The most effective expression of these issues was the panel installation by Mannix Flynn on Leeson Street in Dublin, which translated the Proclamation into five languages: Irish, Polish, Russian, Chinese and Arabic. It prompted a reflection on what relevance the Proclamation had beyond its message of Irish independence.

12   *Irish Times*, 18 November 2010.

13   *Irish Examiner*, 19 November 2010. The 1916 Proclamation ends with the words: 'In this supreme hour the Irish nation must, by its valour and discipline and by the readiness of its children to sacrifice themselves for the common good, prove itself worthy of the august destiny to which it is called.'

Index